BECOMING A
CONFIDENT
READER

BECOMING A CONFIDENT READER

Instructor's Annotated Edition

Carol Kanar

HOUGHTON MIFFLIN COMPANY   Boston   New York

Senior Sponsoring Editor: Mary Jo Southern
Senior Associate Editor: Ellen Darion
Senior Project Editor: Fred Burns
Production/Design Coordinator: Jennifer Meyer Dare
Senior Manufacturing Coordinator: Priscilla Bailey
Senior Marketing Manager: Nancy Lyman

Cover Design: Harold Burch, Harold Burch Design, NYC
Cover Illustration: Harold Birch

Acknowledgments for reprinted materials appear on pages 405–406.

Printed in the U.S.A.

Library of Congress Catalog Card Number: 99-71970

Instructor's Edition ISBN: 0-395-93399-4

Student Edition ISBN: 0-395-71863-5

2 3 4 5 6 7 8 9—FFG—03 02 01 00

CONTENTS

Preface for Instructors   xiii

To the Student: How to Use This Book   xvii

UNIT 1   **Building Confidence for Reading   1**

Chapter 1   **Reading Actively   3**

What Do You Already Know?   4

"Time Management for College Students," Greg Gottesman   4

The author's tips show students how to manage their time.

Vocabulary Preview   4

How Well Did You Comprehend?   5

Have a Positive Attitude   7

Make Time for Reading   9

Control Your Concentration   14

Use Reading Strategies   16

Preview   16

Build Background   16

Ask Guide Questions   19

Review   20

Reflect   21

Real-World Connections   23

How Well Do You Remember?   24

What Do You Think?   25

Chapter Quiz 1   25

Chapter Quiz 2   27

Vocabulary Quiz   29

Chapter 2   **Using Your Dictionary   31**

What Do You Already Know?   32

"600 New Entries Give Dictionary What Was Missing," Associated
  Press   32

The authors give definitions of ten new words added to the 1996 Random House Webster's College Dictionary.

Vocabulary Preview   32

How Well Did You Comprehend?   34

Use Your Dictionary's Guide Words   36

Use the Parts of a Dictionary Entry   38

 Syllables   38

 Pronunciation   39

 Parts of Speech   42

 Definitions and Special Meanings   44

 Word Origins   46

Make Note Cards for Words and Terms   47

Real-World Connections   49

How Well Do You Remember?   51

What Do You Think?   52

Chapter Quiz 1   53

Chapter Quiz 2   55

Vocabulary Quiz   56

Chapter 3   **Using Context Clues   59**

What Do You Already Know?   60

"Four Words," Bob Greene   60

An American's encouraging words help a Japanese college student gain confidence.

Vocabulary Preview   60

How Well Did You Comprehend?   63

What Are Context Clues?   65

The Definition Clue   66

The Example Clue   67

The Contrast Clue   70

The Inference Clue   72

Real-World Connections   74

How Well Do You Remember?   76

What Do You Think?   76

Chapter Quiz 1   77

Chapter Quiz 2   79

Vocabulary Quiz   82

UNIT 2   **Improving Your Comprehension Skills   85**

Chapter 4   **Understanding Sentences and Transitions   87**

What Do You Already Know?   88
"Goofing Off Is Fast Becoming a Lost Art," Ellen Graham   88
The author explains how Americans waste time.
Vocabulary Preview   88
How Well Did You Comprehend?   90
Know the Parts of a Sentence   92
Identify Key Ideas and Details in Sentences   95
Know How Transitions Connect Ideas   97
　　Addition   98
　　Time   99
　　Example   101
　　Comparison and Contrast   102
　　Cause and Effect   104
Analyze Difficult Sentences   106
Real-World Connections   108
How Well Do You Remember   109
What Do You Think?   110
Chapter Quiz 1   110
Chapter Quiz 2   112
Vocabulary Quiz   114

Chapter 5   **Finding Main Ideas   117**

What Do You Already Know?   118
"Making the Grade," Kurt Wiesenfeld   118
The author complains about students who question their grades.
Vocabulary Preview   118
How Well Did You Comprehend?   121
Distinguish General From Specific Ideas   123
Identify the Author's Topic   125
Find the Topic Sentence of a Paragraph   126
Find the Central Idea of a Passage   131
Know How to Find Implied Main Ideas   133

Real-World Connections   137
How Well Do You Remember?   138
What Do You Think?   139
Chapter Quiz 1   140
Chapter Quiz 2   143
Vocabulary Quiz   146

Chapter 6   **Identifying Supporting Details**   149

What Do You Already Know?   150
"What's a Bagel?" Jack Denton Scott   150
The author explains how bagels have become one of America's most popular foods.
Vocabulary Preview   150
How Well Did You Comprehend?   153
Recognize Types of Details   155
Facts   156
Reasons   160
Examples   164
Find Levels of Development in Paragraphs   169
Find Levels of Development in Longer Passages   173
Look for Transitions That Signal Details   175
Real-World Connections   177
How Well Do You Remember?   178
What Do You Think?   179
Chapter Quiz 1   180
Chapter Quiz 2   182
Vocabulary Quiz   185

Chapter 7   **Recognizing and Following Thought Patterns**   188

What Do You Already Know?   189
"How Gender May Bend Your Thinking," Christine Gorman
In this article about the brain, the author answers the question, "Why can't a woman think more like a man?"
Vocabulary Preview   189
How Well Did You Comprehend?   191
Know Six Basic Patterns   193

Pattern 1: Example   194
Pattern 2: Listing   197
Pattern 3: Time Order   199
Pattern 4: Comparison and Contrast   201
Pattern 5: Cause and Effect   203
Pattern 6: Definition   205
Real-World Connections   210
How Well Do You Remember?   211
What Do You Think?   212
Chapter Quiz 1   212
Chapter Quiz 2   214
Vocabulary Quiz   218

UNIT 3   **Reading and Thinking Critically   221**

Chapter 8   **Using Textbook Reading Strategies   223**

What Do You Already Know?   224
"Biases in Judgment," Saul Kassin   224
The authors of this textbook passage explain two ways people make decisions.
Vocabulary Preview   224
How Well Did You Comprehend?   227
Use Your Textbook's Features   229
Preface   229
Table of Contents   231
Typographical Aids   233
Questions or Problems   235
Glossary   236
Graphics   236
Index   236

Know How Chapters Are Organized   238
Use a Reading System   240
SQ3R   241
Skimming and Scanning   243
Marking Your Textbooks   244
Outlining and Mapping   246
Real-World Connections   249
How Well Do You Remember?   249

What Do You Think?   250
Chapter Quiz 1   251
Chapter Quiz 2   252
Vocabulary Quiz   254

Chapter 9   **Reading Graphics with Understanding   256**

What Do You Already Know?   257
"Seizing Nature's Lifeline," Claudia Kalb and Melinda Beck   257
The authors explain new uses for umbilical-cord blood.
Vocabulary Preview   257
How Well Did You Comprehend?   260
Use *PRT* to Read Graphics   262
Purpose   262
Relationship   263
Text   263
Recognize Four Types of Graphics   264
Charts   264
Tables   269
Graphs   273
Diagrams   276
Make Your Own Graphics   279
Real-World Connections   280
How Well Do You Remember?   281
What Do You Think?   281
Chapter Quiz 1   282
Chapter Quiz 2   285
Vocabulary Quiz   288

Chapter 10   **Developing Your Critical Thinking Skills   291**

What Do You Already Know?   292
"The King of the Frogs," Humphrey Harmon   292
This African folktale is based on a Nyanza story.
Vocabulary Preview   292
How Well Did You Comprehend?   295
Determine An Author's Purpose   297
Distinguish Facts From Opinions   304

Make Inferences From Your Reading   311

Evaluate What You Read   315

Reliability   315

Objectivity   316

Usefulness   316

Real-World Connections   318

How Well Do You Remember?   319

What Do You Think?   320

Chapter Quiz 1   320

Chapter Quiz 2   324

Vocabulary Quiz   327

UNIT 4   **Using Your Skills: More Readings   329**

Selection 1   "It's Not My Fault," Carol Tavris   331

Are we becoming a nation of excuse makers? Carol Tavris thinks so.

Selection 2   "Parents Creating Unique Names," Cindy Roberts   337

Choosing unusual names for children is a trend Cindy Roberts discusses.

Selection 3   "The Struggle To Be An All-American Girl," Elizabeth Wong   342

Her childhood as a Chinese-American caused some problems for Elizabeth Wong.

Selection 4   "Solitude Is Casualty of the War with Time," Cynthia Crossen   348

Finding time to be alone is becoming difficult, according to Cynthia Crossen.

Selection 5   "The Unwritten American Bargain," General Colin L. Powell   353

The author urges everyone to support public education.

Selection 6   "I Remember Masa," José Antonio Burciaga   359

The author writes about tortillas, a popular Mexican food.

Selection 7   "Can We Talk?," Diane White   364

According to this author, some researchers believe that men and women may use their brains differently.

Selection 8   "Lotteries: Is It Right to Encourage Gambling?,"
                   W. M. Pride and O. C. Ferrell   370
                   Pride and Ferrell question whether advertising is being
                   used unfairly to promote gambling.
Selection 9   "Replacement Organs Have Been Grown from
                   Animal Tissue, Say Researchers," Ron Winslow   375
                   This author reports on the growth of replacement organs
                   and its possible consequences.
Selection 10   "How the Camel Got His Hump," Rudyard
                   Kipling   380
                   This story, which many generations have enjoyed, is one
                   of
                   Kipling's most famous.

Appendix A: Developing Your Library Skills   387

Appendix B: Preparing for Tests   392

Partial Answer Key   397
Acknowledgments   405
Index   407

PREFACE

Becoming a Confident Reader treats reading as a process students can learn to control by developing and applying active reading strategies. The goal of *Becoming a Confident Reader* is to help students achieve success in reading and thereby gain confidence in their ability to meet the reading demands of college, the workplace, and our information-filled society.

THE READING PROCESS

Becoming a Confident Reader teaches reading as a process that students can discover and control through skill mastery and the use of active reading strategies.

Integration of Skills

Although each chapter is centered on the development of one or two skills such as finding main ideas or identifying details, there is much cross-referencing and reinforcement of skills covered in other chapters. This approach models the reading process itself in which skills are integrated and often applied simultaneously as readers process information.

Transference of Learning

Many students who seem to achieve in the reading class fall back into bad reading habits in their other courses. This may be the result of textbooks that provide examples and exercises that do not reflect actual reading situations students encounter outside the reading class. *Becoming a Confident Reader* is filled with reading selections and excerpts from a variety of sources: periodicals, fiction, nonfiction, textbooks, and others. A strong emphasis on textbook reading prevails throughout the book, giving students practical experience with the type of reading they are likely to encounter in their other college courses and elsewhere.

How Reading, Thinking, Writing, and Studying Connect

Reading, writing, and studying are linked to critical thinking in several chapter features, including the chapter-opening essay and its prereading and postreading activities. *Becoming A Confident Reader* makes the assumption that all writing is meant for an audience, and that authors expect certain responses from readers. Students' comprehension is enhanced by seeing themselves as engaged in a dialog with the author as they read, and by seeing themselves as part of a larger audience. Studying, too, is more productive when students understand an author's purpose and know what they are expected to learn.

Basic and Advanced Reading Skills

The basic skills of vocabulary development, finding main ideas and supporting details, understanding sentences and transitions, and recognizing thought patterns are covered in Units 1 and 2. The advanced skills required to read textbooks effectively and to think critically are covered in Unit 3. In addition, *Becoming a Confident Reader* also introduces three essential skills that are not addressed in most reading texts: reading and interpreting graphic aids, understanding an author's purpose, and evaluating what you read. This coverage is based on the belief that if we want students to achieve more we have to expect more. With a sound foundation in the basics covered in earlier chapters, students are ready to progress to the more demanding skills covered in later chapters.

Exercises

Exercises are integrated throughout chapters so that students practice skills as soon as they are introduced and explained. The exercises are arranged in each chapter according to difficulty. A few exercises are self-checking, followed by the answers with explanations. The student edition contains a partial answer key. An annotated instructor's edition contains the answers to all other exercises and to all the chapter quizzes. One or more exercises in each chapter are designated as collaborative activities for partners or small groups. However, instructors should feel free to use any exercise either collaboratively or individually.

Organization and Content

Becoming a Confident Reader is divided into four parts, or units, each having its own theme. Unit 1, Building Confidence for Reading, introduces students to the concept of reading as an active, controllable process. In addition, students learn vocabulary-building strategies that will give them the confidence they need to tackle diverse reading tasks.

Unit 2, Improving Your Comprehension Skills, covers the fundamentals of the reading process from looking for key ideas in sentences to finding main ideas of paragraphs and longer selections. Identifying supporting details, and discovering idea relationships through transitions and thought patterns, are basic skills covered in Unit 2 that help students read with understanding.

Unit 3, Reading and Thinking Critically, moves students beyond the basics of understanding stated ideas to interpreting an author's meaning. To the basic skills they have learned, students add advanced strategies that will help them read and study from textbooks and interpret the meaning of graphics such as charts and tables. The last chapter in Unit 3 introduces students to critical thinking through the advanced skills of determining an author's purpose, distinguishing fact from opinion, making inferences, and evaluating what they read.

Unit 4, Using Your Skills: More Readings, consists of eight reading selections on topics that echo those addressed in the chapter-opening reading selections. Prereading and postreading activities frame each selection so that students have an opportunity to apply the active-reading strategies they are learning.

Features

Becoming a Confident Reader has several unique features that make it a practical text for both instructors and students.

Introduction and Objectives Each chapter begins with a brief introduction followed by a list of objectives: the specific strategies students are expected to learn.

What Do You Already Know? This prereading activity prepares students for the chapter-opening reading selection. Its purpose is to help students develop a habit of assessing their prior knowledge on a topic before reading.

The Chapter-Opening Reading Selection The selections appeal to a variety of interests and reflect diverse viewpoints. They provide content for skill practice and ideas for reflection. A headnote preceding the reading selection includes biographical data or contains a clue about the selection's content.

How Well Did You Comprehend? Consisting of five parts, this feature is a postreading activity that checks students' comprehension and provides a structure for them to think and write about the selection. The five parts are (1) main idea, (2) details, (3) inferences, (4) working with words, and (5) thinking and writing. The questions consist of both multiple-choice and open-ended items.

Real-World Connections This feature gives students a practical application for skills they are learning. Each *connection* explains how a chapter concept can be applied to solve a problem or reach a goal in a college, work, or life situation, followed by a brief exercise. Real-World Connections challenges students to think critically about what they are learning.

How Well Do You Remember? This interactive summary is a passage that students read and fill in the blanks to test their understanding and recall of chapter concepts. Completed immediately after reading, this feature provides a quick but comprehensive review.

What Do You Think? To aid the transfer of learning from the reading class to other classes and other reading situations, this feature invites students to think about and comment on what they have learned and how they plan to use their knowledge or skills. Whether used as an exercise or journal prompt, this feature can open the channels of communication between student and instructor.

Chapter Quizzes Several quizzes at the end of each chapter can be used for practice or assessment of students' skills on the recall, conceptual, and application levels of learning.

Ancillary

The instructor's annotated edition is a copy of the student text with answers to all exercises and tests filled in, providing a quick and easy-to-use reference.

ACKNOWLEDGMENTS

I am deeply grateful to the Houghton Mifflin family of editors and others for the parts they played in the development and production of *Becoming a Confident Reader* and for their dedication to excellence. I especially thank Mary Jo Southern for her steadfast support and enthusiasm, Ellen Darion for her inspiration and encouragement, Fred Burns for his unique editing gifts, Danielle Richardson, for all kinds of assistance, and all those involved in the design and production of this book. I also thank my husband, Stephen P. Kanar, for his continuing support; my friends and colleagues who shared their ideas; and my students whose dreams and achievements are always with me.

The many excellent suggestions I received from colleagues who reviewed the manuscript helped me develop *Becoming a Confident Reader* into its present form. To them I give special thanks: Mary Lee Bass, Monmouth University; Nancy Gerli, Suffolk County Community College; Mayme Jeffries, Bethune-Cookman College; and Doris Menezes, Nicholls State University.

TO THE STUDENT

HOW TO USE THIS BOOK

Reading is a necessary part of all your courses, and reading will continue to be an important part of your life. Therefore, you need to develop the strategies that will enable you to become a confident reader. This book will help.

The following ten steps explain how to read each chapter of *Becoming a Confident Reader* efficiently and effectively.

1. Allow yourself enough time to read the chapter before it is due. If you have trouble maintaining concentration, do not try to read the chapter in one sitting. Take a break as needed, but when you return to your reading, review what you have already read before going on.

2. Begin by reading the introductory paragraphs, which tell you what the chapter is about. Following the introduction is a list of two or more reading strategies the chapter covers. Your goal is to learn and use the strategies in all your reading.

4. Next, read "What Do You Already Know?" and answer the questions to prepare yourself for the reading selection that follows. The questions help you explore your background (knowledge and experience) on the writer's topic.

5. Read the selection and the vocabulary preview, which highlights words that may be unfamiliar. The selections that begin each chapter are short, interesting, and cover a variety of topics. They have two purposes: to introduce the chapter, and to provide you with an opportunity to practice strategies learned in previous chapters.

6. To check your comprehension of the selection, complete "How Well Did You Comprehend?" The exercise is broken into five parts: main idea, details, inferences, working with words, and thinking and writing. The *main idea* is the most important idea in a whole selection or in a whole paragraph. A *detail* is a fact, reason, or example that helps explain a main idea. An *inference* is an interpretation of an author's meaning based on the details given. The terms *main idea, detail,* and *inference* are explained in detail in the chapters that follow.

7. As you continue reading, do *all* the exercises, including the Real-World Connections either on your own or as your instructor

xvii

directs. The purpose of these exercises is to check your comprehension or provide practice using the strategies covered in the chapter. Real World Connections will help you see the practical value in what you are learning.

8. Pay attention to the *memory cues* at the end of each section. These short paragraphs summarize each section's important ideas.

9. Complete the chapter summary, How Well Do You Remember? This summary asks you to complete statements that test your recall of the chapter's important ideas.

10. Reflection is an important part of learning. You should always reflect (or think deeply) about your progress and how you will use what you have learned. At the end of each chapter, a section called *What Do You Think?* asks you several questions that help you reflect on your progress. Space is provided for you to write your reflections.

With each new chapter, you will learn strategies to improve your reading. As you learn a strategy, look for opportunities to use it either in your classes or in your personal reading.

I hope you have a successful semester or quarter and that the reading strategies you learn will serve you well in college and in the future that awaits you.

Carol C. Kanar

BECOMING A CONFIDENT READER

Unit
1

Building
Confidence
for Reading

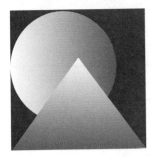

Chapter 1

Reading Actively

M any college students are surprised by the number and length of reading assignments each course requires. Some are overwhelmed by the amount of information they must learn in a single semester or quarter. You too may be feeling the pressure of having too much to read and learn in too little time, especially if family and work obligations compete for your attention. *Active reading* is the key to overcoming these difficulties.

Some students read passively without thinking about what they are reading and why. But active readers get involved in the task. They think about the author's ideas, ask questions, and review what they have learned. Active readers work hard to develop the attitude and study habits that help them get the most they can out of every reading assignment.

Reading actively helps you take control of your learning. Reading actively ensures success, and success builds confidence. Although reading actively is not difficult, it does take practice. These steps will help you get started:

- Have a positive attitude.
- Make time for reading.
- Control your concentration.
- Use reading strategies.

WHAT DO YOU ALREADY KNOW?

To prepare yourself for the reading selection that follows, find out what you already know about time management. Answer the questions below either on your own or in a group discussion.

1. Is it easy or difficult for you to make time for study?

2. What activities and obligations interfere with studying?

3. Have you tried to improve your time management? How?

4. Read the title, headnote, vocabulary preview, and first two paragraphs of the reading selection. What do you think will follow?

Time Management for College Students
Greg Gottesman

The following selection is a list of tips from Greg Gottesman's book College Survival: A Crash Course for Students By Students. *The list also appeared in* Better Homes and Gardens, *September 1997.*

VOCABULARY PREVIEW

eliminate	(ĭ •lĭm´ə•nāt´) get rid of, remove
incentives	(ĭn•sĕn´tĭvz) punishments or rewards that lead to action
retention	(rĭ•tĕn´shən) ability to remember
gorge	(gôrj) to stuff oneself with food
conducive	(kən•dōōs´ĭv) leading to, or resulting in
structure	(strŭk´chər) to construct, make

Pronunciation Key: ā (pay), ĕ (pet), ĭ (pit), ô(paw), ōō (boot), ŭ(cut), ə (about, item)

Use a calendar or planner. During the first week of class, mark down deadlines for each assignment, paper, project, and test you'll encounter that semester. Set daily and weekly goals for progressing through these obligations. 1

Plan to spend at least two nights studying for any major exam. Set aside even more time for writing papers, especially if research is required. Don't forget the time it will take to type and print the paper, especially if you need to schedule computer time. It's also a good idea to allow extra time for computer emergencies—today's version of "the dog ate my homework." 2

Don't get behind in your other classes while concentrating on one. Continue to work ahead in all your classes as much as possible. 3

Read the assignments before class—not right before the test. By reading ahead of time, the lectures will make more sense. 4

Go to class. Your own notes will be more helpful than a friend's. Get in the habit of reading your lecture notes at the end of each day, or at least at the end of each week. This will **eliminate** a lot of cramming at semester's end. 5

Plan your study time. One expert recommends studying for 50 minutes, then breaking for 10 minutes. Allow a cup of coffee or a quick visit with a friend down the hall for those 10 minutes; little **incentives** can keep you going. Rather than highlighting several passages in your reading assignments, write notes or questions to yourself in the margins. This will strengthen your **retention.** 6

Don't **gorge** on caffeinated beverages and foods in an effort to stay awake. You could end up jittery or nauseated—neither condition is **conducive** to effective learning. 7

Even if you're racing to start a paper, take a few extra minutes to prepare a workable outline. It will be easier to **structure** your paper when you start writing. 8

HOW WELL DID YOU COMPREHEND?

Check your comprehension of the ideas presented in Gottesman's list by completing the following items.

Main Idea

1. Which of the following statements best expresses what the entire list is about?
   a. Calendars help college students set goals for meeting obligations.
   b. Students should make a habit of reading their assignments before class.

    (c.) Several tips can help college students improve their time
        management.
    d. Students have many responsibilities that compete for their time.

Details

2. Gottesman says students should spend at least _____
    studying for exams.
    a. several hours
    (b.) two nights
    c. one night
    d. two hours

3. Gottesman says lectures will make more sense if you will
    (a.) read ahead of time.
    b. take your own notes.
    c. share notes with a friend.
    d. read right before a test.

4. According to Gottesman, cramming can be eliminated by
    a. going to class every day.
    b. studying for tests months ahead.
    c. taking your own notes.
    (d.) reading your notes daily or weekly.

Inferences

5. When Gottesman says, "Don't gorge on caffeinated beverages,"
    he probably means:
    a. Don't ever drink coffee.
    (b.) Don't drink too much coffee.
    c. Drink decaffeinated coffee only.
    d. Drink all the coffee you want.

6. All of Gottesman's tips suggest that
    a. you can leave planning to others.
    b. time takes care of itself.
    c. you can't plan for emergencies.
    (d.) you have to plan your time.

Working with Words

Complete the sentences below with these words from the vocabulary
preview:

conducive	eliminate	gorge
incentives	retention	structure

1. Some students need rewards, or ___*incentives*___, for studying.

2. A good way to ___*structure*___ an essay is to begin by making an outline.

3. Staying up all night cramming for a test is not ___*conducive*___ to good grades.

4. Allow time to eat nourishing meals so that you don't ___*gorge*___ on junk food.

5. The more you study the better will be your ___*retention*___.

6. With practice, you can improve your time management and ___*eliminate*___ bad habits.

Thinking and Writing

Review Gottesman's tips for managing your time. Which ones have you tried? Which ones are new to you but seem like good ideas?

Answers will vary. _____

_____

_____

_____

HAVE A POSITIVE ATTITUDE

An *attitude* is a feeling or state of mind. Attitudes can be positive or negative. Positive attitudes promote self-confidence. Negative attitudes lead to feelings of helplessness and insecurity. Attitudes can shape your behavior. People who believe they can succeed are motivated by that belief to keep trying until they reach their goals. But those who expect to fail, often do. Why? Because they are not motivated to keep trying.

As a college student, the most important thing you can learn is that grades and achievement are the direct result of your own effort. Moreover, you have as good a chance as anyone to succeed *if* you maintain a positive attitude and *if* you do the work.

Do you have a positive attitude? To find out, pay attention to the thoughts that run through your mind before you study, read, or take a test. Do these thoughts express self-confidence or self-doubt? For example, which one of the following statements sounds like something you might think when faced with a long reading assignment?

"Thirty pages? I'll never get through this."
"Thirty pages? I'll get started this afternoon."

The first statement expresses self-doubt and a negative attitude toward reading. The second statement expresses self-confidence and a positive attitude toward reading. Also, the second statement shows that the student has a plan to get the work done.

To develop a positive attitude, practice recognizing your own negative thoughts about reading, studying, and learning. Then replace them with positive thoughts that show you have a plan to overcome a problem or to accomplish a task. Over time, you can develop the attitudes and work habits that lead to success.

Exercise 1.1

Following are six negative statements about reading. Turn them into positive statements that express self-confidence and show that you have a plan. The first one is done as an example. *(Student's answers will vary, but some possible ones are given.)*

1. I can't remember what I read.

   I will try to learn better ways to read and study.

   _____

2. I'm not very good at reading, so I probably can't improve.

   I can develop my reading skills.

   _____

3. I have a poor vocabulary.

   I will learn ways to develop my vocabulary.

   _____

4. If I'm not interested in the topic, I can't concentrate.

   No matter what the topic is, I can control my concentration.

   _____

5. This chapter is too difficult for me.

   I will do my best and ask for help if I need it.

   _____

6. I don't like to read.

   I will not let my feelings prevent me from reading my assignments.

   _____

Memory Cue

Attitudes shape behavior. A positive attitude will motivate you to do the reading and studying that leads to academic success. You can change a negative attitude to a positive one by recognizing and eliminating your negative thoughts.

MAKE TIME FOR READING

Like many students, you may think that finding time for reading is difficult when so many desires and obligations compete for your attention. But if you keep trying to *find* time you may not succeed. Instead, you must *make* time for reading.

To make time for reading, you must plan for it as you would any other important task. The key to good planning is no secret. First, determine *how long* it will take you to complete a reading assignment. Next, decide *when* to do the reading and set aside enough time. Then *follow through* on your plan.

Because reading times vary with the individual and with the length and difficulty of the assignment, you need to find out how long it takes *you* to read. To calculate the time you need to read an assignment from any of your textbooks, follow these steps:

1. Choose three consecutive pages from one of your textbooks. Choose pages that contain mostly print.
2. Before you read, write down your starting time in minutes and seconds.
3. Read at a comfortable rate. When you have finished, write down your ending time.
4. Next, subtract your starting time from your ending time to get your total reading time (the number of minutes it took you to read three pages).
5. Divide your total time by three to get your time per page for the textbook you chose. See the following example:

Ending time:	3:20
Starting time:	3:05
Total reading time:	0:15 minutes
Time per page:	$15 \div 3 = 5$ minutes

To figure out how long it will take you to read an assignment, first multiply the number of pages in the assignment by your time per page. Then divide the total by 60 to get the number of hours and minutes you need to set aside for reading. Suppose it takes you 3 minutes to read one page of your biology textbook. How long will it take you to read a chapter that is 40 pages long?

Number of pages:	40
Time per page:	$\times$ 3 (minutes)
Time to set aside:	120 min. $\div$ 60 min. $= 2$ hours

Exercise 1.2   Calculate your time per page for any two of your textbooks. Use the information you get from this exercise to calculate how much time you need to set aside for completing your next reading assignment from each textbook. *(Answers will vary.)*

Textbook _____

Ending time _____

Starting time _____

Total reading time _____

Time per page _____

Time you need to set aside _____

Textbook _____

Ending time _____

Starting time _____

Total reading time _____

Time per page _____

Time you need to set aside _____

Suppose you need to spend 5 hours reading a biology chapter and two hours reading an essay for your composition course—a total of 7 hours. How would you schedule your study time to complete the reading?

Many students make weekly schedules. A weekly schedule lists fixed times and flexible times. *Fixed times* usually do not change, and they include work hours, class times, and regularly scheduled appointments or activities. For example, if you are an athlete, practice times and game times also count as fixed times on your schedule. If you are a parent, you may have to take children to school and other activities at fixed times. The time that remains after you have scheduled your fixed times is your *flexible time*. When to eat, when to sleep, when to go out with friends—the time you spend on activities such as these may vary from day to day and must be arranged around your fixed-time activities.

Is study time a fixed time or a flexible time for you? Many experts recommend that you treat study time as a fixed time, giving it the same importance as you would the hours you spend at work or in class. When study times are flexible, you may never get around to doing the work. Before you know it, time will manage you instead of you managing your time.

Figure 1.1 is a student's schedule for one week. Shaded squares indicate the student's fixed time, which also includes study time. Unshaded squares indicate flexible time.

Exercise 1.3   Using Figure 1.1 as a guide, make your own schedule for one week. First, fill in your fixed times. Next, look at the squares remaining, and set aside enough study time to complete your week's assignments. Finally, add your flexible-time activities to the schedule. *(Students' schedules should reflect Figure 1.1.)*

FIGURE 1.1 A Student's Weekly Schedule

	Sunday	Monday	Tuesday	Wednesday	Thursday	Friday	Saturday
6:00 – 7:00	sleep	exercise, dress, breakfast, travel time →					sleep
7:00 – 8:00	sleep					→	breakfast
8:00 – 9:00	breakfast	algebra	study	algebra	study	algebra	s
9:00 – 10:00	exercise, dress, and travel time	Freshman comp.	Spanish	Freshman comp.	Spanish	Freshman comp.	t
10:00 – 11:00		study/ review	biology lab	study/ review	Spanish lab	study/ review	u
							d
11:00 – 12:00	church	lunch		lunch		lunch	y
12:00 – 1:00	travel time, lunch, chores	biology	lunch, travel time	biology	lunch, travel time	biology	lunch, travel time
1:00 – 2:00		travel, chores	w	travel, chores	w	travel, chores	w
2:00 – 3:00	leisure	s	o	s	o	s	o
3:00 – 4:00		t u d	r	t u d	r	t u d	r
4:00 – 5:00		y	k	y	k	y	k
5:00 – 6:00		leisure	→				
6:00 – 7:00	dinner	→					
7:00 – 8:00	s t u d y	s	→			dinner, leisure	dinner and study or leisure as needed
8:00 – 9:00		t u d	→				
9:00 – 10:00		y	→				
10:00 – 11:00		leisure	study	leisure	study		
11:00 – 12:00	sleep	→					

SCHEDULE FOR EXERCISE 1.3

	Sunday	Monday	Tuesday	Wednesday	Thursday	Friday	Saturday
6:00 – 7:00							
7:00 – 8:00							
8:00 – 9:00							
9:00 – 10:00							
10:00 – 11:00							
11:00 – 12:00							
12:00 – 1:00							
1:00 – 2:00							
2:00 – 3:00							
3:00 – 4:00							
4:00 – 5:00							
5:00 – 6:00							
6:00 – 7:00							
7:00 – 8:00							
8:00 – 9:00							
9:00 – 10:00							
10:00 – 11:00							
11:00 – 12:00							

Memory Cue

Do not depend on finding time for study. Instead, make time for study by making a schedule and sticking to it. For best results, treat your study time as fixed time. Give it the same priority as working and attending classes.

CONTROL YOUR CONCENTRATION

Just as you must make time to read your assignments and study, you must *decide* to concentrate. Reading demands all your attention. To *concentrate* means to focus your attention by thinking about what you are doing and by eliminating distractions.

Do you get bored easily when reading or studying? Do tiredness, hunger, and negative feelings about the assignment keep you from concentrating? These kinds of distractions are called *internal distractions*. Because they originate within you, internal distractions are within your control. You can learn to ignore boredom by focusing your attention on what you hope to achieve and by reminding yourself that reading and studying are necessary steps toward your goals. You can eliminate tiredness by scheduling your time so that you get enough rest. To eliminate distracting feelings of hunger, have a meal or a snack before you sit down to study. Negative feelings can sabotage any effort to concentrate. Developing and maintaining a positive attitude will build your confidence and make concentration easier.

Do you have trouble reading or studying in an environment that is too hot, too cold, or too noisy? Do you have difficulty saying *no* to friends who interrupt your studying? These kinds of distractions are called *external distractions*. Because they originate outside you, they are difficult to control. To overcome external distractions, find or create a comfortable noise-free study environment. Set up a home-study area or find a quiet place on campus. Make a habit of studying in the same place every day and, soon, concentration will become a habit.

To stay focused, set a goal for reading and studying that includes a time limit or a certain number of pages. When you have completed your task, reward yourself with a snack, conversation, or other pleasant activity. Taking frequent breaks is another way to stay focused. After a short break, you will return to your task refreshed and ready to concentrate.

Exercise 1.4   The following statements are typical answers students give to the question *What causes you to lose concentration?* Choose a partner and talk about the statements. Beside each statement write **I** for internal distraction or **E** for external distraction. When you have finished, choose one of the statements and explain what the student can do to eliminate the distraction and improve concentration. Write the number of the statement you chose and your answer on the lines provided. *(Statements chosen and explanations will vary.)*

_____*I*_____ 1.   I get bored when I read.

_____*E*_____ 2.   Ringing phones keep me from concentrating.

_____*E*_____ 3.   If someone asks me out, I put off reading or studying.

_____*I*_____ 4.   I try to read at night, but I'm too tired.

_____*E*_____ 5.   I can't read when people are talking.

_____*E*_____ 6.   The library is either too hot or too cold.

_____*E*_____ 7.   T.V. and music distract me.

_____*I*_____ 8.   If the assignment is too long, my mind wanders.

Statement you chose: _____*3*_____

What can the student do?

Do your assignments first. Then go out with friends as a reward for finishing

your work.

Memory Cue

Internal distractions such as boredom and tiredness originate within you. External distractions such as temperature and noise originate outside you. To control your concentration, find a comfortable study area and eliminate your distractions. Set goals, reward yourself for work completed, and take breaks to stay focused.

USE READING STRATEGIES

A *strategy* is a process, method, or way of doing something. If you read without thinking, your concentration will wander and you will not learn or remember very much. Using a reading strategy will help you think about what you are doing so that you can concentrate, learn, and remember.

Reading strategies give you specific things to do before, during, and after reading that will improve your comprehension and memory. Before reading, you should *preview* the assignment and *build background* for the reading. During reading, you should think and *ask questions*. After reading, you should *review* and *reflect* on what you have read. Now let us examine these strategies one at a time.

Preview

Because you do not want to waste your money, you probably do not go to a movie unless you know enough about it in advance and think that

---

FIGURE 1.2 How to Preview a Textbook Chapter

What to look at:	Why?
The title	The title tells what the chapter is about.
The introduction	The introduction explains the author's purpose and what you are expected to learn.
Major headings	Headings identify the most important idea in each section. The headings together provide an outline of the chapter.
First sentence after a heading	The first sentence introduces the section and may state its central idea.
Graphs, charts, and pictures	The most important ideas are often illustrated by graphic (visual) aids.
Typographical features	Italics, boldfaced type, colored type, marginal notes, numbered items, and underlining make key ideas stand out.
The last paragraph or summary	The last paragraph or summary pulls together the key ideas in the chapter.
End matter	Chapter questions, exercises, or other practice material focus on a chapter's key ideas.

you will like it. A movie preview provides a brief overview of a film that lets you know what to expect: the stars, the basic plot details, and the type of film it is. Similarly, previewing an assignment before you read it lets you know what to expect.

A *preview* is a brief overview that helps you familiarize yourself with the organization and content of something you are about to read. Your goal in previewing an assignment is to find the author's most important ideas and to determine how they are organized. A preview should be rapid and should hit only the high points. Figure 1.2 illustrates how to preview a textbook chapter by showing you what to look for and why.

Exercise 1.5   Preview Chapter 2 of this book by answering the following questions. Words in parentheses at the end of each question tell you where to look to find your answer.

1. What topic is covered in Chapter 2? (title)

   How to use your dictionary is the topic.

2. What are you expected to learn from reading Chapter 2? (introduction)

   You are expected to learn three strategies for

   using your dictionary effectively.

3. What are the three most important ideas? (major headings)

   Use your dictionary's guide words.

   Use the parts of a dictionary entry.

   Make note cards for words and terms.

4. What are two terms that the author wants you to learn? (words in italics)

   etymology, schwa (Students may list any of the chapter's special terms).

Build Background

Use what you can learn from your preview of an assignment to build background for reading. Your *background* consists of anything you have seen, heard, read, or done that relates to the topic. Suppose an author's topic is how the memory works. Try these steps to build background for reading about this topic.

First, *determine what you already know.* What have you read about the human memory? Have you taken any courses that covered this topic? Have you tried any techniques for improving memory?

Second, *determine what else you need to know.* As you think about memory, you decide that you really have no idea how it works or even what it is. So one thing you might need to know is the author's definition of memory. A definition is something specific to look for when you begin reading.

Third, *brainstorm the topic.* Talk it over with a friend or jot down any ideas that come to mind as you think about your own memory. For example, what kinds of things are easy for you to remember? What gives you trouble? Do you think you can improve your memory?

Building background for reading takes only a few minutes and has three advantages:

- Thinking about a topic beforehand puts you in a receptive frame of mind.
- Linking new material with prior knowledge makes learning easier.
- Relating the author's topic to your own experience builds interest.

Two features that come near the beginning of every chapter of this book help you preview the chapter-opening reading selection and build background for reading: *What Do You Already Know?* and *Vocabulary Preview.* As you use these features, remember that previewing and background building are things you should do every time you read.

Exercise 1.6   Working with a partner, imagine that you have been assigned to read a chapter from *Personal Finance,* a textbook by E. Thomas Garman and Raymond E. Forgue. The title of the chapter is "Credit Use and Credit Cards." Brainstorm the topic; then answer the questions below. *(Answers will vary, but here are some possible ones.)*

1. **What do you already know about the topic?** What experience have you had with credit cards and the use of credit?

   Most people today have one or more credit cards.

   Some people overuse credit cards and get in debt.

   Credit cards are convenient if used properly.

2. **What do you need to know about the topic?** What do you want or expect the authors to tell you about credit use and credit cards that you do not already know?

___The authors may explain different types of credit and the appropriate___

___uses of credit cards.___

Ask Guide Questions

Previewing and building background are strategies that help you focus your attention *before* reading. You also need a strategy to help you maintain concentration *during* reading. A proven strategy is to ask guide questions.

A *guide question* keeps you from reading without thinking. Do you ever find yourself staring at a page, wondering what you have read? Do you ever feel as if you are reading words without understanding? These two familiar situations are the result of inattention. Asking questions during reading helps you think about the author's ideas and maintain concentration. These suggestions will help you ask good guide questions.

- Preview first. Previewing helps you find the most important ideas so that you know what questions to ask.
- Turn major headings into questions that focus on what you think is important.
- As you read each section that follows a major heading, look for the answer to your question.
- After reading the section, determine whether your questions have been answered.
- Questions that can be answered *yes* or *no* are not helpful. Instead, ask questions that begin with *who, what, where, when, why,* or *how.*

Exercise 1.7

The chapter headings listed in questions 1 through 4 below are from "Credit Use and Credit Cards." For each of these headings write two guide questions. The first one is done as an example.

1. Reasons For and Against Using Credit *(Answers may vary.)*

   a. ___Why should I use credit?___

   b. ___What is a good reason not to use credit?___

2. Types of Open-Ended Credit Accounts

    a. *What is an open-ended credit account?* _____

    b. *How many types are there, and what are they?* _____

3. The Process for Opening an Open-Ended Charge Account

    a. *Can anyone open an open-ended charge account?* _____

    b. *What are the steps in the process?* _____

4. Managing a Charge Account

    a. *Why is it important to manage a charge account?* _____

    b. *What are the ways to manage an account?* _____

Review

Many students ask, "Why can't I read something one time and remember it?" For one thing, some information is too complex or unfamiliar to be absorbed in only one reading. Even more important, unless you have a photographic memory, just reading the material will not help you remember it. Not only is it normal to forget, but forgetting is sure to occur unless you make an effort to remember.

The best way to keep information fresh in your mind and to make it part of your permanent memory is to review. You should review immediately after reading and frequently thereafter. Your reviews should include the following steps:

1. Get a general overview of the chapter's organization by reading through the introduction, major headings, and summary.
2. Go through the chapter page by page. Review the most important ideas by looking at the headings and trying to recall your guide questions and answers.
3. Review key terms and definitions.
4. Review charts, tables, and other graphics. In your own words be able to explain what they illustrate.
5. Add reciting to your review. Recite (say aloud) important facts, terms and definitions, and other information you want to remember.

How Well Do You Remember, a feature near the end of every chapter of this book, summarizes the chapter's most important ideas for review. Some textbooks do not have chapter summaries, but when they do, make reading the summary an essential part of your previewing and reviewing activities.

Reflect

To *reflect* means to think about the meaning, importance, or effect of what you have learned. Reflection is thinking for yourself rather than accepting without thinking what someone else has said or thought. To reflect on what you have learned, start with a fact or idea, and ask yourself questions like these:

- Why is this information important?
- How can I use the information?
- How does the information relate to what I already know?
- What more can I learn from this information?

What Do You Think, a feature at the end of each chapter of this book, asks you to reflect on what you have learned. Reflection takes you a step beyond the review process to help you apply your knowledge in practical ways.

Memory Cue

Before reading, preview and build background for the topic. During reading, ask guide questions to help you think about the author's most important ideas. After reading, review and reflect to help you remember and apply your knowledge. These strategies help you read actively.

Exercise 1.8

This chapter describes a reading process that includes these steps: *preview, build background, ask guide questions, review,* and *reflect.* To try out the process, select a chapter from one of your textbooks. Preview the chapter, read it, and then answer the following questions. *(Chapters chosen and student's answers will vary.)*

1. What is the chapter's title?

_____

2. In your own words, what is the overall topic covered in the chapter?

_____

_____

3. What do you already know about this topic?

_____

_____

4. What else do you need to know about the topic?

_____

_____

5. List two of the author's headings and your guide questions.

    Headings   Guide Questions

    a. _____   a. _____

    b. _____   b. _____

6. Write the answers to your guide questions.

_____

_____

7. Based on your reading, what do you need to review? List two of the chapter's important ideas that you need to remember.

_____

_____

8. To reflect on your reading, explain the significance of at least one piece of information in the chapter. How can you use this information?

_____

_____

REAL-WORLD CONNECTIONS

You can adapt the textbook reading strategies explained in this chapter to use with other materials such as newspaper and magazine articles. Previewing, building background, asking questions, and reflecting will improve your understanding of everything you read.

Working with a partner, choose a short newspaper article on a topic that interests you. Then follow the directions to complete steps 1, 2, and 3 below.

1. Step 1: Preview

Read the title, first and last paragraphs, and then answer these questions: *(Articles chosen and students' answers will vary.)*

a. What is the title and source of your article?

_____

b. What is the author's topic?

_____

c. What do you already know about the topic?

_____

d. What else do you need to know about the topic?

_____

2. Step 2: Read with a purpose

As you read, pay attention to these features if there are any:

a. Headings: Turn them into guide questions and look for answers.

b. Special terms in bold type or italics: Read the definitions.

c. Photographs, illustrations, charts, tables, and so on: What do they tell you?

3. Step 3: Review and Reflect

Discuss the article and answer these questions:

a.   What do you think is the point or most important idea of the whole article?

_____

b.   What details explain this idea?

_____

c.   What have you learned from your reading?

_____

d.   How can you use this information?

_____

HOW WELL DO YOU REMEMBER?

To review the chapter, read the following summary and fill in the blanks. If you need help, look back through the chapter to refresh your memory.

Confident readers are active readers. Having a __positive__ attitude is your first step toward becoming an active reader. To improve your attitude, replace any feelings of self-doubt with feelings of __self-confidence__ .

Active readers know how to control their time and concentration. To manage your reading time, make a schedule. Your schedule should include __fixed__ times for working and attending classes and __flexible__ times for eating, sleeping, and leisure activities. Many experts recommend that you treat study time as a fixed time.

To improve concentration, eliminate your __internal__ and __external__ distractions. Another way to improve concentration is to _____*preview*_____ an assignment before reading to get an idea of its content and organization. In addition, build background for reading by _____*determining what you know, determining what you need to know,*_____ and _____*brainstorming the topic*_____. To keep your attention focused during reading, ask _____*guide questions*_____. To make knowledge your own, _____*review*_____ and _____*reflect*_____ after reading.

WHAT DO YOU THINK?

Reflect on this chapter's most important ideas: attitude, time management, concentration, and reading strategies. Which one is most important to you now? What have you learned that will help you become an active reader? How do you plan to apply the information? Write your reflections below.

_*Reflections will vary.*_____

_____

_____

_____

_____

CHAPTER QUIZ 1

Part 1 Terms and Definitions

Match this chapter's special terms in Column A with their definitions in Column B.

Column A	Column B
_c_ 1. preview	a. to think about the importance of what you have learned
_a_ 2. reflect	b. a feeling or state of mind
_d_ 3. background	c. an overview to determine content and organization
_f_ 4. reading strategy	d. what you know before reading
_b_ 5. attitude	e. *who, what, where, when,* or *why,* for example
_e_ 6. guide question	f. what to do before, during, or after reading

Part 2 Chapter Review

Read and answer each question below. Write your answer in complete sentences, and use extra paper if needed. *(Answers may vary but should be similar to these.)*

1. How do positive or negative attitudes affect reading and learning?

   Attitudes shape behavior; therefore, a positive attitude may motivate you to do the work that leads to success.

2. What is the purpose of asking guide questions?

   Guide questions focus your attention on headings, which are clues to the author's important ideas.

3. For maximum comprehension, what should you do before, during, and after reading?

   Before reading, preview and build background. During reading, ask guide questions. After reading, review and reflect.

Part 3 Using Your Skills

Suppose you were assigned to read a chapter from *Broadcasting in America,* a communications textbook. The chapter's title is "Network T.V. Sports." As you preview the chapter, you read the following headings. Write a guide question you could ask about each one. *(Answers may vary, but here are some possible ones.)*

1. Evolution of Network Sports

   When did network sports begin?

2. Cable and PPV Sports

   How have cable and PPV sports affected network sports?

3. Scheduling and Buying Sports

   How do networks schedule and buy sports?

4. Issues in Sports Broadcasting

   What are the important issues in sports broadcasting?

Score: 100 − 8 for each one missed = _____ %

CHAPTER QUIZ 2

Part 1 Terms and Definitions

Match this chapter's special terms in Column A with their definitions in Column B.

Column A

_f_	1. fixed time
_d_	2. flexible time
_c_	3. reading time
_a_	4. concentration
_b_	5. internal distraction
_e_	6. external distraction

Column B

a. focused attention
b. hunger, tiredness, boredom
c. the number of minutes per page
d. includes leisure activities
e. temperature, noise
f. hours in class or at work

Part 2 Chapter Review

Read and answer each question below. Write your answer in complete sentences, and use extra paper if needed. *(Answers may vary, but should be similar to these.)*

1. This chapter suggests three things you can do to plan your reading time. What are they?

   First, determine how long it will take to read an assignment. Second,

   decide when you will read and then plan your time. Third, follow through

   on your plan.

2. What should be included on a weekly schedule?

   Your schedule should include fixed times for work, classes, study, and so on,

   and flexible times for other activities.

3. What is the difference between internal and external distractions, and which is harder to eliminate?

   Internal distractions such as boredom and hunger are within you. External

   distractions such as noise and temperature are outside you and are harder

   to eliminate because they may be beyond your control.

Part 3 Using Your Skills

The following passage is the introduction to a textbook chapter titled "Aggression." Read the passage and answer the questions.

> In this chapter, we examine a disturbing aspect of human behavior, aggression. First, we ask "What is *aggression?*" and consider its definition. After describing possible *origins of aggression,* we explore a variety of *social and situational influences.* Finally, specific *scenes of violence,* each of which may serve to induce further aggression, are discussed. Throughout the chapter, we emphasize ways to prevent or reduce aggressive actions.
>
> From Sharon S. Brehm and Saul M. Kassin, *Social Psychology,* second edition. Boston: Houghton Mifflin, 1993.

1. What is the authors' topic?

   The author's topic is aggression.

2. What do the authors expect you to learn from this chapter?

The authors want you to learn what aggression is and how to prevent or

reduce it.

3. What term do the authors plan to define?

The authors plan to define aggression.

4. What are three important ideas that the authors plan to explain in the chapter? (Hint: The key words *after* and *finally* are clues.)

The authors plan to explain the origins of aggression, the social and

situational influences, and scenes of violence that may cause aggression.

5. What term do the authors expect you to learn and remember?

The term the authors expect you to learn is "aggression."

Score: 100 − 8 for each one missed = _____ %

Vocabulary Quiz

Each sentence below contains a word in bold type from the reading selection on page 5. Read the sentence and the definitions that follow it. Then circle the correct one. Turn to the vocabulary preview on page 4 to check your answers.

1. A quiet area with a desk, chair, and appropriate materials is **conducive** to studying.
   a. leading to a result
   b. causing harm
   c. irritating
   d. revealing

2. Favorite snacks or T.V. programs are **incentives** to look forward to after studying.
   a. necessities
   b. rewards
   c. tasks
   d. secrets

3. We watched the monkeys **gorge** themselves on popcorn that people had tossed into their cages.
   a. kill
   b. amuse
   c. stuff
   d. confuse

4. It is best to **structure** your weekly schedule around fixed and flexible times.
   a. postpone
   b. construct
   c. consider
   d. reflect

5. Reviewing and reflecting are two active reading strategies that can improve your **retention** of what you read.
   a. interest
   b. desire to learn
   c. comprehension
   d. ability to remember

6. To improve your concentration, you must **eliminate** your internal and external distractions.
   a. remove
   b. increase
   c. handle
   d. find

Score: 100 − 17 for each one missed = _____%

Chapter 2

Using Your Dictionary

Vocabulary plays an important role in every course you take. The special terms of disciplines such as psychology, biology, and chemistry are essential to your understanding of those subjects. In your composition and speech courses, you must be able to make effective and accurate word choices. When you write a paper for any course, you will probably need to check the definition or spelling of a word. Although some textbooks contain glossaries, and most textbooks define special terms in context, a dictionary is still an indispensable tool.

If you do not own a dictionary, consider investing in two: an unabridged desk dictionary to use in your study area and a paperback version to carry with you. The *American Heritage College Dictionary* and the *Random House Webster's College Dictionary* are two good choices, and both come in hardcover and paperback editions. Not only is a dictionary useful in college, but it is also a reference tool you can use throughout your life.

This chapter explains three strategies that will help you use your dictionary with increased confidence and skill:

- *Use your dictionary's guide words.*
- *Use the parts of a dictionary entry.*
- *Make note cards for words and terms.*

WHAT DO YOU ALREADY KNOW?

To prepare yourself for the reading selection that follows, find out what you already know about dictionaries. Answer the questions below either on your own or in a group discussion.

1. On average, how often do you use a dictionary?

2. What kinds of words do you most often look up: textbook terms, unfamiliar words from other kinds of reading, or unfamiliar words that you hear other people use?

3. How do you think dictionaries get new words?

4. Read the title, headnote, vocabulary preview, and first two paragraphs of the reading selection. What do you think will follow?

600 New Entries Give Dictionary What Was Missing
Associated Press

In the following article, the authors discuss new words that have been added to the Random House Webster's College Dictionary. *The article appeared in* The Orlando Sentinel *in May, 1996.*

VOCABULARY PREVIEW

rife	(rīf) widespread, numerous
strenuous	(strĕn´yoō·əs) requiring great effort or energy
innumerable	(ĭ·noō´mər·ə·bəl) too many to be counted
abundance	(ə·bŭn´dəns) plenty, a great amount
channeled	(chăn´əld) guided or directed along a desired path
exploit	(ĕk´sploit´) to use selfishly or unethically
etiquette	(ĕt´ĭ·kĕt´) rules of conduct
exasperation	(ĭg·zăs´pə·rā´shən) extreme annoyance

apathetic   (ăp´ə•thĕt´ĭk) lacking interest or concern

Pronunciation Key: ā(**pay**), ă(**pat**), ĕ(**pet**), ī(**pie**), ĭ(**pit**), oi (**noise**),
o͞o(**boot**), ə (**about, item**)

New York—Have you tried any fartleks lately? Maybe you made a gazillion attempts but prefer being a domestique wheeling through ecotourism spots **rife** with ixora. [1]

Reaching for the dictionary? Luckily, you'll find these words among the 600 entries in the first "new-words section" of the revised *Random House Webster's College Dictionary.* [2]

The $23.95 hardcover dictionary is the fifth revision of the *Random House Webster's College Dictionary* since its publication in 1991. Random House's first college dictionary—the *American College Dictionary*—came out in 1947. [3]

"They are not necessarily new words, but words that for some reason or another just never made it into the main body of the text, mostly for lack of space," said Sol Steinmetz, head wordmeister* at Random House Reference and Information Publishing. [4]

Any die-hard runner can tell you that fartleks—a training technique involving bursts of effort alternating with less **strenuous** exercise—have been around at least 20 years. And no, a domestique is not a French maid who wears sassy skirts, but a cyclist who sets the pace and provides food and support for team members. [5]

You probably have heard *gazillion* **innumerable** times but never seen it in a Random House dictionary. Computer technology weighs in with an **abundance** of terms such as *bustopology, expansion card, netiquette,* and *screen saver.* [6]

Business phrases include *flex dollars* and *tax deferred annuity.* "Dictionaries are the indexes of current society and the words we use reflect society's concerns," Steinmetz said. [7]

The dictionary includes: shaken baby syndrome, drive-by shooting and deadbeat dad. [8]

New Words

[Here is] a random selection of 10 of the 600 new words—and their definitions—contained in the revised *Random House Webster's College Dictionary,* 1996 edition. [9]

* one who is a master in the use of words

Bustopology, n. An arrangement of computers on a local-area network in which each computer is connected to a central cable through which data is **channeled.**   10

Gazillion, n. An extremely large, indeterminate number.   11

Kleptocracy, n. A government or state in which those in power **exploit** national resources and steal; rule by a thief or thieves.   12

Netiquette, n. The **etiquette** of computer networks, especially the Internet.   13

Sheesh, n. interj. Used to express **exasperation.**   14

Slacker, n. An educated young person who is antimaterialistic, purposeless, **apathetic** and usually works in a dead-end job.   15

HOW WELL DID YOU COMPREHEND?

Main Idea

1. Which statement below best expresses what the whole article is about?
   a. A dictionary often reflects social change.
   b. Computer technology has given us many new words.
   c. New words often do not make it into a dictionary.
   d. Random House has added new words to its dictionary.

Details

2. Random House's first college dictionary was published in
   a. 1900.
   b. 1947.
   c. 1991.
   d. 1996.

3. What prevented the new words explained in the article from being added before 1996?
   a. Lack of space prevented their addition.
   b. They were already in the main body of the text.
   c. These words were not necessarily new.
   d. They were business terms.

4. Sol Steinmetz
   a. wrote the article.
   b. is a die-hard runner.
   c. works for Random House.
   d. sells dictionaries.

Inferences

5. *Deadbeat dad* probably means a father
   a. who is out of work.
   (b.) who does not support his children.
   c. who is exhausted.
   d. who has not received an education.

6. The terms *shaken baby syndrome* and *drive-by shooting* were probably included in the new dictionary because
   a. they are not new words.
   b. they were in a previous edition.
   c. no one knows what they mean.
   (d.) they reflect society's concerns.

Working with Words

Fill in the sentences below with these words from the vocabulary preview.

channeled   innumerable   abundance   apathetic   rife
exasperation   strenuous   etiquette   exploit

1. At Thanksgiving, we had delicious dishes in such ___abundance___ that the table was overflowing with food.

2. Chores such as cleaning windows and scrubbing floors can be ___strenuous___ tasks.

3. This book is ___rife___ with someone else's underlining.

4. If we ___exploit___ our national forests by cutting down trees without planting new ones, we will have no forests left.

5. I have been to ___innumerable___ stores, and I can't find a pair of pants I like.

6. Children whose energy is ___channeled___ into worthwhile activities have little time for drugs.

7. Table manners and good telephone behavior are but two examples of ___etiquette___ that everyone should learn.

8. After trying for two hours to get the lawn mower started, Ben gave up in ___exasperation___ .

9. The math instructor called the students ___*apathetic*___ because they did not want to review their test errors.

Thinking and Writing

Several business and computer terms in the article are not defined. Ask your college librarian to help you find a source that will give you the meanings of *expansion card, screen saver, flex dollars,* and *tax deferred annuity.* Write your definitions and the source where you found them to share with the class.

Answers will vary.

USE YOUR DICTIONARY'S GUIDE WORDS

Open your dictionary to any page, and you will find two *guide words* at the top. Their purpose is to help you determine where to look for a word. The first guide word listed corresponds to the first word on a page. The second guide word listed corresponds to the last word on a page. For an example of guide words, see Figure 2.1, which shows a page with guide words from the *American Heritage College Dictionary,* Third Edition.

Guide words are most helpful when you know how to spell a word you want to find. Suppose you know how to spell *persevere,* but you are unsure of its definition. Can you find the meaning of this word on the page represented in Figure 2.1? No, because all the words on that page begin with the letters *perk* through *perp*—not *pers.* However, you can find the meaning of *permeable* or *permute* because these words fall between the guide words *perky* and *perpetuate.*

Suppose you do not know how to spell a word? The following tips will help you make intelligent guesses so that you can use guide words effectively.

1. Spell a word the way it sounds.
2. If you cannot find the word, try substituting a different letter or letter combination that sounds similar. For example, a word you think begins with *f* may begin with *v* or *ph.* Try *g* in place of *j* or *qu* in place of *kw.*

FIGURE 2.1 Guide Words

1018

perky
perpetuate

guide words →

First and last word correspond to guide words.

perk•y (pûr'kē) adj. -i•er, -i•est. 1. Having a buoyant or self-confident air; briskly cheerful. 2. Jaunty; sprightly. — perk'-i•ly adv. — perk'i•ness n.

per•lite also pearl•ite (pûr'līt') n. A volcanic glass having distinctive concentric cracks and a relatively high water content, used in a heat-expanded form as a lightweight aggregate in insulation and potting soil. [Fr. (< perle, pearl < OFr.; see PEARL¹) or Ger. Perlite (< Perle, pearl, ult. < VLat. *pernula).]

perm (pûrm) Informal. — n. A permanent. — tr.v. permed, perm•ing, perms. To give (hair) a permanent.

Perm (pĕrm, pyĕrm). A city of W-central Russia on the Kama R. in the foothills of the Ural Mts. Pop. 1,056,000.

perm. abbr. Permanent.

per•ma•frost (pûr'mə-frôst', -frŏst') n. Permanently frozen subsoil, occurring throughout the Polar Regions and locally in perennially frigid areas. [PERMA(NENT) + FROST.]

Perm•al•loy (pûr'mə-loi', pûrm-ăl'oi'). A trademark used for any of several alloys of nickel and iron having high magnetic permeability.

per•ma•nence (pûr'mə-nəns) n. The quality or condition of being permanent.

per•ma•nen•cy (pûr'mə-nən-sē) n. Permanence.

per•ma•nent (pûr'mə-nənt) adj. 1. Lasting or remaining without essential change. 2. Not expected to change in status, condition, or place. — n. A long-lasting hair wave produced chemically and with heat. [ME < Lat. permanēns, permanent-, pr.part. of permanēre, to endure : per-, throughout; see PER- + manēre, to remain; see men-³*.] — per'ma•nent•ly adv. — per'ma•nent•ness n.

permanent magnet n. A piece of magnetic material that retains its magnetism after it is removed from a magnetic field.

permanent press n. 1. A chemical process in which fabrics are permanently shaped and treated for wrinkle resistance. 2. A fabric treated by permanent press. — per'ma•nent-press' (pûr'mə-nənt-prĕs') adj.

permanent tooth n. One of the second set of teeth in mammals. Human beings have 32 permanent teeth.

permanent wave n. See permanent.

per•man•ga•nate (pər-măng'gə-nāt') n. Any of the salts of permanganic acid, all of which are strong oxidizing agents.

per•man•gan•ic acid (pûr'măn-găn'ĭk, -măng-) n. An unstable inorganic acid, HMnO₄, existing only in dilute solution.

per•me•a•bil•i•ty (pûr'mē-ə-bĭl'ĭ-tē) n., pl. -ties. 1. The property or condition of being permeable. 2. The rate of flow of a liquid or gas through a porous material.

per•me•a•ble (pûr'mē-ə-bəl) adj. That can be permeated or penetrated, esp. by liquids or gases.

per•me•ance (pûr'mē-əns) n. A measure of the ability of a magnetic circuit to conduct magnetic flux; the reciprocal of reluctance. [< Lat. permeāre, to permeate. See PERMEATE.]

per•me•ase (pûr'mē-ās') n. An enzyme that promotes the passage of a substance across a cell membrane.

per•me•ate (pûr'mē-āt') v. -at•ed, -at•ing, -ates. — tr. 1. To spread or flow throughout; pervade. 2. To pass through the openings or interstices of: liquid permeating a membrane. — intr. To spread through or penetrate something. [Lat. permeāre, permeāt-, to penetrate : per-, through; see PER- + meāre, to pass; see mei-¹*.] — per'me•ant (-ənt), per'me•a'tive (-ā'tĭv) adj. — per'me•a'tion n.

Per•mi•an (pûr'mē-ən, pĕr'-) Geol. — adj. Of, belonging to, or being the geologic time of the seventh and last period of the Paleozoic Era. See table at geologic time. — n. The Permian Period or its deposits. [After Perm in W-central Russia.]

per•mis•si•ble (pər-mĭs'ə-bəl) adj. Permitted; allowable: permissible tax deductions. — per•mis'si•bil'i•ty, per•mis'si•ble•ness n. — per•mis'si•bly adv.

per•mis•sion (pər-mĭsh'ən) n. 1. The act of permitting. 2. Consent, esp. formal consent; authorization. [ME < OFr. < Lat. permissiō, permissiōn- < permissus, p.part. of permittere, to permit. See PERMIT.]

per•mis•sive (pər-mĭs'ĭv) adj. 1. Granting or inclined to grant permission; tolerant or lenient. 2. Permitting discretion; optional. 3. Archaic. Not forbidden; permitted. — per•mis'sive•ly adv. — per•mis'sive•ness n.

per•mit (pər-mĭt') v. -mit•ted, -mit•ting, -mits. — tr. 1. To allow the doing of (something); consent to. 2. To grant leave or consent to (someone); authorize. 3. To afford opportunity or possibility for. — intr. To afford opportunity; allow. — n. (pûr'mĭt, pər-mĭt'). 1. Permission, esp. in written form. 2. A document or certificate giving permission to do something; a license or warrant. [ME permitten < Lat. permittere : per-, through; see PER- + mittere, to let go.] — per•mit•tee' (pûr'mĭ-tē') n. — per•mit'ter n.

Usage Note: In the sense "to allow for, be consistent with," permit is often accompanied by of when its subject is inanimate: The wording permits of several interpretations. But permit of should not be used in the sense "to give permission": The law permits (not permits of) camping.

per•mit•tiv•i•ty (pûr'mĭ-tĭv'ĭ-tē) n., pl. -ties. Phys. A measure of the ability of a material to resist the formation of an electric field within it.

per•mu•ta•tion (pûr'myoō-tā'shən) n. 1. A complete change; a transformation. 2. The act of altering a given set of objects in a group. 3. Math. a. An ordered arrangement of the elements of a set. b. An operation that rearranges the elements of a set. — per'mu•ta'tion•al adj.

per•mute (pər-myoōt') tr.v. -mut•ed, -mut•ing, -mutes. 1. To change the order of. 2. Math. To subject to permutation. [ME permuten < OFr. permuter < Lat. permūtāre : per-, per- + mūtāre, to change; see mei-¹*.] — per•mut'a•bil'i•ty n. — per•mut'a•ble adj. — per•mut'a•bly adv.

per•ni•cious (pər-nĭsh'əs) adj. 1.a. Tending to cause death or serious injury; deadly: a pernicious virus. b. Causing great harm; destructive: pernicious rumors. 2. Archaic. Evil; wicked. [ME < OFr. pernicios < Lat. perniciōsus < perniciēs, destruction < per-, per- + nex, nec-, violent death; see nek-¹*.] — per•ni'cious•ly adv. — per•ni'cious•ness n.

pernicious anemia n. A severe anemia caused by failure of the stomach to absorb vitamin B₁₂ and characterized by abnormally large red blood cells and gastrointestinal disturbances.

per•nick•e•ty (pər-nĭk'ĭ-tē) adj. Persnickety. [?]

Pe•rón (pə-rŏn', pĕ-rŏn'), Juan Domingo. 1895–1974. Argentine soldier who served as president (1946–55 and 1973–74). His second wife, (Maria) Eva Duarte de Perón (1919–52), "Evita," was popular for her charitable works. Perón was succeeded by his third wife, Maria Estela Martínez de Perón (b. 1931), "Isabelita," who was ousted in 1976.

per•o•ne•al (pĕr'ə-nē'əl) adj. Of or relating to the fibula or to the outer portion of the leg. [< Gk. peronē, pin of a brooch, fibula. See per-²*.]

per•o•ral (pər-ôr'əl, -ōr'-) adj. Through or by way of the mouth: a peroral infection. — per•o'ral•ly adv.

per•o•rate (pĕr'ə-rāt') intr.v. -rat•ed, -rat•ing, -rates. 1. To conclude a speech with a formal recapitulation. 2. To speak at great length, often in a grandiloquent manner; declaim. [Lat. perōrāre, perōrāt- : per-, per- + ōrāre, to speak.] — per'o•ra'tion al adj. — per'o•ra'tion n.

per•ox•i•dase (pə-rŏk'sĭ-dās', -dāz') n. Any of a group of enzymes that occur esp. in plant cells and catalyze the oxidation of a substance by a peroxide.

per•ox•ide (pə-rŏk'sīd') n. 1. A compound, such as sodium peroxide, Na₂O₂, that contains a peroxyl group and yields hydrogen peroxide when treated with an acid. 2. Hydrogen peroxide. — tr.v. -id•ed, -id•ing, -ides. 1. To treat with peroxide. 2. To bleach (hair) with hydrogen peroxide. — per•ox'ide' adj. — per'ox•id'ic (pûr'ŏk-sĭd'ĭk) adj.

per•ox•i•some (pə-rŏk'sĭ-sōm') n. A cell organelle containing enzymes, such as catalase and oxidase, that catalyze the production and breakdown of hydrogen peroxide.

peroxy- pref. Containing the bivalent group O₂: peroxybenzoic acid. [PER- + OXY-.]

perp (pûrp) n. Slang. One who perpetrates a crime.

perp. abbr. Perpendicular.

per•pend (pər-pĕnd') v. -pend•ed, -pend•ing, -pends. — tr. To consider carefully; ponder. — intr. To be attentive; reflect. [Lat. perpendere : per-, per- + pendere, to weigh; see (s)pen-*.]

per•pen•dic•u•lar (pûr'pən-dĭk'yə-lər) adj. 1. Math. Intersecting at or forming right angles. 2. Being at right angles to the horizontal; vertical. 3. Often Perpendicular. Of or relating to a style of English Gothic architecture of the 14th and 15th centuries characterized by emphasis of the vertical element. — n. 1. Math. A line or plane perpendicular to a given line or plane. 2. A perpendicular position. 3. A device, such as a plumb line, used in marking the vertical from a given point. 4. A vertical or nearly vertical line or plane. [ME perpendiculer < OFr. < Lat. perpendiculāris < perpendiculum, plumb line < perpendere, to weigh carefully : per-, per- + pendere, to weigh; see (s)pen-*.] — per'pen•dic'u•lar'i•ty (-lăr'ĭ-tē) n. — per'pen•dic'u•lar•ly adv.

per•pe•trate (pûr'pĭ-trāt') tr.v. -trat•ed, -trat•ing, -trates. To be responsible for; commit. [Lat. perpetrāre, perpetrāt-, to accomplish : per-, per- + patrāre, to bring about (< pater, father; see pəter-*).] — per'pe•tra'tion n. — per'pe•tra'tor n.

per•pet•u•al (pər-pĕch'oō-əl) adj. 1. Lasting for eternity. 2. Continuing or lasting for an indefinitely long time. 3. Instituted to be in effect or having tenure for an unlimited duration: perpetual friendship. 4. Continuing without interruption. See Syns at continual. 5. Flowering throughout the growing season. [ME perpetuel < OFr. < Lat. perpetuālis < perpetuus, continuous : per-, per- + petere, to go toward; see pet-*.] — per•pet'u•al•ly adv.

perpetual calendar n. A chart or device that indicates the day of the week corresponding to a date over a period of years.

perpetual motion n. The hypothetical continuous operation of an isolated mechanical device or other closed system without a sustaining energy source.

per•pet•u•ate (pər-pĕch'oō-āt') tr.v. -at•ed, -at•ing, -ates. 1. To cause to continue indefinitely; make perpetual. 2. To prolong the existence of; cause to be remembered. [Lat. perpetuāre, perpetuāt- < perpetuus, continuous. See PERPETUAL.] — per•pet'u•ance, per•pet'u•a'tion n. — per•pet'u•a'tor n.

3. Many words like *commitment, success,* and *shatter* have doubled consonants. If you are having trouble finding a word, try doubling a consonant or leaving one out.
4. Pay attention to vowels. In some words, *a* or *e* can sound like *i*. Try several spellings until you find your word.

Exercise 2.1 The first column below lists pairs of guide words. The second column lists groups of words. Circle the word in each group that can be found on a page containing the guide words listed beside it. The first one is done as an example.

Guide Words	Words to Find
1. all-purpose/alphabetical	also, (along) alpine
2. bird-dog/bishop	bipolar, bisque, (biscuit)
3. chuck wagon/Cincinnati	(churn) cinema, chubby
4. fleece/flight	(fleet) flirt, fleck
5. gamut/garage	gamete, (gape) gargoyle
6. ham/handball	(hammer) handgun, handout
7. job/joker	jive, jostle (joiner)
8. percentile, perfume	perceive, (perceptive) percent
9. subway, suffer	sugar, suffix, (succotash)
10. yokel, youthful	yoke, (york) yowl

USE THE PARTS OF A DICTIONARY ENTRY

A *dictionary entry* consists of a word broken into syllables and all the information needed to explain its meaning. The entries contained in most dictionaries consist of five basic parts:

- Syllables
- Pronunciation
- Parts of speech
- Definitions and special meanings
- Word Origins

Reviewing the parts and improving your use of them will make using your dictionary easier.

Syllables

Generally speaking, a *syllable* represents a vowel sound. A word that has one vowel sound has one syllable. *Cake* is an example of a word with only one vowel sound because the only vowel sound you hear in this word is that of *ā*. A word that has two or more separate vowel sounds has two or more syllables. For example, in the word *catnip* you hear the vowel sounds of *ă* and *ĭ*.

Every dictionary entry begins with a correctly spelled word broken into syllables that are separated by dots as in the following examples.

case
cas•tle
ca•ta•log
con•ti•nen•tal

Case, a one-syllable word, is not separated by dots. As you can tell from the dots in the other three words, *castle* has two syllables, *catalog* has three syllables, and *continental* has four syllables.

Exercise 2.2   Using your dictionary, divide the following words into syllables. Place a dot between each syllable, as in the previous examples.

1. announce *an•nounce*

2. blockbuster *block•bust•er*

3. congregation *con•gre•ga•tion*

4. frustrate *frus•trate*

5. gregarious *gre•gar•i•ous*

6. laminate *lam•i•nate*

7. opportunity *op•por•tu•ni•ty*

8. participation *par•tic•i•pa•tion*

9. questionnaire *ques•tion•naire*

10. thermography *ther•mog•ra•phy*

Pronunciation

Dictionaries not only show words broken into syllables, they also show them spelled *phonetically* (by sound). The phonetic spelling of a word appears in parentheses beside it, as in the following example.

stren•u•ous (strĕn´yŏŏ • əs)

Each sound of a word is indicated by a different mark or *pronunciation symbol*. To pronounce words correctly, you may need to refer to your dictionary's pronunciation key at first. With experience, you will remember the sounds and symbols. Look for the pronunciation key near the front of your dictionary. Some dictionaries also print a key at the bottom of some pages or in the margin. The example shown in Figure 2.2 is from the *American Heritage College Dictionary*, Third Edition. Notice also that an abbreviated version of the key shown in Figure 2.2 is printed in each chapter's *Vocabulary Preview*. For example, see page 33.

To use a pronunciation key, match the symbols and sounds in the key with the sounds of the vowels in each syllable as shown in parentheses beside the word you are trying to pronounce. For example, the *e* in the first syllable of *strenuous* (stren´yoo • əs) sounds like the *e* in *pet*. The *u* in the second syllable sounds like *y* + the *oo* sound in *boot*. The *ou* in the third syllable sounds like the *a* in *about*.

The symbol that looks like an upside-down *e* is called a *schwa*. The sound of this symbol is pronounced "uh." It is the sound you hear in the *a* in *about* and the *e* in *item,* the example words used in Figure 2.2.

Exercise 2.3   Match the following vowel sounds in the words on page 41 with those shown in the key in Figure 2.2 below. The first one is done as an example.

FIGURE 2.2 Pronunciation Symbols

Symbols	Examples	Symbols	Examples	Symbols	Examples	Symbols	Examples
ă	pat	îr	pier	p	pop	zh	vision, pleasure
ā	pay	j	judge	r	roar		garage
âr	care	k	kick, cat, pique	s	sauce	ə	about, item, edible
ä	father	l	lid, needle* (nēd´l)	sh	ship, dish		gallop, circus
b	bib	m	mum	t	tight, stopped	ər	butter
ch	church	n	no, sudden* (sŭd´n)	th	thin		
d	deed, milled	ng	thing	*th*	this	**Foreign**	
ĕ	pet	ŏ	pot	ŭ	cut		
ē	bee	ō	toe	ûr	urge, term,	œ	*French* feu
f	fife, phase, rough	ô	caught, paw, for,		firm, word,		*German* schön
g	gag		horrid, hoarse**		heard	ü	*French* tu
h	hat	oi	noise	v	valve		*German* über
hw	which	ŏŏ	took	w	with	KH	*German* ich
ĭ	pit	ōō	boot	y	yes		*Scottish* loch
ī	pie, by	ou	out	z	zebra, xylem	N	*French* bon

*In English the consonants *l* and *n* often constitute complete syllables by themselves.
Regional pronunciations of *-or-* vary. In pairs such as **for, four; horse, hoarse; and **morning; mourning,** the vowel varies between (ô) and (ō). In this Dictionary these vowels are represented as follows: for (fôr), four (fôr, fōr); horse (hôrs), hoarse (hôrs, hōrs); and morning (môr´ning), mourning (môr´ning, mōr´-). A similar variant occurs in words such as **coral, forest,** and **horrid,** where the pronunciation of *o* before *r* varies between (ô) and (ō): forest (fôr´ĭst, fŏr´-).

1. The *a* in *angel* sounds like the *a* in _____*pay*_____.

2. The double *o* in *blooming* sounds like the double *o* in _____*boot*_____.

3. The *i* in *commit* sounds like the *i* in _____*pit*_____.

4. The *u* in *buckle* sounds like the *u* in _____*cut*_____.

5. The *e* in *stream* sounds like the *e* in _____*bee*_____.

Exercise 2.4 Sound out each of the phonetically spelled words below. On the line beside each word, write the correct spelling. The first one is done as an example.

1. kəm·pēt´ _compete_

2. pik´chûr _picture_

3. dī·am´·ĭ·tûr _diameter_

4. kôm´plĭ·kā´tĭd _complicated_

5. rĭ·lā´shŏn·shĭp _relationship_

6. ar´kē·ŏl´ō·jē _archeology_

An *accent mark* indicates which syllable of a word gets the most stress, or is pronounced more heavily, as in the following words:

express   (ĭk·sprĕs´)
market   (mär´kĭt)
attention   (ə·tĕn´shən)

In *express,* the accent is on the second syllable. In *market,* the accent is on the first syllable. In *attention,* the accent is on the second syllable.

One-syllable words have no accent mark. Some longer words have two accent marks: a *primary* and a *secondary.* The primary accent mark may be larger or darker than the secondary accent mark to show you which syllable gets the most stress. The secondary accent mark shows you which of the remaining syllables gets more stress than any un-marked syllables. Look at the next two examples:

anthropology (ăn´thrə·pôl´ə·jē)
registration (rĕj´ĭ·strā´shən)

In both words, the third syllable gets the primary accent and the first syllable gets the secondary accent. To pronounce either word correctly, you would emphasize the first syllable and give the third syllable a little extra emphasis.

Exercise 2.5   Working with a partner, use your dictionary to look up the following words. On the line beside each word, rewrite the word using pronunciation symbols and accent marks. The first one is done as an example.

1. excel Ĭk·sĕl´ _____

2. reformer rĭ·fôrm´ər _____

3. consequence kŏn´sĭ·kwĕns´ _____

4. remember rĭ·mĕm´bər _____

5. photography fa·tŏg´rə·fē _____

6. radiology rā´dē·ŏl´ə·jē _____

Parts of Speech

A word may be a noun, pronoun, verb, adjective, or other part of speech. Some words function as more than one part of speech. To find a word's part of speech, look for an abbreviation in italics following the pronunciation symbols in parentheses as in the following words.

apologize (ə·pôl´ə·jīz) *v.*
better (bĕt´ər) *adj.*

In these words, the abbreviations tell you that *apologize* is a verb, and *better* is an adjective.

Although most nouns form their plurals by adding *-s* as in *solids* or *-es* as in *gases,* some do not. For example, the plural of *mouse* is *mice.* A dictionary entry for *mouse* looks like this:

mouse (mous) *n., pl.* mice (mīs)

In this entry, *pl.* stands for *plural* and indicates that an irregular spelling follows.

Following is a list of the parts of speech and their abbreviations as found in most dictionaries.

noun (n.)	verb (v.)	adverb (adv.)
pronoun (pro.)	adjective (adj.)	interjection (interj.)

FIGURE 2.3 A Word Having More Than One Meaning

con•tract (kŏn′trăkt′) *n.* **1.a.** An agreement between two or more parties, esp. one written and enforceable by law. **b.** The writing or document containing such an agreement. **2.** The branch of law dealing with formal agreements between parties. **3.** Marriage as a formal agreement; betrothal. **4.** *Games.* **a.** The last and highest bid of a suit of one hand in bridge. **b.** The number of tricks thus bid. **5.** A paid assignment to murder someone. — *v.* (kən-trăkt′, kŏn′trăkt′) **-tract•ed, -tract•ing, -tracts.** — *tr.* **1.** To enter into by contract; establish or settle by formal agreement. **2.** To acquire or incur. **3.a.** To reduce in size by drawing together; shrink. **b.** To pull together; wrinkle. **4.** *Gram.* To shorten (a word or words) by omitting or combining letters or sounds. — *intr.* **1.** To enter into an agreement. **2.** To become reduced in size by or as if by being drawn together. [ME < Lat. *contrāctus,* p.part. of *contrahere,* to draw together : *com-,* com- + *trahere,* to draw.] — con•tract′i•bil′i•ty, con•tract′i•ble•ness *n.* — con•tract′i•ble *adj.*

> Noun Meanings

> Verb Meanings

Words can have more than one meaning, and they are grouped and numbered according to their parts of speech. The entry for *contract* in Figure 2.3 is an example. The source of the entry is the *American Heritage College Dictionary,* Third Edition.

As a noun, *contract* has five meanings. As a verb, it has four meanings. Notice that when *contract* is used as a verb, you can pronounce it with the accent on either the first or second syllable. But when you use *contract* as a noun, the accent is on the first syllable.

Exercise 2.6   The words listed below are from the reading selection on pages 33–34, and all of them can be used as more than one part of speech. First, write the name of the dictionary you are using. Then look up each word and list the parts of speech and number of definitions that appear in the entry. The first one is done as an example. *(Answers may vary depending on the dictionary used.)*

Name of dictionary: *American Heritage College Dictionary, Third Edition*

1. reason *noun (4), verb (3)*

2. space _____

3. burst _____

4. support _____

5. concern _____

6. network _____

Definitions and Special Meanings

In a dictionary entry, definitions follow the part of speech. Definitions are numbered, and the first one indicates the word's most common usage. Those that come after the first definition indicate less frequent usages. In some dictionaries, a list of *synonyms* (words having similar meanings) follows the definitions.

A label such as *informal* or *slang* before a word indicates a special meaning, one you would use only in certain situations. An abbreviation such as *chem.* (chemistry) or *biol.* (biology) may come before a definition. These labels indicate that the definitions apply only in those scientific fields. For example, a word may have one meaning when used in your biology class and a different meaning when used in other situations.

Listed below are some common labels and their definitions found in most dictionaries. Look near the front of your dictionary to find a list of the abbreviations and labels it uses.

- Nonstandard   unacceptable to educated people
- Informal   limited to conversation and informal writing
- Slang   improper for formal conversation and writing
- Offensive   used for words or expressions that are insulting
- Geol.   applies to the field of geology
- Electron.   applies to the electronics field
- Mus.   applies to the field of music
- Archaic   out of date, no longer in use

The following example from the *American Heritage College Dictionary*, Third Edition, shows two entries for *flat*. Read the entries and notice this word's parts of speech, number of definitions, and special meanings.

flat¹ (flăt) *adj.* **flat·ter, flat·test. 1.** Having a horizontal surface without a slope, tilt, or curvature. **2.** Having a smooth, even, level surface: *a skirt sewed with fine flat seams.* **3.** Having a relatively broad surface in relation to thickness or depth: *a flat board.* See Synonyms at **level. 4.** Stretched out or lying at full length along the ground; prone. **5.** Free of qualification; absolute: *a flat refusal.* **6.** Fixed; unvarying: *a flat rate.* **7.** Lacking interest or excitement; dull: *a flat scenario.* **8.a.** Lacking in flavor: *a flat stew that needs salt.* **b.** Having lost effervescence or sparkle: *flat beer.* **9.a.** Deflated. Used of a tire. **b.** Electrically discharged. Used of a storage battery. **10.** Of or relating to a horizontal line that displays no ups or downs and signifies the absence of physiological activity: *A flat electroencephalogram indicates a loss of brain function.* **11.** Commercially inactive; sluggish: *flat sales for the month.* **12.** Unmodulated; monotonous: *a flat voice.* **13.** Lacking variety in tint or shading; uniform: "*The sky was bright but flat, the color of oyster shells*" (Anne Tyler). **14.** Not glossy; mat: *flat paint.* **15.** *Music.* **a.** Being below the correct pitch. **b.** Being one half step lower than the corresponding natural key: *the key of B flat.* **16.** Designating the vowel *a* as pronounced in *bad* or *cat.* **17.** *Nautical.* Taut. Used of a sail. —**flat** *adv.* **1.a.** Level with the ground; horizontally. **b.** On or up against a flat surface; at full length. **2.** So as to be flat. **3.a.** Directly; completely: *went flat against the rules; flat broke.* **b.** Exactly; precisely: *arrived in six minutes flat.* **4.** *Music.* Below the intended pitch. **5.** *Business.* Without interest charge. —**flat** *n.* **1.** A flat surface or part. **2.** Often **flats.** A stretch of level ground: *salt flats.* **3.** A shallow frame or box for seeds or seedlings. **4.** Stage scenery on a movable wooden frame. **5.** A flatcar. **6.** A deflated tire. **7.** A shoe with a flat heel. **8.** A large flat piece of mail. **9.** A horse that competes in a flat race. Also called *runner.* **10.** *Music.* **a.** A sign (♭) affixed to a note to indicate that it is to be lowered by a half step. **b.** A note that is lowered a half step. **11.** *Football.* The area of the field to either side of an offensive formation. —**flat** *v.* **flat·ted, flat·ting, flats.** —*tr.* **1.** To make flat; flatten. **2.** *Music.* To lower (a note) a semitone. —*intr. Music.* To sing or play below the proper pitch. [Middle English, from Old Norse *flatr.* See **plat-** in Appendix.] —**flat′ly** *adv.* —**flat′ness** *n.*

flat² (flăt) *n.* **1.** An apartment on one floor of a building. **2.** *Archaic.* A story in a house. [Alteration of Scots *flet,* inner part of a house, from Middle English, from Old English, floor, dwelling. See **plat-** in Appendix.]

The first entry for *flat* shows seventeen adjective meanings, five adverb meanings, eleven noun meanings, and two verb meanings. *Mus.*

before several definitions indicates that *flat* has several usages in the field of music. *Naut.* before a definition means that *flat* has a special meaning to people in nautical fields such as sailing or shipping. The second entry for *flat* shows two more noun meanings, one of which is no longer in use.

Because a word can have more than one meaning, the way it is used in a sentence determines its definition. Now read the next five example sentences and the explanation that follows them:

1. The performance was too long and the jokes were *flat.*
2. Maria's cat lay *flat* on its back.
3. Last summer, we visited the great salt *flats.*
4. Bob *flattened* the roach with one blow.
5. When Sarah went to London last summer she stayed in her aunt's *flat* on the second floor of a large building.

Sentences 1 through 4 use definitions from the first entry for *flat.* In the first sentence flat means *dull* as in definition *adj. 7* in the example. In the second sentence, flat means *at full length* as in definition *adv. 1b.* In the third sentence, flat means *a stretch of level ground* as in *n. 2.* In the fourth sentence, flattened means *made flat* as in *v. 1.*

In sentence 5, *flat* means *apartment,* as in definition 1 of the second entry.

When you need to look up the definition of an unfamiliar word that has several meanings, how do you know which meaning fits your sentence? The following tips will help.

- If you can identify an unfamiliar word's part of speech as it is used in a sentence, look only at the definitions following that part of speech. For example, if you know the word is used as a noun, look only at the noun definitions.
- If you cannot identify the part of speech, read each definition until you find one that seems to fit.
- For most college reading, ignore definitions preceded by the labels *slang* or *nonstandard.*
- When you think you have found the right definition, read your sentence, substituting the definition for the unfamiliar word. If the new sentence makes sense, you probably have found the definition.

Exercise 2.7   Working with a partner, read the following dictionary entry for *fast.* Then define *fast* as used in each sentence. Write the part of speech and number of the definition on the line beside each sentence. The first one is done as an example.

fast¹ (făst) *adj.* **fast·er, fast·est. 1.** Acting, moving, or capable of acting or moving quickly; swift. **2.** Accomplished in relatively little time: *a fast visit.* **3.** Indicating a time somewhat ahead of the actual time: *The clock is fast.* **4.** Adapted to or suitable for rapid movement: *a fast running track.* **5.** Designed for or compatible with a short exposure time: *fast film.* **6.a.** Disposed to dissipation; wild: *ran with a fast crowd.* **b.** Flouting conventional moral standards; sexually promiscuous. **7.** Resistant, as to destruction or fading: *fast colors.* **8.** Firmly fixed or fastened: *a fast grip.* **9.** Fixed firmly in place; secure: *shutters that are fast against the rain.* **10.** Firm in loyalty: *fast friends.* **11.** Lasting; permanent: *fast rules and regulations.* **12.** Deep; sound: *in a fast sleep.* —**fast** *adv.* **1.** In a secure manner; tightly: *hold fast.* **2.** To a sound degree; deeply: *fast asleep.* **3.** In a rapid manner; quickly. **4.** In quick succession: *New ideas followed fast.* **5.** Ahead of the correct or expected time: *a watch that runs fast.* **6.** In a dissipated, immoderate way: *living fast.* **7.** *Archaic.* Close by; near. [Middle English, from Old English *fæst,* firm, fixed. See **past-** in Appendix.]

SYNONYMS: *fast, rapid, swift, fleet, speedy, quick, hasty, expeditious.* These adjectives refer to something, such as activity or movement, marked by great speed. *Fast* and *rapid* are often used interchangeably, though *fast* is more often applied to the person or thing in motion, and *rapid,* to the activity or movement involved: *a fast car; a fast plane; a rapid mountain stream; rapid development; a fast runner; rapid strides. Swift* suggests smoothness and sureness of movement (*a swift current; swift but unclear handwriting*), and *fleet,* lightness of movement (*The cheetah is the fleetest of animals*). *Speedy* refers to velocity (*a speedy worker*) or to promptness or hurry (*hoped for a speedy resolution to the problem*). *Quick* most often applies to what takes little time or to promptness of response or action: *Let's eat a quick snack. Only her quick reaction prevented an accident. Hasty* implies hurried action (*a hasty visit*) and often a lack of care or thought (*regretted the hasty decision*). *Expeditious* suggests rapid efficiency: *sent the package by the most expeditious means.* See also Synonyms at **faithful.**

fast² (făst) *intr.v.* **fast·ed, fast·ing, fasts. 1.** To abstain from food. **2.** To eat very little or abstain from certain foods, especially as a religious discipline. —**fast** *n.* **1.** The act or practice of abstaining from or eating very little food. **2.** A period of such abstention or self-denial. [Middle English *fasten,* from Old English *fæstan.* See **past-** in Appendix.]

---

adj. 12   1.   The children were *fast* asleep.

intr. v.2   2.   In some religions, people *fast* on certain days.

adv. 6   3.   Have you heard the old saying "Live *fast,* die young"?

adv. 5   4.   Do you have the time? I think my watch is *fast.*

adj. 6b   5.   My mother warned me to avoid a person who has a reputation for being *fast.*

adv. 1   6.   Are the windows and doors locked *fast*?

Word Origins

Etymology means the origin or history of a word: the language it came from and how it developed over time. Most of the words in the English language originated from other languages. To find a word's origin, read the information printed in brackets at the end of the entry. For example, look at the end of the entry for *contract* in Figure 2.3 and find the word's origin. *ME* and *Lat.* in brackets trace this word's history from Latin, to Middle English, to its present day use. (The last origin listed is the earliest one known.)

Following is a short list of the languages from which many English words originated and their abbreviations. The list is excerpted from the *American Heritage College Dictionary,* Third Edition.

Afrikaans	Afr.	Greek	Gk.
Arabic	Ar.	Hebrew	Heb.
Old English	OE	Latin	Lat.
French	Fr.	Middle English	ME
German	Ger.	Spanish	Sp.

Memory Cue

Syllables, pronunciation, parts of speech, definitions, and origins are the five parts of a dictionary entry. Syllables represent vowel sounds. Pronunciation symbols and accent marks help you pronounce words correctly. Abbreviations for parts of speech and special meanings help you find the right definition. A word's origin tells you its history.

MAKE NOTE CARDS FOR WORDS AND TERMS

In your college reading you are likely to encounter new words and terms every day. In your courses you are learning about different fields of study such as biology, psychology, finance and marketing, computer technology, and others. Each of these disciplines introduces you to special terms that you must learn so that you can speak and write clearly and accurately about the field. Moreover, a knowledge of each discipline's special terms is essential to your understanding of the textbook and related reading materials.

Take the first step toward expanding your vocabulary by identifying the words and terms you need to study. Textbook authors call attention to important terms by making them stand out. Look for words and terms printed in italics, bold type, or a different color. Some authors list essential vocabulary at the beginning or end of a chapter. Pay attention to the terms your instructor uses in lectures and discussions. Make a master list of the terms you need to learn. As the semester or quarter progresses, add to your list.

Because the human memory needs prodding, you must review words and terms frequently and systematically, or you will forget them. To help you prod your memory, make a note card for each word or term

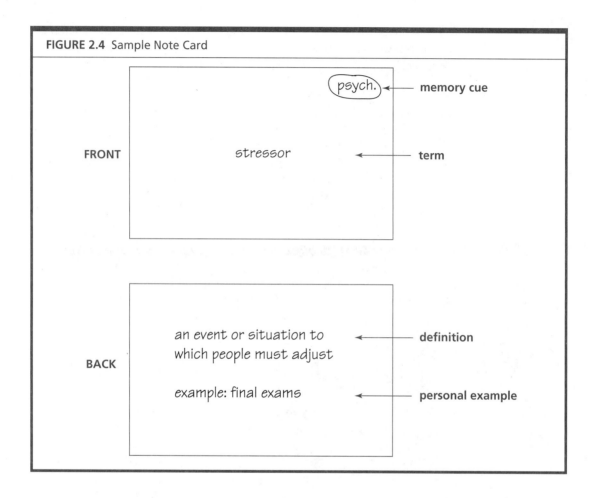

FIGURE 2.4 Sample Note Card

on your list. Look at the sample note card in Figure 2.4 and follow these suggestions.

1. Buy a pack of 3-by-5 inch note cards. They are easy to carry in your purse, pocket, or backpack.
2. Write the word or term on the front of the card.
3. Write a memory cue also on the front of the card to remind you of the source of the word or term. For example, write *biol.* for biology if the term is from your biology course, *psych.* for psychology, and so forth. A chapter number or book title could also serve as a memory cue.
4. Write the definition on the back of the card. You could also write the word in a sentence or add an example.

5. Review your note cards every day. Begin by turning all the cards so that only the words show. Look at the word and recite its definition. Then check yourself by looking on the back of the card.

When you can go through the whole pack of cards without missing a word or term, you may not need to continue reviewing every day. Instead, review your cards as often as needed to keep the definitions fresh in your mind.

Exercise 2.8　　The following list contains this chapter's important words and terms. Make a note card for each one. The words and terms are listed in the order that they appear in the chapter. Read back through the chapter to find the definitions. Review your note cards and use your new vocabulary in class discussions, writing assignments, and on tests. *(Students' note cards should resemble the one in Figure 2.4.)*

1. guide words
2. dictionary entry
3. syllable
4. pronunciation symbols
5. accent marks
6. part of speech
7. synonym
8. etymology

Memory Cue

New words and terms are easier to learn and remember if you have a system. Make a master list of words and terms for study. Make note cards from your master list and review them often. To make a note card, write the term and a memory cue on the front. Write the definition on the back.

REAL-WORLD CONNECTIONS

The following ad appeared in *Time* magazine during the second week of September, 1997. The ad makes clear that your vocabulary can make a positive or negative impression on people. For example, the way you use language tells a college admissions officer or future employer as much about you as the grades on your transcript or the qualifications listed on your résumé.

Read and discuss the ad with a partner. Then answer the questions that follow. Share your answers with the rest of the class.

By permission. Merriam-Webster, Incorporated at http://www.m-w.com

1. Why do you think the advertisers chose to run the ad during September?

   Most colleges begin the school year in September. Students buy

   books early in the term.

2. What audience does the ad appeal to, and how can you tell?

   The ad appeals to college students. The young women, the college

   dictionary, the phrase "good friends," and the slang use of "like" tell you so.

3. Write your definition of *commitment* below. Then look up the word in your dictionary. Revise your definition as needed.

   A commitment is an emotional bond between people in a relationship.

4. An advertisement tells a story that is revealed in pictures and words. Look at the picture and read the ad's text. Then briefly describe what you think the two women are talking about.

   One woman puts down her boyfriend for lacking commitment. She says

   he can't even spell the word. The woman who says, "Neither can you"

   suggests that the other woman may also have trouble with commitment.

   In other words, she needs a dictionary.

5. The ad's purpose is to sell dictionaries. If you were planning to buy a dictionary, would this ad convince you to consider the *Merriam Webster's Collegiate Dictionary?* Why or why not?

   Answers will vary.

HOW WELL DO YOU REMEMBER?

To review the chapter, read the following summary and fill in the blanks. If you need help with an answer, look back through the chapter to refresh your memory.

Using a dictionary consistently will help you in all your courses. Whether you need to look up a definition or check a word's spelling, your dictionary is an indispensable tool. To find a word quickly, use your dictionary's _____*guide*_____ words listed at the top of each page. In addition, know what kind of information a dictionary entry contains.

Each entry consists of a word followed by several important pieces of information. First, a word is broken down into ____*syllables*____ that represent vowel sounds. Next, the ____*phonetic*____ spelling of a word shows you how to pronounce it. Each sound is indicated by a mark or symbol. The ____*accent mark*____ tells you which part of a word gets the most stress. Some entries include ____*synonyms*____, words that have similar meanings. Near the end of an entry is an explanation of the word's ____*etymology*____: its origin or history. For example, if you see *Lat.* in brackets following a definition, you know that the word comes from ____*Latin*____.

Make a habit of learning new words and special terms. The ____*note*____ ____*card*____ technique explained in this chapter is a proven method that has worked for many students.

The dictionary skills you develop in college will follow you into the workplace and other areas of your life where a good vocabulary is not only helpful but may be essential.

WHAT DO YOU THINK?

Reflect on your use of a dictionary. What have you learned from this chapter that will help you use your dictionary more effectively? Which of this chapter's strategies can you use immediately? Write your reflections below.

Reflections will vary.

_____

CHAPTER QUIZ 1

Part 1 Terms and Definitions

Match this chapter's special terms in Column A with their definitions in Column B.

Column A

_c_ 1. syllable
_e_ 2. phonetic spelling
_d_ 3. guide words
_b_ 4. dictionary entry
_a_ 5. discipline

Column B

a. a field of study
b. gives information about a word
c. vowel sound
d. help you find a specific word
e. the way a word sounds

Part 2 Chapter Review

Read and answer each question below. Write your answer in complete sentences, and use extra paper if needed. *(Answers may vary but should be similar to these.)*

1. What are the five parts of a dictionary entry?

   The five parts of an entry are syllables, pronunciation, parts of speech,

   definitions and special meanings, and origins.

2. How do you find a word that you do not know how to spell?

   Spell it the way it sounds. Try several spellings. Try doubling consonants,

   substituting different letters or combinations, or leaving out a letter.

3. What do these labels mean when placed before a definition: *chem.,*
   informal, and *nonstandard?*

   These labels indicate a special meaning follows. "Chem." means "chemistry."

   "Informal" means "used for speech or informal writing." "Nonstandard"

   means "unacceptable to educated people."

Part 3 Using Your Skills

1. Match vowel sounds in the words given with those in the key.

Pronunciation Key. a(păt), ā(pāy), e(pĕt), ē(bee), i(pĭt), ī(pīe), o(pŏt),
ō(tōe), oo(boot), u(cŭt), û(ûrge)

a. The *e* in *wheat* sounds like the *e* in _____ bee _____ .

b. The *u* in *umbrella* sounds like the *u* in _____ cut _____ .

c. The *o* in *remove* sounds like the *o* in _____ boot _____ .

d. The *i* in *revise* sounds like the *i* in _____ pie _____ .

e. The *e* in *etymology* sounds like the *e* in _____ pet _____ .

f. The *a* in *remain* sounds like the *a* in _____ pay _____ .

2. Circle a word in each group in Column B that can be found on a
   page containing the guide words in Column A.

Column A	**Column B**
a. appear/appreciate	appeal, (appoint) approach
b. Columbus Day/comet	comfort, (comedy) compare
c. haystack/headquarters	harvest, hayloft, (headpiece)
d. likelihood/limp	lighthouse, likable, (limbo)
e. organ/orphan	(organize), oregano, orphanage
f. time bomb/tip	timber, (tinker) titanic

Score: 100 − 5 for each one missed = _____ %

CHAPTER QUIZ 2

Part 1 Terms and Definitions

Match this chapter's special terms in Column A with their definitions in Column B.

Column A

_c_ 1. accent mark

_e_ 2. etymology

_d_ 3. part of speech

_a_ 4. schwa

_b_ 5. synonym

Column B

a. a pronunciation symbol

b. a word that means about the same as another word

c. indicates which part of a word gets the most stress

d. a verb or noun, for example

e. a word's origin or history

Part 2 Chapter Review

Read and answer each question below. Write your answer in complete sentences, and use extra paper if needed. *(Answers may vary but should be similar to these.)*

1. Why is it necessary to learn the terms of a discipline?

   A word may have a special meaning when used in a discipline such as

   chemistry or biology.

2. Some words have more than one meaning. How do you know which definition is the one you want?

   A word's part of speech and the way it is used in a sentence determines

   which definition to choose.

3. What is the note-card system for learning new words as explained in this chapter?

   Write words to learn on note cards. Write the word and a memory cue on

   one side and a definition and example on the other side. Review often.

Part 3 Using Your Skills

Read the following entry from the *American Heritage College Dictionary,* Third Edition, and answer the questions.

for·mu·la (fôr′myə-lə) *n., pl.* **-las** or **-lae** (-lē′). **1.a.** An established form of words or symbols for use in a ceremony or procedure. **b.** An utterance of conventional notions or beliefs; a hackneyed expression. **2.** A method of doing or treating something that relies on an established uncontroversial model or approach. **3.** *Chem.* **a.** A symbolic representation of the composition or of the composition and structure of a compound. **b.** The compound so represented. **4.a.** A prescription of ingredients in fixed proportion; a recipe. **b.** A liquid food for infants, containing most of the nutrients in human milk. **5.** *Math.* A statement, esp. an equation, of a rule, principle, or other factual relation. **6. Formula.** *Sports.* A set of specifications that determine a class of racing car. [Lat. *fŏrmula,* dim. of *fŏrma,* form.] **—for′mu·la′ic** (-lā′ĭk) *adj.* **—for′mu·la′i·cal·ly** *adv.*

1. What does *formula* mean as applied to mathematics?

   a statement of a rule, principle, or other factual relation

2. What does *formula* mean as applied to chemistry?

   symbolic representation of a compound's composition and/or structure

3. What is the number of the definition that refers to baby's formula?

   4b

4. Can *formula* be used as a verb? How can you tell?

   No, because the entry does not list any verb definitions.

5. What is the origin of *formula?*

   "Formula" comes from the Latin "formula" or "forma."

Score: 100 − 8 for each one missed = _____%

Vocabulary Quiz

Each sentence below contains a word in bold type from the reading selection on pages 33–34. Read the sentence and the definitions that follow it. Turn to the vocabulary preview on pages 32–33 to check your answers.

1. My boyfriend does not observe conversational **etiquette** because he does not let anyone else get a word in.
   a. tone of voice
   b. topic
   c. rules of conduct
   d. skills

2. If you really want to burn calories, then you must do **strenuous** exercise so that you get a hard workout.
   a. frequent
   b. light
   c. minimal
   d. energetic

3. My grandmother's apples grew in such **abundance** that we had them at almost every meal.
   a. plenty
   b. trees
   c. ways
   d. types

4. No matter how much the cheerleaders tried, they could not arouse the **apathetic** crowd.
   a. sleeping
   b. uninterested
   c. quiet
   d. unruly

5. When the children tired of one project, their teacher **channeled** their interests into another project.
   a. guided
   b. videotaped
   c. forced
   d. distracted

6. Rumors about the latest scandal in Washington were **rife** in the media; every newspaper and T.V. news show reported it.
   a. numerous
   b. confirmed
   c. disproved
   d. outrageous

7. Because the students' mistakes were **innumerable,** the instructor decided to give a retest.
   a. infrequent
   b. unimportant
   (c.) too many to count
   d. careless

8. The people standing in line could not conceal their **exasperation** when they learned that the movie was sold out.
   a. surprise
   (b.) annoyance
   c. amusement
   d. tickets

9. Do not **exploit** my labor by paying me too little for my work.
   a. bargain for
   b. request
   c. reward
   (d.) use unethically

Score: 100 − 10 for each one missed = _____ %

Chapter 3

Using Context Clues

*Y*our vocabulary reflects your personality and education. Your vocabulary can create a favorable or unfavorable impression on others. Overwhelmingly, employers in a wide variety of fields say that they want employees to have good *communication skills*. These skills include reading, speaking, writing, and listening. If your vocabulary is limited, then your ability to express your ideas or to understand others' ideas is also limited. Fortunately, you can develop your vocabulary.

As explained in Chapter 2, you can begin to develop your vocabulary by using your dictionary efficiently and by using the note-card method for learning new words and terms. This chapter explains how to use *context clues:* words or phrases within a sentence or paragraph that act as clues to the meaning of an unfamiliar word or term. You can increase your reading comprehension, speed, and vocabulary by using four types of context clues:

- *The definition clue*
- *The example clue*
- *The contrast clue*
- *The inference clue*

WHAT DO YOU ALREADY KNOW?

To prepare yourself for the reading selection that follows, find out what you already know about the power of words to affect others. Answer the questions below either on your own or in a group discussion.

1. What kind or cruel words have made a lasting impression on you?

2. Suppose you had to do something even though you believed you lacked the skill. What would be the most encouraging words someone could say to you?

3. What words of encouragement have you offered to others?

4. Read the title, headnote, vocabulary preview, and first two paragraphs of the reading selection. What do you think will follow?

Four Words

Bob Greene

Bob Greene is a journalist and the author of several books. His columns have appeared in many newspapers across the United States. In this essay from He Was a Midwestern Boy on His Own, *Greene tells about a Japanese college student who felt encouraged by a young man's words.*

VOCABULARY PREVIEW

assured	(ə·sho͞ord´) made certain, guaranteed
naive	(nä·ēv´) lacking worldly knowledge
gymnasium	(jĭm·nā´zē·əm) room or building equipped for indoor sports
lousy	(lou´zē) inferior or worthless
humiliated	(hyo͞o·mĭl´ē·āt·ĭd) feeling a loss of pride or respect

undoubtedly	(ŭn·dout´ĭd·lē) without doubt, certainly
perceived	(pər·sēvd´) understood, made aware
coed	(kō´ĕd) coeducational, educating both men and women

Pronunciation Key: ā (**pay**), ä(**father**), ē(**bee**), ĭ(**pit**), ō(**toe**), o͞o (**boot**), o͝o(**took**), ou(**out**), ŭ(**cut**), ə(**about**, **item**)

If anyone has said anything cruel to you—something that has stuck with you for a long time; if anyone has ever said anything very kind to you—something that has stuck with you for a long time. . . .   1

Well, be **assured** that you're feeling emotions that have nothing to do with national boundaries.   2

In the city of Fujisawa, Japan, which is near Yokohama, lives a woman named Atsuko Saeki. She is twenty-six years old; she is single and lives with her parents. She has a job as a sales clerk at the Yurindo Bookstore in her town.   3

When she was a teenager, she dreamed of coming to the United States. Most of what she knew about American life she had read in textbooks. "I had a picture of the daddy sitting in the living room," she said, "and of the mommy baking chocolate chip cookies, and of a big dog lying by the couch. In my mind, the teenage girl goes to the movies on the weekends with her boyfriend. . . ."   4

She arranged to attend a college in the United States—Lassen College, in Susanville, California. When she arrived in the United States, though, it was not the dream world she had imagined. She couldn't blame anyone; it was no one's fault, and certainly not the college's fault. She considered herself **naive** to have pictured American life in such storybook terms.   5

"People were struggling with their own problems," she said. "People had family troubles, and money worries, and often they seemed very tense. I felt very alone."   6

At college, one of the classes that was hardest for her was physical education.   7

"We played volleyball," she said. "The class was held in an indoor **gymnasium.** The other students were very good at it, but I wasn't."   8

She tried to have fun playing volleyball, and often she was able 9
to. But the games made her nervous. "I was very short, compared to
the other students," she said. "I felt I wasn't doing a very good job.
To be very honest, I was a **lousy** player."

One afternoon, the physical education instructor told Atsuko 10
Saeki that she was assigned to set the volleyball up for the other
players on her team. "I was told that it was my job to hit the ball to
them, so that they could hit it over the net."

No big deal for most people, but it terrified Atsuko Saeki. For 11
some reason, she feared she would be **humiliated** if she failed—
if she was unable to set the shots up for her teammates.
Undoubtedly they would have forgiven her. But in this world
each person's fears—each person's **perceived** humiliations—are
private and are real.

Apparently a young man on her team sensed what she was going 12
through. This was a **coed** class; he was on her side of the net.

"He walked up to me," she said. "He whispered to me: 'Oh, 13
come on. You can do that.'

"He said it in a nice way, but he was serious. If you are the kind 14
of person who has always been encouraged by your family or your
friends or somebody else, maybe you will never understand how
happy those words made me feel. Four words: 'You can do that.' "

She made it through the phys ed. class. She may have thanked 15
the young man; she is not sure.

But now five years have passed; she is out of college, and back in 16
Japan, and living in her parents' house.

"I have never forgotten the words," she said. " 'You can do that.' 17
When things are not going so well, I think of those words."

She is quite sure that the young man had no idea how much his 18
words meant to her. "I'm sure that he was just a nice guy," she said.
"I'm sure that he was the kind of guy who would say those words to
anyone.

"But at the time it made a big difference to me. When I left the 19
gymnasium I felt like crying with happiness. He probably doesn't even
remember saying the words."

Which, perhaps, is the lesson here. You say something cruel to a 20
person, you have no idea how long it will stick. You say something
kind, you have no idea how long that will stick.

"I remember the young man's name," Atsuko Saeki said. "His 21
name was William Sawyer. I do not know what happened to him, but
he helped me just by whispering to me."

She's all the way over there in Japan. But still she hears his words: 22
"You can do that." 23

HOW WELL DID YOU COMPREHEND?

Main Idea

1. Which statement best expresses what the whole essay is about?
   a. Your emotions have nothing to do with the country you live in.
   b. For years Atsuko Saeki had dreamed of coming to the United States.
   c. Most people have a false picture of life in other countries.
   (d.) You have no idea how long your cruel or kind words will be remembered.

Details

2. What is the name of the college that Atsuko Saeki attended?
   a. Fujisawa
   b. Yokohama
   (c.) Lassen
   d. Susanville

3. According to Atsuko Saeki, the United States was not the dream world she had imagined because
   (a.) people were struggling with their own problems.
   b. teenage girls go to movies on the weekends.
   c. Americans live storybook lives.
   d. American families are like Japanese families.

4. Besides his kind words, what else did Atsuko Saeki remember about the young man?
   a. what he looked like
   b. what happened to him
   c. where he lived
   (d.) his name

5. Playing volleyball made Atsuko Saeki nervous for several reasons. Which of the following is *not* one of the reasons?
   a. She was shorter than the other students.
   (b.) She often had fun playing volleyball.
   c. She was not very good at it.
   d. The other students were good players.

Inferences

6. Which of the following is the author's unstated message to the reader?
   a. Some people are more sensitive to personal remarks than others.
   b. What people say to you does not matter because you will probably forget it.
   c. You should think about what you say because words make a lasting impression.
   d. People who criticize others are not popular.

Working with Words

Complete the sentences below with these words from the vocabulary preview.

| naive | assured | undoubtedly | coed |
| gymnasium | humiliated | perceived | lousy |

1. A student giving a serious speech may be ___humiliated___ when classmates laugh.

2. Chelsea Clinton chose to attend a ___coed___ university instead of a women's college.

3. It is normal to feel ___lousy___ about hurting a friend's feelings.

4. People who are ___naive___ may not suspect that someone is trying to take advantage of them.

5. The teacher ___perceived___ the student's remark to be an insult, but it was really a compliment.

6. The ___gymnasium___ was filled to overflowing during the basketball playoff.

7. The dark clouds and the weather make me think that we ___undoubtedly___ will have rain today.

8. Raymond has ___assured___ me that he will be here on time.

Thinking and Writing

As you read Greene's essay, did Atsuko Saeki's story seem familiar? Have you ever lacked confidence in your ability to do something that you wanted to do? What happened? Did you achieve your goal? Write about your experience.

Answers will vary.

_____

_____

_____

_____

WHAT ARE CONTEXT CLUES?

Having a dictionary available when you are reading is a good idea. But in some situations you may not be able to use a dictionary. What do you do during a test when you see an unfamiliar word in one of the questions or in a reading passage? Using context clues is a strategy that may help you determine a word's meaning without having to look it up.

The *context* of a word or term is the sentence or paragraph in which it appears. *Context clues* are words or phrases that help you figure out the meaning of an unfamiliar word or term. As an example, read the following sentence.

Susan felt **elated** when she saw a grade of A on her midterm biology exam.

As you read this sentence, you probably concluded that *elated* means *happy* because that is the way you feel when you have earned a high grade on a difficult test such as a midterm exam. The phrases *grade of A* and *midterm biology exam* are context clues that help you figure out the meaning of the unfamiliar word. If you were to look up *elated* in the dictionary, you would find that it means *filled with pride or joy*, so *happy* is an acceptable *synonym*—a word that has a similar meaning.

Suppose that *elated* is a new word for you. If you make a conscious effort to learn its meaning, then the next time you see *elated*, it will not be an unfamiliar word.

As you can see, using the context to define words has several advantages:

- You will save time.
- You will not be at a disadvantage in situations where you cannot use a dictionary.
- The more often you define a word in context, the more likely you are to remember it.
- You will gain an understanding of how to use words in sentences.

On the other hand, context alone may not give you a word's exact meaning. Similarly, using the dictionary alone may not be helpful if you are looking up a word that has several meanings such as *flat* or *fast*—two examples explained in Chapter 2. Instead, you may need to use both context clues and your dictionary to get an accurate sense of a word's meaning or to select the right meaning.

THE DEFINITION CLUE

The context of an unfamiliar word may contain a synonym or a brief explanation of a word's meaning. Key words such as *is, means,* and *refers to* are clues that a definition follows. In some sentences, commas, parentheses, or dashes set off the synonym or definition. In the following examples, definitions and synonyms of the words in bold type are underlined.

Several shops in the mall sell formal **apparel,** or <u>clothing</u>, for weddings and other special occasions.
To have **empathy** means <u>to understand another person's feelings</u>.
Following the death of a pet, a child must be **consoled** <u>(comforted)</u>.
Oil is not **soluble**—<u>capable of being dissolved</u>—in water.

Exercise 3.1

As you read each sentence below, look for key words, synonyms, or punctuation marks that help you define the word in bold type. Then underline the definition, as in the examples above.

1. Scratching will **exacerbate,** or <u>worsen</u>, a wound.

2. Vernon **sauntered** (<u>walked at a leisurely pace</u>) across the street.

3. Commenting on Pat's <u>glowing</u> complexion, Al said, "You look absolutely **radiant** today."

4. The student population at colleges today is more **diverse,** or <u>varied,</u> than it used to be.

5. American cars **depreciate**—<u>decrease in value</u>—quicker than foreign cars.

Exercise 3.2   The following sentences contain words you are likely to find in your textbooks. As you read each sentence, look for key words, synonyms, or punctuation marks that help you define the word in bold type. Then underline the definition.

1. Some people have **phobias,** or <u>unnatural fears,</u> that prevent them from leading normal lives.

2. <u>Participating in the election process</u>—**electioneering**—is a tactic many interest groups use.

3. **Anthropology** is <u>the study of human origins and culture.</u>

4. The formula for the **circumference** <u>(the distance around a circle)</u> is $C = pi$ *times the radius squared.*

5. **Photosynthesis,** <u>the process by which plants use light to break down nutrients extracted from the soil</u>, is an important biological concept.

Memory Cue

Look for definition clues *such as synonyms or punctuation marks that set off definitions. Also look for key words such as* means *and* refers to.

THE EXAMPLE CLUE

Writers often use examples to help you define the meaning of unfamiliar words and terms. Examples are illustrations or explanations that help you associate a new word or term with a familiar object, idea, or situation.

The words *for example, for instance, to illustrate,* and *such as* are additional clues that an example follows. In the next three examples, words defined in context appear in bold type; clue words appear in italics. An explanation follows each sentence.

I like a variety of **condiments,** *such as* mustard, onions, and relish, on hot dogs.

In this sentence, the examples of mustard, onions, and relish make clear that condiments are *chopped foods or sauces that improve the flavor of other foods.* Ketchup is another condiment. What additional examples can you provide?

You can vary your fitness routine with **calisthenics;** *for example,* do some sit-ups and leg raises.

In this sentence the examples of sit-ups and leg raises tell you that calisthenics are *physical exercises that develop strength.* What additional examples can you provide?

To illustrate the **camaraderie** Jane feels with her friends, she explained how much they enjoy each other's company.

In this sentence, the example tells you that camaraderie is a feeling of good will among friends. Sharing interests is another example of camaraderie. What additional examples can you provide?

Exercise 3.3   In each sentence below, look for the key words and examples that can help you define the word in bold type. Then circle the letter of the definition.

1. Only a few **arachnids,** such as black widows and tarantulas, are poisonous.
   a. spiders
   b. insects
   c. snakes
   d. plants

2. The lecture was so long and **tedious** that I fell asleep.
   a. lively
   b. amusing
   c. boring
   d. serious

3. The restaurant serves **exotic** foods, for example pickled eel and candied lizard.
   a. unknown
   b. common
   c. tasteless
   d. unusual *(circled)*

4. Alcohol abuse has many **adverse** effects; for instance, impaired judgment, lowered reaction times, and loss of health.
   a. harmful *(circled)*
   b. unnecessary
   c. costly
   d. advantageous

5. The two most common **queries** handled by the reference librarians are "Where are the encyclopedias?" and "What time is it?"
   a. statements
   b. remarks
   c. questions *(circled)*
   d. observations

Exercise 3.4

The following sentences contain words you are likely to find in your textbooks. As you read each sentence, look for key words and examples that help you define the word in bold type. Then underline the definition.

1. Polls measure **public opinion,** for example people's evaluations of political issues, policies, and politicians.

2. This novel has a good **plot;** in fact, I enjoy reading books that have an interesting story line.

3. **Entitlements** such as social security benefits and military pensions are payments for which people must meet certain requirements.

4. Although we commonly think of **appendages** as arms and legs, they also include the wings of insects and birds.

5. Situations that cause anxiety, such as a divorce, a change in job, or a death in the family, are a few of life's common **stressors.**

Memory Cue

To define unfamiliar words in context, look for example clues *that help you associate new words with familiar objects or ideas. Also, look for key words such as* for example, *and* for instance.

THE CONTRAST CLUE

Sometimes the context of an unfamiliar word or term contains an *antonym* or an explanation that suggests an opposite meaning. An antonym is a word that has an opposite meaning. *Hot* and *cold* are antonyms, as are *rough* and *smooth*. Antonyms and certain key words such as *though, although, yet, but, however, on the contrary,* and *on the other hand* act as contrast clues that can help you determine the meaning of an unfamiliar word or term.

Read the next two sentences in which the words defined appear in bold type, key words appear in italics, and antonyms are underlined.

> *Although* one tennis player seemed <u>energetic</u>, the other player appeared **enervated.**

> John had been a <u>thin</u> active young man, *but* as he grew older he began to eat more, exercise less, and grow **corpulent.**

In the first sentence, *enervated* means "lacking energy," which is the opposite of *energetic*. In the second sentence, *corpulent* means "fat," which is the opposite of *thin*. Now read the next sentence in which the word defined appears in bold type, key words appear in italics, and the brief definition that suggests the opposite of the boldfaced word is underlined.

> <u>I would like to go</u> to the party; *on the other hand,* I must **abstain** because I have another commitment.

In this sentence, *abstain* means "to choose not to do something." Although the writer of this sentence says she would like to go to the party, she has chosen instead to keep another commitment.

Exercise 3.5   As you read each sentence below, look for key words and antonyms to help you define the word in bold type. Then write your definition.

1. Today's forecast is for clear weather, yet the sky is **obscured** by clouds.

   hidden

2. The space shuttle made its **ascent** without difficulty; however, the crew had some minor problems during landing.

   takeoff

3. In general, I **concur** with your opinion about the movie even though I disagree on one or two points.

   agree

4. We thought the painting was real, but it turned out to be a **forgery.**

   fake

5. I would like to live where a mild temperature is **invariable;** on the contrary, where I live the temperature is always changing.

   unchanging

Exercise 3.6   The following sentences contain words you are likely to find in your textbooks. As you read each sentence below, look for key words and antonyms that help you define the word in bold type. Then write your definition.

1. Although most ground beetles are **nocturnal,** you can find them during the day in moist places, under rocks, logs, or leaves.

   active at night

2. Children who are unable to work cooperatively with others may be **maladjusted.**

   poorly adjusted

3. Sometimes it is better to **paraphrase** an author's words than to copy the author's words exactly.

   put in your own words

4. Unlike the **turbulent** ocean waves, the water along the gulf coast is calm.

_____disturbed, not calm_____

5. The patient's problem is a **physiological** disorder rather than a psychological, or mental, disorder.

_____physical_____

Memory Cue

Look for contrast clues *in the form of antonyms and key words such as* but *and* however *to help you define an unfamiliar word in context. Also look for any brief definitions that suggest the word's opposite meaning.*

THE INFERENCE CLUE

Example and contrast clues by themselves may not help you define an unfamiliar word. You may have to use your prior knowledge and experience to *infer,* or guess, the meaning.

An *inference* is an educated guess based on what you know and what is stated. The inference clue, therefore, is one *you* bring to your reading.

The examples you have read on previous pages contain context clues. Some of them also require you to make inferences to determine a word's meaning, as in this example:

A fitness routine should include an **aerobic** exercise; running or fast walking are good choices.

An aerobic exercise is one that is *designed to strengthen the cardiovascular system (heart, veins, and arteries).* The examples of running and fast walking are clues to this definition. What do these exercises have in common? If you know that they both increase your heart rate and that this, in turn, strengthens the cardiovascular system, then you can infer the meaning of *aerobic.* Here is another example:

The queen was dressed in stunning **raiment**—silks and satins of the finest quality.

You know that silks and satins are fabrics. These words and the word *dressed* help you infer that *raiment* is clothing.

Making inferences not only helps you define words in context, but it also helps you interpret an author's message. Making inferences is one of the critical thinking skills explained in Chapter 10.

Exercise 3.7 As you read each sentence below, make inferences and use other context clues to define the word in bold type. Then write your definition.

1. Rachel's **amazement** was clear to all when she opened the door and everyone yelled "Happy Birthday."

    surprise

2. When you have finished your research paper, **compile** your note cards, outline, and final draft into one folder.

    arrange or put together

3. Some people believe that taking Vitamin C is **beneficial** to your health because it may reduce your chances of infection.

    good, helpful

4. It is more healthful to lose weight **gradually** than to try to lose too much too fast.

    over a period of time

5. Rachel is a **vivacious** person, unlike her sister who seems unlively by comparison.

    lively

Exercise 3.8 Working with a partner, read and discuss the following paragraph. Make inferences and use other context clues to define the words in bold type. Write your definitions on the lines provided, then use a dictionary to check your answers.

A **commotion** broke out in the college bookstore. Several students were involved in an **altercation** about the last book on a shelf. One student needed the book to replace one he had lost. The other student had just signed up for a course in which the textbook was **mandatory.** The bookstore manager offered to **retrieve** a copy of the book from another store. Both students left happy, their differences having been **resolved.**

1. commotion: *violent motion, agitation*

2. altercation: *argument*

3. mandatory: *required*

4. retrieve: *get, acquire, obtain*

5. resolved: *settled*

Memory Cue

An inference *is an educated guess. Use key words, other context clues (definition, example, contrast), and your own experience to make inferences about the meaning of an unfamiliar word.*

REAL-WORLD CONNECTIONS

When you see an unfamiliar word, you have two choices: You can skip the word and keep reading, or you can try to define the word. If you skip the word, your understanding will be incomplete. If you take the time to define the word, you are less likely to lose comprehension. Context clues and your dictionary can help—but only if you remember to use them.

The following paragraph is from *Child and Adolescent Development,* Fourth Edition, a textbook by Kelvin L. Seifert and Robert J. Hoffnung. Apply what you have learned about context clues to read the paragraph and answer the questions. You can do this exercise on your own or with a partner.

How much are you the result of genetic, inborn qualities, and how much the result of learning and experience? The first alternative (genetics and inborn qualities) is your **nature,** and the second (learning and experience) is your **nurture.** It seems sensible to expect that each of us combines nature and nurture in a lot of ways. Your height depends on how tall your parents are (nature), but it also depends on the nutrition and exercise you get as you grow up (nurture).

1. What do a. *genetic* (first sentence), b. *alternative* (second sentence), and c. *nutrition* (last sentence) mean? Write your definitions on the lines below, then check them with your dictionary.

    a. *inborn*

    b. *choice*

    c. *food, nourishment*

2. The author calls your attention to which two special terms?

    a. *nature*

    b. *nurture*

3. What are the definitions of these terms?

    a. *Nature means genetics and inborn qualities.*

    b. *Nurture means learning and experience.*

4. Which two types of context clues listed below do the authors provide to define *nature* and *nurture?*

    definition, example, contrast, inference

    definition, example

5. Does eye color depend on nature or nurture? How do you know?

    Eye color depends on nature because it is inherited from parents.

6. Are reading to a child and exposing a child to new experiences examples of nature or nurture? How do you know?

    Reading to a child and exposing a child to new experiences are examples

    of nurture because they describe ways children learn.

HOW WELL DO YOU REMEMBER?

To review the chapter, read the following summary and fill in the blanks. If you need help with an answer, look back through the chapter to refresh your memory.

Employers want employees to have good *communication* skills. These skills include reading, speaking, writing, and listening. A good vocabulary is essential to all of these skills. You can increase your reading comprehension, speed, and vocabulary by using context clues.

Four types of context clues are *definition, example, contrast,* and *inference* . Synonyms and terms such as *refers to* and *means* are *definition* context clues. Explanations that create images in your mind and phrases such as *for example* and *to illustrate* are *example* context clues. Antonyms, punctuation clues, and words such as *although* and *however* are *contrast* context clues. When you use your experience and prior knowledge along with the author's details to help you define a word, you are using *inference* context clues.

WHAT DO YOU THINK?

Reflect on what you have learned about using context clues. Do you think this strategy will be as helpful to you as using a dictionary? What else are you doing to develop your vocabulary? Write your reflections below.

Reflections will vary.

_____

_____

_____

CHAPTER QUIZ 1

Part 1 Terms and Definitions

Match this chapter's special terms in Column A with their definitions in Column B.

Column A

_c_ 1. antonym

_d_ 2. infer

_e_ 3. context clues

_b_ 4. communication skill

_a_ 5. context

Column B

a. a sentence or paragraph in which a word appears

b. reading, speaking, writing, or listening

c. a word having an opposite meaning

d. to guess, figure out

e. key words or punctuation marks that help you define a word

Part 2 Chapter Review

Read and answer each question below. Write your answer in complete sentences, and use extra paper if needed. *(Answers may vary but should be similar to these.)*

1. What are four types of context clues?

   Four types of context clues are definition, example, contrast, and inference.

   _____

2. What are two advantages of using context clues?

   Answers may vary but should provide any two of the four advantages

   listed on page 66.

3. What is one example of a key word or phrase that can help you determine a word's meaning in context, and how does it help?

_____"For example" is a key phrase that tells you an example follows that may_____

_____explain the meaning of a word._____

_____

Part 3 Using Your Skills

Circle the meaning of each word in bold type that best fits the context of the sentence.

1. Whenever I am interrupted by an interesting conversation, I find it difficult to **resume** my work.
   a. put off
   b. start again
   c. ignore
   d. stop

2. Although some people feel a burst of energy when the weather is cold, they may feel lazy when temperatures are **torrid.**
   a. colder
   b. changeable
   c. hot
   d. uncertain

3. The civic center is a place where we often **convene** because it is large enough to hold our group.
   a. decorate
   b. avoid
   c. buy
   d. meet

4. Which **option** do you prefer as an elective: a music appreciation course or an art class?
   a. choice
   b. activity
   c. plan
   d. requirement

5. It seems **apparent** from the way you are frowning that you do not like this recipe.
    a. strange
    b. unpleasant
    c. clear
    d. annoying

6. While the neighbors were gone, their security alarm went off and the noise could not be **quelled** because no one had the key to their house.
    a. transmitted
    b. heard
    c. increased
    d. stopped

Score: 100 − 7 for each one missed = _____%

CHAPTER QUIZ 2

Part 1 Terms and Definitions

Match the context clues in Column A with the key words in Column B that help you identify them.

Column A

_c_	1. the definition clue
_d_	2. the example clue
_a_	3. the contrast clue
_b_	4. the inference clue

Column B

a. although, however, but
b. your ideas plus author's key words
c. means, refers to
d. for example, for instance

Part 2 Chapter Review

Read and answer each question below. Write your answer in complete sentences, and use extra paper if needed. *(Answers may vary but should be similar to these.)*

1. Why is the dictionary alone not always helpful?

    A word may have more than one meaning. You must use the context

    to choose the right one.

2. How can punctuation marks help you define a word in context?

Sometimes synonyms or definitions are surrounded by commas, dashes,

or parentheses. They are definition clues.

3. Inferences about word meanings are based on what two things?

Inferences are based on what you know and what is stated.

Part 3 Using Your Skills

Each textbook passage below contains a word in bold type that is necessary to your understanding of the passage. Use context clues to define the words, and write your definitions on the lines provided. *(Answers may vary but should approximate those given.)*

> Competent speakers come across as informed, intelligent, and well prepared. You can seem competent only if you know what you are talking about. People listen more respectfully to those who speak from both knowledge and personal experience. You can build this perception of **competence** by selecting topics that you already know something about and by doing research as a responsible speaker.
>
> From Michael Osborn and Suzanne Osborne, *Public Speaking*, third edition, Boston: Houghton Mifflin, 1994.

1

Competence means:

having the necessary knowledge or qualifications

> A speaker who conveys **integrity** appears ethical, honest, and dependable. Listeners are more receptive when speakers are straightforward, responsible, and concerned about the consequences of their words. You can enhance your integrity by presenting all sides of an issue and then explaining why you have chosen your position. It also helps if you can show that you are willing to follow your own advice. . . .
>
> From Michael Osborn and Suzanne Osborne, *Public Speaking*, third edition. Boston: Houghton Mifflin, 1994.

2

Integrity means:

ethical behavior, honesty and dependability

Chemistry has played an important role in the processing of foods.   3
Foods are processed so that they remain fresh and free of harmful
toxins for a longer period of time. Chemists are hard at work seeking
and researching ways to **alleviate** the world food shortage. . . .

From Alan Sherman, Sharon J. Sherman, and Leonard Russikoff,
Basic Concepts of Chemistry, sixth edition. Boston: Houghton Mifflin,
1996.

Alleviate means:

relieve

Before we try to discuss the atom, we should recall that until very   4
recently no one had ever seen one. How, then, did we know what an
atom was like? We really didn't, exactly. But scientists have put
together observations, experimental results, and a good deal of
reasoning and have come up with a **model.** This model of the atom
is just a representation of what scientists believe the atom is like.

From Alan Sherman, Sharon J. Sherman, and Leonard Russikoff, *Basic
Concepts of Chemistry,* sixth edition. Boston: Houghton Mifflin, 1996.

Model means:

example, representation

At birth, one particular tactile sensation, pain, seems less developed   5
than among slightly older infants or children. It is possible to **evoke** a
response of pain or other negative reaction to a pinprick, such as that
a baby might receive for a blood test, in one-day-old infants . . .

From Kelvin L. Seifert and Robert J. Hoffnung, *Child and Adolescent
Development,* fourth edition. Boston: Houghton Mifflin, 1997.

Evoke means:

_____bring out, cause_____

_____

Score: 100 − 8 for each one missed = _____%

Vocabulary Quiz

Each sentence below contains a word in bold type from the reading selection on pages 61–62. Read the sentence and the definitions that follow it. Then circle the correct one. Turn to the vocabulary preview on pages 60–61 to check your answers.

1. Everyone gathered in the **gymnasium** to watch the cheerleading tryouts.
   a. college cafeteria
   b. learning resources building
   c. student union
   (d.) indoor sports area

2. This **lousy** answer key is numbered incorrectly, and I cannot find the answers I need.
   a. required
   (b.) worthless
   c. easy to use
   d. inexpensive

3. I chose a **coed** university because I was used to working and attending classes in places where the sexes were not separated.
   a. male only
   b. female only
   (c.) both male and female
   d. more males than females

4. When I forgot part of my speech, I was more **humiliated** than angry.
   a. amused.
   b. annoyed.
   (c.) embarrassed
   d. upset

5. It is **naive** to think that if you cheat on an exam you will never get caught.
   a. unwise
   b. using common sense
   c. immoral
   d. unnatural

6. I will **undoubtedly** be able to attend the wedding because I have nothing else scheduled for that day.
   a. not likely
   b. reluctantly
   c. only
   d. certainly

7. Although the company **assured** me that my order would arrive within a week, I did not receive it until two weeks later.
   a. believed
   b. guaranteed
   c. teased
   d. remarked

8. Because the two were not well suited to each other, their friends **perceived** that the relationship would not last.
   a. questioned
   b. hoped
   c. understood
   d. announced

Score: 100 − 12 = _____%

Unit
2

Improving Your Comprehension Skills

Chapter 4

Understanding Sentences and Transitions

A sentence is a basic unit of meaning. Paragraphs are made up of sentences, and longer passages are made up of paragraphs. To improve your comprehension of these larger units of meaning, you may need to review that basic unit of meaning: the sentence.

You probably learned a long time ago that every sentence has a *subject* and a *verb*. These two parts express a *key idea*. A sentence may also contain *details* that explain the key idea. Words and phrases called *transitions* connect key ideas and details within and between sentences. Reading for the key idea and details in a sentence helps you unlock its meaning. An understanding of transitions helps you see how ideas are related. As you gain experience, you will be able to follow an author's train of thought and predict what comes next. As a result, your comprehension will improve.

This chapter explains several strategies that will help you understand sentences and transitions:

- ■ *Know the parts of a sentence.*
- ■ *Identify key ideas and details in sentences.*
- ■ *Know how transitions connect ideas.*
- ■ *Analyze difficult sentences.*

WHAT DO YOU ALREADY KNOW?

To prepare yourself for the reading selection that follows, find out what you already know about wasting time. Answer the questions below either on your own or in a group discussion.

1. Are your time-management skills good, average, or poor?

2. When are you most likely to waste time?

3. If you had to guess what most people consider their biggest waste of time, what would be your answer?

4. Read the title, headnote, vocabulary preview, and first two paragraphs of the reading selection. What do you think will follow?

Goofing Off Is Fast Becoming a Lost Art
Ellen Graham

Ellen Graham, a journalist who writes for newspapers and magazines, talks about ways Americans waste time.

VOCABULARY PREVIEW

cited	(sīt′ ĭd) to state or mention
dwarfs	(dwôrfs) causes to appear smaller
fritter	(frĭt′ər) to waste
petty	(pĕt′ē) of little importance, secondary in importance or rank
vices	(vīs′ ĭs) shortcomings, personal failings
chides	(chīds) scolds
multitasking	(mŭl·tĭ·tăsk′ ĭng) a business term that means doing more than one task at once
drudgery	(drŭj′ər·ē) boring or unpleasant work

mundane	(mŭn·dān') ordina

Pronunciation Key: ī(pie), ĭ (pit), ô
ŭ (cut), ă (pat), ā (pay), ə (about,

So much for America's love affair with the
the list of time-wasters **cited** by busy Americans,
on the phone and junk reading. But a surprising 19% den
waste any time at all.

Television was deliberately excluded from the choices because   2
typically it **dwarfs** all other responses.

Women, far more than men, say they waste time on the phone.   3
While 16% of women believe they **fritter** away hours shopping, only
3% of men do. On the other hand, more than twice as many men as
women—15% against 6%—say they waste time playing on the
computer or video games. And the older they get, the more likely
people are to say they don't waste time: 33% of those 65 and older
make this claim.

Most Americans are inclined to forgive themselves these **petty**   4
vices as ways to combat stress. Michael Bray, a 48-year-old software
support analyst in Corvallis, Ore., says his job consists of trouble-
shooting problems all day. "So, when I have time off," he says, "I
tend to vegetate."

Steven Johnston, a 22-year-old in Gainesville, Fla., mildly **chides**   5
himself for spending as much as three hours a day on-line. "I could
budget my time better," he says.

John White, president of Priority Management, a Rochester, N.Y.,   6
consulting firm, observes that some people squirm in lines, while
others use that time pleasurably to people-watch. "If you are getting
or contributing value, it's not a waste of time," he adds.

In roughly equal numbers, women and men say they have   7
trimmed all waste time from their schedules. Susan Stillwell of Key
Largo, Fla., says, "It seems I don't get to waste much time." The
resort reservations clerk and mother of two is a master at
multitasking: As she is being interviewed, she is folding her
husband's socks.

For most Americans, goofing off is preferable to errands and other   8
drudgery. By a large margin, waiting in line is the biggest annoyance,
followed by household chores and "people who talk too much."

Priority Management's Mr. White says few actually pay to farm   9
out **mundane** tasks—"only the very rich and the very impressed with
themselves," he asserts.

HOW WELL DID YOU COMPREHEND?

Main Idea

1. Which statement best expresses what the whole selection is about?
   a. People should avoid wasting time.
   b. Americans waste time in different ways.
   c. Men waste time differently than women.
   d. There is no such thing as wasting time.

Details

2. According to the author, Americans' biggest time waster is
   a. shopping.
   b. junk reading.
   c. talking on the phone.
   d. driving.

3. According to the author, which time waster is the most annoying?
   a. people talking too much
   b. waiting in line
   c. household chores
   d. daydreaming

4. More men than women waste time by
   a. waiting in line.
   b. doing household chores.
   c. playing on the computer.
   d. talking on the phone.

5. More women than men waste time by
   a. waiting in line.
   b. doing household chores.
   c. playing on the computer.
   d. talking on the phone.

6. Who said, "If you are getting or contributing value, it's not a waste of time"?
   a. John White
   b. Michael Bray
   c. Stephen Johnston
   d. Susan Stillwell

Inferences

7. According to the author, watching television was not one of the survey items because
    a. people watch television less than they used to.
    b. most Americans do not consider watching T.V. a waste of time.
    c. the response to television would have made the responses to the other items surveyed seem too small.
    d. few people would have chosen this item.

Working with Words

Complete the sentences below with these words from the vocabulary preview:

cited   fritter   vices   multitasking   mundane
dwarfed   petty   chides   drudgery

1. So many women have worn scrunchies around their ponytails that these hair ornaments have become ____*mundane*____.

2. My sister is so tall that she ____*dwarfs*____ me by comparison.

3. Many convicted criminals committed ____*petty*____ crimes before they committed more serious ones.

4. A mother who wants to protect her children ____*chides*____ them for playing in the street.

5. Don't ____*fritter*____ away my time with these annoying phone calls.

6. For some students, homework is a challenge, but for others it is a ____*drudgery*____.

7. Eating chocolate is one of my small ____*vices*____.

8. ____*Multitasking*____ may be necessary for students who work, take care of children, and attend classes.

9. Marcia ____*cited*____ "close to home" as one of her reasons for attending a community college.

Thinking and Writing

Explain what you think the following quotation from Ellen Graham's article means: "If you are getting or contributing value, it's not a waste of time." Do you agree or disagree with the quotation? Explain your answer in writing.

Answers will vary. _____

_____

_____

_____

KNOW THE PARTS OF A SENTENCE

To understand paragraphs and longer passages, you must first master the sentence. A quick review of its parts will help. A sentence is a unit of meaning that has three parts: a *subject,* a *verb,* and a *thought that can stand alone.*

The *subject* tells you who or what the sentence is about. A subject can be one word or a group of words, and a sentence can have more than one subject. In the following examples, the subjects are underlined.

A large green <u>lizard</u> escaped from its owner.

<u>Having a pet</u> requires commitment.

My <u>dog</u> and <u>cat</u> get along well together.

The first sentence has a one-word subject: *lizard.* The subject of the second sentence is a group of words: *having a pet.* The third sentence has two subjects: *dog* and *cat.* To find the subject of a sentence, ask yourself, "Who or what is this sentence about?"

Exercise 4.1

Underline the subjects in the sentences below. Remember that the subject can be one word or a group of words. If a sentence has more than one subject, underline each subject. The first one is done as an example.

1. <u>Nicholas</u> wanted a pet for his birthday.

2. His <u>mother and father</u> are both allergic to cats.

3. <u>They</u> decided to buy Nicholas a golden retriever.

4. <u>Nicholas's sisters</u> would also enjoy having a pet in the family.

5. However, <u>taking care of the dog</u> would be Nicholas's responsibility.

6. <u>Nicholas, his sisters, and his parents</u> were all pleased with their choice.

7. <u>Feeding, walking, and brushing</u> Max were tasks Nicholas enjoyed.

8. Sometimes his <u>sisters</u> asked to help.

9. <u>Everyone</u> enjoyed playing with Max.

10. <u>Caring for a pet</u> teaches children responsibility.

A *verb* tells you what the subject is doing or feeling or what is happening to the subject. A verb can be one word or a group of words, and a sentence can have more than one verb. In the following examples, the verbs are underlined.

Raymond <u>caught</u> a cold.
Raymond <u>has been feeling</u> sick all week.
Raymond <u>coughs</u> or <u>sneezes</u> several times a day.

The first sentence has a one-word verb: *caught.* The verb in the second sentence is a group of words: *has been feeling.* The third sentence has two verbs: *coughs* and *sneezes.* To find the verb of a sentence, ask yourself, "What is the subject doing or feeling" or "What is happening to the subject?"

Exercise 4.2   Underline the verbs in the sentences below. Remember that the verb can be one word or a group of words. If a sentence has more than one verb, underline each verb. The first one is done as an example.

1. Carla <u>could not decide</u> on a major.

2. She <u>wanted</u> a career in business.

3. Carla <u>talked</u> with her advisor and <u>took</u> some tests in her college's career center.

4. The test results <u>showed</u> Carla's aptitude for math.

5. Carla always <u>had earned</u> high grades in math.

6. A number of careers and job opportunities <u>require</u> a knowledge of math.

7. Drafting, engineering, and marketing <u>are</u> three examples.

8. Carla <u>decided</u> to major in accounting.

9. Later, she <u>might become</u> a CPA (Certified Public Accountant).

10. As a CPA, she <u>would have</u> even more career opportunities.

Some word groups that have a subject and verb are not sentences. To be a sentence, a word group must be able to stand alone and still make sense. The third part of a sentence is *a thought that can stand alone.* Read the next two examples, and decide which one is a sentence.

When Reva arrived home.
When Reva arrived home, she went to bed.

The first group of words has a subject, *Reva,* and a verb, *arrived.* However, this group of words seems incomplete. What happened when Reva arrived home? This group of words cannot stand alone; therefore, it is not a sentence. The second group of words is a sentence because it has all three parts. The subject is *Reva* and the two verbs are *arrived* and *went.* The thought can stand alone because you know what Reva did when she arrived home: *She went to bed.* To find the thought that can stand alone, ask yourself, "Do the subject and verb and any other words in the sentence tell me everything I need to know?"

Exercise 4.3

Read each group of words below and underline the subject once and verb twice. Decide whether the group of words expresses a thought that can stand alone. Then write yes in front of the group of words if it is a sentence; write no if the group of words is not a sentence. The first one is done as an example.

yes 1. <u>I</u> just <u>bought</u> a new set of tires.

no 2. Because a <u>car</u> <u>requires</u> upkeep.

yes 3. <u>We</u> <u>washed and waxed</u> the car together.

no 4. When <u>rain</u> <u>spatters</u> the windshield.

yes 5. <u>Wiper blades that are getting old</u> <u>should be replaced</u>.

yes 6. <u>Body work</u> <u>can be</u> very expensive.

no 7. If <u>you</u> <u>own</u> a foreign car.

yes 8. <u>Regular oil changes</u> <u>will extend</u> the life of an engine.

yes 9. <u>Some cars</u> <u>are</u> old before their time.

no 10. Unless <u>they</u> <u>receive</u> proper care.

Memory Cue

A sentence has three parts: a subject, verb, and a thought that can stand alone. Identifying the parts can help you master sentences and improve your comprehension of paragraphs and longer selections.

IDENTIFY KEY IDEAS AND DETAILS IN SENTENCES

The subject and the verb together express a *key idea*. Every sentence has at least one key idea, and some sentences have more than one key idea. Most sentences contain other words and phrases that help explain or clarify the key idea. These words and phrases are *details*. Read the following sentence and find the key idea and details.

> Yesterday afternoon, you received a telephone call from your dentist.

This sentence contains a lot of information. The subject is *you* and the verb is *received*. The key idea is *you received*. The detail *yesterday afternoon* explains when the call came in, and the detail *from your dentist* explains who called.

The sentences in your textbooks may not all be as clear as the previous example. But even in a long or complicated sentence, you should still be able to find the key idea and understand what the details in the sentence tell you about the key idea. Read the following sentence and find the key idea.

> Georgia O'Keeffe, an American painter of the twentieth century, is known for her many oil paintings of oversized flowers.

In this sentence, *Georgia O'Keeffe* is the subject, and *is known* is the verb. *Georgia O'Keeffe is known* is the key idea. What do the details in the sentence tell you about the key idea? They tell you who Georgia O'Keeffe was (American painter), when she lived (twentieth century), what kind of painting she was known for (oil painting), and the subject of many of her paintings (oversized flowers).

To find the key idea in a sentence, identify the subject and verb. To find the details, look at the remaining words in the sentence. Then determine what they tell you about the subject and verb. Ask yourself three questions:

1. Who or what is the sentence about?
2. What action or state of being does the sentence describe?
3. What do the other words tell me about the key idea?

Exercise 4.4   Identify the key idea and details in each of the following sentences. The first one is done as an example.

1. Francis Scott Key, a lawyer of the late eighteenth and early nineteenth centuries, wrote "The Star Spangled Banner."

   a. key idea: *Francis Scott Key wrote . . .*

   b. details: *lawyer, late eighteenth and early nineteenth centuries, "The Star Spangled Banner"*

2. The words of the song came to Key during the War of 1812.

   a. key idea: *The words of the song came . . .*

   b. details: *to Key, during the War of 1812*

3. "The Star Spangled Banner" became the national anthem of the United States.

   a. key idea: *The Star Spangled Banner became . . .*

   b. details: *the national anthem of the United States*

4. Vocalists such as Aretha Franklin, Whitney Houston, Robert Goulet, and many others have sung the national anthem at public events.

   a. key idea: *Vocalists have sung . . .*

   b. details: *Aretha Franklin, Whitney Houston, Robert Goulet, and others; the national anthem at public events*

5. Another song, "Oh Columbia, the Gem of the Ocean," was once considered as a possible anthem for the United States.

   a. key idea: *Another song was once considered . . .*

   b. details: *"Oh Columbia, the Gem of the Ocean"; a possible anthem for the United States*

6. Some people have expressed a preference for yet another patriotic song, "America the Beautiful."

a. key idea: _Some people have expressed . . ._

b. details: _a preference for yet another patriotic song, "America the_

Beautiful"

Memory Cue

The subject and verb together express a sentence's key idea. Every sentence has at least one key idea, and some sentences have more than one. The other words in a sentence provide the details that explain the key idea.

KNOW HOW TRANSITIONS CONNECT IDEAS

Some sentences have more than one key idea, as in the following sentence:

Cindy would have called yesterday, but she forgot.

This sentence has two parts, separated by a comma and the word *but*. The key idea in the first part of the sentence is *Cindy would have called*. The key idea in the second part of the sentence is *she forgot*. How are these ideas related? The word *but* shows a contrast between the two parts of the sentence. The second part of the sentence explains why Cindy did not call. Compare the previous example with the next one.

Grant should have called yesterday, and he should have come over.

Like the previous sentence, this one has two parts separated by a comma and a connecting word. But the connecting word and one of the key ideas are different. How are the two parts of this sentence related? The word *and* shows addition: One idea is being added to another. Grant should have done two things: called *and* come over.

Transitions are words that connect ideas. *And* is a transition, so is *but*. Many other words and phrases act as transitions to show how ideas are related within and between sentences. A transition can appear at the beginning, middle, or end of a sentence. Transitions express the following types of relationships:

FIGURE 4.1 Transitions That Signal Addition	
also	first, second, (and so on)
and	furthermore
another	in addition
besides	moreover
finally	next

- addition
- time
- example
- comparison and contrast
- cause and effect

Addition

In an *addition* relationship, one key idea or detail is *added* to another. These key ideas or details continue along the same line of reasoning. Read the following examples, and notice the transitions in bold type.

1. Rod bought a new shirt. **Also,** he bought a new tie.
2. No, I will not go to the party; **furthermore,** I will not change my mind.
3. I like bananas on my cereal **in addition** to strawberries.

In the first example, the transition, *also,* comes between two sentences. This transition tells you that the key ideas expressed in this pair of sentences are following the same line of reasoning. The key ideas and the details in the sentences explain that Rod bought two items of clothing.

In the second example, the transition, *furthermore,* separates two key ideas within the same sentence. This transition tells you that the key ideas expressed in both parts of the sentence are following the same line of reasoning. The key ideas and the details in the sentence explain two things that the subject will not do.

In the third example, the transition, *in addition,* comes within the sentence. The key idea is *I like.* The details tell you what the subject likes: *bananas on my cereal* and *strawberries.* The transition, *in addition,* tells you that one kind of fruit is added to the other.

Figure 4.1 lists transitions that show addition.

Exercise 4.5   Choose a transition from the list below to complete each sentence. Use each transition only once. *(Students' choices may vary.)*

| another | furthermore | besides |
| also | in addition | second |

1. I am buying new furniture. _____*Also*_____, I am buying a new carpet.

2. One child wants to be a ghost for Halloween. _____*Another*_____ child wants to be a witch.

3. To prepare for a hurricane, buy batteries, canned goods, and bottled water. _____*In addition*_____, stay tuned to your radio and follow evacuation procedures.

4. First, I want a raise in pay. _____*Second*_____, I want a reduction in my hours. Third, I want more time off.

5. _____*Besides*_____ mowing the lawn, you must weed the flower beds.

6. Rhoda told Fred he had to move out; _____*furthermore*_____, he had to clear out his things today.

Memory Cue

Transitions are words or phrases that connect key ideas and details to show how they are related. Transitions help you follow an author's train of thought. Look for transitions within or between sentences. Look for transitions at the beginning, middle, or end of a sentence.

Time

A *time* relationship explains when or in what order things happen. In a history class, you read about important events and when they occurred, such as the signing of the Declaration of Independence in 1776. In a science class, you read about various processes (such as digestion and circulation), the steps of each process, and the order in which they occur. A sequence of events, hours or parts of a day, months, weeks, and days of the year are time relationships. Read the following examples and notice the transitions in bold type.

1. **As** Clark listened to the lecture, he took notes.
2. Tara will not go to bed **until** she finishes studying.
3. Ed and Janet went to a movie. **Later** that evening, they met some friends for a snack.

FIGURE 4.2 Transitions That Signal Time	
as	later
after	next
at last	often
before	then
during	until
finally	when
first, second, etc.	while

In the first example, the transition, *as,* comes at the beginning of the sentence. This transition tells you that the two events, listening to the lecture and taking notes, took place at the same time.

In the second example, the details following the transition *until* tell you when Tara will go to bed—after she finishes studying.

In the third example, the transition, *later,* comes between two sentences to help you follow the sequence of events from the first sentence to the second. The transition makes clear that meeting friends for a snack occurred after the trip to the movies.

Figure 4.2 lists transitions that express time relationships.

Exercise 4.6   Choose a transition from the list below to complete each sentence. Use each transition only once.

before	while	then
next	during	after

1. First, you open the package. Second, you slide out the tray. _____*Next*_____ you microwave the dinner for three minutes.

2. _____*After*_____ the 1996 Olympic Games in Atlanta, the city had a lot of cleaning up to do.

3. The electricity went out _____*while*_____ I was looking up information on the Internet.

4. The process of digestion begins in the mouth. _____*Then*_____ food travels to the stomach where digestion continues.

5. I enjoy eating a snack _____*during*_____ the football games on T.V.

6. On a cold morning, you should warm up your car's engine _____*before*_____ you drive.

Example

Sometimes a statement is followed by an *example,* which is a short explanation or illustration. *For example* and *such as* are two transitions writers use to tell you that an example follows. An example may appear within a sentence, or the example may follow in a separate sentence. Read the next group of sentences and notice the transitions in bold type.

1. Vernon likes desserts, **for example** chocolate mousse, lemon meringue pie, and carrot cake.
2. Some children's books, **including** *Mary Poppins* and *Charlotte's Web,* are both entertaining and instructive.
3. You have many costumes to choose from. **For instance,** you could go to the party as Frankenstein.

In the first sentence, the transition *for example* tells you that the details in the last part of the sentence are examples that explain what kinds of desserts Vernon likes: chocolate mousse, lemon meringue pie, and carrot cake.

In the second sentence, the key idea and details tell you that some children's books are entertaining and instructive. The transition *including* signals that examples of these kinds of books will follow.

In the last pair of sentences, the transition *for instance* relates the second sentence to the first by providing an example of one kind of costume.

Figure 4.3 lists transitions that signal readers to look for an example.

Exercise 4.7

Choose a transition from the list below to complete each sentence. Use each transition only once.

once	to illustrate	including
example	for instance	such as

1. People should be polite to each other. Opening a door for anyone whose hands are full is one _____*example*_____.

2. Always use good table manners _____*such as*_____ putting your fork down between bites, not talking with your mouth full, and offering a roll to the person seated next to you before taking one for yourself.

FIGURE 4.3 Transitions That Signal Example

example	once
for example	such as
for instance	to illustrate
including	to show

---

3. Rules of conduct change with the times. _____*Once*_____, men were expected to open doors for women, but now whoever gets to the door first should open it for the other person.

4. What is polite in one culture may not be polite in another. _____*For instance*_____, some people are offended if you look them in the eye, but others are offended if you do not.

5. Some items of clothing, _____*including*_____ blue jeans, baseball caps, and athletic shoes, are considered inappropriate dress for formal occasions.

6. _____*To illustrate*_____ what I mean by "bad manners," think of someone who burps in public or spits on the sidewalk.

Comparison and Contrast

A *comparison* relationship explains how one thing is like another. A *contrast* relationship explains how one thing differs from another. Comparison and contrast are often used together. In fact, the word *compare* often implies contrast.

When comparing automobiles to determine which one would be a better buy, you might consider their similarities and differences in price, gas mileage, safety features, and various options that are offered. The transitions of comparison and contrast can help you spot details that show similarities or differences. As you read the following examples, notice the transitions in bold type.

1. You think I don't want to go to the party. **On the contrary,** I would love to go.
2. Lyn enjoys movies **just as** much as Larry does.
3. I have a dress **similar** to the one you are wearing, **but** it is a different color.

FIGURE 4.4 Transitions That Signal Comparison and Contrast

Comparison

comparable	like
equal	likely
in the same way	similar
just as	the same

Contrast

although	however
but	in contrast
conversely	instead
despite	on the contrary
differ	on the other hand
different	unlike
even though	yet

In the first example, *on the contrary* signals a contrast between the ideas expressed in the two sentences. "You think I don't want to go" is contrasted with "I would love to go."

In the second example, the transition *just as* tells you that Lyn's enjoyment of movies is being compared to Larry's enjoyment of movies.

The third example contains both a comparison and a contrast. In the first part of the sentence, the transition *similar* relates one dress to the other by comparison. The transition *but* in the second part of the sentence signals that the detail following shows how the dresses differ.

Figure 4.4 lists transitions that relate ideas by comparison or contrast.

Exercise 4.8

Choose a transition from the list below to complete each sentence. Use each transition only once.

the same	on the other hand	although
like	in contrast	despite

1. "_____*Like*_____ two peas in a pod" is not a remark you could make about me and my sister.

2. Beverly is tall and blonde. _____*In contrast*_____, I am short and dark.

3.   _____*Although*_____ I enjoy outdoor activities, Beverly prefers dancing and reading.

4.   Beverly is an accomplished dancer. I, _____*on the other hand*_____, have won several trophies for my horse riding.

5.   We do have some things in common _____*despite*_____ our differences.

6.   Beverly does like to cook _____*the same*_____ food as I do.

Cause and Effect

A *cause* is a reason. An *effect* is a result. Transitions that signal causes tell you to look for the reasons why something happens or the reasons why someone feels, acts, or thinks a certain way. Transitions that signal effects tell you to look for the results of actions, behaviors, or ideas. Read the following examples and notice the transitions in bold type.

1.   I was late to class this morning. **As a result,** I did not have time to finish my test.
2.   **Because** David has a terrible cold, he has decided to stay home.
3.   Some students do not get enough rest. This **leads to** drowsiness and poor concentration.

In the first example, the transition *as a result* relates the second sentence to the first by explaining an effect of arriving to class late.

In the second example, why has David decided to stay home? The transition *because* tells you that the reason follows.

In the third example, the transition *lead to* tells you that drowsiness and poor concentration are the effects students can expect if they do not get enough rest.

Figure 4.5 lists transitions that relate ideas by cause and effect.

FIGURE 4.5 Transitions That Signal Cause and Effect	
as a result	lead to
because	reason
cause	result
effect	so
finally	therefore
in conclusion	thus

Exercise 4.9   The following paragraph is similar to one you might read in a psychology textbook. Working with a partner, read the paragraph and fill in the blanks with the transitions listed below. Use each transition only once.

lead to   in conclusion   results   effect
causes   therefore   reason   because

Why Do We Forget?

1. Psychologists have determined two common ____*causes*____ of forgetting. 2. One ____*reason*____ we forget can be explained by a process called **decay.** Information we take in gradually disappears, or decays, if we do not make an attempt to remember it. 3. _*Therefore*_, if you need to remember a date, a name, or some other piece of important information, you must review it often to keep it from decaying. 4. **Interference** is another process that may ____*lead to*____ forgetting. Suppose you are taking a Spanish class and are having difficulty remembering the vocabulary. 5. ____*Because*____ you took French last semester, the words you learned and stored in your memory may interfere with, or block, the Spanish vocabulary you are now trying to learn. 6. Similarly, not being able to remember a phone number you have just dialed could be another ____*effect*____ of interference. 7. _*In conclusion*_, to prevent forgetting, you must seek ways to combat decay and interference. 8. ____*Results*____ may be successful with recitation and frequent review.

Memory Cue

Addition *transitions tell you that one idea is added to an idea already mentioned.* Time *transitions help you follow sequences or steps.* Example *transitions tell you that an explanation of an idea already stated follows.* Comparison and contrast *transitions signal similarities and differences.* Cause and effect *transitions point out reasons and results.*

ANALYZE DIFFICULT SENTENCES

Sometimes when you are reading, you may feel lost because the sentences are long and difficult. When this happens, do not keep reading. Try to figure out what the sentence says before going on. To *analyze,* or figure out, a sentence, try this five-step strategy:

1. Find the key idea (subject and verb).
2. Identify the details.
3. Define unfamiliar words.
4. Look for transitions.
5. State in your own words the thought expressed in the sentence.

Try to analyze this sentence from paragraph 7 of Ellen Graham's article before you read the explanation that follows.

"The resort reservations clerk and mother of two is a master at multitasking: As she is being interviewed, she is folding her husband's socks."

This sentence may be difficult because it contains two key ideas separated by a colon. The subject stated in the first part of the sentence is *clerk and mother.* When you first read this part of the sentence, you may have thought that the clerk and mother were two different people. But the verb *is* tells you that they are the same person. The details tell you that she is a *master at multitasking.*

The details in the second part of the sentence define multitasking. The clerk is being interviewed and is folding clothes. The transition *as* tells you that she is doing these tasks *at the same time.* Even though *multitasking* may have been a new word for you, the context provides a strong clue to its meaning. Also, you can look back at the definition in the vocabulary preview if you are still unsure.

To state the sentence's expressed thought in your own words, you could say, "The reservations clerk who is also a mother has learned to do more than one thing at a time."

Taking the time to analyze a difficult sentence may save you time in the long run because you will get more out of your reading.

Exercise 4.10   Working with a partner, select any two sentences from Ellen Graham's article on pages 89–90 that you think are difficult. Analyze the sentences by completing the items that follow. Share your results with the rest of the class. *(Sentences chosen and answers will vary.)*

1. Write your first sentence here:

   _____

   _____

   a. What is(are) the subject(s)?

   _____

   b. What is(are) the verb(s)?

   _____

   c. List the details.

   _____

   _____

   d. List and define any unfamiliar words.

   _____

   _____

   e. List any transitions you find.

   _____

   f. In your own words, what thought do the key ideas and details
      express?

   _____

   _____

2. Write your second sentence here:

   _____

   _____

a. What is(are) the subject(s)?

_____

b. What is(are) the verb(s)?

_____

c. List the details.

_____

_____

d. List and define any unfamiliar words.

_____

_____

e. List any transitions you find.

_____

f. In your own words, what thought do the key ideas and details express?

_____

_____

Memory Cue

To analyze a difficult sentence, find the key idea and details, define unfamiliar words, look for transitions, and state the thought expressed in the sentence in your own words.

REAL-WORLD CONNECTIONS

You can also use this chapter's reading strategies in a writing class or for any writing situation.

Read your own sentences the way you would read those of an author. Find your key ideas. Look for transitions. Ask yourself whether your sentences express meaningful thoughts and whether a reader would be able to follow your ideas. As an example of how to put these strategies into practice, try the following exercises.

Thinking and Writing on page 91 asks you to explain a quotation from Ellen Graham's article and agree or disagree with it. First, answer these questions about the sentences you wrote. Then rewrite your sentences, improving them as much as you can. Use extra paper as needed. *(Answers will vary.)*

1. How many sentences did you write?

2. Does each sentence have a subject and verb?

3. Does each sentence express a thought that can stand alone?

4. What transitions could you add to your sentences to connect your ideas?

HOW WELL DO YOU REMEMBER?

To review the chapter, read the following summary and fill in the blanks. If you need help with an answer, look back through the chapter to refresh your memory.

To improve your reading of paragraphs and longer passages, you must first be able to unlock the meaning of a sentence. Every sentence has at least one key idea that consists of a subject and a _____*verb*_____. Most sentences have additional words, or _____*details*_____, that explain the key idea. Also, a sentence must express a thought that can stand alone.

Transitions are words or phrases that connect ideas within and between sentences. *Addition* transitions indicate that one idea or detail is added to another. _____*Time*_____ transitions show when or in what order things happen. _____Example_____ transitions point out an illustration or explanation. _____Comparison_____ transitions signal that similarities follow, and _____contrast_____ transitions signal that differences follow. Cause and _____effect_____ transitions point out reasons and results.

This chapter also explains a five-step strategy that will help you *analyze* difficult sentences.

WHAT DO YOU THINK?

Reflect on what you have learned about transitions. Do you see a connection between the transitions explained in this chapter and the key words and context clues explained in Chapter 3? How will you use this information to help you analyze difficult sentences and improve your reading comprehension?

Reflections will vary.

_____

_____

_____

_____

CHAPTER QUIZ 1

Part 1 Terms and Definitions

Match this chapter's special terms in Column A with their definitions in Column B.

Column A	Column B
_d_ 1. analyze	a. expresses action or state of being
_e_ 2. subject	b. the subject and verb together
_b_ 3. key idea	c. connects ideas
_a_ 4. verb	d. to figure out by reasoning
_c_ 5. transition	e. who or what a sentence is about

Part 2 Chapter Review

Read and answer each question below. Write your answer in complete sentences, and use extra paper if needed. *(Answers may vary but should be similar to these.)*

1. What are the parts of a sentence?

    The parts of a sentence are the subject, verb, and a thought that can

    stand alone.

2. How are the parts of a sentence related?

    The subject tells who or what the sentence is about. The verb expresses the

    action or state of the subject. The subject and verb together, depending on

    the context, may express a complete thought.

3. What is the difference between key ideas and details?

    The key idea consists of the subject and verb. The details explain or

    clarify the key idea.

Part 3 Using Your Skills

1. In each of the following sentences, underline the subject once and the verb twice.
   a. At the hardware store, Ron and Ray sorted nuts and bolts into bins.
   b. Gabby, a Yorkshire terrier, barks and nips at my heels when we play.

    c. <u>Eating green apples</u> <u><u>may give</u></u> you a stomach ache.

    d. <u>Riding to work on a <u>bicycle</u></u> <u>provides</u> exercise as well as cheap transportation.

2. In each of the following sentences, identify the key idea and details.

    a. My new computer works much faster than my old one.

    key idea: *My new computer works*

    details: *faster than my old one*

    b. Yesterday a tornado uprooted trees and damaged several houses.

    key idea: *a tornado uprooted and damaged*

    details: *yesterday, trees, several houses*

    c. I bought beach towels and sports equipment on sale yesterday.

    key idea: *I bought*

    details: *beach towels, sports equipment, on sale yesterday*

    d. I wish you would not be so noisy while I am trying to sleep.

    key idea: *I wish*

    details: *you would not be so noisy while I am trying to sleep*

Score: 100 − 5 for each one missed = _____ %

CHAPTER QUIZ 2

Part 1 Terms and Definitions

Match each type of relationship in Column A with its definition in Column B.

Column A	Column B
_b_ 1. addition	a. similarities and differences
_d_ 2. time	b. added to or following
_c_ 3. example	c. explanation or illustration
_a_ 4. comparison and contrast	d. when or in what order
_e_ 5. cause and effect	e. how or why things happen

Part 2 Chapter Review

Read and answer each question below. Write your answer in complete sentences, and use extra paper if needed. *(Answers may vary but should be similar to these.)*

1. What are *transitions* and what examples can you give?

   Transitions are words that connect ideas. Two examples are "and"

   and "but."

2. Why is it important to be able to recognize transitions?

   Transitions help you follow an author's train of thought.

3. What steps should you follow to analyze the meaning of a difficult sentence?

   Find the key idea, details, and transitions. Define unfamiliar words. State

   in your own words the thought expressed in the sentence.

Part 3 Using Your Skills

1. Choose a different word or phrase from the list below to complete each sentence.

   because   for example   like   result   after

   a. As a ____result____ of studying, Terry earned a high score on the test.

   b. Please put out the trash _____after_____ you finish cleaning up the kitchen.

   c. Chris likes all kinds of berries; ___for example___, she likes strawberries, blackberries, and raspberries.

   d. _____*Like*_____ you, I too have an allergy to dust.

   e. _____*Because*_____ I have a cold today, I think I will stay home.

2. Read the following textbook passage and identify all the transitions that show example and contrast.

> One of the most dramatic changes in society has been the growing importance of women in the work force. In 1987, for instance, the Census Bureau reported that for the first time in American history more than half of all women with children under the age of one were either working or actively seeking employment. Yet women's wages still lag behind those of men. To some extent the wage gap between men and women represents the failure of employers to abide by the Equal Pay Act of 1963, which requires "equal pay for equal work." A large part of the difference, however, is explained by the fact that so many women work in low-paying, traditionally female occupations, such as teaching, nursing, and secretarial work.

> From Gitelson, Dudley, and Dubnick, *American Democracy,* fourth edition. Boston: Houghton Mifflin, 1996.

   a. example: _for instance, such as_

   b. contrast: _yet, however_

Score: 100 − 7 for each one missed = ____%

Vocabulary Quiz

Each sentence below contains a word in bold type from the reading selection on pages 89–90. Read the sentence and the definitions that follow it. Then circle the correct one. Turn to the vocabulary preview on pages 88–89 to check your answers.

1. I do not like to **fritter** away my time by waiting in lines.
   a. spend
   b. waste
   c. use
   d. schedule

2. Washing the car is a **drudgery,** and I would rather do almost anything else.

    a. required task
    b. necessary evil
    c. pleasant activity
    (d.) boring job

3. Eating too much, drinking to excess, and smoking are **vices** that can endanger your life.
    (a.) personal failings
    b. healthy habits
    c. mortal sins
    d. good deeds

4. California's giant redwood **dwarfs** other trees, even the tall pine for which Maine is famous.
    a. takes over
    b. crowds out
    (c.) causes to appear smaller
    d. is a substitute for

5. When proofreading a research paper, make sure that you have correctly **cited** all the sources you have quoted.
    (a.) mentioned
    b. hidden
    c. saved
    d. located

6. Because punctuality is important to Professor Morris, he always **chides** his students for being late.
    a. praises
    b. rewards
    c. beats
    (d.) scolds

7. In your writing you should avoid **mundane** sayings such as "better late than never" because they are unimaginative.
    a. incorrect
    b. inventive
    (c.) ordinary
    d. obscene

8. Completing her own work while doing that of a co-worker who was sick showed that Tina was good at **multitasking.**
    a. delegating responsibility to others
    b. doing more than one thing at once
    c. procrastinating
    d. networking

9. Do not make **petty** complaints about the assignment being too long or too hard—just do the work.
    a. valid
    b. frequent
    c. unkind
    d. unimportant

Score: 100 − 10 for each one missed = _____%

Chapter 5

Finding Main Ideas

Do you have trouble remembering what you read? Do you ever find yourself wondering what your instructor expects you to get out of an assignment, or which ideas in a chapter are the most important? If your answer to any of these questions is *yes,* then learning how to find a main idea is one step you can take to improve your reading comprehension.

The main idea is the most important idea in a whole paragraph or longer passage. All the other ideas in a paragraph or passage support, or explain, the main idea. Often, a main idea of a paragraph is stated in a *topic sentence* that may be easy for you to find. Sometimes, a main idea is unstated, or *implied,* and you must read carefully for clues to help you determine the main idea.

A main idea guides your reading in two ways: by telling you what is important and by helping you predict what comes next. This chapter explains several strategies that will help you find the main idea:

- *Distinguish general from specific ideas.*
- *Identify the author's topic.*
- *Find the topic sentence of a paragraph.*
- *Find the central idea of a passage.*
- *Know how to find implied main ideas.*

117

WHAT DO YOU ALREADY KNOW?

To prepare yourself for the reading selection that follows, find out what you already know about grades. Answer the questions below either on your own or in a group discussion.

1. What do grades mean to you?

2. What do you think grades mean to your instructors, parents, and employers?

3. What do you do when you receive a grade that you do not like?

4. Read the title, headnote, vocabulary preview, and first two paragraphs of the reading selection. What do you think will follow?

Making the Grade
Kurt Wiesenfeld

Kurt Wiesenfeld is a physicist who teaches at Georgia Tech in Atlanta. In this essay, which appeared in Newsweek, *the author discusses students' attitudes about grades.*

VOCABULARY PREVIEW

tentative	(tĕn´tə•tĭv) hesitant, uncertain
disgruntled	(dĭs•grŭn´tld) discontented, ill-humored
cynicism	(sĭn´ĭ•sĭsm) a belief that people are motivated by selfishness
wheedling	(hwēd´lĭng) persuading by flattery or cleverness
overwrought	(ō´vər•rôt´) nervous or excited
intrinsically	(ĭn•trĭn´zĭk•lē) by its nature, inborn
eccentric	(ĭk•sĕn´trĭk) unusual, out of the ordinary

superficial	(so͞o′pər·fĭsh′əl) unimportant, on the surface
blatant	(blāt′nt) obvious to the point of being offensive
expertise	(ĕk′spûr·tēz′) expert skill or knowledge

Pronunciation Key: ā (**pay**), ĕ (**pet**), ē (**bee**), ĭ (**pit**), ō (**toe**), ô (**caught, paw**), o͞o (**boot**), ŭ (**cut**), û (**urge, term**), ə (**about, item**)

It was a rookie error. After 10 years I should have known better, but I went to my office the day after final grades were posted. There was a **tentative** knock on the door. "Professor Wiesenfeld? I took your Physics 2121 class? I flunked it? I wonder if there is anything I can do to improve my grade?" I thought: "Why are you asking me? Isn't it too late to worry about it? Do you dislike making declarative statements?"

After the student gave his tale of woe and left, the phone rang. "I got a D in your class. Is there any way you can change it to 'incomplete'?" Then the e-mail assault began: "I'm shy about coming in to talk to you, but I'm not shy about asking for a better grade. Anyway, it's worth a try." The next day I had three phone messages from students asking *me* to call *them.* I didn't.

Time was, when you received a grade, that was it. You might groan and moan, but you accepted it as the outcome of your efforts or lack thereof (and, yes, sometimes a tough grader). In the last few years, however, some students have developed a **disgruntled**-consumer approach. If they don't like their grade, they go to the "return" counter to trade it in for something better.

What alarms me is their indifference toward grades as an indication of personal effort and performance. Many, when pressed about why they think they deserve a better grade, admit they don't deserve one but would like one anyway. Having been raised on gold stars for effort and smiley faces for self-esteem, they've learned that they can get by without hard work and real talent if they can talk the professor into giving them a break. This attitude is beyond **cynicism.** There's a weird innocence to the assumption that one expects (even deserves) a better grade simply by begging for it. With that outlook, I guess I shouldn't be as flabbergasted as I was that the 12 students asked me to change their grades *after* final grades were posted.

That's 10 percent of my class who let three months of midterms, quizzes and lab reports slide until long past remedy. My graduate student calls it hyperrational thinking: if effort and intelligence don't

1

2

3

4

5

matter, why should deadlines? What matters is getting a better grade through an unearned bonus, the academic equivalent of a freebie T shirt or toaster giveaway. Rewards are disconnected from the quality of one's work. An act and its consequences are unrelated, random events.

Their arguments for **wheedling** better grades often ignore academic performance. Perhaps they feel it's not relevant. "If my grade isn't raised to a D I'll lose my scholarship." "If you don't give me a C, I'll flunk out." One sincerely **overwrought** student pleaded, "If I don't pass, my life is over." This is tough stuff to deal with. Apparently, I'm responsible for someone's losing a scholarship, flunking out or deciding whether life has meaning. Perhaps these students see me as a commodities broker with something they want—a grade. Though **intrinsically** worthless, grades, if properly manipulated, can be traded for what has value: a degree, which means a job, which means money. The one thing college actually offers—a chance to learn—is considered irrelevant, even less than worthless, because of the long hours and hard work required.

In a society saturated with surface values, love of knowledge for its own sake does sound **eccentric.** The benefits of fame and wealth are more obvious. So is it right to blame students for reflecting the **superficial** values saturating our society?

Yes, of course it's right. These guys had better take themselves seriously now, because our country will be forced to take them seriously later, when the stakes are much higher. They must recognize that their attitude is not only self-destructive, but socially destructive. The erosion of quality control—giving appropriate grades for actual accomplishments—is a major concern in my department. One colleague noted that a physics major could obtain a degree without ever answering a written exam question completely. How? By pulling in enough partial credit and extra credit. And by getting breaks on grades.

But what happens once she or he graduates and gets a job? That's when the misfortunes of eroding academic standards multiply. We lament that schoolchildren get "kicked upstairs" until they graduate from high school despite being illiterate and mathematically inept, but we seem unconcerned with our college graduates whose less **blatant** deficiencies are far more harmful if their accreditation exceeds their qualifications.

Most of my students are science and engineering majors. If they're good at getting partial credit but not at getting the answer right, then the new bridge breaks or the new drug doesn't work. One finds examples here in Atlanta. Last year a light tower in the Olympic Stadium collapsed, killing a worker. It collapsed because an engineer miscalculated how much weight it could hold. A new 12-story dormitory could develop dangerous cracks due to a foundation that's uneven by more than six inches. The error resulted from incorrect data being fed into a computer. I drive past that dorm daily on my way to work, wondering if a foundation crushed under kilotons of weight is repairable or if this structure will have to be demolished. Two 10,000-pound steel beams at the new natatorium collapsed in March, crashing into the student athletic complex. (Should we give partial credit since no one was hurt?) Those are real-world consequences of errors and lack of **expertise.**

But the lesson is lost on the grade-grousing 10 percent. Say that   11 you won't (not can't, won't) change the grade they deserve to what they want, and they're frequently bewildered or angry. They don't think it's fair that they're judged according to their performance, not their desires or "potential." They don't think it's fair that they should jeopardize their scholarships or be in danger of flunking out simply because they could not or did not do their work. But it's more than fair; it's necessary to help preserve a minimum standard of quality that our society needs to maintain safety and integrity. I don't know if the 13th-hour students will learn that lesson, but I've learned mine. From now on, after final grades are posted, I'll lie low until the next quarter starts.

HOW WELL DID YOU COMPREHEND?

Main Idea

1. Which statement *best* expresses what the whole selection is about?
    a. Students believe that grades are the result of performance.
    b. In the past, students accepted their grades without question.
    c. Students today expect good grades whether they deserve them or not.
    (d.) "Making the grade" has a new meaning for today's students.

Details

2. According to the author, grades are
    (a.) intrinsically worthless.
    b. considered irrelevant.
    c. properly manipulated.
    d. generally desired.

3. Which of the following is a real-world consequence of an engineer's error as explained in paragraph 10?
   a. A new bridge collapsed.
   b. A new drug didn't work.
   c. A light tower in the Olympic Stadium collapsed.
   d. A 12-story dormitory was built.

Inferences

4. In paragraph 1, what does the author mean by, "It was a rookie error. After 10 years I should have known better."
   a. Students usually do not complain about grades.
   b. It was a mistake only inexperienced teachers make.
   c. He was not an experienced teacher.
   d. He should have given the students better grades.

5. In paragraph 9, the author says that illiterate and mathematically inept schoolchildren get "kicked upstairs." What does he mean?
   a. Children who cannot read, write, or figure are promoted anyway.
   b. The children have not been taught to read and write.
   c. Many children in the upper grades are poor in mathematics.
   d. Schoolchildren are the victims of physical abuse.

Working with Words

Complete the sentences below with these words from the vocabulary preview.

tentative	disgruntled	cynicism	eccentric
wheedling	overwrought	intrinsically	superficial
blatant	expertise		

1. Despite your ___*wheedling*___, I am not going to buy you a car for your sixteenth birthday.

2. You expect the doctors who treat you to have a great deal of ___*expertise*___ in their fields.

3. Erin was ___*tentative*___ about accepting a date with Eric because she did not know him very well.

4. The ___*eccentric*___ kindergarten teacher wore combat boots and other military gear to class.

5. It is normal for students to become __*overwrought*__ as the final exam period approaches.

6. Whenever Congress votes to raise its members' salaries, taxpayers accuse them of ____*cynicism*____.

7. Your wounds are only ____*superficial*____, not deep.

8. Professor Sims caught a student looking at notes during a test, which was a ____*blatant*____ act of cheating.

9. These fake gems are ____*intrinsically*____ worthless.

10. The ____*disgruntled*____ child could not be persuaded to smile.

Thinking and Writing

The author says that students are indifferent to grades as indicators of effort and performance. He says students believe they can get by without hard work. Do you agree or disagree? What is your attitude towards grades? Do you think most students share your attitude?

Answers will vary. _____

_____

_____

_____

DISTINGUISH GENERAL FROM SPECIFIC IDEAS

A main idea is a *general,* or broad, idea. On the other hand, a *specific* idea is narrow. To see the difference between general and specific ideas, read the following three sentences.

1. I want a sports utility vehicle.
2. A Jeep Cherokee is one of the vehicles I have considered.
3. Also, I have test-driven a Ford Explorer.

In the first sentence, *sports utility vehicle* is a general idea because it describes all possible vehicles that fit into this category. In the second and third sentences, *Jeep Cherokee* and *Ford Explorer* are specific ideas because they both are examples of certain kinds of sports utility vehicles.

Exercise 5.1   Read each group of words, then circle the most general idea. The first one is done as an example.

1.	baseball	tennis	(sports)	football	golf
2.	magazine	journal	newspaper	newsletter	(periodical)
3.	diamond	ruby	emerald	(gemstone)	sapphire
4.	collie	boxer	poodle	(dog)	terrier
5.	candy	(dessert)	pie	pudding	ice cream
6.	pear	apple	peach	(fruit)	plum
7.	(flower)	rose	daisy	tulip	daffodil
8.	country	rock	rap	jazz	(music)
9.	chair	sofa	table	(furniture)	bed
10.	(tree)	maple	elm	pine	palm

Some ideas are more specific than others. For example, *seafood* is a general idea. *Shellfish* is a specific kind of seafood. Shrimp, lobster, and crab are specific kinds of shellfish.

Exercise 5.2   In each item below, the first word is the most general idea, and the second word is a more specific idea. On the blank that follows the second word, add an even more specific idea. The first one is done as an example. *(Answers may vary but should be of the type listed here.)*

1. plant   flower   _____rose_____

2. vehicle   automobile   _____Ford Taurus_____

3. required course   mathematics course   _____Algebra I_____

4. accessory   jewelry   _____bracelet_____

5. T.V. program   situation comedy   _____Seinfeld_____

6. periodical   magazine   _____Time_____

7. entertainment   movie   _____Titanic_____

8. kitchen equipment   cookware   _____frying pan_____

9. fiction   children's story   _____Charlotte's Web_____

10. household pet   cat   _____Siamese_____

The main idea of a paragraph is the most general idea in the paragraph. The other ideas in a paragraph are specific ideas that support, or explain, the main idea. Therefore, to find the main idea, you must first be able to distinguish between general and specific ideas.

Memory Cue

General ideas are broad. Tree *is a general idea. Specific ideas are narrow.* Evergreen *is a specific kind of tree. Some ideas are more specific than others. A type of evergreen tree, such as the* Douglas fir, *is an even more specific idea.*

IDENTIFY THE AUTHOR'S TOPIC

The first step toward finding a main idea is to identify the author's topic. To find the topic, ask yourself, "What is the author's subject" or "What is the author writing about?" You should be able to state the topic in a single word or a short phrase.

The title, if there is one, is a good place to start looking for the topic. For example, what came to mind as you read the title of Kurt Wiesenfeld's article "Making the Grade"? Did you think of a general idea such as *measuring up to a standard* or *meeting a requirement?* Or did you think of a specific idea such as *students' grades?*

The next place to look for the topic is the first paragraph. An author usually begins with an introduction that makes clear what the topic is. In Wiesenfeld's first paragraph, for example, the phrase "final grades" and the student's question "Is there anything I can do about my grade?" make clear that the author's topic is *students' grades.*

If reading the title and first paragraph do not help you determine the author's topic, read further for more clues.

Exercise 5.3   Working with a partner, read the following three paragraphs and identify the author's topic in each.

1. The Mt. Dora Craft Festival is fun for the whole family. The festival is an annual October event, and it draws crowds of people from all across the state. Men and women display and sell their crafts. Local bands provide entertainment, and a variety of food vendors satisfy every appetite.

Topic: <u>*Mt. Dora Craft Festival*</u>

2. Some students enter college having already made a career choice. Others arrive not knowing what they want to do with their lives. Choosing a major is an important decision you will have to make. Your major should be a field that interests you. Moreover, your major should prepare you for a variety of careers, one of which is right for you. To choose a major, you must consider your interests, skills, and talents. Moreover, you must have an idea of the kind of work that you would enjoy doing.

Topic: <u>*choosing a major*</u>

3. The newest shopping malls are not what we have come to expect. The malls we are used to are self-contained buildings with shops, restaurants, and theaters opening onto connecting walkways. These buildings are temperature controlled, and many are connected to covered parking garages. The newest malls, however, are composed of separate, free-standing buildings arranged around a center court. They resemble an old-fashioned town square with ample parking and green areas where people can stop to chat or rest. Some think the new malls are a passing trend. Others predict they will catch on.

Topic: <u>*the newest shopping malls*</u>

Memory Cue

The author's topic is his or her subject. You should be able to state in a single word or short phrase what a whole paragraph or longer passage is about.

FIND THE TOPIC SENTENCE OF A PARAGRAPH

Not every paragraph has a topic sentence, but every paragraph does have a main idea. Sometimes the main idea is stated, sometimes not. If the main idea is stated, then you will be able to point to a sentence in the paragraph that states the main idea. This sentence is the *topic sentence.*

To find the topic sentence, ask yourself two questions. Then look for a sentence that combines your answers:

- What is the author's topic?
- What is the author's opinion about the topic?

The following examples are sentences that could be the topic sentences of paragraphs. The writer's *topic* (T) and *opinion* (O) are underlined and labeled in each one.

1. *T* <u>Advertising</u> *O* <u>has several benefits for consumers</u>.
2. *T* <u>Commercials during children's programs</u> *O* <u>encourage bad habits</u>.
3. *T* <u>Consumer Economics</u> is a *O* <u>worthwhile</u> course for students.

In the first sentence, the author's topic is *advertising*. The author's opinion is that advertising *has several benefits*. If this were the topic sentence of a paragraph, then you would expect the rest of the paragraph to explain what the benefits are.

In the second sentence, the author's topic is *commercials during children's programs*. The author's opinion is that they *encourage bad habits*. If this were the topic sentence of a paragraph, then you would expect the rest of the paragraph to explain what the bad habits are and how commercials encourage them.

In the third sentence, the author's topic is *Consumer Economics*. The author's opinion is that this course is *worthwhile* for students. If this were the topic sentence of a paragraph, you would expect the rest of the paragraph to describe the course and explain why the author thinks it is worthwhile.

Exercise 5.4

Do this exercise on your own or with a partner. In each of the sentences below, underline the topic once and the author's opinion twice. Write *T* above the topic and *O* above the opinion. The first one is done as an example. *(Underlining may vary as long as topic and opinion are correctly identified.)*

1. *T* <u>Florida's beaches</u> *O* <u>provide something for everyone</u>.
2. *O* <u>A highlight of the Olympic games</u> is *T* <u>the lighting of the torch</u>.
3. *T* <u>Sailing</u> is a summer activity *O* <u>I enjoy for several reasons</u>.
4. *T* <u>These guidelines</u> *O* <u>can help students improve their note-taking skills</u>.

5. The <u>high salaries of some</u> ^T sports celebrities have become <u>a contro-</u> ^O <u>versial topic</u>.

6. <u>Being an astronaut</u> ^T is a job that <u>requires special training</u> ^O.

7. <u>Nutrition and exercise</u> ^T are two <u>components of an effective weight-</u> ^O <u>loss program</u>.

8. <u>Loons</u> ^T <u>have characteristics that make them unique</u> ^O among waterbirds.

9. <u>Automobile buyers</u> ^T are <u>interested in price, dependability, and service</u> ^O.

10. <u>You should learn to use</u> ^O your <u>college library's resources</u> ^T.

A topic sentence can be anywhere in a paragraph. It can be the first sentence, the last sentence, or any sentence in between. If there is a topic sentence, it is often the *first* sentence. The following examples show topic sentences in three positions. These examples are from textbooks such as the ones used in your classes. In each example, the topic sentence is underlined.

Example 1: The Topic Sentence as First Sentence

<u>TNT began in October 1988, promoted as the first cable network designed expressly to challenge the major television broadcast networks.</u> Initially reaching some 17 million subscribers, the service offered mostly movies but began more original programming in the 1990s. It was the fastest-growing new cable network, reaching 60 million subscribers by 1994. . . .

From Sydney W. Head, Christopher H. Sterling, Lemuel B. Schofield, *Broadcasting in America.* Boston: Houghton Mifflin, 1996.

In this example, the writer's topic is TNT, which stands for "Turner Network Television." The writer's opinion is that TNT was designed to challenge the major networks. The details in the rest of the paragraph explain the kinds of programs offered and the number of cable subscribers the network reached. *When the topic sentence is the first sentence in a paragraph, the details come after the main idea.*

Example 2: The Topic Sentence as Last Sentence

Within the organization, information may be transmitted from superiors to subordinates (downward communication), from subordinates to superiors (upward communication), among people at the same level on the organizational chart (horizontal communication), and among people in different departments within the organization (cross-channel communication). <u>These four types of communication make up the organization's **formal communication network.**</u>

From Scot Ober, *Contemporary Business Communication*, second edition. Boston: Houghton Mifflin, 1995.

In this example, the writer's topic is the formal communication network. The writer's opinion is that four types of communication make up the network. The details in the rest of the paragraph explain the four types of communication: their names and how communication flows. *When the topic sentence is the last sentence in a paragraph, the details come before the main idea.*

Example 3: The Topic Sentence Between First and Last Sentences

All organisms must ensure that their offspring have a reasonable chance to survive and begin a new generation. <u>Plants, however, face special challenges.</u> Plants do not have nervous systems, and they are not able to run away from predators or pests. Because nearly all plants live in fixed positions, they must also manage to find mates without being able to move around. Therefore they have evolved strategies for dealing with these problems that are essentially passive. An important part of such strategies is a reproductive pattern enabling each individual to produce large numbers of offspring.

From Joseph S. Levine and Kenneth R. Miller, *Biology.* Lexington, MA: D. C. Heath, 1991.

In this example, the writer's topic is plants. The writer's opinion is that plants face special challenges. The details before the topic sentence explain that the special challenges relate to plant reproduction and survival. The details after the topic sentence explain three challenges for plants: They do not have nervous systems, they cannot run from predators, and they cannot move around to find mates. However, special strategies and a high reproductive rate help them meet these challenges. *When the topic sentence comes between the first and last sentences of a paragraph, the details come before and after the main idea.*

Exercise 5.5   This exercise will help you practice looking for main ideas in textbook passages. Working with a partner, read and discuss each paragraph. Then underline the topic sentence.

1. <u>Anyone who has ever stood near the restrooms at a baseball park on a hot day knows that there is a relationship between beer and urination</u>. The casual drinker may think that this is due to the amount of liquid he has drunk, but this is only partly true. A heavy drinker feels "hung over" the next morning, and one of the symptoms of the hangover is a powerful thirst. The need to visit the restroom and the hangover thirst are related. Alcohol inhibits the release of ADH, and this increases the rate at which water is lost from the kidneys. Excessive drinking therefore causes a great deal of water to be lost, producing an unusually large amount of urine and dehydrating the body. Consider the case of two fans sitting side-by-side at the ball park, one drinking beer and the other drinking an equal volume of soft drink. The non-alcohol drinker will not only see more of the game (fewer visits to the restroom) but will also feel better in the morning!

From Joseph S. Levine and Kenneth R. Miller, *Biology*. Lexington, MA: D.C. Heath, 1991.

2. *Roots,* a 14-hour adaptation of a bestseller about the evolving role of blacks in American life, ran for eight successive nights in 1977. It started a trend toward miniseries. At the time, experts doubted the drawing power of the subject matter and its ability to sustain viewership for so many hours, but *Roots* took them by surprise. The audience increased for each episode, breaking all records on the eighth night. A western miniseries, *Lonesome Dove,* scored a similar surprise success in the late 1980s. <u>Miniseries proved able to compete well against pay-cable movies and to attract new viewers, especially upscale professionals, who may otherwise watch little entertainment television</u>.

From Sydney W. Head, Christopher H. Sterling, Lemuel B. Schofield, *Broadcasting in America*. Boston: Houghton Mifflin, 1996.

3. <u>Those who view diversity among employees as a source of richness and strength for the organization can help bring a wide range of benefits to their organization</u>. Whether you happen to belong to the majority culture or one of the minority cultures where you work, you will share your work and leisure hours with people different from yourself—people who have values, mannerisms, and speech habits different from your own. This is true today, and it will be even truer in the future. The same strategies apply whether the cultural differences exist at home or abroad.

From Scot Ober, *Contemporary Business Communication,* second
edition. Boston: Houghton Mifflin, 1995.

4. "You can't have everything," as the old saying goes, but many
young Americans certainly try. This is one of the reasons why the
average household headed by someone under age 25 spends 17
percent more than its disposable income. (How? By using credit,
of course.) <u>What is important to realize is that although one
cannot have everything right now, planning will help keep things
in perspective.</u> Comparing what one has to parents or older
relatives and friends is fine. But recognize that it takes a lot of time
to build up the quantity and quality of possessions that they may
have. Intelligently setting short-term goals and recognizing budget
limitations will enable you to reach goals for major purchases but
not at the expense of financial security.

From E. Thomas Garman and Raymond E. Forgue, *Personal
Finance,* fourth edition. Boston: Houghton Mifflin, 1994.

FIND THE CENTRAL IDEA OF A PASSAGE

Longer passages are made up of several paragraphs. Each paragraph
has a main idea. The entire passage has an overall main idea, sometimes
called the *central idea*. The main ideas and details of each paragraph
support the central idea of the whole passage.

To find the central idea of a longer passage, first determine the
topic. What is the passage about? The title, if there is one, may provide a clue. For example, the title of this chapter is *Finding Main Ideas*.
You can tell from the title that the topic is *main ideas*. What is the author's opinion about the topic? The chapter introduction tells you
that main ideas are important and that you can learn how to find the
main idea.

To find the central idea of a longer passage, look for a sentence
near the beginning of the passage that states the author's topic and
opinion. If that does not work, try looking for a sentence that explains
what the author expects you to learn. In this chapter, the central idea
is stated in the last sentence of the third paragraph: "This chapter explains several strategies that will help you find the main idea."

If reading the title and first paragraph do not help you find the central idea, try reading further. The details may help. If the passage is

broken up into sections with headings, these may provide additional clues. First sentences of paragraphs are another good place to look.

Besides textbook chapters, longer passages also include chapters or sections from other types of books as well as articles from magazines and newspapers. In these passages also, reading the title and first paragraph may help you determine the author's topic and central idea. If not, then you may have to read further.

Exercise 5.6   Read the following longer passage and find the central idea. The hints stated in parentheses at the end of each question will help you think through the passage. Do the exercise on your own or with a partner.

How to Buy

There are numerous suggestions on how to buy, and probably the most valuable is to plan ahead for purchases. To reach your long-term goals, you must buy the goods and services that you need and want; you do not need to wastefully spend money on things you do not really desire. Thus, making a list to plan what you want to buy is a crucial step. The following are some other suggestions.   1

Make an effort to keep up with the current prices on goods and services that you want to buy.   2

Use newspaper advertisements to get information on product availability and prices. Clip the ads to your shopping list to have more reference information available.   3

Use the Yellow Pages and the telephone to find out whether stores carry certain items and get price information as appropriate.   4

Comparison shop to protect yourself from overpricing. . . .   5

From E. Thomas Garman, *Consumer Economic Issues in America.* Boston: Houghton Mifflin, 1991.

1. What is the author's topic? (Hint: Read the title.)

   The author's topic is "How to buy."

2. What is the author's opinion? (Hint: What does the author think or want you to know about the topic?)

   The author wants you to follow his suggestions on how to buy.

3. What more do the first sentences of paragraphs 2 through 5 tell you? (Hint: How do the ideas expressed in these sentences relate to the author's topic?)

   These sentences list the author's suggestions on how to buy.

4. What is the central idea of the whole passage? (Hint: Look in the first paragraph for a sentence that states the author's topic and opinion.)

   The first sentence states the central idea of the passage.

Memory Cue

To find a main idea of a paragraph, look for a topic sentence. The topic sentence states the author's topic and opinion. The topic sentence can appear anywhere in a paragraph, but not all paragraphs have topic sentences. The main idea of a longer passage is called the central idea, and it is often stated near the beginning of the passage. The title, if there is one, may provide a clue. If not, you may have to read further.

KNOW HOW TO FIND IMPLIED MAIN IDEAS

Every paragraph has a main idea. You know that main ideas are stated in topic sentences. If a paragraph has no topic sentence, then the main idea is unstated or *implied*. As a reader, you must be able to figure out what the main idea is. Ask yourself these questions. Your answers will lead you to the implied main idea.

1. What is the author's topic?
2. What seems to be the author's opinion about the topic?
3. What more can I learn from the details?
4. In my own words, what is the main idea?

    The following paragraph does not have a topic sentence. Read the paragraph and determine the main idea.

One day last week I was driving the speed limit on an interstate highway, and traffic was very heavy. Suddenly, the car behind me bumped into my car, pushing me into the car ahead of me. I later found out that the driver's brakes had failed, causing him to lose control of his car. Although the accident tied up traffic for hours, no one was hurt, and little damage was done.

The author's topic is *an automobile accident.* The author's opinion is that the accident caused little damage. The details tell you what happened. Putting topic, opinion, and details together, what is the main idea? The following statement would work as a topic sentence for the paragraph: *An automobile accident I had recently turned out to be a minor one.*

As you can see, finding an unstated main idea does not have to be difficult if you look for clues in the details.

Exercise 5.7   Like the example paragraph about the accident, each of the following paragraphs has an unstated main idea. Read each paragraph and answer the questions that follow to determine the main idea. Do the exercise on your own or with a partner. *(Answers may vary in wording but should be similar to these.)*

1. My job is different and exciting every day. Also, my company pays for me to take courses that advance my skills and make me eligible for promotions. Best of all, my job provides opportunities for me to travel and work with interesting people.
   a. What is the author's topic?

   The author's topic is "my job."

   b. What seems to be the author's opinion about the topic?

   The author likes the job.

   c. What more do the details tell you?

   The details explain the author's reasons.

   d. In your own words, what is the main idea?

   I like my job for several reasons.

2. David Walker is a recently retired astronaut. Before becoming an astronaut, he was a fighter pilot in Vietnam and a test pilot for the

Navy. During his career at NASA, he made four flights into space. He was the commander of three of these flights, the most recent of which was the flight of the Endeavor in 1995. Walker's missions have included a spacewalk, the release and retrieval of satellites, and the gathering of scientific data. Walker says that being an astronaut was always exciting, never routine.

a. What is the author's topic?

   The author's topic is "David Walker."

b. What seems to be the author's opinion about the topic?

   The author seems to think Walker has led an interesting life.

c. What more do the details tell you?

   The details tell you what Walker has done as a pilot and astronaut.

d. In your own words, what is the main idea?

   David Walker has had an interesting career.

In some longer passages the central idea may be unstated. Asking the same four questions as in Exercise 5.7 will help you determine the implied central idea. For example, Kurt Wiesenfeld's article on pages 118–121 has an unstated main idea. Wiesenfeld's topic is *students' grades*. His opinion is that students want good grades even when they do not deserve them. From the details, you learn that students' attitudes about grades have changed over the years. Wiesenfeld thinks that students did not used to complain about grades; now they do. In the past, students worked hard for good grades. Wiesenfeld thinks that now they expect to receive good grades whether they work for them or not.

What is the central idea of the whole article? The following statement combines the author's topic, opinion, and details: *Making the grade has a new meaning for today's students.*

Exercise 5.8 Read the following longer passage and determine the implied central idea. The hints stated in parentheses will help you think through the passage. Do the exercise on your own or with a partner.

Photographs and Pictures

  The old Chinese proverb that a picture is worth a thousand   1
words is not always true in public speaking. . . . On the plus side, a
good photograph can demonstrate or authenticate a point in a
speech in a way that words alone cannot. It can make a situation
seem more vivid and realistic. For instance, if you were trying to
describe the devastation caused by a flood, tornado, or hurricane,
photographs could be quite useful.

  On the negative side, photographs and pictures frequently   2
include distracting details that are not relevant to your message.
Their vividness can also be a disadvantage, especially when speakers
rely on them too heavily to make a point, forgetting that language is
the primary medium of communication in a speech. Such aids
should reinforce, not replace the speaker's words. . . .

Adapted from Michael Osborn and Suzanne Osborn, *Public Speaking,*
third edition. Boston: Houghton Mifflin, 1994.

1. What is the authors' topic in the passage as a whole? (Hint: Read the
   title and first sentence.)

   The topic is "photographs and pictures in public speaking."

2. What seems to be the authors' opinion about the topic? (Hint: What
   does the author think about using photographs and pictures?)

   Using photographs and pictures has both good and bad points.

3. What do the details in the first paragraph tell you about the authors'
   topic? (Hint: The phrase "on the plus side" is a clue.)

   The first paragraph explains the good points.

4. What do the details in the second paragraph tell you about the authors' topic? (Hint: The phrase "on the negative side" is a clue.)

   The second paragraph explains the bad points.

5. In your own words, what is the main idea of the whole passage? (Hint: Write a sentence that combines the authors' topic and opinion, and details in 1 through 4 above.)

Using photographs and pictures in public speaking has advantages

and disadvantages.

Memory Cue

To find an unstated main idea, read carefully. Ask yourself questions about the author's topic, details, and opinion. Use this information to come up with a main idea statement of your own.

REAL-WORLD CONNECTIONS

This chapter's strategies for finding stated and implied main ideas are useful not only for your college assignments but for outside reading as well. Being able to find main ideas will improve your reading comprehension and your enjoyment of reading.

Practice your strategies by reading a short newspaper article on a topic of your choice and by answering the following questions about it. Be prepared to bring your article to class and share what you have learned. _(Students' articles and answers will vary.)_

Title of your article: _____

Author: _____

Source: _____

1. What is the author's topic?

    _____

2. What is the author's opinion about the topic?

    _____

    _____

3.   What more do the details in each paragraph tell you?

_____

_____

4.   What is the central idea of the whole article, and is it stated or implied?

_____

_____

5.   Explain one interesting piece of information you have learned from the article.

_____

_____

HOW WELL DO YOU REMEMBER?

To review the chapter, read the following summary and fill in the blanks. If you need help with an answer, look back through the chapter to refresh your memory.

The main idea is the most important idea in a whole paragraph or longer passage. All the other ideas in a paragraph or passage support, or explain, the _____*main*_____ idea.

The author's topic is the author's _____*subject*_____: what a whole paragraph or passage is about. The main idea states the author's opinion about the topic. The main idea is also the most general idea. The supporting details are _____*specific*_____ ideas.

Every paragraph and every longer passage has a main idea. Often the main idea of a paragraph is stated in a topic sentence. The two parts of a topic sentence are the author's _____topic_____ and the author's _____opinion_____. The topic sentence is often the _____first_____ sentence of a paragraph. Two other places you can find the topic sentence are between the first and _____last_____ sentence or at the _____end_____ of the paragraph.

In some paragraphs, the main idea is unstated or _____implied_____. To find an unstated main idea, you must read the _____details_____ carefully for clues. Then try to determine the general idea that all the _____details_____ support.

The main idea of a longer passage is often called the central idea, and it is usually stated near the beginning of the passage. The main ideas and details in each paragraph support the _____central_____ idea of the entire passage.

WHAT DO YOU THINK?

Reflect on this chapter's strategies for finding main ideas. What have you learned about main ideas that you did not know before? In which of your courses is the assigned reading the most demanding? How can you use this chapter's strategies to improve your reading of difficult material? Write your reflections below.

Reflections will vary. _____

_____

_____

_____

_____

CHAPTER QUIZ 1

Part 1 Terms and Definitions

Match this chapter's special terms in Column A with their definitions in Column B.

Column A

_d_ 1. general
_a_ 2. specific
_e_ 3. main idea
_b_ 4. detail
_c_ 5. implied

Column B

a. narrow
b. supporting idea
c. not stated
d. broad
e. most important idea

Part 2 Chapter Review

Read and answer each question below. Write your answer in complete sentences, and use extra paper if needed. *(Answers may vary but should be similar to these.)*

1. What is a main idea?

   The main idea is the most important idea in a paragraph or longer passage.

2. How is the main idea different from the rest of the ideas stated in a paragraph?

   The main idea is a general idea. The rest of the ideas in a paragraph are

   specific ideas that support the main idea.

3. Where in a paragraph will you find the main idea stated?

   Often, the main idea is the first sentence. However, the main idea can be

   anywhere in the paragraph.

Part 3 Using Your Skills

I. In each group of words below, circle the most general idea.

1. broccoli   carrot   (vegetable)   radish
2. pork   (meat)   beef   chicken
3. pelican   gull   heron   (water bird)
4. (rock)   granite   marble   limestone
5. canyon   cave   (land form)   mountain
6. Leprechaun   giant   elf   (mythical creature)
7. (religion)   Islam   Hinduism   Buddhism

II. Read each paragraph and answer the questions that follow.

Until just a few hundred years ago, children in Western society were not perceived as full-fledged members of society or even as genuine human beings (Aries, 1962). During medieval times, infants tended to be regarded rather like talented pets: at best interesting and even able to talk, but not creatures worth caring about deeply. Children graduated to adult status early in life, around age seven or eight, by taking on major, adultlike tasks for the community. At that time, children who today would be attending second or third grade might have been caring for younger siblings, working in the fields, or apprenticed to a family to learn a trade.   1

From Seifert and Hoffnung, *Child and Adolescent Development,* fourth edition. Boston: Houghton Mifflin, 1997.

a. What is the author's topic?

   children in Western society

b. What is the main idea?

   Until just a few hundred years ago . . . (first sentence)

Intelligence refers to adaptability, or, put differently, to a general ability to learn from experience. Usually intelligence also refers to the ability to reason abstractly, sometimes using language to do so, and it includes the ability to integrate old and new knowledge. In recent years, some psychologists have also used the term *intelligence* to refer to social skills, talents of various kinds (such as a talent for music), or bodily skills. The traditional orientation toward reasoning and problem solving, however, still dominates discussions of intelligence, and partly as a result, many standardized tests have been developed to measure these forms of intelligence.   2

From Seifert and Hoffnung, *Child and Adolescent Development,* fourth edition. Boston: Houghton Mifflin, 1997.

a. What is the author's topic?

  intelligence

b. What is the main idea?

  Intelligence can be defined in different ways. (implied)

Poll findings suggest that Americans do not believe that their elected representatives respond to their demands and expectations. For example, when asked whether "having elections makes the government pay attention to what the people think," 56 percent of those questioned said that it does so only "some" or "not much of the time." In a recent survey of citizens who call in to radio talk shows, 87 percent indicated that "generally speaking, elected officials in Washington lose touch with the people pretty quickly." And when asked whether they felt that things in this country were generally going in the right direction, two out of three voters felt we were on the wrong track.   3

From Gitelson, Dudley, Dubnick, *American Government,* fourth edition. Boston: Houghton Mifflin, 1996.

a. What is the author's topic?

  what Americans think about elected officials

b. What is the main idea?

  Poll findings suggest . . . (first sentence)

If there is a container provided to pay for the coffee, do so every time you take a cup; don't force others to treat you to a cup of coffee. Also, take your turn making the coffee and cleaning the pot if that is a task performed by the group. Although in most offices it is acceptable to drink coffee or some other beverage while working, some offices have an unwritten rule against snacking at one's desk. Regardless, never eat while talking to someone in person or on the telephone.   4

From Scot Ober, *Contemporary Business Communications,* second edition. Houghton Mifflin, 1995.

a. What is the author's topic?

eating and drinking at work

b. What is the main idea?

Follow these rules for eating and drinking at work. (implied)

People often assume that if a behavior or mental process has a   5
strong biological basis, it is beyond control, that "biology is destiny."
Accordingly, many smokers don't even try to quit because they
assume that a biological addiction to nicotine will doom them to
failure. This is not necessarily true, as millions of ex-smokers can
attest. Indeed, the fact that all behavior and mental processes are
based on biological processes does not mean that they can be fully
understood through the study of biological processes _alone_. Those
who would reduce all of psychology to the analysis of brain
chemicals vastly oversimplify the interactions between our biological
selves and our psychological experiences, between our genes and
our environments.

From Bernstein et al., _Psychology,_ fourth edition. Boston: Houghton
Mifflin, 1997.

a. What is the author's topic?

behavior or mental processes

b. What is the main idea?

Indeed, the fact that all behavior and mental processes . . . (fourth

sentence)

Score: 100 − 5 for each one missed = _____%

CHAPTER QUIZ 2

Part 1 Terms and Definitions

Match this chapter's special terms in Column A with their definitions
in Column B.

Column A	Column B
__e__ 1. topic sentence	a. unstated main idea
__c__ 2. author's topic	b. parts of a topic sentence
__f__ 3. author's opinion	c. subject
__a__ 4. implied main idea	d. main idea of a longer passage
__b__ 5. topic plus opinion	e. stated main idea
__d__ 6. central idea	f. a thought or belief

Part 2 Chapter Review

Read and answer each question below. Write your answer in complete sentences, and use extra paper if needed. *(Answers may vary but should be similar to these.)*

1. What is a topic sentence, and do all paragraphs have one?

   A topic sentence states a paragraph's main idea. Not all paragraphs

   have a topic sentence.

2. How can you identify the topic sentence?

   Look for the most general sentence. Look for a sentence that states the

   author's topic and opinion.

3. If there is no topic sentence, how can you find the main idea of a paragraph?

   Read the details to determine the author's topic and opinion. Put topic

   and opinion together to find the implied main idea.

Part 3 Using Your Skills

I. The following sentences could be topic sentences of paragraphs. In each sentence, underline the topic once and the author's opinion twice.

   1. The Consumer's Bill of Rights is designed to protect you against unfair business practices.
   2. My major in English will prepare me for careers in several fields.
   3. Exercising is the best way I have found to reduce stress.

4. Many experts believe that <u>having a pet</u> is <u>good for the elderly.</u>

5. <u>Studying, preparing for tests, and avoiding procrastination</u> are the <u>three keys to success in college.</u>

II. Read the following textbook passage and answer the questions.

Fill-in-the-Blank Tests

A fill-in test may require you to recall an answer from memory or choose an answer from a list of options. In either case, the information provided in the incomplete statements may provide clues to the answers. Three strategies will help you fill in the blanks correctly.   1

First, decide what kind of answer the statement requires. For example, are you asked to supply a name, a date, or a place? Knowing what kind of answer you need may help you recall or select the right one.   2

Second, the way a statement is written may provide a clue. Your answer should complete the statement logically and grammatically. For example, if you must choose options from a list to fill in the blanks and the statement you are working on requires a verb to complete it, scan the list for verbs and choose among them.   3

Third, key words in a statement may help you determine what topic a question covers. For example, if a question asks you to explain *Piaget's third stage of development,* these key words tell you that the topic is Piaget's stages. If you can't remember the third stage, try to recall the others. Thinking about all the stages may lead you to the one you need.   4

Adapted from Carol C. Kanar, *The Confident Student,* third edition. Boston: Houghton Mifflin, 1998.

1. What is the author's topic?

   fill-in-the-blank tests

2. Which sentence in paragraph 1 states the central idea of the whole passage?

   Three strategies will help . . . (last sentence)

3. What is the topic sentence of paragraph 2?

   First, decide . . . (first sentence)

4. What is the topic sentence of paragraph 3?

   Second, the way . . . (first sentence)

5. What is the topic sentence of paragraph 4?

   Third, key words . . . (first sentence)

6. How do the ideas expressed in the topic sentences of paragraphs 2–4 help explain the central idea of the whole passage?

   These ideas tell you what the strategies are.

Score: 100 − 5 for each one missed = _____ %

Vocabulary Quiz

Each sentence below contains a word in bold type from the reading selection on pages 118–121. Read the sentence and the definitions that follow it. Then circle the correct one. Turn to the vocabulary preview on page 118–119 to check your answers.

1. Students who arrive late to class day after day are showing **blatant** disrespect for their instructor and classmates.
   a. unintentional
   b. unconventional
   c. excusable
   d. obvious

2. When students receive passing grades for work they have not done, employers can expect them to lack **expertise** in their fields.
   a. confidence
   b. skill
   c. experience
   d. interest

3. No matter how hard we tried to please Jim, he remained **disgruntled.**
   a. ill at ease
   b. uninterested
   c. discontented
   d. cooperative

4. Although tattoos have become commonplace, to many people they still seem **eccentric.**

a. normal
b. harmful
c. unusual
d. artistic

5. In spite of your **wheedling,** I am not convinced that you really do want to date only me.
   a. flattery and cleverness
   b. crying and begging
   c. arguing
   d. deception

6. When Nick got up to give his speech, he became so **overwrought** that he forgot what he was going to say.
   a. overconfident
   b. nervous and excited
   c. well prepared
   d. angry

7. Some people seem **intrinsically** depressed even when they have no reason to be.
   a. unusually
   b. artificially
   c. uncontrollably
   d. by nature

8. June was so **tentative** about setting a date for the wedding that her friends thought she did not want to get married.
   a. quick
   b. secret
   c. uncertain
   d. frightened

9. Some people would rather discuss **superficial** topics like the weather instead of important ones.
   a. unimportant
   b. well known
   c. inappropriate
   d. significant

10. Students who cheat on tests because "everybody else does" are showing **cynicism.**
    a. team spirit
    b. leadership qualities
    c. that they have studied
    (d.) motivation by selfishness

Score: 100 − 10 for each one missed = _____%

Chapter 6

Identifying Supporting Details

As explained in Chapter 5, the main idea is the author's most important idea. The main idea tells you what an author thinks, knows, or believes about a chosen topic. But why does an author hold a certain opinion? On what information is an author's opinion based? In paragraphs as well as in longer passages, the details provide answers to these questions.

What are *supporting details*? Whereas main ideas are general ideas, details are specific ideas. They are the bits and pieces of information that support, or explain, an author's main idea. Details answer the questions *who, what, where, when, why,* and *how.*

Reading is not a mystery when you know the difference between a main idea and a detail. Studying is easier when you can pick out the most important ideas in a textbook chapter and identify the details that support them. This chapter explains four strategies that will help you identify supporting details:

- *Recognize types of details.*
- *Find levels of development in paragraphs.*
- *Find levels of development in longer passages.*
- *Look for transitions that signal details.*

149

WHAT DO YOU ALREADY KNOW?

To prepare yourself for the reading selection that follows, find out what you already know about bagels, a type of bread. Answer the questions below either on your own or in a group discussion.

1. Have you ever eaten a bagel? Describe how it looks and tastes.

2. What are some of the ways you can eat bagels?

3. What restaurants or bakeries do you know that sell bagels?

4. Read the title, headnote, vocabulary preview, and first two paragraphs of the reading selection. What do you think will follow?

What's a Bagel?

Jack Denton Scott

In this article from Reader's Digest, *Jack Denton Scott answers the question "What's a Bagel?" with some surprising facts. Scott is an author and fan of one of America's most popular foods: the bagel.*

VOCABULARY PREVIEW

aficionados	(ə·fĭsh′ē·ə·nä′dōs) fans, enthusiasts
phenomenon	(fĭ·nŏm′ə·nŏn) unusual fact or event
croissant	(krə·sänt′) crescent-shaped roll
hearth	(härth) brick oven, fireplace
automated	(ô′tə·māt′ĭd) mechanical, operated automatically
quirky	(kwûrk′ē) odd, eccentric
delicacy	(dĕl′ĭ·kə·sē) a fine-quality food
tutus	(tōō′tōōs) short ballet skirts
baffling	(băf′əl·ĭng) frustrating, discouraging, puzzling or difficult to understand

lox	(lŏks) smoked salmon
Yiddish	(yĭd´ĭsh) the historical language of Central and Eastern European Jews
spirited	(spĭr´ĭ·tĭd) lively

Pronunciation Key: ä (**father**), ă (**pat**), ā (**pay**), ē (**bee**), ĕ (**pet**), ĭ (**pit**), ō (**toe**), ŏ (**pot**), ô (**caught, paw**), o͞o (**boot**), û (**urge, term**), ə (**about, item**)

If bread is the staff of life, the bagel may be the laugh of life. "Brooklyn jawbreakers," "crocodile teething rings," even "doughnuts with rigor mortis" are affectionate terms invoked by bagel **aficionados.** 1

For those who haven't tried one, the flavorful bagel is a shiny, hard, crisp yet chewy roll with a hole in the middle, and it is booming in popularity. Eight million are consumed daily in the United States— worth about $400 million a year. Bakery experts call the **phenomenon** "the Americanization of the bagel." To bagel believers it's "the bagelization of America." In the past four years retail sales of bagels have about doubled. Over 80 percent of these sales are now to non-Jewish consumers, a dramatic sociological switch. Moreover, the "bagel belt," always on the East Coast, is starting to stretch across the country. In fact, the world's largest bagel bakery is now located in Mattoon, Ill., producing over a million rolls a day. 2

Walter Heller of *Progressive Grocer* magazine calls the bagel's rise to stardom an example of "America's current love affair with ethnic foods." Yet, unless sliced in half, toasted and eaten warm, the bagel isn't easy to handle. It may make messy sandwiches and challenge the teeth. What's more, bagels become stale and hard after 12 hours— "something you can fight wars with," as one bagel expert said. 3

For the health conscious, however, the bagel has a lot going for it. The plain, two-ounce toaster-size has just 150 calories and one gram of fat. (The popular buttery **croissant,** by comparison, contains 235 calories and 12 grams of fat.) Furthermore, the plain bagel has no cholesterol, preservatives, or artificial color. 4

Bagels are made with unbleached, protein-rich, high-gluten flour, lightly seasoned with malt, salt and sugar, and raised with yeast. They then get a brief bath in boiling water. This results in the shiny surface after they are baked. (Most are **hearth**-baked to give them a crusty exterior and chewy interior.) 5

Some U.S. bakeries still use the Old World method of rolling and shaping the stiff dough by hand. This requires about six months to 6 learn, but one expert bagel baker can whip out about 700 an hour. (One **automated** machine can turn up to 9000 an hour.)

Where did this **quirky** roll originate? One version has the bagel created by an Austrian baker in 1683, honoring the king of Poland who had defeated Turkish invaders. It was first formed to resemble a stirrup (*beugel,* from the German *bugel,* for stirrup), because the king's favorite hobby was riding. 7

Another account puts the bagel in Cracow, Poland, in 1610, where poor Jews, who normally ate coarse black bread, considered their uncommon white-flour roll a **delicacy.** Bagels were officially approved as presents for women after childbirth, and mothers used them as teething rings for their children. In the 1600s in Russia, bagels were looped on strings, and were thought to bring good luck and have magical powers. 8

Bagels were brought to New York City and New Jersey by Jewish immigrants about 1910. Among the most successful immigrant bagel bakers was Harry Lender, who arrived from Lublin, Poland, in 1927 and settled in New Haven, Conn. His sons—Sam, Murray and Marvin—have almost made Lender's Bagels household words by using humor to push sales. For their bakery's 55th anniversary party, Murray and the executive staff attended a ballet class for two months; then, dressed in orange leotards and yellow **tutus,** they gracefully tiptoed to what was announced as "The Dance of the Bagels." 9

Today the **baffling** bagel surge to the top is even inspiring bagel restaurants. They offer as many as 17 flavors, from raisin and honey to zippy onion, plus bagel sandwiches, burgers, clubs, grilled cheese, French toast, salad sandwich combos, an egg-and-sausage bagelwich and a rancher's bagel breakfast. Big also are bagelettes—one-inch bagels—served by the basket with dinners. Then there are hero, hoagie, pizza and taco bagels—even Bagel Dogs. Where there's a bagel, there's a way. 10

Bagel bakeries are opening in Alaska, England, Japan and Israel. Ron Stieglitz, founder of the New York Bagels bakery in London, where few people had ever seen a bagel, had trouble raising money from banks. "A lot of them thought we were a football team," he said. But the bakery now supplies four large retail chains and many small shops and restaurants. 11

Lyle Fox, from Chicago, sees more potential for the bagel in Japan than in the United States. Young Japanese view the bagel as trendy and upscale—so much so that he easily sells 6000 a day. Fox discovered that the Japanese associate the bagel with New York, and New York with fashion. Thus, a lot of his customers are young women who consider the bagel as "sort of another accessory." A long-time bagel lover, Fox says his stomach does a sickly flip when Japanese customers ask for **lox** and cream cheese on a cinnamon-raisin bagel. 12

Cashing in on the new bagel awareness, innovators have come up with some really neat twists. Three Philadelphians started Bagels in Bed, a home-delivery business. Mike Bretz, owner of Simon Brothers Bakery in Skokie, Ill., has borrowed an idea from Chinese fortune cookies. He stuffs slips with **Yiddish** wisdom into his Schlepper Simon's Yiddish Fortune Bagels. One cheerfully advises, "Smile, bubeleh, success is assured."   13

A **spirited** cookbook, *The Bagels' Bagel Book* (Acropolis Books), has recipes like "Mexicali Bagel Fondue," the "Kojak Bagel" with feta cheese and Greek olives, "Tofu Bagels," and "Delhi Bagels" with whipped cream cheese, curry and chutney. The book also captures some of the laughter inspired by baking's most remarkable roll. Here's comedienne Phyllis Diller: "President Reagan was so gung-ho to get ethnic votes, he went into a deli and ordered a bagel. The waiter asked, "How would you like that?" Ronnie said, 'On rye.' "   14

What's a bagel? Fun you can eat.   15

HOW WELL DID YOU COMPREHEND?

Main Idea

1. The central idea of the entire essay is stated in
   a. paragraph 1, first sentence "If bread is . . ."
   b. paragraph 1, second sentence "Brooklyn . . ."
   c. paragraph 2, first sentence "For those who . . ."
   d. paragraph 15, last sentence "What's a bagel . . ."

2. Which sentence states the main idea of paragraph 9?
   a. the first sentence "Bagels were brought . . ."
   b. the second sentence "Among the most . . ."
   c. the third sentence "His sons . . ."
   d. the last sentence "It was first . . ."

Details

3. According to the author, bagels may have originated in
   a. Austria.
   b. Israel.
   c. New York.
   d. Connecticut.

4. Lyle Fox sees more potential for the bagel in Japan than in the United States because
   a. more bagels are sold in Japan.
   b. Japanese eat more bread than Americans.
   c. bagels have not been popular in the United States.
   d. Japanese view the bagel as trendy.

5. According to the author, bagels contain
   a. artificial color.
   b. one gram of fat.
   c. preservatives.
   d. cholesterol.

Inferences

6. Bagels may have been used as teething rings in the 1600s because
   a. babies like bagels.
   b. bagels are smooth and shiny.
   c. bagels are hard and chewy.
   d. a bagel is easy to handle.

7. The author calls the bagel's rise in popularity baffling, or difficult to understand. Why?
   a. Bagels are hard to eat and do not stay fresh long.
   b. Ethnic foods are not popular in the United States.
   c. Bagels are not widely available.
   d. They do not come in a variety of flavors.

Working with Words

Complete the sentences below with these words from the vocabulary preview:

automated	aficionados	spirited	baffling
croissant	phenomenon	delicacy	Yiddish
hearth	quirky	lox	tutus

1. At some Chinese restaurants, meats are cooked on an open _____*hearth*_____.

2. _____*Aficionados*_____ of Italian cooking enjoy the foods of Northern Italy.

3. Hardly anyone makes doughnuts by hand anymore because most bakeries are _____*automated*_____.

4. Like bagels, pumpernickel bread is a _____*quirky*_____ treat that some people do not like.

5. Margaret eats on the run, stopping at a bakery on her way to work to buy coffee and a _____*croissant*_____.

6. I like restaurants where the servers are _____*spirited*_____ and friendly.

7. Like the Hard Rock Cafe, Planet Hollywood is also a _____*phenomenon*_____ in the restaurant business.

8. At the wedding reception, servers offered us small crackers with _____*lox*_____ and cream cheese.

9. Kitty thought it was _____*baffling*_____ that her favorite deli would be closed so early in the day.

10. In some countries, candied lizards are considered a _____*delicacy*_____.

11. We wondered why David could not get the financing he wanted for a cafe where the servers wear _____*tutus*_____ and roller skates.

12. In some Jewish neighborhoods, you can still find a _____*Yiddish*_____ bakery or deli.

Thinking and Writing

Think about a food you enjoy that is part of your cultural background or family traditions. Then describe the food and explain why you like it or why it is important to you.

Answers will vary. _____

_____

_____

_____

RECOGNIZE TYPES OF DETAILS

Details are the bits and pieces of information that support a main idea. Why does an author feel, think, or believe a certain way? On what

FIGURE 6.1 Types of Details		
Types	**Definitions**	**Questions to Ask**
FACTS	figures and statistics, names of people and places, dates, times, measurements	Who? What? Where? When? How many or how much? How long or how often?
REASONS	causes and their results	Why? How? What for?
EXAMPLES	illustrations, images, and descriptions	What does it look, sound, smell, taste, or feel like?

information is an author's knowledge or opinion based? To find the answer to either question, you must read for details. Three types of details you should be able to recognize are *facts, reasons,* and *examples.*

Read Figure 6.1, which lists types of details, their definitions, and questions you can ask to identify them.

Facts

A *fact* is something you can prove by direct observation, by reading, or by asking an expert. Facts include dates, times, measurements, figures and statistics, names of people and places, and recorded events. Facts also include mathematical rules, principles, and scientific laws.

If one of your legislators proposed a one penny increase in sales tax in your state, how would you decide whether to vote for it? For one thing, you would probably read about the tax in your local newspaper to get the facts that would answer such questions as these: How much money will the tax raise? How will the tax affect the prices you pay for products and services? How will the money be spent?

As an example of the way facts support main ideas, read the following paragraph in which the topic sentence is underlined and the facts are printed in bold type.

> Visitors to the Sanders Art Center, which opened today, learned all about this new facility. The center was named for **Robin L. Sanders,** a wealthy businesswoman and art lover. Sanders donated **$15,000,000** toward the construction price. The center houses the **James Gray Theater** and the **Springwood museum.** In addition, the center provides **classes in painting and sculpture** taught by local artists. Fees for classes are billed at **$10.00 an hour plus costs** for materials. Special rates are available for children and groups.

The topic sentence tells you that visitors to the art center learned about the facility. The details in the following sentences tell you exactly what they learned. The facts that support the main idea include names of people and places and dollar amounts. These facts tell you *who* the center was named for, *who* paid for the center, *how much* money she donated, *what* the center provides, and *how much* these services cost.

Exercise 6.1 On the lines beneath each paragraph, write the main idea and the facts that support it. One fact in each paragraph is identified for you.

Gina knows exactly what she wants in a new apartment. First of all, she wants approximately 750 square feet of living space. She wants a bedroom that is at least 12 feet by 12 feet to accommodate the furniture she already has. Moreover, she needs an apartment that is available on December 1 because that is when her current lease expires.

1. main idea: *Gina knows exactly what she wants in a new apartment.*

   a. fact: *She wants about 750 square feet of living space.*

   b. fact: *She wants a bedroom at least 12 feet by 12 feet.*

   c. fact: *She needs an apartment that is available on December 1.*

The Bahama Islands enjoy a warm, subtropical climate. Rainfall in the Bahamas averages about 30–60 inches a year. Also, hurricanes can blow through these islands from June to November. Finally, temperatures rarely drop below 70 degrees.

2. main idea: *The Bahama Islands enjoy a warm subtropical climate.*

   a. fact: *Rainfall averages about 30–60 inches a year.*

   b. fact: *Hurricanes blow from June to November.*

   c. fact: *Temperatures rarely drop below 70 degrees.*

When Mt. St. Helens erupted in 1991, most people in the United States were astonished. We tend to think that volcanic eruptions are rare, but they occur quite regularly. During the 1970s and 1980s, 33 eruptions were recorded. Between 1990 and 1996, volcanic eruptions occurred in 12 countries. In fact, of the world's 42 major volcanoes, only 3 are extinct.

3. main idea: <u>*Volcanic eruptions occur quite regularly.*</u>

    a. fact: <u>*Mt. St. Helens erupted in 1991.*</u>

    b. fact: <u>*During the 1970s and 1980s, 33 eruptions were recorded.*</u>

    c. fact: <u>*Between 1990 and 1996, eruptions occurred in 12 countries.*</u>

    d. fact: <u>*Of the world's 42 major volcanoes, only 3 are extinct.*</u>

Exercise 6.2

Answer each of the following questions with a fact from the reading selection at the beginning of this chapter. Scan (look quickly) through the selection to identify the facts.

1. How many bagels are consumed each day in the United States?

    Eight million bagels are consumed daily in the U.S. (paragraph 2)

2. What percent of bagel sales are to non-Jewish consumers?

    Over 80 percent of sales are to non-Jewish customers. (paragraph 2)

3. Where is the world's largest bagel bakery?

    The world's largest bakery is in Mattoon, Ill. (paragraph 2)

4. How many calories does a bagel contain?

    A two-ounce bagel contains 150 calories. (paragraph 4)

5. Who was one of the most successful bagel bakers?

    Harry Lender was one of the most successful bakers. (paragraph 9)

6. What countries besides the United States have opened bagel bakeries?

    Bakeries have opened in England, Japan, and Israel. (paragraph 11)

Exercise 6.3

The next two paragraphs are from the textbook *American Government,* fourth edition, by Alan R. Gitelson, Robert L. Dudley, and Melvin J. Dubnick. Read each paragraph and answer the questions about the facts that support the main idea.

1. Article I of the Constitution specifies only three criteria for membership in the U.S. Congress. Before taking office, senators must have reached

the age of thirty, must have been citizens of the United States for at least nine years, and must reside in the states from which they are elected. Representatives may enter office at the age of twenty-five and after only seven years of citizenship. Members of the House must also reside in the states from which they are chosen, but the Constitution does not require residence in the districts they represent.

a. What is the main idea?

___*Article I of the Constitution . . . (first sentence)*___

b. What is the minimum age for senators?

___*The minimum age for senators is 30.*___

c. What is the minimum age for representatives?

___*The minimum age for representatives is 25.*___

d. A senator must have been a U.S. citizen for how many years before taking office? How many years must a representative have been a citizen?

___*Senators must have been U.S. citizens for at least 9 years, representatives*___

___*for at least 7 years.*___

e. Do senators and representatives have to live in the states from which they are chosen?

___*Senators and representatives must live in the states from which they*___

___*are chosen.*___

f. Which one does not have to live in the district he or she represents, a senator or a representative?

___*Representatives do not have to live in their districts.*___

2. Americans buy nearly 60 million newspapers and keep their television sets on an average of more than six hours each day. Simultaneously, they can choose among ten thousand or so weekly and monthly periodicals and almost nine thousand radio stations. The attentive media watcher faces an incessant flow of information on topics ranging from foreign affairs to domestic scandals. Yet it has not always been this way.

A mere 150 years ago news of Washington or the state capital arrived, if at all, days, weeks, or even months after the events occurred.

a.   What is the main idea?

The attentive media watcher . . . (third sentence)

b.   About how many weekly and monthly periodicals are available to Americans?

About ten thousand periodicals are available.

c.   Approximately how many radio stations are available?

Almost nine thousand radio stations are available.

d.   About how long is the average T.V. set on each day?

The average T.V. set is on more than six hours each day.

e.   Americans buy about how many newspapers each day?

Americans buy about 60 million daily newspapers.

f.   What do the words *incessant* and *domestic* mean? (Use your dictionary.)

"Incessant" means continuing without interruption.

"Domestic" means relating to a particular country.

Reasons

Reasons are the explanations that tell you why or how something happens. Reasons explain why people think or feel the way they do. Why did you earn a good grade on a test? Was it because you studied? Was it because the test was easy? What are the reasons?

Think about the decision you made to come to college. At some point, you had to decide which college to attend and how you would pay for tuition and books. What were the reasons behind your decision?

As a reader, you should expect authors to back up their claims and opinions with reasons. As a reader, you should continually ask *why?* and *how?* and look for the answers to your questions.

As an example of the way reasons support main ideas, read the following paragraph in which the topic sentence is underlined and the reasons are printed in bold type.

<u>What should have been a lovely evening at the theater turned out</u> <u>badly.</u> First of all, **we could not find our tickets.** We spent at least fifteen minutes searching for them in our pockets and desk drawers. **Then we arrived late** at the theater. We spent another twenty minutes looking for a parking space because **the parking lot was full.** As if this were not bad enough, when we finally did get in, **we did not have good seats.** All in all, we felt we had wasted the evening.

The topic sentence tells you that the evening turned out badly. The detail sentences tell you the reasons: lost tickets, a late arrival, a full parking lot, and bad seats. These reasons clearly explain why the evening was not a success.

Exercise 6.4

On the lines beneath each paragraph, write the main idea and the reasons that support it. One reason in each paragraph is identified for you.

Taking vitamins may be beneficial to your health for several reasons. For one thing, vitamins provide essential nutrients that may be lacking in your diet. Also, some vitamins may reduce your risk of cancer and other diseases. Finally, vitamins may increase your energy and improve your well-being.

1. main idea: *Taking vitamins may be beneficial . . . (first sentence)*

    a. reason: *Vitamins provide essential nutrients.*

    b. reason: *Some vitamins may reduce risk of cancer and other diseases.*

    c. reason: *Vitamins increase energy and improve well-being.*

Bookstore chains such as Borders and Barnes and Noble are opening in every major town or city. It is not unusual for a best-selling novel to sell millions of copies. People turn out in large numbers to meet famous authors and have them autograph copies of their books. These reasons suggest that reading has become one of our most popular pastimes.

2. main idea: *These reasons suggest . . . (last sentence)*

    a. reason: *Bookstore chains are opening in major towns and cities.*

    b. reason: *Best-selling novels sell millions of copies.*

    c. reason: *People turn out to meet famous authors.*

You may have wondered "Why do I have to take math? I'll never use it after I graduate." But a math course could be one of the most important courses you will take. Mathematics requires you to think logically and critically. The problem-solving skills you learn in a math course can be applied to making decisions and solving problems in daily life. A knowledge of mathematics is essential to careers in many fields such as architecture, engineering, and nursing. A final reason you should take math is that it teaches you discipline and patience, two valuable qualities.

3. main idea: *But a math course could be . . . (second sentence)*

    a. reason: *Math requires logical, critical thinking.*

    b. reason: *Math teaches you problem-solving skills.*

    c. reason: *A knowledge of math is essential to many careers.*

    d. reason: *Math teaches you discipline and patience.*

Exercise 6.5   Read again this paragraph from Jack Denton Scott's essay and answer the questions that follow it.

Lyle Fox, from Chicago, sees more potential for the bagel in Japan than in the United States. Young Japanese view the bagel as trendy and upscale—so much so that he easily sells 6000 a day. Fox discovered that the Japanese associate the bagel with New York, and New York with fashion. Thus, a lot of his customers are young women who consider the bagel as "sort of another accessory." A long-time bagel lover, Fox says his stomach does a sickly flip when Japanese customers ask for lox and cream cheese on a cinnamon-raisin bagel.

1. What is the paragraph's main idea?

    Lyle Fox, from Chicago, sees . . . (first paragraph)

2. What are three reasons that support the main idea?

    a. *Young Japanese view the bagel as trendy.*

    b. *The Japanese associate bagels with New York and fashion.*

    c. *Young women consider the bagel an accessory.*

Exercise 6.6 The next two paragraphs are from the textbook Personal Finance, fifth edition, by E. Thomas Garman and Raymond E. Forgue. Read each paragraph and answer the questions about the reasons that support the main idea.

1. There are several reasons people may choose to rent housing. They may not have the funds for the down payment and high mortgage costs associated with buying a home. Alternatively, they may prefer the easy mobility of renting or may prefer to avoid many of the responsibilities associated with buying. Prospective renters need to consider the monthly rental fee and related expenses, the lease agreement and restrictions, and tenants' rights.

   a. What is the main idea?

   There are several reasons . . . (first sentence)

   b. According to the author, why do some people rent instead of buying a home? (list three reasons)

   They may lack funds for a down payment or mortgage costs, may prefer

   the mobility of renting, or may want to avoid the responsibilities

   associated with buying.

   c. What three things do prospective renters need to consider?

   They need to consider rental fees and related expenses, the lease

   agreement and restrictions, and tenants' rights.

2. A primary cause of many marital problems is conflict over money. Couples often disagree about what to spend their money on and how much to spend. Sometimes one person in a relationship will make a crucial financial decision without consulting the other person, thereby creating resentment and perhaps setting the stage for a series of retaliatory actions. Many couples simply seem unable to work together to perform the fundamental tasks of managing money, such as reconciling the checking account, creating a workable budget, and paying bills on time. Others get into financial trouble because they use credit too often.

   a. What is the main idea?

   A primary cause of many marital problems . . . (first sentence)

b. What are two disagreements about spending money that may cause marital conflict?

Couples disagree on how much money to spend and what to spend it on.

c. What can happen in a relationship when one person makes a financial decision without consulting the other?

Resentment is created.

d. What three fundamental tasks of managing money do the authors identify?

The tasks are reconciling the checking account, creating a budget, and

paying bills on time.

e. What is the last reason the authors state as causing financial trouble for couples?

Couples get in trouble for using credit too often.

Examples

Examples are illustrations, images, and descriptions that appeal to one or more of your five senses: sight, hearing, smell, touch, and taste. Examples clarify and explain main ideas by encouraging you to picture in your mind exactly what an author is describing or relating.

Think about a friend of yours who has met someone new. One of your first questions is "What is this person like?" Your friend then provides examples of the way the person looks, talks, acts, dresses, or thinks. If these examples are good ones, then you will have a clear image of the person in your mind. In fact, you may have said to someone (or someone may have said to you) "I have heard so much about you that I feel as if I know you." Such feelings are based on clear and vivid examples.

As a reader, you should look for examples. Try to picture an author's illustrations and descriptions in your mind. Ask yourself what something *looks, sounds, smells, feels,* or *tastes* like. Then read on to find the answers.

To see how examples support main ideas, read the following paragraph in which the topic sentence is underlined and the examples are printed in bold type.

The cottage looked warm and inviting. **Smoke from a roaring fire curled** out of the chimney. **Light shone** through the windows **onto the sparkling snow** outside. A **holiday wreath** brightened the door, and a **straw mat** placed on the front porch for visitors to wipe their feet announced **"Welcome friends."**

The topic sentence gives a general description of the cottage: *warm* and *inviting.* These key words tell you to look for the specific examples that describe what the author means. *Smoke curling from the chimney* is a strong visual image. A *roaring fire* appeals to your sense of touch and indicates warmth. The *sparkling snow* is a visual as well as tactile image: You can see the snow in your mind's eye, and you can feel its coldness. The cold weather outside the cottage contrasts with the warmth inside. Two examples of the holiday wreath and the straw mat that says "welcome friends" suggest that visitors are expected.

Exercise 6.7   On the lines beneath each paragraph, write the main idea and the examples that support it. One example in each paragraph is identified for you.

Rolanda's is a bakery in our neighborhood that has a cookie for everyone. For example, kids love Rolanda's sugar cookies that are decorated with sweet icings and candies. Chocolate lovers can choose chocolate chip cookies or chocolate macaroons. For someone who likes a cookie that is not too sweet, Rolanda's oatmeal raisin is a great choice.

1. main idea: *Rolanda's is a bakery in our neighborhood . . . (first sentence)*

   a. example: *Kids love Rolanda's sugar cookies.*

   b. example: *Chocolate chip cookies and macaroons are for chocolate lovers.*

   c. example: *Oatmeal raisin are for those who like cookies not too sweet.*

The Crocketts were tired of their drab front yard. They wanted something that was more colorful. First, they planted pink and white azaleas close to the house. Next, they put in two dogwood trees on either side of the walkway. Finally, they dug beds around the new trees and planted pansies in assorted colors.

2. main idea: *They wanted something . . . (second sentence)*

   a. example: *They planted pink and white azaleas.*

b. example: *They put in two dogwood trees.*

c. example: *They planted pansies in assorted colors.*

The elementary school is within walking distance of our home. Also, a major shopping mall with restaurants and theaters is only blocks away. Our children have lots of neighborhood kids to play with. As an added advantage, the street we live on is quiet and shady. Our new home has several advantages.

3. main idea: *Our new home . . . (last sentence)*

a. example: *School is within walking distance.*

b. example: *A mall, restaurants, and theaters are close.*

c. example: *Children have lots of neighborhood kids to play with.*

d. example: *Our street is quiet and shady.*

Exercise 6.8

Read again the following paragraph from Jack Denton Scott's essay and answer the questions below.

Today the baffling bagel surge to the top is even inspiring bagel restaurants. They offer as many as 17 flavors, from raisin and honey to zippy onion, plus bagel sandwiches, burgers, clubs, grilled cheese, French toast, salad sandwich combos, an egg-and-sausage bagelwich and a rancher's bagel breakfast. Big also are bagelettes—one-inch bagels—served by the basket with dinners. Then there are hero, hoagie, pizza and taco bagels—even Bagel Dogs. Where there's a bagel, there's a way.

1. What is the paragraph's main idea?

   Today the baffling . . . (first sentence)

2. What are two examples of bagel flavors?

   Two flavors are raisin and honey and zippy onion.

3. What are two examples of bagel sandwiches?

   Two bagel sandwiches are grilled cheese and egg-and-sausage.

4. What are two examples of breakfast items?

Two breakfast items are French toast and rancher's bagel breakfast.

5. What is a bagelette?

A bagelette is a one-inch bagel.

Exercise 6.9   The next two paragraphs are adapted from the textbook Biology by Joseph S. Levine and Kenneth R. Miller. Read each paragraph and answer the questions about the examples that support the main idea.

1. The term **environment** refers to all the conditions surrounding an organism. Those conditions are often divided into two subgroups: the physical environment and the biotic, or biological, environment. The **physical environment** includes all the conditions created by the nonliving components of the organism's surroundings such as sunlight, heat, moisture, the speed of wind and water currents, the size of sand or sediment grains, and so on. The **biotic environment** consists of the living organisms in the habitat—that is, other species that may serve as food, parasites, predators, or competitors.

    a. What is the main idea?

    The term environment . . . (first sentence)

    b. What are two examples of conditions that the physical environment includes?

    Sunlight and heat are two examples. (Students may list others.)

    c. What are two examples of the kinds of organisms living in the biotic environment?

    Parasites and predators live in the biotic environment. (Students may

    list others.)

2. All organisms produce metabolic waste products. For example, animals exhale carbon dioxide and excrete nitrogen. Plants release oxygen by day, give off carbon dioxide by night, and often discard leaves and stems on a seasonal basis. In most cases, waste products

such as these undergo chemical changes in which they are broken down or carried away. But in certain microenvironments, wastes can accumulate. In mud, for example, poisonous gases such as hydrogen sulfide (responsible for the odor of rotten eggs) and methane (commonly called marsh gas) may build up, making the immediate environment unsuitable for many organisms.

a. What is the main idea?

   All organisms produce . . . (first sentence)

b. What are two examples of animal waste products?

   Carbon dioxide and nitrogen are animal waste products.

c. What are the authors' examples of plant waste products?

   Oxygen, carbon dioxide, and leaves and stems are plant wastes.

d. Which waste products of plants are seasonal?

   Leaves and stems are seasonal waste products.

e. What is an example of an environment in which wastes can accumulate?

   Wastes can accumulate in mud.

f. Which gas is responsible for the odor of rotten eggs?

   Hydrogen sulfide smells like rotten eggs.

g. What is another name for methane?

   Methane is also called marsh gas.

Memory Cue

Facts, reasons, and examples are three common types of details that you should be able to identify. Facts include such things as numbers, figures, and names of people and places. Reasons explain why and how things happen. Examples are illustrations and descriptions that create mental images.

FIND LEVELS OF DEVELOPMENT IN PARAGRAPHS

Paragraphs often have three levels of development: *main idea, major details,* and *minor details.* The main idea is the first level of development. As you already know, the main idea is the most important, most general idea in a paragraph. Major details are the second level of development. Major details support the main idea because major details are more specific than the main idea. Minor details are the third level of development. Minor details support major details. Minor details are even more specific than either major details or the main idea.

The following three sentences illustrate the three levels of development.

> 1 The college's nursing department is having a bake sale.
> > 2 Several kinds of cookies are available.
> > > 3 The chocolate chip cookies are going fast.

The main idea is that the students are having a bake sale. The major detail explains the type of baked goods that are for sale. The minor detail gives an example of the kinds of cookies you can buy.

As you can see, *bake sale* (level 1) is the most general idea. *Cookies* (level 2) is a more specific idea. *Chocolate chip cookies* (level 3) is the most specific idea.

Exercise 6.10   The following items illustrate three levels of development. In each item, the main idea and a major detail are given. Add a minor detail. The first one is done as an example.

a.
> 1 Bookstores offer a variety of magazines for sale.
> > 2 I prefer to read news magazines.
> > > 3 *Newsweek is one of my favorites.*

b.
> 1 Fruit is an important part of a balanced diet.
> > 2 Citrus fruits are one possible choice.
> > > 3 *(Answers should name a citrus fruit.)*

c.
> 1 Colleges require students to take certain courses.
> > 2 One or more English courses may be required.
> > > 3 *(Answers should name a course.)*

d. | 1 I enjoy going to the movies with my friends.
| 2 I always like to see a good action film.
| 3 *(Answers should name an action film.)*

e. | 1 This restaurant is famous for its desserts.
| 2 Several kinds of pies appear on the menu.
| 3 *(Answers should list one or more kinds of pies.)*

f. | 1 Flowers are always a welcome gift.
| 2 I have received flowers on two special occasions.
| 3 *(Answers should specify the occasions.)*

Exercise 6.11   Read the next paragraph and fill in the outline that follows it. The outline will help you find the paragraph's three levels of development. A portion of the outline has been completed for you.

Chicken Neckin'

Chicken Neckin' is my uncle's new fast-food restaurant, and it is unusual for two reasons. First of all, he offers take-out only from a drive-up window. He saves money by not having to provide a place for people to sit. Also, he does not have to clean up after the customers. The second reason is that the menu is different. Chicken sandwiches are not available. At Chicken Neckin' you will not find the usual assortment of chicken parts such as breasts, thighs, wings, and drumsticks. At my uncle's restaurant you can order boiled chicken necks and fried livers and gizzards. "Chitlins"—pieces of intestine that are split open, breaded, and fried—are also available in a handy pack with sauce for dipping. Although Chicken Neckin' may appeal to some, I have a feeling that many people read his menu and just drive through.

I. (main idea) *My uncle's restaurant is unusual for two reasons.*

a. (major detail) *First of all, he offers take-out only from a drive-up window.*

1. (minor detail) *He saves money by not providing a place for people to sit.*

   2. (minor detail) *He does not have to clean up after customers.*

b. (major detail) *The second reason is that the menu is different.*

   1. (minor detail) *Chicken sandwiches are not available.*

   2. (minor detail) *You will not find chicken parts such as breasts, thighs, wings, and drumsticks.*

   3. (minor detail) *You can order chicken necks, livers, and gizzards.*

   4. (minor detail) *"Chitlins" are also available.*

Exercise 6.12   The following paragraph is typical of one you might find in a history textbook. Read the paragraph and complete the outline.

On December 15, 1791, the House of Representatives ratified ten amendments to the Constitution, which we call the Bill of Rights. The First Amendment guarantees the right to freedom of expression. The freedoms of speech, press, peaceful assembly, and petition are First Amendment rights. The Second Amendment permits the right to bear arms. The Third Amendment says that troops cannot be stationed in anyone's home without prior consent. People are protected against unreasonable searches and seizures by the Fourth Amendment. The Fifth and Sixth Amendments provide for fair treatment under the law. The Fifth Amendment guarantees the right to due process, and the Sixth Amendment provides for the right to a speedy and public trial in criminal cases. Under certain conditions, the Seventh Amendment provides for a jury trial in civil suits. The Eighth Amendment protects against cruel and unusual punishment and excessive fines. The Ninth and Tenth Amendments allow for the exercise of rights and powers that neither belong to nor are prohibited by the federal government. For example, the Ninth Amendment reserves these rights and powers to the people, but the Tenth Amendment reserves them to the states. These two amendments also give states the authority to provide public education and build roads and highways.

I. main idea *The Bill of Rights lists Americans' rights and freedoms. (Implied)*

A. The First Amendment guarantees the right to freedom of expression.

   1. *freedom of speech*

   2. *press*

   3. *peaceful assembly*

   4. *petition*

B. *The Second Amendment permits the right to bear arms.*

C. The Third Amendment says that troops cannot be stationed in anyone's home without prior consent.

D. *The Fourth Amendment protects against unreasonable search and seizure.*

E. *The Fifth and Sixth Amendments provide fair treatment under the law.*

   1. The Fifth Amendment guarantees the right to due process.

   2. *The Sixth Amendment provides trial rights in criminal cases.*

F. *The Seventh Amendment provides a jury trial in civil suits.*

G. *The Eighth Amendment protects against cruel and unusual punishment and excessive fines.*

H. The Ninth and Tenth Amendments allow for the exercise of rights and powers that neither belong to nor are prohibited by the federal government.

   1. *The Ninth Amendment reserves these rights and powers to the people.*

   2. *The Tenth Amendment reserves them to the states.*

   3. *Both Amendments provide for public education, roads, and highways.*

FIND LEVELS OF DEVELOPMENT IN LONGER PASSAGES

Do you have trouble deciding what is important in a longer passage such as a textbook chapter? A simple prereading strategy may help.

Before you read a textbook chapter, turn to the table of contents and read the chapter's title, headings, and subheadings. This list reveals the author's hidden outline of the chapter and is a clue to what is most important.

As an example, read the following outline excerpted from the table of contents of *Child and Adolescent Development* by Kelvin L. Seifert and Robert J. Hoffnung. Labels show three levels of development.

Topic ⟶ Chapter 5 The First Two Years: Physical Development

First Section (main idea) ⟶ **Appearance of the Young Infant**

Major details ⟶
- The First Few Hours
- Is the Baby All Right? The Apgar Scale
- Newborn Weight
- Size and Bodily Proportions

Second Section (main idea) ⟶ **Development of the Nervous System**

Major details ⟶
- Growth of the Brain
- States of Sleep and Wakefulness

Third Section (main idea) ⟶ **Sensory Development**

Major details ⟶
- Visual Acuity
- Auditory Acuity

Fourth Section (main idea) ⟶ **Motor Development**

Major details ⟶
- Early Reflexes
- The First Motor Skills
- Variations in Motor Skill Development

Fifth Section (main idea) ⟶ **Variations in Infant Growth**

Major details ⟶
- Low-Birth-Weight Infants
- Helping Low-Birth-Weight Infants

Sixth Section (main idea) ⟶ **Nutrition During the First Two Years**

Major details ⟶
- Breast Milk Versus Formula
- Nutrition in Later Infancy
- Infant Mortality . . .

What is the chapter about? From the title you can tell that the topic is *a child's physical development during the first two years.* In other words, the chapter explains how a child grows. A question you could ask about this topic is "What happens during the first two years?"

To answer your question, look at the major headings in bold type. These headings break up the chapter into six sections. Each section explains a different aspect of a child's physical development: appearance, nervous system, sensory and motor development, infant growth, and nutrition.

Using the title and major headings as clues, can you guess the chapter's central idea? Here is one possibility: *Certain physical developments take place during the first two years of a baby's life.* If you were to read the chapter's introduction, you would probably find a central idea statement very similar to this one.

Reading the subheadings under a boldfaced heading on the outline will help you determine the major details that support that section's main idea. For example, development of the nervous system (main idea) depends on two things: growth of the brain and states of sleepfulness and wakefulness (major details).

As you read through the headings and subheadings, you may see some unfamiliar terms such as *Apgar Scale, visual acuity,* and *auditory acuity.* Noticing these terms before you read may help you pay attention to them and look for their definitions as you read the chapter.

In conclusion, the table of contents is merely a shorthand list of each chapter's main ideas and major details. As you can see, reading the contents beforehand can alert you to a chapter's important ideas. However, you should follow up your overview of the contents with a slow and careful reading of the chapter.

Exercise 6.13   To practice what you have learned about levels of development, use the outline on physical development, page 173, to help you complete the following items.

1. In what section of the chapter can you learn about the size and bodily proportions of newborns?

     The first section explains size and bodily proportions.

2. In what section would you expect to find definitions of visual and auditory acuity?

     Visual and auditory acuity are explained in the third section.

3. What major details are explained in the section on nutrition?

   The major details explained in the nutrition section are breast milk versus

   formula, nutrition in later infancy, and infant mortality.

4. What does *mortality* mean? (Use your dictionary.)

   "Mortality" means death rate.

5. Why do you suppose the authors discuss infant mortality in the section on nutrition?

   Death can result from improper nutrition.

6. Write guide questions for each of the following subheadings. Low-Birth-Weight Infants:

   What causes low-birth-weight infants? (Answers may vary.)

   Helping Low-Birth-Weight Infants:

   How can we help them? (Answers may vary.)

Memory Cue

You can follow an author's ideas by identifying three levels of development. The first and most general level is the main idea. Major details are the second and more specific level. Minor details are the third and most specific level. A book's table of contents provides an overview of each chapter's levels of development.

LOOK FOR TRANSITIONS THAT SIGNAL DETAILS

As explained in Chapter 4, *transitions* are words and phrases that connect ideas. Transitions can occur within or between sentences. Transitions act as signals, telling you what to expect. Very often, transitions signal major or minor details. As an example, read again the following excerpt from Jack Denton Scott's essay. In this excerpt, transitions appear in bold type.

FIGURE 6.2 Transitions that Signal Details	
Type of Detail	**Transitions to Watch for**
FACTS	one, another, first, second, next, finally, also, in addition
REASONS	one reason, another reason, cause, because, lead to
EXAMPLES	for example, for instance, such as, to illustrate, to show, that is

. . . Where did this quirky roll originate? **One version** has the bagel created by an Austrian baker in 1683, honoring the king of Poland who had defeated Turkish invaders. It was first formed to resemble a stirrup (*beugel*, from the German *bugel*, for stirrup), because the king's favorite hobby was riding.

Another account puts the bagel in Cracow, Poland, in 1610, where poor Jews, who normally ate coarse black bread, considered their uncommon white-flour roll a delicacy. . . .

The implied main idea of both paragraphs is *several stories explain how the bagel originated.* The transition *one version* tells you that you are about to read one of these stories. The transition *another account* in the next paragraph tells you that you are about to read another story of the bagel's origin. Both transitions signal major details that support the main idea.

Figure 6.2 lists some of the transitions you read about in Chapter 4 that writers use to signal facts, reasons, and examples.

Exercise 6.14   Read again the paragraph Chicken Neckin' from Exercise 6.11 and answer the following questions about transitions.

1. What two transitions tell you to look for major details that are reasons?

   first of all, the second reason

2. What transition *at the beginning* of the fourth sentence signals a minor detail?

   also

3. What transition *within* the seventh sentence signals a minor detail?

   such as

Exercise 6.15 This exercise will help you review transitions and practice identifying them. Follow the directions in each of the items below to complete the exercise. Item 1a is done as an example.

1. Read again the paragraphs in Exercise 6.1, pages 157–158. And list any transitions that you find.

   a. paragraph 1 _first of all, moreover_

   b. paragraph 2 _also, finally_

   c. paragraph 3 _but, during, between, in fact_

2. Read again the paragraphs in Exercise 6.4, pages 161–162. And list any transitions that you find.

   a. paragraph 1 _several reasons, for one thing, also, finally_

   b. paragraph 2 _such as, these reasons_

   c. paragraph 3 _but, such as, a final reason_

3. Read again the paragraphs in Exercise 6.7, pages 165–166. And list any transitions that you find.

   a. paragraph 1 _for example_

   b. paragraph 2 _first, next, finally_

   c. paragraph 3 _also, an added advantage, several advantages_

REAL-WORLD CONNECTIONS

How are your note-taking skills? Do your lecture notes seem skimpy and unconnected? Do you feel frustrated because you cannot tell what is important and do not know what notes to take? It may surprise you to know that you can use the reading strategies you have learned from this chapter to help you take better notes.

Most lecturers speak from an outline or notes. The lecturer usually begins by stating the topic. For example, "Today's lecture is on plant reproduction." Next, the lecturer may state a main idea. For example, "Plants reproduce in two ways: by sexual or asexual reproduction." The lecturer then adds details (facts, reasons, and examples that explain the main idea). The lecturer may also write on the board, draw diagrams, or project pictures on a screen to illustrate important ideas.

Some lecturers are better speakers than others, but by listening for and taking notes on the topic, main idea, and major details, you can get all the information you need. Here are some guidelines to follow:

1. Write the topic at the top of your page.

2. As soon as you know the main idea, write it down.

3. Listen for transitions such as "first," "next," and "for example." These transitions will help you identify major details.

4. If you hear phrases like "three parts," "four steps," or "five ways," number your paper and leave space to write in the parts, steps, or ways as the lecturer comes to them.

5. Pay attention to notes or diagrams written on a chalkboard or projected on a screen. These are major details that you should copy into your notes.

6. When in doubt about what you are hearing, ask questions if the lecturer does not mind being interrupted. Some lecturers save time for answering questions at the end of the lecture.

Try out these strategies by doing the following exercise: Use the six guidelines above to take notes in one of your classes for one week. Compare the notes you take with an old set of notes. Do you see any improvement? Share your results with your reading instructor and classmates. *(Students' results will vary.)*

HOW WELL DO YOU REMEMBER?

To review the chapter, read the following summary and fill in the blanks. If you need help with an answer, look back through the chapter to refresh your memory.

You can improve your reading comprehension by learning to tell the difference between a main idea and a detail. ____Details____ are the bits and pieces of information that support, or explain, an author's main idea.

Three types of details you should be able to recognize are ____facts____, ____reasons____, and ____examples____. A ____fact____ is something you can prove by direct observation, by reading, or by asking an expert. A ____reason____ is an explanation that tells you why or how things happen. ____Examples____ are illustrations, images, and descriptions that appeal to one or more of your five senses.

The ideas within a paragraph have different levels of development. A main idea is the first, or most general, level of development. A ____major detail____, the second level of development, supports a main idea. A ____minor detail____ is the third, or most specific, level of development.

Words and phrases called ____transitions____ connect ideas. They act as signals for certain types of details and levels of development.

The ____table of contents____ in a textbook lists each chapter's main ideas and major details.

WHAT DO YOU THINK?

Reflect on the way you read textbook chapters. Did you know that the headings and subheadings are clues to the chapter's main ideas and major details? Were you aware that authors use different types of details to support their ideas? How will you use this chapter's strategies

to help you get more out of your assigned reading? Write your reflections below.

Reflections will vary.

_____

_____

_____

_____

CHAPTER QUIZ 1

Part 1 Terms and Definitions

Match this chapter's special terms in Column A with their definitions
in Column B.

Column A

___d___ 1. examples

___a___ 2. reasons

___b___ 3. facts

___e___ 4. supporting details

___c___ 5. Ask who?, what?, why?

Column B

a. explanations of why or how

b. dates, times, and
   measurements, for example

c. how to identify details

d. illustrations, images,
   descriptions

e. information that explains a
   main idea

Part 2 Chapter Review

Read and answer each question below. Write your answer in complete
sentences, and use extra paper if needed. *(Answers may vary but should
be similar to these.)*

1. What is the difference between a main idea and a detail?

A main idea is a general idea. Details are specific ideas. Details support, or

explain, main ideas.

2. Why is it important to be able to distinguish between main ideas and details?

   It is important because you are able to see how the ideas are organized. As

   a result, comprehension improves and studying is easier.

3. What are levels of development, and why should you be able to recognize them?

   The levels of development are main idea, major details, and minor details.

   Recognizing them helps you follow the author's organization.

Part 3 Using Your Skills

Read each paragraph and circle whether the underlined details are facts, reasons, or examples. The paragraphs are from *The Practical Entomologist* by Rick Imes.

The name <u>centipede means "one hundred feet,"</u> and centipedes are characterized by having <u>one pair of legs per segment</u>; while few centipedes have exactly one hundred legs, the number is a fair estimate. Their long, flattened, multisegmented <u>bodies comprise between 15 and 181 segments.</u> The <u>head bears a pair of long antennae</u>, a <u>pair of mandibles</u> for chewing, and <u>two pairs of maxillae</u> for handling food. <u>A pair of poison claws on the first segment behind the head</u> enables a centipede to deliver a painful bite if handled carelessly. Most species live under stones or logs, emerging at night to prey upon earthworms and insects, which they kill with their <u>venomous bite.</u>

(The paragraph provides facts and figures about the insects' life and appearance.)

(a.) facts   b. reasons   c. examples

Wings have evolved to serve a number of other purposes besides flight. <u>Male crickets and katydids, for example, have developed specialized structures on their forewings</u>; when rubbed together on warm summer nights, <u>these structures produce the pulsing songs by which the males seek to attract females.</u>

(The paragraph illustrates the use of wings to produce sound.)

a. facts   b. reasons   (c.) examples

. . . a reasonably strong argument can be made for saying that insects, not mammals, are the dominant life form on earth. Consider that the <u>number of insect species is greater than the number of all other species of organisms combined</u>; beetle species alone outnumber all plant species in the world. Despite their conspicuous scarcity in

(The paragraph explains why insects are the dominant life form.)

marine environments, <u>insects inhabit every other conceivable habitat</u>, sometimes in mind-boggling densities. Then consider <u>the remarkable resiliency of insects</u>—their short life spans and tremendous reproductive capacity result in their being extraordinarily responsive to environmental changes that would stress the populations of other organisms.

a. facts   b. reasons   c. examples

Insects may destroy crops in one of two ways. Most obviously, their <u>consumption of the plant</u> means there is less for us. Grasshoppers, true bugs, aphids, and beetles are the most serious offenders in this category. <u>Infestation of our stored grains and cereals</u> is also a serious problem, but most of this damage is caused by only a few species of beetle. Perhaps more serious are the many <u>plant diseases</u> introduced through the wounds where insects have been feeding, boring, or laying eggs.   4

(The paragraph explains how insects destroy crops.)

a. facts   b. reasons   c. examples

Score: 100 − 8 for each one missed = _____%

CHAPTER QUIZ 2

Part 1 Terms and Definitions

Match this chapter's special terms in Column A with their definitions in Column B.

Column A

_d_ 1. levels of development
_e_ 2. major details
_a_ 3. minor details
_b_ 4. transitions
_c_ 5. main idea

Column B

a. third level of development
b. may signal major or minor details
c. first level of development
d. how ideas are organized
e. second level of development

Part 2 Chapter Review

Read and answer each question below. Write your answer in complete sentences, and use extra paper if needed. *(Answers may vary but should be similar to these.)*

1. What are three types of details? Give an example of each.

   The three types of details are facts, reasons, and examples. (Students'

   examples of each type may vary.)

2. What questions should you ask to identify a fact? A reason? An example?

   To identify facts ask, Who? What? Where? When? To identify reasons ask,

   Why? or How? To identify examples ask, What kind? What color?, etc.

3. In what way do examples appeal to your five senses?

   Examples tell you how things look, smell, taste, feel, and sound.

Part 3 Using Your Skills

Read the following textbook passage and answer the questions about its levels of development. Use extra paper if needed.

Meditation, Health, and Stress

Meditation provides a set of techniques intended to create an altered   1
state of consciousness characterized by inner peace and tranquility
(Shapiro & Walsh, 1984). Some claim that meditation increases
awareness and understanding of themselves and their environment,
reduces anxiety, improves health, and aids performance in
everything from work to tennis.

  In the most common meditation methods, attention is focused   2
on just one thing—a word, sound, or object—until the meditator
stops thinking about *anything* and experiences nothing but "pure
awareness" (Benson, 1975).

  What a meditator focuses on is far less important than doing so with   3
a passive attitude. To organize attention, meditators may, for example,
inwardly name every sound or thought that reaches consciousness, focus
on the sound of their own breathing, or slowly repeat a *mantra*, which is a
soothing word or phrase. During a typical meditation session, breathing,
heart rate, muscle tension, blood pressure, and oxygen consumption
decrease (Wallace & Benson, 1972). Most forms of meditation induce
alpha-wave EEG activity, the brain-wave pattern commonly found in a
relaxed, eyes-closed, waking state. . . .

Meditators often report significant reductions in stress-related problems such as general anxiety, high blood pressure, and insomnia (Beauchamp-Turner & Levinson, 1992). More generally, meditators' scores on personality tests indicate increases in general mental health, self-esteem, and social openness (Sakairi, 1992; Janowiak & Hackman, 1994). Exactly how meditation produces its effects is unclear. Many of its effects can also be achieved by biofeedback, hypnosis, and just relaxing (Holmes, 1984).

4

From Bernstein et al., *Psychology,* fourth edition. Boston: Houghton Mifflin, 1997.

1. What is the central idea of the whole passage?

   Meditation provides . . . (first sentence, paragraph 1)

2. How does a meditator *focus* attention?

   To focus attention, think about one thing until you stop thinking about

   anything at all.

3. How does a meditator *organize* attention?

   To organize attention, inwardly name sounds or thoughts, focus on

   breathing, or repeat a mantra.

4. What happens during a typical meditation session?

   Breathing, heart rate, muscle tension, blood pressure, and oxygen

   consumption decrease.

5. What are some of the reported *effects* of meditation?

   Some effects are increased awareness and self-understanding, reduced

   anxiety, improved health and performance.

6. How does meditation produce these effects?

   How meditation produces these effects is unclear, according to the authors.

7. Are the details in paragraph 3 mostly facts, reasons, or examples?

The details are mostly examples of what the authors mean by focusing

with a passive attitude.

8. Are the details in paragraph 4 mostly facts, reasons, or examples?

The details are facts that state research findings.

9. What is a *mantra?*

A mantra is a soothing word or phrase.

10. According to the authors, the effects of meditation can be achieved by what other means?

They can be achieved by biofeedback, hypnosis, and just relaxing.

Score: 100 − 6 for each one missed = _____%

Vocabulary Quiz

Each sentence below contains a word in bold type from the reading selection on pages 150–153. Read the sentence and the definitions that follow it. Then circle the correct one. Turn to the vocabulary preview on pages 150–151 to check your answers.

1. In Disney's cartoon *Fantasia,* the dancing hippos are dressed in pink ruffled **tutus.**
   a. pants
   b. ribbons
   c. skirts
   d. hats

2. At Christmas, children like to hang stockings over the **hearth.**
   a. Christmas tree
   b. fireplace
   c. doorway
   d. bed posts

3. Rosie's grandfather speaks **Yiddish** with the family because he prides himself on being from "the old country."
   a. a heavy accent
   b. slang words and phrases
   (c.) language of European Jews
   d. speech that is slow and careful

4. When "Madame Butterfly" opened, the theater was filled to overflowing with the **aficionados** of this famous opera.
   a. musicians
   b. actors
   c. writers
   (d.) fans

5. "Mad Max," the horse that won the race, was so **spirited** that he pranced and trotted all the way back to his stable.
   (a.) lively
   b. tired
   c. sick
   d. afraid

6. **Lox** and cream cheese on a bagel is a traditional snack that many people enjoy.
   a. mayonnaise
   (b.) smoked salmon
   c. hot peppers
   d. bacon

7. The solid black puzzle pieces were **baffling** because we could not tell how to put them together.
   a. surprising
   (b.) frustrating
   c. fun
   d. clever

8. A hot **croissant** tastes good with butter and jelly.
   a. chocolate
   b. vegetable
   (c.) crescent roll
   d. roast beef

9. Although caviar may be a **delicacy** to some people, to me it is just fish eggs.
   a. habit
   b. jewel
   c. good wine
   d. fine food

10. A comet is a **phenomenon** you may not be lucky enough to see because it is only visible every few thousand years.
    a. regular occurrence
    b. feat of science
    c. natural disaster
    d. unusual event

11. Although the Ford assembly plant is partly **automated,** workers still do many jobs by hand.
    a. unionized
    b. closed
    c. mechanical
    d. remodeled

12. My brother's habit of always putting on his clothes in a certain order is one example of his **quirky** behavior.
    a. odd
    b. polite
    c. insane
    d. childish

Score: 100 − 8 for each one missed = _____%

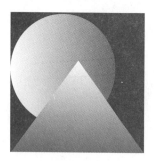

Chapter 7

Recognizing and Following Thought Patterns

*I*n a discussion, someone is sure to ask your opinion. Suppose the topic is what to do on spring break. You may give an *example* of a fun place to go. Someone else may offer a *definition* of the perfect spring break. One friend may *list* favorite activities or events. Another may *compare and contrast* two popular beaches.

In a discussion about personal achievements, someone may ask you to explain the *cause and effect* of your success in a course—how you studied and the grades you earned—or the *time order* you followed to reach a goal. In each case, the explanation follows a recognizable thought pattern. Although you may not always realize that you are using a thought pattern such as comparison and contrast or cause and effect, the fact is that these and other patterns come naturally to you.

Thought patterns are as common to reading as they are to conversation. Authors organize details in meaningful ways. Discovering an author's thought pattern will help you follow the ideas and anticipate what comes next. Moreover, patterns serve as clues to what is important to remember.

This chapter explains two strategies that will help you find and follow an author's thought pattern:

- ■ *Know six basic patterns.*
- ■ *Recognize transitions that signal patterns.*

WHAT DO YOU ALREADY KNOW?

To prepare yourself for the reading selection that follows, find out what you already know about the ways men and women think. Answer the questions below either on your own or in a group discussion.

1. In your opinion, do men and women think differently? What examples can you give to support your opinion?

2. Do certain issues or problems seem to concern one sex more than the other? Explain your answer.

3. Does one sex outperform the other in some activities? Explain your answer.

4. Read the title, headnote, vocabulary preview, and first two paragraphs of the reading selection. What do you think will follow?

How Gender May Bend Your Thinking

Christine Gorman

In the following article from Time *magazine, the author presents evidence to suggest that men and women may use their brains differently.*

VOCABULARY PREVIEW

chauvinist	(shō′və·nĭst) one who feels superior to those who are different
tantalizing	(tăn′tə·līz·ĭng) teasing, kept out of reach
orienting	(or′ē·ənt·ĭng) locating or placing in relation to the compass points
cerebral	(sĕr′ə·brəl) of the brain, intellectual rather than emotional
crucial	(krōō′shəl) extremely important, vital
innately	(ĭ·nāt′lē) inborn characteristically
delving	(dĕlv′ĭng) searching deeply

predispose	(prē′dĭ·spōz′) to make someone likely to do something in advance
uncanny	(ŭn·kăn′ē) unsettling, strange
versatile	(vûr′sə·təl) able to do many things, having many uses

Pronunciation Key: ā (**pay**), ă (**pat**), ē (**bee**), ĕ (**bet**), ī (**pie**), ĭ (**pit**), ō (**toe**), o͞o (**boot**), ô (**horrid**), ŭ (**cut**), û (**urge**, **term**), ə (**about**, **item**)

Why can't a woman think more like a man? That's the sort of question one would expect to hear from an unrepentant **chauvinist** like Shaw's Professor Higgins.* But a growing number of scientists have begun wondering the same thing. Relying in part on advanced brain-scanning techniques, they have amassed **tantalizing** hints that men and women may use their heads in subtly distinctive ways.

Recently, a new study showed that in science tests teenage boys who scored in the top 5% outnumbered girls 7 to 1, while girls outperformed boys in reading comprehension. In general, men as a group excel at tasks that involve **orienting** objects in space—like reading a map without having to turn it so it lines up with the road. Women, on the other hand, seem to be more adept at communication, both verbal and nonverbal. Readings of MRI scans suggest one reason: women seem to have stronger connections between the two halves (hemispheres) of their brain.

What's sauce for the goose need not be a problem for the gander, however. The relative lack of cross talk between their hemispheres may actually benefit men by allowing each half of the brain to concentrate on what it does best. Studies have shown that when men are confronted with problems that deal with spatial orientation—a function that can be handled by both the left and right hemispheres—they tend to use the right hemisphere only. Thus there aren't many distracting messages coming in from the left hemisphere, which concentrates on language. This **cerebral** division of labor could also explain why there are so many more male architects and chess champions. Their brains may simply be better able to concentrate on solving problems involving spatial relations.

Just because scientists can measure these differences, however, does not mean they understand their causes. Are men born with better spatial abilities, or do they develop them by playing sports in which eye-hand coordination is **crucial?** Are women **innately** better

*Professor Higgins is a character in *Pygmalion,* a play by George Bernard Shaw, on which the stage and film versions of *My Fair Lady* are based.

at reading words and understanding emotions, or do they just get more practice? If heredity and biology are important, though, then it's a pretty good bet that the sex hormones are somehow involved. For that reason, researchers have begun **delving** into the effects of testosterone and estrogen on the brain.

Although romantics of all ages can recall occasions when lust interfered with reason, scientists once believed sex hormones had very little effect on the brain. The chemicals' only target was supposed to be a tiny structure called the hypothalamus, buried deep in the brain, which is the seat for sexual drive and other urges, such as appetite and aggression. Recent research, however, has shown that the entire brain, including the thought-processing cortex, is awash in sex hormones, even before birth. The larger amounts of testosterone produced by males may **predispose** men's brains toward greater specialization of the two hemispheres.

This oversimplifies the case, of course. There are men whose brains are not especially compartmentalized, and women whose brains are. And even when a brain fits the mold, performance is not always predictable. Consider Judit Polgar, who at 15 became the world's youngest chess grand master. Her success does not mean she has a male-wired brain. Nor did Shakespeare, whose intuitions about women were **uncanny,** necessarily have female wiring. The variation between the sexes pales in comparison with individual differences—and shows how marvelously **versatile** a 3-lb. mass of nerve cells can be.

HOW WELL DID YOU COMPREHEND?

Main Idea

1. Which of the following sentences states the central idea of Christine Gorman's article?
   a. paragraph 1, first sentence "Why can't . . ."
   b. paragraph 1, last sentence "Relying in part . . ."
   c. paragraph 2, first sentence "Recently . . ."
   d. paragraph 2, last sentence "Readings of . . ."

2. Which sentence best expresses the unstated main idea of paragraph 6?
   a. Men's brains tend to be more compartmentalized than women's.
   b. Men's and women's brains are "wired" differently.
   c. Performance is not always predictable.
   d. Individual differences are more significant than sexual differences.

Details

3. According to a study, boys scored higher on science tests while girls outperformed boys in
   a. reading comprehension.
   b. reading a map.
   c. understanding spatial relations.
   d. playing chess.

4. The hypothalamus, a structure buried deep in the brain, controls all of the following *except*
   a. the sex drive.
   b. aggression.
   c. intelligence.
   d. appetite.

Inferences

5. The author would probably agree with which of the following statements?
   a. Scientists know why men and women think differently.
   b. Women's abilities are the result of reading.
   c. Men's abilities are influenced by their involvement in sports.
   d. Both biology and heredity may influence the ways men and women think.

Working with Words

Complete the sentences below with these words from the vocabulary preview:

cerebral   tantalizing   orienting   predispose   delving
uncanny   versatile   chauvinist   innately   crucial

1. As Halloween approaches, stores tempt us with _____tantalizing_____ candies and other sweets.

2. Many readers think that Mary Shelley's *Frankenstein* is a terrifying and _____uncanny_____ story.

3. Horror movies usually appeal to our emotional natures rather than to our _____cerebral_____ qualities.

4. Dressed in a pig costume and wearing a button that said "down with women," Brian went to the party as a male _____chauvinist_____.

5. Some people enjoy ___*delving*___ into ancient tales of witch-craft and the supernatural.

6. "I'll be happy to take the children trick-or-treating," said Barbara, "but it is ___*crucial*___ that we all stay together."

7. Bettina's costume is so ___*versatile*___ that she can be a witch, a goblin, or a vampire.

8. Listening to ghost stories may ___*predispose*___ you to have night-mares.

9. Inside the haunted house attraction, Brad had difficulty ___*orienting*___ himself to the way out.

10. Some children seem ___*innately*___ more fearful of the unknown than others.

Thinking and Writing

Do you think that your choices or activities have been limited in any way because of your sex? Why or why not?

Answers will vary.

_____

_____

_____

_____

KNOW SIX BASIC PATTERNS

Patterns are ways of organizing details: They show how ideas are related. Also, patterns are connected to an author's purpose and main idea. For example, in a chapter of a biology textbook, the author's purpose may be to explain the process of cell reproduction. The main idea may be that cells reproduce in one of two ways: by sexual or asexual reproduction. The author may use *time order* to explain the stages in each process and the order in which they occur. In addition, the author may

FIGURE 7.1 Six Common Thought Patterns	
Patterns	**Explanations**
EXAMPLE	A general *statement* is followed by an *example* that illustrates it.
LISTING	*Listing* provides a series of details that support a main idea.
TIME ORDER	*Time order* shows a sequence of events, a series of steps, or the stages in a process.
COMPARISON AND CONTRAST	*Comparison* shows how things are alike. *Contrast* shows how they differ. *Comparison* and *contrast* often occur together.
CAUSE AND EFFECT	*Causes* are the reasons that explain why things happen. *Effects* are the results of what happens. *Cause* and *effect* often work together as a pattern.
DEFINITION	*Definition* may occur by itself or in combination with another pattern. A definition may be followed by an example, a comparison, or a contrasting word or idea.

use *comparison and contrast* to explain the similarities and differences between sexual and asexual reproduction.

Figure 7.1 lists six basic patterns and a brief explanation of each. Figure 7.2 lists transitions that signal each pattern and help you identify details.

PATTERN 1: EXAMPLE

As explained in Chapter 6, *examples* are one type of detail that an author uses to support a main idea. Examples help clarify or explain a more general statement. The example pattern consists of a general statement followed by one or more examples. Now read the following paragraph.

Some Barbie dolls are designed as collectibles for adults rather than as toys for children. For example, Marilyn Monroe Barbie comes in a

---

FIGURE 7.2 Transitions That Signal Thought Patterns

Patterns	Transitions
EXAMPLE	for example, to illustrate, for instance, specifically, such as
LISTING	first, next, then, last, finally, other, another, in addition, also, moreover, furthermore
TIME ORDER	first, second, third . . ., next, after, before, one, two, three . . ., soon, later, finally, during (Also look for dates, hours, and minutes.)
COMPARISON AND CONTRAST	alike, like, similar, resembles, same, different, unlike, however, as opposed to, on the other hand, in contrast
CAUSE AND EFFECT	cause, because, reason, thus, leads to, since, effect, result, therefore
DEFINITION	for example, for instance, such as, to illustrate, to define, means, is defined as

---

choice of three outfits that recall the star's famous film roles. Another example is the Lily Barbie, one of several dolls whose dresses are made to look like flowers. A doll in the American Beauties series is dressed to look like George Washington.

The first sentence, or topic sentence, is a general statement. The next three sentences contain examples that support the general statement. These examples make clear which Barbie dolls are designed as collectibles. Also, the transitional phrases *for example* in the first sentence and *another example* in the second sentence are signals that tell you to look for the examples.

Exercise 7.1   In the following paragraphs, several examples support the main idea. For each paragraph, one example is given. Read the paragraph and answer the questions that follow.

I. Many developments that we take for granted were not available to our grandparents when they were growing up. Television is but one example. The first television was developed in the 1940s. Computers are another example. Most schoolchildren have access to computers in their homes and schools. However, personal computers did not come into widespread use until the seventies. Video recorders, videocameras, and CD players are three more examples of new technology unavailable to anyone who was of school age in the 1960s or earlier.

1. What is the main idea?

   Many developments . . . (first sentence)

2. List the examples that support the main idea.

   a. _television_

   b. _computers_

   c. _video recorders_

   d. _videocameras_

   e. _CD players_

3. What are the transitions that help you find the examples?

   one example, another example, three more examples

II. Do you know anyone who has had tuberculosis? Because of advancements in medicine, tuberculosis and many other diseases have been nearly wiped out. Polio, for instance, used to claim hundreds of children's lives and cripple others. Thanks to the Salk vaccine, polio is now quite rare. Yellow fever and scarlet fever are two more examples of diseases that have become rare. Although some children still get chicken pox, this disease occurs less frequently.

1. What is the main idea?

   Because of advancements in medicine . . . (second sentence)

2. List the examples that support the main idea.

   a. _Polio is now quite rare._

   b. _Yellow fever and scarlet fever have become rare._

   c. _Chicken pox occurs less frequently._

3. What are the transitions that help you find the examples?

   for instance, two more examples
   _____

PATTERN 2: LISTING

A *list* is a series of items. When a series of details, such as facts or reasons, supports a main idea, the pattern is *listing*. Transitions such as *first, next, also,* and *in addition* may help you identify the items in a list. Sometimes the items are numbered 1, 2, 3, and so on. Occasionally, the items may be preceded by a little dot, or bullet. Listing is a pattern many textbook authors use to help readers identify important details quickly and easily. For example, an author may list guidelines for taking notes or the signs of alcoholism or depression.

As you read the next paragraph, try to identify the main idea and the author's list of details.

> Psychologists have identified several common signs of stress that everyone should recognize. For one thing, people under stress are often depressed for no reason that they can identify. A change in sleep pattern is another sign of stress. Irritability, a third sign of stress, is also common. Other signs of stress include difficulty making decisions, mood swings, and a sudden change in appetite.

The main idea is stated in the first sentence. The following sentences list six signs of stress: depression, a change in sleep pattern, irritability, difficulty making decisions, mood swings, and a change in appetite. The transitions that help you identify the items in the list are *for one thing, another sign, a third sign,* and *other signs.*

Even though these items are listed one after the other, the order of items is not important. For example, it does not matter whether depression or appetite change comes first, second, or last on the list since they are all signs of depression.

For an additional example of the listing pattern, review Greg Gottesman's "Time Management for College Students," Chapter 1, page 5. The author lists eight tips for managing your time. Each one is explained in a separate paragraph.

Exercise 7.2   In the following paragraphs, a list of details supports the main idea. For each paragraph, one detail is given. Read the paragraph and answer the questions that follow.

I. A good study area should contain the following items. First, you need a desk or table where you can spread out your work. Second, a chair that provides enough back support is essential. Third, you should have paper, pencils, and pens within reach. A calendar on which you can post important dates and deadlines is a fourth item to include in your study area.

1. What is the main idea?

   A good study area . . . (first sentence)

2. What are the details?

   a. *a desk or table*

   b. *a chair that provides back support*

   c. *paper, pencils, and pens within reach*

   d. *a calendar*

3. What transitions help you identify the details?

   first, second, third, fourth

II. Many students wonder how they can improve their grades. Classroom performance is one key to success. Most instructors agree on several essential classroom skills. First of all, be punctual—arrive on time. Second, attend regularly. You cannot receive instruction if you are absent. Always do required assignments, and turn them in on time. Class participation is one of the most essential skills. Do not miss an opportunity to participate in class.

1. What is the main idea?

   Most instructors agree . . . (third sentence)

2. What are the details?

   a. *Arrive on time.*

   b. *Attend regularly.*

   c. *Do assignments and turn them in on time.*

   d. *Participate in class.*

3. What transitions help you identify the details?

___*several, first, second, one of the most*_____

PATTERN 3: TIME ORDER

Time order is a pattern that organizes details according to time. *Chronological order* is another name for time order. Authors use time order when the order, or sequence, in which events occur is important. For example, the steps or stages of certain processes occur in a sequence that is necessary to the successful completion of the process. For instance, if you do much cooking, you have probably learned that ingredients do not blend well, or a dish may not cook evenly unless you follow the order of steps in a recipe.

When you realize that an author is using the pattern of time order, be sure you understand what series of events or what process is being described. Then identify and follow the sequence. Practice this strategy on the following paragraph.

> Before buying a new fertilizer for my lawn, I decided to test the soil for its content. A nursery recommended that I follow these four steps. First, pour a few spoonfuls of dirt into a glass jar. Next, fill the jar with water. Third, shake the jar to thoroughly mix the soil and water. As a final step, let the jar stand for several hours until the contents of the soil separate into bands of sand, silt, and clay. The amount of sand in relation to the soil's other parts will determine which fertilizer to buy.

The process being described is how to test soil for its content. The main idea is that you must follow four steps. The details are the four steps and the order in which they occur. The transitions *first, next, third,* and *a final step* help you follow the steps. Dates or times (hours and minutes) may also serve as transitions to help you follow events.

How is time order different from listing? Both patterns list details, and both patterns use some of the same transitions. Remember that in time order, sequence is important. In listing, however, it is not. Time order describes events and processes that happen over time or in a certain sequence. Listing merely lists a number of facts or reasons, like the signs of stress, that support a main idea.

Exercise 7.3   In the following paragraphs, a sequence of events or steps support the main idea. For each paragraph, one event or step is given. Read the paragraph and complete the items that follow.

I. Jim always seems to score well on tests. How does he do it? Jim offers these tips for successful studying. The first step is to decide what to study. Find out what topics will be covered on the test. Next, organize your notes and other materials on these topics. Third, make study guides to use as memory aids. Your final step is to review your notes and study guides until you feel confident about taking the test.

1. What is the main idea?

   Jim offers these tips . . . (third sentence)

2. List the events, steps, or stages in order.

   a. *Decide what to study.*

   b. *Organize notes and other materials.*

   c. *Make study guides.*

   d. *Review notes and study guides.*

3. What transitions help you follow the time order?

   The first step, next, third, the final step

II. Diana, the late Princess of Wales, had a short but full life. She was born in 1961 to Earl Spenser and his wife Frances. In 1981, she married Prince Charles. Diana gave birth to two sons: Prince William in 1982 and Prince Harry in 1983. Unfortunately, the marriage between the Prince and Princess was in trouble from the beginning. By 1996, they were divorced. On August 29, 1997, an automobile accident claimed Diana's life. Millions of people the world over mourned her death. She was admired for her charity work, especially with AIDS patients and land mine victims.

1. What is the main idea?

   Diana, the late Princess . . . (first sentence)

2. List the events, steps, or stages in order.

   a. *She was born in 1961.*

   b. *She married in 1981.*

c. *She gave birth to sons in 1982 and 1983.* _____

d. *She was divorced by 1996.* _____

e. *She died on August 29, 1997.* _____

3. What transitions help you follow the time order?

_____ *1961, 1981, 1982, 1983, 1996, 1997* _____

PATTERN 4: COMPARISON AND CONTRAST

Authors use *comparison and contrast* to explain similarities and differences. Although comparison and contrast can occur separately, they often occur together.

Comparison and contrast is a pattern you will often recognize in psychology and biology textbooks. In a psychology text, authors may compare and contrast personality theories, results of experiments, and normal versus abnormal behavior. In a biology text, authors compare and contrast the life processes of plants, animals, and humans.

Transitions such as *alike, different, comparatively,* and *in contrast* help you identify the points of comparison and contrast as in the following paragraph excerpted from Christine Gorman's article on pages 189–191.

> Recently, a new study showed that in science tests teenage boys who scored in the top 5% outnumbered girls 7 to 1, while girls outperformed boys in reading comprehension. In general, men as a group excel at tasks that involve orienting objects in space—like reading a map without having to turn it so it lines up with the road. Women, on the other hand, seem to be more adept at communication, both verbal and nonverbal. Readings of MRI scans suggest one reason: women seem to have stronger connections between the two halves (hemispheres) of their brain.

This paragraph supports the author's central idea that men and women may use their brains in distinctive ways. According to the author, men excel at orienting objects in space, but women are better at communicating. In a study, boys did better in science, but girls did better in reading. The transition *on the other hand* signals a contrast between men's and women's use of their brains.

Exercise 7.4   In the following paragraphs, several points of comparison or contrast support the main idea. For each paragraph, one point of comparison or contrast is given. Read each paragraph and complete the items that follow.

> I. Although spiders and insects are creepy creatures that have many legs, a spider is not an insect. Like an insect, a spider has an external skeleton that protects its internal organs. Also, spiders and insects have jointed legs. However, spiders and insects differ in three important ways. Spiders have eight legs, but insects have only six. An insect's body is divided into three parts: head, thorax, and abdomen. The spider's body, on the other hand, has only a head and abdomen. Finally, most insects have wings, but spiders do not.

1. What is the main idea?

   Although spiders . . . (first sentence)

2. What is being compared and/or contrasted?

   spiders and insects

3. What are the points of comparison and/or contrast?

   a. *Both spiders and insects have an external skeleton.*

   b. *Both spiders and insects have jointed legs.*

   c. *Spiders have eight legs, but insects have six.*

   d. *Spiders have two body parts, but insects have three.*

   e. *Most insects have wings, but spiders do not.*

4. What transitions help you identify a comparison or contrast?

   like, However, differ, on the other hand

> II. Many first-year college students find out that high school and college differ in several important ways. Motivation is a major difference. In high school, parents and teachers motivate you to study. In college, you are expected to motivate yourself. Another difference is the availability of instructors. In high school, teachers are available when you need them. In college, you usually have to

make an appointment to see a professor. The work load differs too.
College courses are more difficult and students usually have more
homework than they had in high school. Perhaps the greatest
difference for many students is that in college they are on their own.

1. What is the main idea?

   Many first-year college students . . . (first sentence)

2. What is being compared and/or contrasted?

   high school and college

3. What are the points of comparison and/or contrast?

   a. _Motivation is a major difference._

   b. _Another difference is the availability of instructors._

   c. _The work load differs too._

   d. _In college, students are on their own._

4. What transitions help you identify a comparison or contrast?

   differ, difference, more, greatest difference

PATTERN 5: CAUSE AND EFFECT

A *cause* is a reason, and an *effect* is a result. Causes explain the reasons,
or why, things happen. Effects explain the results of certain events or
decisions. As a pattern, *cause and effect* often work together.

   In college you read about important events and discoveries, the
causes behind them, and their lasting effects. Whenever you ask "What
caused this?" or "Why did this happen?" or "What would happen if I did
this?" you are asking about causes and effects.

   Transitions that help you identify causes and effects are *because, for
this reason, as a result,* and *therefore.* As you read the following paragraph,
try to identify causes and effects.

   Tiger Woods is one of the most successful young golfers of our time.
   Many fans have wondered what are the causes of his success. One
   cause is skill. Tiger began playing golf at an early age, so he has had

many years to build his skill. Ask any athlete, "What makes you successful?" and the answer is likely to be "Practice." For Tiger, too, regular practice has led to success. Strong support of his parents is a third reason Tiger has done well. His parents have helped him develop the self-confidence and positive attitude needed to excel in any field.

In this paragraph, the main idea is stated in the second sentence. The rest of the paragraph states three causes of Tiger Woods's success: skill, practice, parental support. Transitions that help you identify causes are *one cause, has led to,* and *a third reason.*

Exercise 7.5   In the following paragraphs, several causes or effects support the main idea. For each paragraph, one cause or effect is given. Read each paragraph and complete the items that follow.

I. I used to love living in my apartment, but now I have decided to move. A major cause of my dissatisfaction is the rent increase. Even though no improvements have been made, my landlord is still raising the rent. Another cause is noise. Recently I have had difficulty getting in and out of my apartment complex because the road is under construction. It may be a year or more before the road is finished. This also has influenced me to move out. My utility bill was the final cause. Utilities used to be included in the rent but not anymore.

1. What is the main idea?

   I used to love . . . (first sentence)

2. List the causes and/or effects that support the main idea.

   a. *rent increase*

   b. *noise*

   c. *road under construction*

   d. *utilities no longer included*

3. What transitions help you identify a cause or effect?

   major cause, another cause, because, final cause

II. We could not get along without volunteers. Their services not only benefit the recipients but also have a positive effect on themselves. As any school volunteer knows, reading to children leads to an appreciation of literature. After-school sports programs help kids build athletic skills and team spirit. Hospital volunteers relieve the nursing staff of housekeeping chores such as delivering food trays to rooms. They also take time to chat with patients, offering words of comfort and cheer. Volunteers and recipients enjoy these positive effects.

1. What is the main idea?

   Their services not only benefit . . . (second sentence)

2. List the causes and/or effects that support the main idea.

   a. *Reading leads to an appreciation of literature.*

   b. *Sports programs build skills and team spirit.*

   c. *Volunteers relieve nursing staff of chores.*

   d. *They also comfort and cheer patients.*

3. What transitions help you identify a cause or effect?

   effect, leads to, effects

PATTERN 6: DEFINITION

Textbooks and other written materials are filled with terms that may be new or unfamiliar. Authors use *definition* to explain the meaning of a term. This pattern consists of a brief definition followed by examples that may describe, compare, contrast, or explain uses and functions.

When you encounter a definition in your reading, you need to ask yourself two questions: "What is being defined?" and "What are its characteristics?" Transitions that signal a term's definition are *means, is,* and *to define.* Transitions that signal characteristics are the same as those used in the example pattern: *such as, for example,* and *to illustrate.*

As you read the following paragraph, find the main idea, the definition, and characteristics.

My nephew is hoping to receive a Lava Lamp for his birthday. The Lava Lamp is a light that became popular during the 1960s. Now it is enjoying a revival. The lamp's globe is made of glass, and it sits on a metal base. The globe is filled with a clear liquid. Globs of a gooey substance that look like lava are suspended in the liquid. A light shines up through the liquid from the lamp's base. The light heats the "lava," causing it to bubble and circulate through the liquid and form strange shapes. When you turn off the lamp, the lava cools and settles to the bottom.

In this paragraph, the main idea is stated in the first sentence. The term defined is *Lava Lamp.* The definition of the term is *a light that became popular during the 1960s.* The examples explain the lamp's characteristics: what it looks like and how it works.

For an example of definition as used in a longer passage, review "What's a Bagel?" on pages 150–153, Chapter 6. In this essay, the author defines bagels in several ways. He describes how they look and taste, he traces their history, and he explains all the clever and tasty ways you can eat bagels.

As an example of the way textbook authors use definition, see the following paragraph from a psychology text:

> In the first few weeks and months after birth, babies demonstrate involuntary, unlearned reactions called **reflexes.** These are swift, automatic movements that occur in response to external stimuli. Figure 12.2 illustrates the *grasping reflex;* more than twenty other reflexes have been observed in newborn infants. For example, in the *rooting reflex* the infant turns its mouth toward a finger or nipple that touches its cheek. In the *sucking reflex* the newborn sucks on anything that touches its lips. . . .
>
> From Bernstein et al., *Psychology,* fourth edition. Boston: Houghton Mifflin, 1994, p. 389.

In this paragraph, the main idea is stated in the first sentence. The term defined is *reflexes.* The definition of the term is *an involuntary, unlearned reaction.* Several examples explain the characteristics of a reflex: what it is like (a swift, automatic movement), why it happens (in response to external stimuli), and how many types of reflexes occur (more than twenty). Examples of the grasping, rooting, and sucking reflexes are also included.

Notice, too, that the authors refer readers to a figure that illustrates the grasping reflex. Very often, definitions of complex terms are accompanied by figures and other graphics that help explain them. You should always take time to read charts, tables, and figures. See Chapter 9 for an explanation of how to read graphics.

Exercise 7.6   In each paragraph, a word or term is defined by facts or examples. Read the paragraphs and answer the questions that follow. For each definition, one characteristic is given.

I. Test anxiety is defined as stress related to a testing situation. Test anxiety has three forms. For some students, test anxiety is physical. These students may develop a headache, upset stomach, dizziness, or fatigue just before a test. After the test, these physical symptoms disappear. For other students, test anxiety is mental. These students may have "butterflies" in the stomach, jitters, or feelings of helplessness. For still other students, test anxiety may include both physical and mental symptoms. What is the best cure for test anxiety? Study and be well-prepared for tests.

1. What is the main idea?

   Test anxiety has three forms. (second sentence)

2. What is being defined?

   test anxiety

3. What are its characteristics?

   a. _For some students, test anxiety is physical._

   b. _For other students, test anxiety is mental._

   c. _For still others, it may be both physical and mental._

4. What transitions help you follow the pattern?

   is defined, for some, for other students, for still others

II. What is your definition of the perfect mate? According to sociologists, most people seek the same qualities in an ideal mate. For example, an ideal mate is one who shares your values and interests. Also, this person would be about the same age as you. A similar background and educational level are additional qualities of an ideal mate. For many people, an ideal mate is one who values family and wants children.

1. What is the main idea?

   According to sociologists . . . (second sentence)

2. What is being defined?

_____ *the perfect mate* _____

3. What are its characteristics?

    a. *shares values and interests* _____

    b. *about the same age* _____

    c. *similar background and education* _____

    d. *values family and wants children* _____

4. What transitions help you follow the pattern?

_____ *definition, for example, also, additional* _____

Exercise 7.7   Working with a partner, read and discuss the following paragraphs. Then identify the pattern from the list that is given. Use each pattern only once, and be able to explain your choices to the rest of the class.

    a. example   c. comparison and contrast   e. time order
    b. listing   d. cause and effect   f. definition

_____*b*_____ 1.   Several years ago, I started an exercise program. Now I cannot imagine how I ever got along without exercising. If someone were to ask me why I think exercise is important, I would list these benefits. For one thing, exercising makes me feel great. Second, exercising gets my heart rate up and raises my level of fitness. In addition, through regular exercise, I am able to keep my weight down.

_____*f*_____ 2.   In any market transaction, a **seller-consumer conflict** will always be present. This term simply means that sellers and consumers are motivated by different needs. For example, a person who is selling a house wants to make a certain profit on the sale. A buyer, on the other hand, wants to buy the house for as little as possible.

_____*c*_____ 3.   Buddhism and Confucianism are two of the world's religions that predate Christianity. Buddhism, founded by Prince Siddhartha

Gautama (Buddha), originated in India around 500 B.C. Confucianism, founded by K'ung Fu-tzu, originated in China during the 6th century, B.C. Buddhism's major beliefs are the Four Noble Truths and The Eight-Fold Path. Confucianism teaches that human beings are perfectible and that people can shape their own destinies. Buddhist festivals include celebrations of the Buddha's birth, enlightenment, first sermon, and death. The festivals of Confucianism include Chinese New Year, Lantern Festival, and All Souls' Festival.

_a_   4.   Although many people hate and fear insects, some of these creatures are not only harmless to humans but are also beneficial to the environment. Specifically, the dragonfly feeds on mosquitoes and other small biting insects. Ladybugs, too, are helpful creatures. They feed on small insects like aphids, which attack rose bushes. Another example of a "good bug" is the dung beetle. This insect burrows in animal droppings to feed on undigested seeds and other matter. In the process, it spreads the dung and aids soil fertilization.

_e_   5.   Arnold Gesell was the first psychologist to determine the stages of motor development in infants. The first stage occurs at about three months when an infant is able to roll over. At about four-and-a-half months, an infant can push up with the hands bearing weight on the legs. Around five-and-a-half months, an infant can sit without support. Often at about 6 months, an infant can push up to a standing position by holding onto furniture. Somewhere between the ninth and tenth month an infant will walk, holding onto furniture. Most infants can stand alone before their twelfth month, and between their twelfth and thirteenth months, many infants are walking alone. Although the age at which an infant arrives at each stage varies, the order in which the stages occur does not vary.

_d_   6.   Everyone is concerned about excessive drinking among college students. What are the causes of this behavior? Some students drink because it is one of the privileges of adulthood. They are away from home, and drinking makes them feel grown up. Other students drink for the fun of it. Their friends are doing it, and they don't want to feel left out. Still other students drink because it helps them relax and forget about their troubles. In each case, the students are using alcohol to hide from a problem instead of seeking an appropriate solution.

Memory Cue

Thought patterns are ways of organizing details. Finding and following an author's thought pattern will help you identify what is important and anticipate what comes next. Six common thought patterns are example, listing, time order, comparison and contrast, cause and effect, *and* definition.

REAL-WORLD CONNECTIONS

Thought patterns are as common to writing as they are to reading and conversation. You can apply what you have learned in this chapter about thought patterns in reading to any writing that you do for your other courses. As a writer, you must choose a topic, state your main idea, and support it with details. Moreover, you must organize your details in a meaningful way. Patterns can help you achieve good organization in writing.

How do you choose a thought pattern for organizing your details? Your topic and your purpose will help you decide. Ask yourself three questions:

1. What is my topic?

2. What is my purpose, or reason, for writing about this topic?

3. Which thought pattern is best for my topic and purpose?

Suppose you choose the topic *an event that changed my life.* If your purpose is to trace the event step by step, you might choose *time order* as your pattern. If your purpose is to explain how or why your life changed, you might choose *cause and effect.* If your purpose is to show what your life was like before and after the event, you might choose *comparison and contrast.*

Patterns help you arrange details in a clear and meaningful way. To experiment with patterns, try this simple exercise:

Think about yourself as a college student. Why are you here? What motivated you to choose this college? Write a paragraph in which you use the listing pattern to state your reasons for coming to college. Use transitions such as *one reason, another reason,* and *also.* If you need an example, review the paragraphs in Exercise 7.2 on page 197–199. Share your paragraph with the rest of the class. *(Paragraphs will vary but should state the main idea and list reasons.)*

HOW WELL DO YOU REMEMBER?

To review the chapter, read the following summary and fill in the blanks. If you need help with an answer, look back through the chapter to refresh your memory.

Thought patterns help authors organize details in meaningful ways. An author's choice of pattern is connected to purpose and ___main idea___. Sometimes ___transitions___ may serve as clues to an author's pattern. You should learn to recognize six common thought patterns.

The ___example___ pattern begins with a general statement followed by one or more examples.

When a series of details, such as facts or reasons, supports a main idea, the pattern is ___listing___.

___Time order___ is a pattern that organizes details according to time. This pattern is also called *chronological order.*

Authors use ___comparison and contrast___ to explain similarities and differences.

The ___cause and effect___ pattern provides reasons and results.

Authors use ___definition___ to explain the meaning of a term.

Thought patterns are as common to ___writing___ as they are to reading and conversation. In fact, we would probably have trouble communicating without them.

WHAT DO YOU THINK?

Reflect on what you have learned about thought patterns. What thought patterns have you been able to recognize in your reading? What thought patterns have you used recently in writing or in conversation? How do you plan to use what you have learned about thought patterns? Write your reflections below.

Reflections will vary.

CHAPTER QUIZ 1

Part 1 Terms and Definitions

Match each thought pattern in Column A with its brief definition in Column B. Use each answer only once.

Column A

___c___ 1. example

___f___ 2. definition

___e___ 3. listing

___a___ 4. time order

___b___ 5. comparison and contrast

___d___ 6. cause and effect

Column B

a. a series of details, order is important

b. similarities and differences

c. general statement followed by examples

d. reasons and results

e. a series of details, order not important

f. meanings alone or with other patterns

Part 2 Chapter Review

Read and answer each question below. Write your answer in complete sentences, and use extra paper if needed. *(Answers may vary but should be similar to these.)*

1. What are thought patterns?

   Thought patterns are ways of organizing details. They show how ideas

   are related.

2. How can you determine an author's thought pattern?

   The main idea, details, and transitions may provide clues to the

   author's pattern.

3. Besides in your reading, where else do you encounter thought patterns?

   You encounter thought patterns in writing and in conversation as well

   as in reading.

Part 3 Using Your Skills

Read each brief passage below and write the letter of the author's thought pattern beside it. Circle any transitions in the passage that help you identify the author's thought pattern. You may use an answer more than once.

a. example	c. comparison and contrast	e. cause and effect
b. definition	d. time order	f. listing

__b__ 1. What does **self** mean? Everyone has three selves: a physical self, an emotional self, and a social self. In a well-adjusted person, the three selves strike a balance so that neither one dominates the others.

__c__ 2. Vacationers differ in two important ways. First of all, some want lots of activity, but others just want to relax. Also, some have an unlimited budget while others must watch what they spend.

__e__ 3. About 80 percent of those who are called retarded have been the victims of inorganic causes such as physical abuse or neglect.

__d__ 4. At first, Dan's eyes became sensitive to light. Next, he felt a numbness in the fingers of his left hand. These symptoms were followed by a severe headache and nausea. Dan knew he was having a migraine.

__a__ 5. Employers today are looking for applicants whose personal qualities are strong. For example, they are seeking employees whose attitudes are positive and who can work cooperatively with others.

___b___   6.   Having good manners (means) doing what is socially acceptable in a given circumstance.

___f___   7.   The reference section of your college library contains many helpful resources. Encyclopedias, biographical indexes, almanacs, and atlases are a short (list.)

___e___   8.   (Why) am I attending college? I am here to pursue a career in business. I am here also (because) I want to improve my mind and broaden my interests.

___c___   9.   Choosing a vacation destination may depend on (whether) you want to relax in a quiet place (or) spend a few days mingling with tourists and seeing popular attractions.

___d___   10. The Democrats and Republicans (began) a struggle for power in the early nineties that would last through the (end) of the decade. In (1992,) Bill Clinton was elected President. In (1994,) the Republicans took control of Congress, and many thought that Clinton would be a one-term president. In (1996,) however, he was re-elected.

Score: 100 − 5 for each one missed = _____%

CHAPTER QUIZ 2

Part 1 Terms and Definitions

Match each thought pattern in Column A with the transitions that signal it in Column B. Use each answer only once.

Column A

___e___ 1. example
___d___ 2. definition
___b___ 3. listing
___f___ 4. time order
___c___ 5. comparison and contrast
___a___ 6. cause and effect

Column B

a. because, leads to, thus
b. in addition, also, another
c. like, however, in contrast
d. refers to, means
e. for instance, such as
f. first, second, third . . .

Part 2 Chapter Review

Read and answer each question below. Write your answer in complete sentences, and use extra paper if needed. *(Answers may vary but should be similar to these.)*

1. How can determining an author's thought pattern improve your reading comprehension?

   Determining the pattern helps you follow an author's ideas and

   anticipate what comes next.

2. What is another name for *time order* and how can you recognize this pattern?

   Time order is also called chronological order. Look for dates, time periods,

   and the transitions first, next, then, etc.

3. Which thought pattern is the most familiar to you, and what is its purpose?

   Answers will vary.

Part 3 Using Your Skills

Read the following textbook passages, and write the author's main idea and dominant thought pattern on the lines provided. Circle any transitions that help you identify the thought pattern. Use each pattern only once.

a. example   c. comparison and contrast   e. cause and effect
b. definition   d. time order   f. definition

In the late (1700s,) the French decided to change their own system of   1
measurement. To replace it they developed a logical and orderly
system called the **metric system.** The advantages of this system led to
its adoption in most countries of the world and in all branches of
science. The British held out until (1965) and then began a
changeover to the metric system.

   In countries using the metric system, almost everything is
measured in metric units—distances between cities, the weight of a
loaf of bread, the size of a sheet of plywood. Nearly all countries have
adopted the metric system. In (1975) the United States Congress
passed a bill establishing a policy of voluntary conversion to the
metric system and creating the U.S. Metric Board. A program of

gradual conversion was the goal of this board, whose funding ended in (982) . . .

From Alan Sherman, Sharon J. Sherman, and Leonard Russikoff, *Basic Concepts of Chemistry,* sixth edition. Boston: Houghton Mifflin, 1996.

a. main idea: *The metric system has had a long history. (Implied)*

b. pattern: *time order*

. . . There are (two types) of consumer credit: installment credit and   2
noninstallment credit. With **installment credit,** the consumer must
repay the amount owed in a specific number of equal payments,
usually monthly. For example, a $12,000 automobile loan might
require monthly payments of $255 for 60 months.

   Noninstallment credit includes single-payment loans [such as a
loan of $2000 plus $2000 at 12 percent interest with a single
payment of $2240 ($2000 plus $2000 × 0.12 due at the end of one
year)] and open-ended credit.

From E. Thomas Garman and Raymond E. Forgue, *Personal Finance,* fifth edition. Boston: Houghton Mifflin, 1997.

a. main idea: *There are two types . . . (first sentence)*

b. pattern: *comparison and contrast*

Simple restraint will help you avoid **impulse buying,** which is simply   3
buying without fully considering needs and alternatives. (For example,)
you may have shopped carefully by comparing various personal
computers and then selected one at a discount store. While at the
store, you impulsively pick up some games and entertainment
software that you had not planned to buy. The extra $245 spent on
an unplanned purchase ruins some of the benefits of the careful
shopping for the computer itself.

From Garman and Forgue, *Personal Finance,* fifth edition. Boston: Houghton Mifflin, 1997.

a. main idea: *Simple restraint . . . (first sentence)*

b. pattern: *example*

(An **element** is) *a pure substance that cannot be broken down into simpler*   4
substances, with different properties, by physical or chemical means. The
(elements are) the basic building blocks of all matter. There are now
109 known elements. Each has its own unique set of physical and
chemical properties. . . . The elements can be classified into three
types: **metals, nonmetals,** and **metalloids.**

From Sherman, Sherman, and Russikoff, *Basic Concepts of Chemistry,*
sixth edition. Boston: Houghton Mifflin, 1996.

a. main idea: *The elements are . . . (second sentence)*

b. pattern: *definition*

The environmental responsibility of firms is to avoid the contamination   5
of land, air, and water. Surveys by the Roper Organization Inc. found
that 62 percent of Americans believe that pollution is a very serious
threat to their health and the environment, and 75 percent say that
business should handle clean-up. (Because) business activities are a vital
part of the total environment, businesspeople have a responsibility to
help provide what society wants and to minimize harmful products and
conditions that it does not want.

From O. C. Ferrell and John Fraedrich, *Business Ethics,* second
edition. Boston: Houghton Mifflin, 1994.

a. main idea: *The environmental . . . (first sentence)*

b. pattern: *cause and effect*

To become a biochemist, you will need to take courses in biology,   6
chemistry, physics, and mathematics. You will need a minimum of a
baccalaureate degree and preferably a master's degree or doctorate in
biochemistry. Biochemists are employed by pharmaceutical companies,
chemical firms, hospitals, government research facilities, and universities.

From Sherman, Sherman, and Russikoff, *Basic Concepts of Chemistry,*
sixth edition. Boston: Houghton Mifflin, 1996.

a. main idea: *These are the requirements for a career as a biochemist. (Implied)*

b. pattern: *listing*

Score: 100 − 7 for each one missed = _____%

Vocabulary Quiz

Each sentence below contains a word in bold type from the reading selection on pages 189–191. Read the sentence and the definitions that follow it. Then circle the correct one. Turn to the vocabulary preview on pages 189–190 to check your answers.

1. May's employer says that she is **versatile** because she can type, do bookkeeping, and meet with the customers.
   a. a perfectionist
   b. punctual
   c. well liked by others
   (d.) able to do many things

2. Chris called Terry a **chauvinist** when Terry said that men are better drivers than women.
   a. one who does not care
   b. an imposter
   (c.) one who feels superior
   d. a whiner

3. Candy did not cry when she saw *Titanic*. In fact, her response was more **cerebral** because she was interested in the acting skill and camera work.
   (a.) intellectual
   b. emotional
   c. physical
   d. unprofessional

4. The only way to get good reception from a satellite dish is by **orienting** it in the right direction.
   a. removing
   b. turning off
   c. destroying
   (d.) locating

5. Instead of accepting someone else's word, John preferred **delving** into the facts himself.
   a. ignoring
   (b.) searching deeply
   c. not believing
   d. proving

6. Hearing a new song on the radio may **predispose** some listeners to buy the recording from which it is taken.
   a. alienate
   b. entertain
   (c.) cause to decide in advance
   d. increase popularity

7. It is **uncanny** how you always seem to know when I am going to call.
   (a.) strange
   b. embarrassing
   c. reassuring
   d. amusing

8. Why do you keep **tantalizing** me with that cake when you know I am on a diet?
   a. hurting
   b. humoring
   c. angering
   (d.) teasing

9. Finding the main idea is **crucial** to your understanding of the author's meaning.
   a. beside the point
   (b.) very important
   c. not necessary
   d. a major detail

10. Feeling grief over the loss of a loved one is an **innately** human reaction.
    a. occasional
    b. unexpected
    (c.) inborn
    d. unimportant

Score: 100 − 10 for each one missed = _____%

Unit

3

 Reading and Thinking Critically

Chapter 8

Using Textbook Reading Strategies

*I*n college, one of your major tasks is to read assigned textbook chapters. Many of your homework assignments, in-class assignments, group activities, and tests are based on the information presented in textbooks. In fact, you could say that the textbook is the core of almost any course.

How confident are you about your ability to read textbooks, learn the information, and recall it as needed? How would you describe the way you read a textbook chapter? Some students start at the beginning and read straight through to the end without stopping to think about what they have read. Reading this way is inefficient, and it results in poor comprehension and in memory loss. Instead, you should do what many successful students do: Use textbook reading strategies. What are these strategies, and how do they work?

This chapter explains how you can read your textbooks efficiently and confidently by using these strategies:

- ■ *Use your textbook's features.*
- ■ *Know how chapters are organized.*
- ■ *Use a reading system.*

WHAT DO YOU ALREADY KNOW?

To prepare yourself for the reading selection that follows, find out what you already know about making decisions. Answer the questions below either on your own or in a group discussion.

1. Do you usually make decisions quickly or slowly?

2. What kinds of decisions seem to be the most difficult?

3. How do you make a decision? Describe your thought process.

4. Read the title, headnote, vocabulary preview, and first two paragraphs of the reading selection. What do you think will follow?

Biases in Judgment

Saul Kassin

In this passage excerpted from a chapter in Psychology, *the author explains two ways people make decisions.*

VOCABULARY PREVIEW

intuitive	(ĭn tōō´ĭ tĭv) based on a sense or feeling rather than reasoning
probability	(prŏb´ə·bĭl´ĭ tē) likelihood
heuristics	(hyōō·rĭs´tĭ ks) methods used to solve problems
relevant	(rĕl´ə·vənt) related or connected to a topic under discussion
bias	(bī´əs) an error in statistics caused by favoring some outcomes over others; a preference for or against
consequence	(kŏn´sĭ·kwĕns´) result or effect
symptomatic	(sĭm´tə·măt´ĭk) based on

graphic (grăf′ĭc) represented in pictures; described clearly and vividly

random (răn′dəm) chance, having no pattern or purpose

Pronunciation Key: ă (p**a**t), ĕ (p**e**t), ē (b**ee**), ĭ (p**i**t), ī (p**ie**), ŏ (p**o**t), o͞o (b**oo**t), ə (**a**bout, it**e**m)

Should I buy the Toyota wagon or a Ford Taurus, a Macintosh or an IBM PC? Should my wife and I have more children? Should I coach little-league baseball again? Like everyone else, I could continue to list forever the kinds of decisions that are made every day—decisions that are based on **intuitive** judgments of **probability,** estimates we make of the likelihood of good and bad outcomes. How do we go about making these judgments? Do the decisions we make match those we *should* have made, based on actual, observable probabilities? In a series of studies, Daniel Kahneman, Amos Tversky, and others (1982) have found that people consistently use two **heuristics** in making these kinds of judgments: availability and representativeness.

Availability   One mental shortcut people use is the availability heuristic, the tendency to estimate the likelihood of an event based on how easily instances of that event come to mind. To demonstrate, Tversky and Kahneman (1973) asked subjects to judge whether there are more words in English that begin with the letter *k* or the letter *t.* To answer this question, subjects tried to think of words that started with each letter. More words came to mind that started with *t,* so most subjects correctly chose *t* as the answer. In this case, the availability heuristic was useful. It sure beat counting all the **relevant** words in the dictionary.

As demonstrated, the availability heuristic enables us to make judgments that are quick and easy—but often these judgments are in error. For example, Tversky and Kahneman asked some subjects the following question: Which is more common, words that start with the letter *k,* or words that contain *k* as the third letter? In actuality, the English language contains many more words with *k* as the third letter than the first; yet, out of 152 subjects, 105 guessed it to be the other way around. The reason for this disparity is that it's easier to bring to mind words that start with *k,* so these are judged more common.

The letter-estimation **bias** may seem cute and harmless, but the availability heuristic can lead us astray in important ways—as when

1

2

3

4

uncommon events pop easily to mind because they are very recent or highly emotional. One possible **consequence** concerns the perception of risk. Which is a more likely cause of death in the United States, being killed by falling airplane parts or being attacked by a shark? Shark attacks get more publicity, and most people say it is a more likely cause of death. Yet the chances of dying from falling airplane parts are thirty times greater ("Death Odds," 1990). Similarly, people who are asked to guess the major causes of death tend to overestimate the number of those who die in shootings, fires, floods, terrorist bombings, accidents, and other dramatic events (Slovic et al., 1982). With stories of drug dealing featured so prominently in the news, it is no wonder that Americans think that drug abuse is on the rise when, in fact, it is not (Eisenman, 1993).

A second consequence of the availability heuristic is that we are influenced more by one vivid life story than by hard statistical facts. Have you ever wondered why so many people buy lottery tickets despite the low odds, or why so many travelers are afraid to fly even though they're more likely to perish in a car accident? These behaviors are **symptomatic** of the fact that people are relatively insensitive to numerical probabilities and, instead, are overly influenced by **graphic** and memorable events like the sight of a multi-million dollar lottery winner rejoicing on TV, or a photograph of bodies being pulled from the wreckage of a plane crash (Bar-Hillel, 1980). It may not be logical, but one memorable image is worth a thousand numbers.

Representativeness   A second rule of thumb that people use to make probability estimates is the *representativeness heuristic*—the tendency to judge the likelihood of an event by how typical it seems (Kahneman & Tversky, 1973). Like other heuristics, this one enables us to make quick judgments. With speed, however, comes bias and a possible loss of accuracy. For example, which sequence of boys (B) and girls (G) would you say is more likely to occur in a family with six children: (1) B,G,B,G,B,G, (2) B,B,B,G,G,G, or (3) G,B,B,G,G,B? In actuality, these sequences are all equally likely. Yet most people say that the third is more likely than the others because it looks typical of a **random** sequence. . . . This use of the representativeness heuristic can give rise to a "gambler's fallacy" in games of chance.

The problem with this heuristic is that it often leads us to ignore numerical probabilities, or "base rates." Suppose I told you that there is a group of thirty engineers and seventy lawyers. In that group I randomly select a conservative man named Jack, who enjoys mathematical puzzles and has no interest in social or political issues. Question: Is Jack a lawyer or an engineer? When Kahneman and

Tversky (1973) presented this item to subjects, most guessed that Jack was an engineer (because he seemed to fit the stereotyped image of an engineer)—even though he came from a group containing a 70 percent majority of lawyers. In this instance, representativeness overwhelmed the more predictive base rate. . . .

HOW WELL DID YOU COMPREHEND?

Main Idea

1. Which of the following sentences best expresses the main idea of the reading selection?
   a. Each person's decision-making process differs.
   b. Everyday we make decisions based on expected outcomes.
   c. People consistently use two methods to make decisions.
   d. Some decisions are the result of bad judgments.

2. Which of the following sentences states the main idea of paragraph 5?
   a. the first sentence, "A second consequence . . ."
   b. the second sentence, "Have you ever . . ."
   c. the third sentence, "These behaviors . . ."
   d. the last sentence, "It may not be . . ."

Details

3. The experiment that asked subjects to judge whether there are more words in English that begin with the letter *k* or the letter *t* illustrates
   a. representativeness.
   b. availability.
   c. probability.
   d. intuition.

4. The experiment that asked subjects to predict the sequence of boys and girls in a family of six illustrates
   a. representativeness.
   b. availability.
   c. probability.
   d. intuition.

5. Most subjects guessed that Jack was an engineer because
    a. they paid attention to the base rate.
    b. they used a mental shortcut.
    c. they lacked sufficient information.
    (d.) they responded to a stereotype.

Inferences

6. The "gambler's fallacy" (paragraph 6) probably means that gamblers
    a. do not expect to win.
    b. often cheat at games of chance.
    (c.) believe they can predict winning numbers.
    d. do not know that the odds are against them.

Working with Words

Complete the sentences below with these words from the vocabulary preview.

intuitive	probability	heuristics	relevant	random
bias	consequence	symptomatic	graphic	

1. In a lottery, the winning numbers are selected at _____*random*_____.

2. Therefore, choosing a winning number is neither _____*intuitive*_____ nor rational but a matter of luck.

3. Although the _____*probability*_____ of selecting a winning lottery number is very low, many people still play.

4. Advertisements for state lotteries often show _____*graphic*_____ examples of luxuries winners will be able to afford.

5. One unfortunate _____*consequence*_____ of lotteries is that people who cannot afford to play often do.

6. A belief that your number will eventually come up could be _____*symptomatic*_____ of a gambling problem.

7. Some state officials have shown a _____*bias*_____ in favor of lotteries as a source of income.

8. These officials seem unwilling to consider other _____*relevant*_____ sources of public funding.

9. In fact, our leaders' policies often show a lack of the _____*heuristics*_____ that can foster good decision making.

Thinking and Writing

Try out the availability experiment explained in paragraph 2. On a sheet of paper, list as many words as you can think of that begin with the letter *k*. Then list as many words as you can think of that begin with the letter *t*. Time yourself for two minutes. When you have finished your lists, count the number of words in each. Which list is longer? Do your results match those of the experimenters? Write your results below.

Answers will vary. _____

_____

_____

_____

USE YOUR TEXTBOOK'S FEATURES

Although textbooks differ and some may be more difficult than others, they do have two things in common. All textbooks contain large amounts of information for you to learn. Also, textbooks have certain *features,* or learning aids, that make reading and studying easier. To use a textbook efficiently and confidently, you must take advantage of seven common features described in Figure 8.1 on page 230.

Preface

The *preface,* or introduction, comes at the beginning of the textbook and may provide some or all of the following information:

- The author's purpose for writing the book
- The author's topics or major points
- How the book is organized
- How to use the book's learning aids

This information gives you an overview of the text so that you know what to expect. For an example, read or review "To the Student" on

FIGURE 8.1 Seven Textbook Features	
PREFACE	The *preface* provides information such as the book's topic, purpose, organization, and learning aids.
TABLE OF CONTENTS	The *table of contents* breaks down the book into parts and chapters.
TYPOGRAPHICAL AIDS	*Typographical aids* include the type, size, and color of print; numbers or letters; headings and subheadings.
QUESTIONS OR PROBLEMS	Most textbooks contain exercises for practice and review.
GLOSSARY	The *glossary* lists terms and their definitions.
GRAPHICS	*Graphics* include charts, tables, figures, and diagrams.
INDEX	The *index* lists topics alphabetically for easy reference.

page xvii of this text. As you can see, the *author's purpose* is to help you become a confident reader. The book's *topics* include the reading strategies that will help you become a confident reader. The book is *organized* into several units, or parts, that include chapters and additional reading selections. The author also lists and explains how to use each chapter's *learning aids.*

Exercise 8.1

Working with a partner, choose any textbook that you have with you and read the introduction together. Then answer the following questions. *(Answers will vary depending on textbook chosen.)*

1. What is the book's title?

    _____

    _____

2. What is the author's purpose?

    _____

    _____

3. What topics or points are covered?

_____

_____

4. How is the book organized?

_____

_____

5. What learning aids are provided?

_____

_____

6. What else did you learn from the introduction that is not covered
    in questions 1–4?

_____

_____

Table of Contents

One way to get a quick overview of a textbook is to glance through
its table of contents, which may provide some or all of the following
information.

- The parts, units, or other major divisions of the text
- The chapters or other material contained in each part
- The topics that are covered in each chapter

The table of contents not only illustrates how the text is organized,
but it also provides a detailed outline of the book. For an example, turn
to the table of contents on pages v–xii and briefly glance over it. As you
can see, *Becoming a Confident Reader* contains five units. Units 1–3 contain Chapters 1–10, and Unit 4 contains additional readings. Headings
and subheadings are listed and indented under each chapter title.

Headings and subheadings divide chapters into sections. They call
your attention to main ideas and major details within each section.
Also, they help you predict what a section is about. Chapter headings

and subheadings listed in order in the table of contents reveal an author's hidden outline.

As mentioned in Chapters 1 and 6, a good prereading step is to turn to the table of contents and glance over a chapter's headings and subheadings to familiarize yourself with the topics covered.

Exercise 8.2 Choose any textbook that you have with you and glance over the table of contents. Then answer the following questions. *(Answers will vary but should reflect the chosen textbook's contents.)*

1. What is the textbook's title?

    _____

    _____

2. How many parts is the book divided into? Write the title of one of the parts.

    _____

    _____

3. How many chapters does the book contain? Write the title of one of the chapters.

    _____

    _____

4. Select a chapter that is broken down into headings with subheadings. On the lines below, list one heading and the subheadings that follow it.

    _____

    _____

    _____

    _____

    _____

Typographical Aids

Typographical aids include the size, type, and color of print and the way lines of print are arranged on a page. These aids make important ideas stand out so that you will be sure to notice them. The typographical aids do not exist merely to make the book attractive. On the contrary, their purpose is to guide your reading and keep your attention focused. Several typographical aids you should look for include:

- Italic, bold, or colored type
- Numbers, letters, or bullets
- Headings and subheadings

Italic type is slanted. *Bold* type is thick and dark. These types of print call your attention to words, terms, and definitions that you should learn and remember. Colored type can be used for different purposes: to emphasize terms, definitions, or important ideas. In some textbooks, headings and subheadings are printed in color to make them stand out. Headings and subheadings also separate the chapter into sections that can be read as units.

Numbers (1,2,3, and so on) or *letters* (a,b,c, and so on) help you find important ideas or facts. Numbers and letters have two purposes: They make ideas or facts stand out, and they break down complex ideas or concepts into steps or parts, making them easier to read. In some textbooks *bullets* (small dots, squares, or other shapes) are used in place of numbers or letters. Notice how the numbers in the following excerpt from *Personal Finance* by E. Thomas Garman and Raymond E. Forgue make the major details stand out:

What Employers Want

In a survey of more than 100 corporate employers, Rensselaer Polytechnic Institute's Tom Tarantelli reports that employers are most interested in (1) interpersonal skills, (2) ability to solve problems, (3) communications skills, (4) technical knowledge, (5) energy level, and (6) judgment. While grades are very important in getting the initial chance at an interview, employers want to hire people who are well-rounded, can get along well with others, and can participate effectively as a member of a team.

The main idea of this excerpt is that employers want employees to have certain qualities or skills. The numbered details tell you what the qualities and skills are.

Memory Cue

The preface *and* table of contents *both provide an overview of the textbook's organization. In addition, the preface explains the author's purpose and topic and any learning aids that are included.* Typographical aids *include italics, bold, and colored type; numbers and letters; and headings and subheadings. These textbook features call your attention to what is important.*

Exercise 8.3

Select a chapter from any textbook you have available. Briefly glance through the chapter to determine its typographical aids. Then answer the following questions. *(Answers vary depending on the typographical aids present in students' chosen textbooks.)*

1. What is the textbook chapter's title?

   _____

2. Which of the following types of print are used?

   _____ a.   italics

   _____ b.   bold

   _____ c.   colored type

3. For each type of print you checked above, how it is used?

   italics

   _____ a.   for terms

   _____ b.   for definitions

   _____ c.   to make an important idea stand out

   bold

   _____ a.   for terms

   _____ b.   for definitions

   _____ c.   to make an important idea stand out

   colored type

   _____ a.   for terms or definitions

   _____ b.   to make an important idea stand out

   _____ c.   for headings or subheadings

4. Did you find any numbered lists or items identified by letters or bullets?

_____ yes

_____ no

5. If you answered *yes* above, what type of information was listed by number or identified by letter or bullets?

_____

_____

6. Write one of the chapter headings on the line below.

_____

7. Read the information between the heading you listed above and the one that follows it. Then briefly explain in your own words what the section covers.

_____

_____

_____

8. Based on the chapter heading you listed in question 6 above, did the section contain what you thought it would?

_____ yes

_____ no

9. Did paying attention to the heading improve your understanding of what you read in the section following it? How?

_____

_____

Questions or Problems

An important part of the learning process is to be able to use, or apply, what you have learned. This is what tests are all about. Can you apply what you have learned in a new situation? To be able to perform successfully on a test, you must practice applying your knowledge. *Questions* and *problems* given as exercises provide the practice.

In this textbook, the exercises appear throughout the chapter. However, in some textbooks, exercises come at the end of the chapter. If you do not answer the questions or solve the problems, you miss out on an essential step in your learning process. Taking time to do the questions and problems—even when they are not assigned—has four important benefits:

- To help you prepare for tests
- To help you discover what you do and do not know
- To provide essential skill practice
- To encourage critical thinking

Glossary

As explained in Chapter 2, a dictionary entry may provide several different definitions for a single word. One or more definitions may be identified as a special term of a discipline. For example, *psych.* before a definition indicates that this definition is used only in psychology.

The special terms in your textbooks are usually printed in italic, bold, or colored type and are usually defined in context. In addition, these terms may be collected into a *glossary* found near the end of the textbook. A glossary is a brief dictionary of the terms used in the text. These definitions may vary a little from chapter definitions. Therefore, when you are learning new terms, it is a good idea to read both definitions. One of them may be easier for you to understand.

Does one or more of your textbooks have a glossary? If you do not know, then glance through all your textbooks as soon as you can to determine whether they contain this useful feature. See also Figure 8.2, which shows an excerpt from the glossary of a psychology textbook.

Graphics

Because textbook information may be difficult and unfamiliar to many students, authors use graphics to illustrate their ideas. *Graphics* include charts, tables, figures, diagrams, and pictures. When you are pressed for

---

FIGURE 8.2 Excerpt From a Textbook Glossary

A-27

self-control, and seek parental help for even the slightest problems. *(p 410)*

Personality   The pattern of psychological and behavioral characteristics by which each person can be compared and contrasted with other people; the unique pattern of characteristics that emerges from the blending of inherited and acquired tendencies to make each person an identifiable individual. *(p. 458)*

Personality disorder   Long-standing, inflexible ways of behaving that are not so much severe mental disorders as styles of life, which, from childhood or adolescence, create problems, usually for others. *(p. 520)*

Personality psychologist   A psychologist who focuses on the unique characteristics that determine individuals' behavior. *(p. 16)*

Person-centered therapy   See *client-centered therapy.*

Person-oriented leaders   Leaders who provide loose supervision, ask for group members' ideas, and are generally concerned with subordinates' feelings; they are usually well liked by those they lead. *(p. 623)*

Phallic stage   The third of Freud's psychosexual stages, lasting from approximately ages three to five, in which the focus of pleasure shifts to the genital area; the Oedipus complex occurs during this stage. (See also *Oedipus complex.*) *(p. 461)*

From Douglas A. Bernstein, et al., *Psychology,* fourth edition. Boston: Houghton Mifflin, 1997, p. A-27.

time, you may be tempted to skip over these graphics and continue reading. However, you should avoid the temptation. Graphics contain important information essential to your understanding. The key to graphics is knowing how to read them. Chapter 9 explains a strategy you can use to read graphics with understanding.

Index

The *index* lists topics alphabetically, and it is found near the end of most textbooks. All the important topics, including names of people mentioned, are listed in the index along with the pages where you can find them. If you need to review a topic but cannot remember exactly where to find it, use the index.

Memory Cue

Questions or problems *provide essential practice.* Graphics *illustrate key concepts and processes. The* glossary *and* index *are reference tools.*

Exercise 8.4

As a review, match the textbook features in Column A with their definitions in Column B.

Column A

<u> b </u> 1. preface
<u> e </u> 2. typographical aids
<u> g </u> 3. questions or problems
<u> f </u> 4. table of contents
<u> c </u> 5. glossary
<u> d </u> 6. graphics
<u> a </u> 7. index

Column B

a. lists topics covered in the book
b. a textbook's introduction
c. lists definitions of terms
d. charts, tables, and so on
e. italic, bold, or colored print
f. lists the book's chapters
g. exercises for practice

KNOW HOW CHAPTERS ARE ORGANIZED

Although textbooks vary, most chapters follow a basic organizational plan that may include these five important features:

- Title
- Chapter introduction
- Learning goals or objectives
- Headings and subheadings
- Summary

The *title* states the author's topic and may be a key to the chapter's central idea. For example, this chapter's title tells you that the topic is reading strategies.

The *chapter introduction* may build background for the topic, state the author's purpose, or provide a brief preview of what to expect. Some introductions consist of only the first paragraph. Others may be longer. For example, this chapter's introduction consists of the first three paragraphs. The author's purpose is to show you how to read textbooks efficiently and confidently. Three reading strategies listed at the end of the introduction tell you what to expect.

Some authors provide *learning goals* or *objectives.* These explain what you are supposed to learn or be able to do after reading the chapter. Goals or objectives may be listed either before or after the introduction. For example, this chapter's learning goals follow the introduction. The three strategies listed explain what you should be able to do after reading the chapter.

Headings and *subheadings* break up the chapter into smaller units both for easier reading and to highlight important ideas. As explained in Chapters 1 and 6, the title, headings, and subheadings together provide an outline of the chapter. For example, the first heading in this chapter is "Use Your Textbook's Features." The first subheading is "Preface." As you can see from the heading and subheading, *textbook features* is the overall topic. *Preface* is one of the features.

The chapter summary, if there is one, comes near the end of the chapter. The *summary* is a brief review of the chapter that restates the author's most important ideas. For example, this chapter's summary on pages 249–250 is titled "How Well Do You Remember?"

Why is it important to determine how a textbook's chapters are organized? First of all, different authors organize chapters in different ways. For example, in some textbooks the chapters do not have summaries. Some authors do not list objectives at the beginning. The number of headings and subheadings also varies. *However, each chapter within a single textbook is organized the same way.* So if you know how the chapters in your textbook are organized, you will know what to expect. Also, when you review a chapter, you will know where to find the information you need.

Exercise 8.5 Examine a chapter from one of your other textbooks for the five features of chapter organization. Then answer the following questions. *(Answers vary depending on the features of the textbook chapter chosen.)*

1. What is the chapter's title?

_____

2. Based on the title, what do you think is the author's topic?

_____

3. Does the chapter have an introduction? How many paragraphs?

_____

4. Based on the introduction, what do you think is the author's purpose? What are you expected to learn?

_____

_____

5. Does the chapter list learning goals? If so, where?

_____

6. List one of the chapter headings.

_____

7. Turn the heading into a question to guide your reading.

_____

8. Does the chapter have a summary? If so, what else does the summary tell you about the chapter?

_____

_____

Memory Cue

Most textbook chapters have five important features: title, introduction, learning goals or objectives, headings and subheadings, *and* summary. *Use these features to guide your reading and review.*

USE A READING SYSTEM

A reading system is a method or process that helps you read actively. The best reading system is one that you develop after trying several strategies and determining which ones work best for you. Figure 8.3 lists six strategies for you to try.

FIGURE 8.3 Six Reading Strategies

Strategy	Purpose
SQ3R	Use this system for reading textbook chapters.
SKIM	Glance over a page or section to get an idea of what it is about. (topic and main idea)
SCAN	Glance over a page to find a specific piece of information such as a name or a date.
MARK	Highlight, underline, or write marginal notes to make important information stand out.
OUTLINE	Outline textbook sections or whole chapters to use as review sheets.
MAP	Make diagrams or charts to use as study guides.

SQ3R

SQ3R is a system you may have heard of that has helped many students. SQ3R stands for *survey, question, read, recite,* and *review.* These five steps tell you how to preview, read, and review a textbook chapter.

Survey   A survey is a preview or overview of a chapter to get an idea of what it covers. To survey a chapter, start at the beginning and briefly look over its features. Read the title, introduction, headings, subheadings, and summary. These will give you the chapter's outline. Your survey should help you answer two questions: "What is this chapter about?" and "What am I supposed to learn?" Surveying chapters before you read lets you know what to expect.

Question   During your survey, and at any time during your reading process, turn headings and subheadings into questions and use them to guide your reading. As you read, look for the answer to your question. For example, this section's heading is "Use a Reading System." Two questions you could ask yourself are "What is a reading system?" and "What system should I use?" Both questions are answered in the first paragraph under "Use a Reading System" on page 240.

Read   After you survey the chapter, begin reading slowly and carefully. Take one section at a time. Look at the heading, turn it into a question, then read to find the answer. If your question is not answered, look at the heading again. Try to determine how the heading relates to what you have read. Be sure you understand a section before you start reading the next one. In addition, take time to read and think about graphics such as charts, diagrams, and pictures. Pay special attention to terms and definitions.

Recite　When you finish a section, take a moment to recite in your own words the important points you have learned. What ideas stand out? What terms are important to know? Remember that words in italics, bold, or colored print are clues.

Review　After you have read the chapter one section at a time, review the whole chapter. Begin your review by looking again at the summary, which is a condensed version of the important ideas stated throughout the chapter. Or you could survey the chapter again as part of your review. Read each heading and try to recall what is in the section following it. As you become aware of gaps in your understanding, you may need to reread and review certain sections of the chapter.

Do these steps sound familiar? If you have read and completed this chapter's exercises so far, you have already had some practice with the steps of SQ3R. For example, the questions in Exercises 8.1–8.3 require you to *survey* textbooks and chapters and turn a heading into a *question*. The Memory Cue on page 238 and Exercise 8.4 help you *review* what you have read up to that point. To complete an exercise successfully, you must *read* carefully the section that comes before. Now try out the *recite* step by completing the next exercise.

Exercise 8.6　Do this exercise with a partner. The following questions are based on the information presented so far in this chapter. Let one person read a question aloud while the other recites the answer. Look back through the chapter to check the answer before going to the next question. Then repeat the process so that each person has a chance to read questions and recite answers.

1. What kind of information is contained in a book's preface?

   The preface may explain the author's topic, purpose, organization,

   and learning aids.

2. Where in a textbook can you look up the meaning of an unfamiliar term?

   The glossary contains terms and definitions.

3. What textbook feature includes type, size, and color of print?

   Typographical aids include type, size, color, and so on.

4. What is the purpose of questions and problems?

Questions and problems provide skill practice and review.

5. Why are graphics (charts, pictures, diagrams) important?

They contain information essential to your understanding.

6. Why should you read a chapter summary?

The summary reviews the author's most important ideas.

7. Where in a textbook will you find the page number of a topic you want to review?

Topics are listed in the index.

8. What is the purpose of SQ3R?

SQ3R is a system for reading textbooks actively.

9. When should you survey a chapter?

Survey a chapter before you read it or as part of a review.

10. How do you survey a chapter?

Read title, introduction, objectives, headings and subheadings,

and summary.

Skimming and Scanning

When you _skim,_ you briefly glance over a paragraph or passage to get a rough idea of what it is about: its topic, purpose, or main idea. For example, when you quickly look through a newspaper article to get a quick idea of what the story is about, you are skimming. You also use skimming when you survey a chapter or glance through the introduction before you do your careful reading.

When you _scan,_ you glance over a page or more to find a specific bit of information. For example, you scan the page of a telephone book to find a number. When you look up a word in the dictionary or glance through an article to find a name or a date, you are scanning.

Skimming and scanning are useful review activities. If you are looking for the answer to a question, first find the section in your textbook that covers the information. Skim the headings (main ideas) until you find the right section. Then scan the section to find the answer to your question.

Exercise 8.7 Listed below are several kinds of activities for which skimming or scanning may be useful. Identify which activities call for skimming and which call for scanning. The first one is done as an example.

skim 1. Determine the point of a newspaper article.

scan 2. Find a website on the Internet.

skim 3. Find the main idea of a textbook section.

scan 4. Look for a restaurant in the phonebook.

skim 5. Determine the subject of a paperback book.

scan 6. Find a topic in an index.

scan 7. Locate a city on a map.

Marking Your Textbook

Your memory works in interesting ways. You remember some things and forget others. Usually, you remember best what you decide to remember. For example, when you mark your textbook, you are saying to yourself, "I will remember this."

Marking strategies include *underlining, highlighting,* and *writing notes in the margin.* Some students develop their own marking systems. For example, a star in the margin means, "This is important." Some students use common abbreviations to call their attention to important material. For example, *def.* beside a sentence means that sentence contains the definition of an important term. *Ex.* beside a sentence means an example is given. When steps are listed but not numbered, some students write 1, 2, 3, and so on, in front of the sentences that state the steps. Whatever marking system you use is fine because the best marking systems are those you develop through trial and error. In general, here are some suggestions:

- Read before you mark.
- Read and then mark one section at a time.
- Underline or highlight main ideas and important details.
- Do not underline or highlight too much.

Many students ask, "How can I tell what is important?" The following guidelines may help.

1. **Main ideas are important.** Look for main ideas near the beginning of sections. Remember that headings are clues to main ideas of sections.
2. **Details are important.** Use typographical aids such as numbers and letters to help you locate details. Watch for transitions (*for example, such as, also, another*, and so on) that signal details.
3. **Graphics are important.** Charts, tables, and diagrams illustrate key concepts. Read the graphic. Then find and underline the part of the text that explains it. Chapter 9 explains how to read graphics.
4. **Exercises are important.** Exercises always require you to recall or apply key concepts. The answers to some exercise questions are stated in the text. Find these answers and underline them.

Now read the following textbook passage from *Personal Finance* by E. Thomas Garman and Raymond E. Forgue and notice the way it is marked.

Why do women earn less than men?

According to the bureau of the Census, the median earnings of all women workers now stands at 74 percent of the median earnings of men—a higher ratio than the 59 percent seen in 1977. <u>A Working Woman survey revealed that women earn 5 to 15 cents less on the dollar than men in similar jobs.</u> This pay gap exists <u>because</u> the overall labor force remains sharply segregated by gender, with

first reason

①<u>women typically being concentrated in many traditionally low-paying careers.</u> The gap is most pronounced for older women workers. Women make up the great majority of employees in health services, social work, public teaching, bookkeeping, banking, retail trade, insurance, and clerical work; these fields have been dominated by women for decades. Many employers continue to quietly label such positions as "female" jobs and pay low wages to the

second reason

people who perform them. ②<u>Another reason for the differential in pay is that women have traditionally found it difficult to break through the so-called **glass ceiling** (an informal barrier to promotion) and reach higher-paid positions.</u>

similar qualifications may mean similar pay.

The Pacific Research Institute reports that when men and women with the same level of education, field of study, and work experience are compared, pay is virtually identical.

According to the authors, most women make less than men for two reasons: More women than men typically work at low-paying jobs, and women have difficulty being promoted to high-paying positions. However, when men and women have the same qualifications, they receive virtually the same pay. The underlining and marginal notes make these ideas stand out.

Exercise 8.8   Select a section from a chapter in one of your textbooks that you have been assigned to read. First, read the section. Next, mark the section using the guidelines explained on pages 244–246. Show your work to your instructor for evaluation and suggestions. *(Textbooks chosen and students' marking will vary. They should mark main ideas, major details, and important terms.)*

Outlining and Mapping

Reading textbooks is difficult for many students because the information is often new or unfamiliar. Reading systems such as SQ3R, skimming and scanning, and marking your textbook take you only so far. These strategies help you read with understanding and find important information.

To remember what you have read, you need two additional strategies: *outlining* and *mapping*. Using these strategies, you can make study guides that will refresh your memory as you review. An *outline* is a list of related ideas. A *map* is a diagram of related ideas. Figure 8.4 shows an outline and a map of the same information.

According to psychologist Abraham Maslow, people are motivated by five levels of need. Lower-level needs must be met first. Biological needs are at the lowest level. Psychologists refer to these needs as *Maslow's hierarchy*. Suppose you were taking a psychology course, and you knew that you would be responsible for remembering Maslow's hierarchy. Either the map or the outline in Figure 8.4 could serve as a memory aid. Notice that both the outline and map provide the same information. However, some students will prefer the map for two reasons. First of all, the diagram may be easier to remember. Second, the diagram shows that biological levels are the lowest level. They are at the base of the triangle.

Exercise 8.9   Review the excerpt titled "What Employers Want" on page 233. Then complete the outline that follows.

1. Employers are most interested in

   a. *interpersonal skills*

   b. *ability to solve problems*

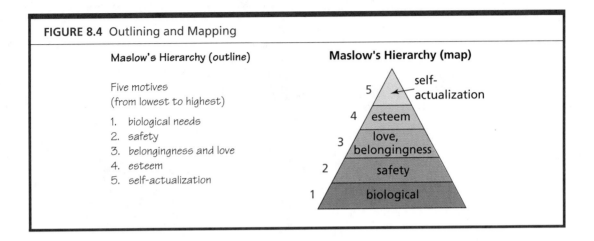

FIGURE 8.4 Outlining and Mapping

Maslow's Hierarchy (outline)

Five motives
(from lowest to highest)

1. biological needs
2. safety
3. belongingness and love
4. esteem
5. self-actualization

Maslow's Hierarchy (map)

5 self-actualization
4 esteem
3 love, belongingness
2 safety
1 biological

c. <u>*communications skills*</u>

d. <u>*technical knowledge*</u>

e. <u>*energy level*</u>

f. <u>*judgment*</u>

2. Employers also want people who

a. <u>*are well-rounded*</u>

b. <u>*can get along well with others*</u>

c. <u>*can participate as a team member*</u>

Exercise 8.10   Read the following passage and complete the map that follows.

Fringe Benefits

In addition to their salaries, most employees expect to receive fringe benefits. A *fringe benefit* is a type of payment, or compensation, for work that is not part of an employee's regular salary or commission. For example, *paid leave* for vacations, holidays, and illness is one kind of fringe benefit. *Insurance and health services* are another type of fringe benefit. Employees expect employers to pay for health insurance, life insurance, maternity leave, and other such services. Some companies

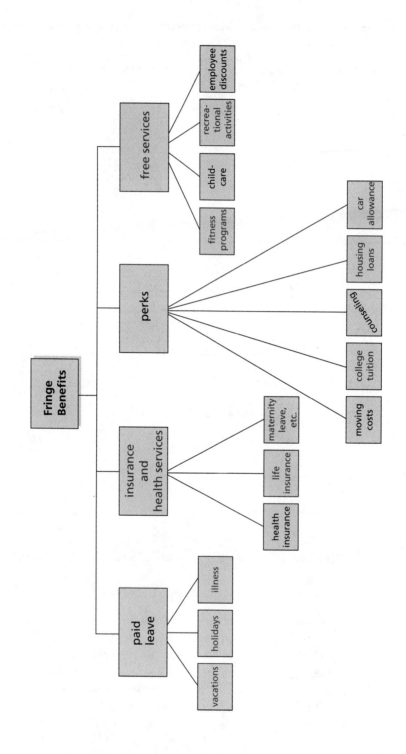

offer *perquisites,* or "perks." These fringe benefits may include paid moving costs, college tuition, counseling, housing loans, and a car allowance. In addition to these benefits, some employers provide various *free services* such as fitness programs, child care, recreational activities, and employee discounts on company products.

REAL-WORLD CONNECTIONS

Outlining is a versatile strategy you can use for reading and studying and for planning reports, speeches, and essays.

Working in a group, use outlining to plan a short report that you will present to the rest of the class. The topic of your report will be "a useful reading strategy." Choose any reading strategy covered in Chapters 1–8. In your report, cover these three major points:

1. What is the strategy?
2. Where and how have you used it?
3. What were the results?

To plan your report, discuss the three major points and decide what you will say. Outline your report on one side of a 5 × 8 card. Write the names of group members on the other side. Choose one group member to present the report to the class. *(Students' reports and outlines should follow the instructions given.)*

HOW WELL DO YOU REMEMBER?

To review the chapter, read the following summary and fill in the blanks. If you need help with an answer, look back through the chapter to refresh your memory.

Textbooks have several features that make reading and learning more efficient. For example, the ____preface____ may state the author's purpose or tell you how to use the book. The ____contents____ show you how the book is organized. *Typographical aids* include the size, type, and color of print. ____Questions____ and ____problems____ are for skill practice.

Use the ___glossary___ to look up terms and definitions. To look up a topic or a name, use the ___index___. Also, pay attention to ___graphics___ such as charts, tables, and diagrams.

Textbook chapters are organized in predictable ways. The ___title___ states the topic. The ___introduction___ may state the author's purpose or tell you what to expect. Some chapters begin with a list of ___learning goals___ or ___objectives___. ___Headings___ and ___subheadings___ break down a chapter into sections. The ___summary___ is a brief review of the author's important ideas.

To improve the way you read and learn, develop a reading system that includes some of these strategies. *SQ3R*, an old reliable system, has five steps: ___survey___, ___question___, ___read___, ___recite___, and ___review___. To find information quickly, use ___skimming___ or ___scanning___. Marking your textbook and making study guides are also useful strategies.

WHAT DO YOU THINK?

Everyone's approach to reading and learning is different. This chapter emphasizes the importance of trying different strategies then choosing the ones that work best for you. What have you learned from this chapter that seems especially helpful? Write your reflections below.

Reflections will vary. _____

_____

_____

_____

CHAPTER QUIZ 1

Part 1 Terms and Definitions

Match this chapter's special terms in Column A with their definitions in Column B.

Column A

   d   1. features
   f   2. preface
   b   3. glossary
   e   4. index
   a   5. graphics
   c   6. table of contents

Column B

a. charts, tables, diagrams, and so on
b. lists terms and definitions
c. lists parts and chapters
d. textbook learning aids
e. lists topics alphabetically
f. introduction

Part 2 Chapter Review

Read and answer each question below. Write your answer in complete sentences, and use extra paper if needed. *(Answers will vary but should be similar to these.)*

1. What are the steps of SQ3R, and what is the purpose of this reading system?

   SQ3R helps you read actively. The steps are survey, question, read, recite,

   review.

2. How can you tell what is important in a chapter?

   Headings, subheadings, typographical aids, and graphics are clues to a

   chapter's important ideas.

3. What is the purpose of outlining and mapping?

   Outlining and mapping help you see how ideas are related. You can

   use these strategies to make study guides.

Part 3 Using Your Skills

Read the following paragraphs that describe students engaged in typical reading or study tasks. Decide which step of SQ3R each one is using. Write the step on the line beside the paragraph.

<u>read</u> 1. Cindy learned in her reading class that underlining and making notes as you read are active reading strategies. While doing an assignment for her biology class, she underlines important ideas and makes notes in the margin.

<u>question</u> 2. Carlos has just finished reading a section of a psychology chapter that he does not understand. He decides to try again. As he comes to a heading, he turns it into a question that he will try to answer as he reads.

<u>survey</u> 3. Bonnie is in the library researching articles on Attention Deficit Disorder. One article looks good, but she is not sure whether it provides the information she needs. To find out, she does a preview of its title, introduction, and summary.

<u>review</u> 4. Lawrence has an important American government test coming up this week. Fortunately, he has highlighted the important ideas in the chapters that he knows will be on the test. Rather than rereading the chapter, he looks over the parts he has marked.

<u>recite</u> 5. After reading any chapter, Ping makes a list of its important terms. Then she repeats aloud the terms and their definitions.

Score: 100 − 7 for each one missed = _____ %

CHAPTER QUIZ 2

Part 1 Terms and Definitions

Match this chapter's special terms in Column A with their definitions in Column B.

Column A

<u>e</u>	1. objectives
<u>d</u>	2. headings
<u>b</u>	3. boldface
<u>f</u>	4. italic
<u>a</u>	5. summary
<u>c</u>	6. typographical aids

Column B

a. brief review
b. thick, dark type
c. size and color of print
d. divide chapters into sections
e. learning goals
f. slanted type

Part 2 Chapter Review

Read and answer each question below. Write your answer in complete sentences, and use extra paper if needed. *(Answers may vary but should be similar to these.)*

1. What is the purpose of exercises and problems?

   Exercises and problems help you apply what you have learned. They

   provide needed practice.

2. What is the difference between skimming and scanning?

   Use skimming to get an overall idea of what a chapter, section, or entire

   article is about. Use scanning to find a specific piece of information.

3. What are the steps of an effective textbook-marking system?

   Read before you mark, do one section at a time, mark main ideas and

   important details, and do not mark too much.

Part 3 Using Your Skills

Read the following paragraphs that describe students engaged in typical reading or study tasks. Decide whether each student is applying the skill of skimming or scanning. Write *skim* or *scan* on the line beside the paragraph.

skim 1. Noelle has decided to do a research paper on the effects of cigarette advertising on women. She looks through the *Reader's Guide* for recent magazine articles on smoking and women.

scan 2. Rick is studying for a chemistry test. As he reviews his notes, he cannot remember the difference between a mixture and a compound. He checks the glossary for definitions of these terms.

skim 3. Jeff plans to take a science elective next term. He has always had an interest in rock formations and thinks he might enjoy taking geology. While in the campus bookstore, he picks up a copy of the book that is required for the course. He does a quick survey of it to get an idea of what the course might cover.

scan 4. Rosa's student success class is discussing the effectiveness of birth control methods. The professor hands out a chart that lists birth control methods and their effectiveness rates. The professor asks Rosa which of the methods has the lowest rate of effectiveness.

skim 5. Hank has been following the progress of an investigation into cellular phone fraud. As he is leaving for campus, he notices that the headline in the morning newspaper concerns the case. Having no time to read the article, he quickly looks over it to get to the point.

<u>*scan*</u>   6.   Stephanie has just finished reading an assignment for her personal finance course and is now doing the questions at the end of the chapter. The first one asks her to explain the difference between installment and noninstallment credit. She turns to the section in the chapter that covers this topic and looks for the answer.

Score: $100 - 7$ for each one missed = _____ %

Vocabulary Quiz

Each sentence below contains a word in bold type from the reading selection on pages 224–227. Read the sentence and the definitions that follow it. Then circle the correct one. Turn to the vocabulary preview on pages 224–225 to check your answers.

1.   With reliable **heuristics,** you should be able to solve most problems.
     a. medications
     b. relaxation techniques
     c. problem-solving methods
     d. partners or groups

2.   Winning lottery numbers are chosen at **random** rather than in any particular order.
     a. well organized
     b. having no pattern
     c. in order
     d. beforehand

3.   Most of the time a poor grade is the **consequence** of not studying.
     a. result
     b. fear
     c. effort
     d. blame

4.   Movies that show **graphic** scenes of sex and violence may get an "adults only" rating.
     a. fully edited
     b. dark

(c.) clearly pictured
d. gloomy

5. Child or spouse abuse is almost always **symptomatic** of a personality disorder.
   a. improper
   b. unbelievable
   c. unrelated
   (d.) based on

6. Although the tennis players were evenly matched, Rachel had the **intuitive** belief that she would win the game.
   a. logical
   (b.) feeling or sensing
   c. insupportable
   d. strange

7. Instead of discussing the issues, politicians will often speak on topics that are not **relevant.**
   a. well known
   b. appropriate
   c. interesting
   (d.) related

8. In all **probability** the weather will be bad because the forecast calls for rain, and it is already cold and cloudy.
   (a.) likelihood
   b. honesty
   c. humility
   d. occasions

9. This report shows **bias** because the people surveyed were carefully selected on the basis of their political beliefs.
   a. persuasion
   b. clear thinking
   (c.) a statistical error
   d. lack of effort

Score: 100 − 10 for each one missed = _____%

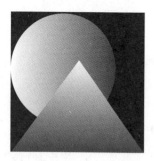

Chapter 9

Reading Graphics with Understanding

O pen any textbook, thumb through it, and you will see charts, tables, diagrams, and other visual aids. These aids are called *graphics,* and they are very important because they illustrate and often simplify difficult ideas.

Graphics are *visual* aids, meaning that they appeal to your sense of sight. You've heard the old saying, "A picture is worth a thousand words." For example, what takes several paragraphs or pages to explain may be condensed into one small chart or table. A difficult process involving many steps may be illustrated by a single diagram that enables you to visualize the process.

Graphics can serve as memory aids. Suppose you are given an exam question that asks you to explain the steps of a process such as the water cycle that leads to cloud formation and rain. At first you do not know where to begin. Then you recall the diagram that you studied. You can see the steps clearly in your mind. Now all you have to do is write your explanation.

This chapter explains three strategies that will improve the way you read and use graphics:

- Use PRT to read graphics.
- Recognize four types of graphics.
- Make your own graphics.

WHAT DO YOU ALREADY KNOW?

To prepare yourself for the reading selection that follows, find out what you already know about diseases of the blood and their treatment. Answer the questions below either on your own or in a group discussion.

1. What do you know about diseases of the blood?

2. As far as you know, are such diseases curable?

3. What have you read or heard about the uses of umbilical cord blood?

4. Read the title, headnote, vocabulary preview, and first paragraph of the reading selection. What do you think will follow?

Seizing Nature's Lifeline

Claudia Kalb and Melinda Beck

In this article from Newsweek, *the authors discuss possible uses for the blood from an infant's umbilical cord.*

VOCABULARY PREVIEW

vivacious	(vĭ·vā′shəs) lively, full of spirit
revive	(rĭ·vīv′) bring back to life or health
chemotherapy	(kē′mō·thĕr′ə·pē) a treatment for cancer and other diseases that uses drugs or chemicals
platelets	(plāt′lĭts) disks in the blood that promote clotting
donor	(dō′nər) one that contributes, gives, or donates
invasive	(ĭn·vās′ĭv) spreading into healthy tissue
enthusiastic	(ĕn·thoo′zē ăs′tĭk) greatly interested or excited
viable	(vī′ə·bəl) capable of living or surviving
leery	(lĭr′ē) distrustful, suspicious

> **relapsed**   (rĭ·lăpst′) returned to a former condition
>
> Pronunciation Key: ă (**pat**), ā (**pay**), ĕ (**pet**), ē (**bee**), ĭ (**pit**), ī (**pie**), ō (**toe**), o͞o (**boot**), ə (**about, item**)

Paulette Lebed's feet dangle several inches above the carpet as she cradles her newborn sister in her lap. "I love to kiss her and hold her," says the **vivacious** 7-year-old as she tenderly pinches the baby's cheeks. So far, Paulette shows no outward signs of the acute lymphocytic leukemia that she has battled for more than two years. If all goes well, her tiny sister may help her survive to enjoy a healthy sibling rivalry. When Mariajose was born, on April 4, doctors at Jackson Memorial Hospital in Miami drained three ounces of blood from her umbilical cord and froze it in liquid nitrogen. In a few weeks, those blood cells will be injected into Paulette; doctors hope that they will **revive** her immune system damaged by high-dose **chemotherapy.** "I haven't slept for months," says their father, Jaime. "This is a gift from God."

1

Umbilical cords are ordinarily discarded at birth. But researchers now know they are a rich source of stem cells, which produce **platelets** and red and white blood cells, even when transplanted into ailing patients. Traditionally, stem cells have been extracted from bone marrow, but that process is expensive (as much as $25,000) and painful to the **donor.** Extracting cord blood costs far less, requires no **invasive** surgery and donors and recipients need not match perfectly. Since 1988, only 200 cord-blood transplants have been performed worldwide. But doctors are excited about this new source of stem cells, private firms are seeking to get into the business and the National Institute of Health plans to establish four cord-blood donor banks.

2

To date, cord blood has been used mainly to treat leukemia and severe **anemia** in children. It doesn't always work miracles; last week baseball star Rod Carew's 18-year-old daughter, Michelle, died of leukemia even after a transplant. But 65 percent of cord-blood recipients are still living, researchers say. "It's given us years, birthdays and Christmases we would not have had," says Barbara Miller, whose son, Eric, received cord blood from his newborn brother six years ago. Today, at 12, Eric shows no signs of Fanconi anemia, a rare blood disease that once threatened his life, and he plays competitive ice hockey.

3

Several private firms are so **enthusiastic** that they are trying to persuade expectant parents to preserve their newborn's cord-blood in case the child or a sibling needs it in the future. One of the largest, ViaCord in Boston, promotes the service as "biological insurance" in direct-mail appeals to pregnant women. ("You are expecting a baby, and we have something important to tell you," begins one solicitation letter.)

4

ViaCord charges $1,500 to harvest the cord blood and $95 a year for storage. CEO Cynthia Fisher says interest is growing at a "phenomenal rate," particularly among couples with a family history of blood diseases. "I thought it was a great idea," says Moira Motyka of Westborough, Mass., whose brother died of leukemia for a lack of a bone-marrow donor. She had her children's cord blood saved so they could serve as their own donors, if necessary. Families with no history of disease are signing on, too. Says Penny Osborne, who banked her son's cord blood last August: "This was a small price to pay to be able to save a child."

Some researchers think it's not such a small price—particularly when the chances that a child will develop a severe blood disease are only about 1 in 10,000. There are other unknowns, too: experts aren't sure how long frozen cord blood will stay **viable,** or what diseases it will prove useful in treating. ViaCord's literature lists AIDS and lung cancer among its possible uses, but NIH officials are **leery** of overpromising. "It could get a bad name before we know how good it is," says NIH's Paul McCurdy. Critics also think private firms are preying on vulnerable parents. It may make more sense, medically and economically, to donate cord blood to a public bank instead. A matching sample could be found later if needed, and children who need transplants sooner would have a ready supply.

The Food and Drug Administration has proposed subjecting cord blood to clinical trials and licensing procedures. But some doctors fear that a long review could deny kids transplants they need now. The Lebeds couldn't wait. Last fall, Paulette's mother was in her first trimester of pregnancy with Mariajose when Paulette's leukemia **relapsed** and they suddenly needed a stem-cell donor. Tests showed

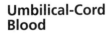

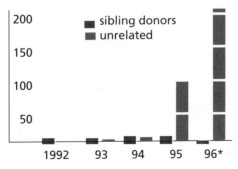

Umbilical-Cord Blood

■ sibling donors
■ unrelated

*Estimate.
Source: INT'L CORD
BLOOD TRANSPLANT REGISTRY

that her sister was a close match, and ViaCord provided fast assistance. Now Paulette's doctors are optimistic, and she is planning her future. She wants to be a model—or a doctor.

HOW WELL DID YOU COMPREHEND?

Main Idea

1. Which of the following best states the main idea of the selection?
    a. The umbilical cord is a structure attached to the navel of a fetus.
    b. Because the umbilical cord has no further use, it is discarded at birth.
    c. Umbilical cord blood is a promising new treatment in the field of blood diseases.
    d. Umbilical cord blood is both difficult and expensive to extract.

2. Which sentence states the main idea of paragraph 2?
    a. the first sentence "Umbilical cords . . ."
    b. the second sentence "But researchers . . ."
    c. the third sentence "Traditionally, stem cells . . ."
    d. the last sentence "But doctors are excited . . ."

Details

3. Cord blood has been used mainly to treat
    a. asthma.
    b. childhood anemia.
    c. AIDS.
    d. lung cancer.

4. Umbilical cords are a rich source of
    a. stem cells.
    b. bone marrow.
    c. platelets.
    d. red blood cells.

Inferences

5. Which group below thinks that cord blood may not be worth its high price?
    a. ViaCord
    b. private firms

c. the National Institute of Health
d. the Food and Drug Administration

6. Which is the most convincing evidence that cord blood may prove to be a useful treatment?
   a. Rod Carew's daughter died of leukemia.
   b. To date, 65 percent of cord-blood recipients are still living.
   c. Six years after receiving cord blood, Eric Miller shows no signs of anemia.
   d. Paulette Lebed's doctors are optimistic.

Working with Words

Complete the sentences below with these words from the vocabulary preview.

chemotherapy	enthusiastic	donor	platelets	revive
invasive	relapsed	leery	vivacious	viable

1. I am _____ *leery* _____ of taking over-the-counter medications unless I first check with a doctor.

2. Most patients would rather have a nurse who is _____ *vivacious* _____ than one who lacks spirit.

3. The doctor was _____ *enthusiastic* _____ about the new treatment that seemed to be working so well.

4. When Gerald needed a kidney transplant, his doctor was able to find an organ _____ *donor* _____ much sooner than expected.

5. Emergency room doctors were able to _____ *revive* _____ the accident victim from unconsciousness.

6. Because of new _____ *chemotherapy* _____ treatments, many cancers can be cured.

7. If an illness has not _____ *relapsed* _____ after several years, the chances are good that the patient will survive.

8. _____ *Invasive* _____ surgeries are those that require a doctor to make an incision in the body.

9. People who bleed more freely than others may have fewer _____ *platelets* _____ in their blood.

10. Because of improvements in infant care, babies born prematurely have a better chance of remaining ___*viable*___.

Thinking and Writing

Because of government regulations, new drugs and treatments are not made available to the public until long after they are discovered. How much testing is enough? Should some people be allowed to try a new medication even if the drug has not been thoroughly tested? What do you think?

Answers will vary.

_____

_____

_____

USE *PRT* TO READ GRAPHICS

To read graphics successfully and make the most of the information they contain, you need to know three things:

1. Graphics have a *purpose.*
2. Graphics show the *relationship* among ideas.
3. Graphics illustrate ideas that are explained in the *text.*

PRT stands for *purpose, relationship,* and *text.* To understand graphics, follow the steps of PRT. Determine the graphic's *purpose.* Discover the *relationship* among the ideas presented in the graphic. Read the *text* that comes before and after the graphic. Also, read any text that is part of the graphic.

Purpose

To determine a graphic's purpose, ask yourself two questions:

■ What does the graphic show?
■ Why is it important?

To answer these questions, look for a *title.* The title tells you the subject of the graphic and may provide a clue to its purpose. Look for the title above or to the side of the graphic. Not all graphics have a title.

Relationship

Different types of graphics illustrate different kinds of relationships. For example, some graphics trace events through time, and some illustrate steps in a process. Graphics also illustrate other relationships such as the parts of a whole or an increase or decrease in number or amount.

First, identify what type of graphic you are reading. Then you may be able to determine how the ideas are related. Four types of graphics and how to recognize them are explained later in this chapter.

Text

Look for a *caption,* or brief explanation of what the graphic contains. The caption may follow the title or it may appear beneath the graphic or to the side.

When there is no caption, a paragraph placed before or after the graphic may contain an explanation. Sometimes the explanation is on another page. As you look at a graphic, refer to its explanation in the text. For example, if a graphic shows steps in a process, look for an explanation of the steps in the text.

Figure 9.1 illustrates the PRT strategy. This graphic lists the steps to follow, explains how to do each step, and provides questions to ask.

As you can see, the title of Figure 9.1 states the topic (PRT) and suggests the graphic's *purpose* (how to use the strategy). There is no caption. The *relationship* of ideas presented in the graphic is process—the

FIGURE 9.1 How to Use PRT

Step	How to	Questions to Ask
Determine the PURPOSE	Read the title.	What is the subject?
		Why is it important?
Find the RELATIONSHIP	Look at all the information.	What type of graphic is it?
		What information is given?
		How are ideas related?
Read the TEXT	Read the caption.	What more does the text tell me?
	Read the paragraphs before and after the graphic.	

steps of the PRT strategy are listed. The *text* explains the steps in the paragraphs that come before the figure.

Memory Cue

PRT is a strategy for reading graphics. PRT stands for purpose, relationship, *and* text. *To read graphics, determine the purpose, find the relationship, read the text.*

RECOGNIZE FOUR TYPES OF GRAPHICS

All graphics show how ideas are related. However, each type of graphic looks different and relates ideas differently. This section explains four types of graphics that occur frequently in textbooks, magazines, newspapers, and other printed materials. Following the explanation of each type of graphic is an exercise that will help you apply the PRT strategy.

- Charts
- Tables
- Graphs
- Diagrams

Charts

You should be able to recognize three kinds of charts: pie chart, organizational chart, and flow chart.

A *pie chart* is round and divided into slices like a pie. Pie charts illustrate part-to-whole relationships. The whole pie, or circle, represents a single idea or thing. The slices of the pie, or segments of the circle, represent the parts that make up the idea or thing.

You will find pie charts in almost any textbook. Now look at the following example, which is from a psychology textbook.

The title is "Cultural Diversity in the United States." The caption says that people of the United States come from many cultural backgrounds. How are the ideas related? The whole pie represents all the people in the United States. Each slice of the pie represents a different cultural group. Some slices are larger than others, meaning that the percent of people in each group varies. European Americans make up the largest percent of the population. American Indians account for the smallest percent. For a more detailed explanation, you would have to read the section of the textbook from which this chart is taken.

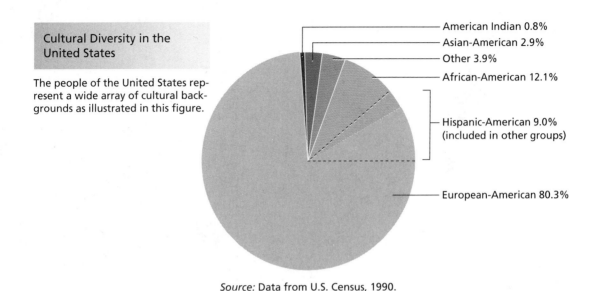

Cultural Diversity in the United States

The people of the United States represent a wide array of cultural backgrounds as illustrated in this figure.

American Indian 0.8%
Asian-American 2.9%
Other 3.9%
African-American 12.1%
Hispanic-American 9.0% (included in other groups)
European-American 80.3%

Source: Data from U.S. Census, 1990.

From Douglas A. Bernstein, et al., *Psychology,* fourth edition. Boston: Houghton Mifflin, 1997, p. 22.

An *organizational chart* can be almost any shape except round, and it is divided into levels that show rankings from high to low or low to high. You have already seen one example of an organizational chart. Turn to Figure 8.4 on page 247 and look at the map of Maslow's hierarchy of needs. As you can see, this chart is shaped like a triangle. Each level of the triangle represents a different need that motivates human behavior. The levels are ranked from lowest at the base of the triangle to highest at the tip of the triangle.

You will find organizational charts in almost any textbook, especially business and government texts. For another example, look at the following chart from a business text.

The title is "Urban Systems Organizational Chart." Although the chart has no caption, you can tell from the title and from the information printed in each box that this chart illustrates a company's (Urban Systems) corporate levels—who reports to whom. The board of directors is at the highest level followed by the president. The vice presidents and executive secretary report directly to the president, and so on. R & D (research and development), advertising, and finance are at the lowest level indicated on the chart. For a more detailed explanation, you would have to read the section of the textbook from which this chart is taken.

A *flow chart* looks like boxes connected with arrows, and it illustrates a process. Inside each box is an explanation of what happens. The arrows show the direction of the process—where it starts and ends.

Urban Systems Organizational Chart

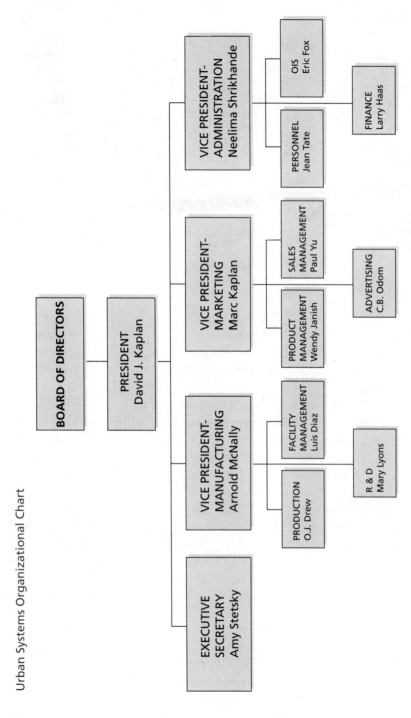

From Scot Ober, *Contemporary Business Communications*, second edition. Boston: Houghton Mifflin, 1995, p. 30.

You will find flow charts in almost any textbook, but they are especially typical of business texts, science texts, and those in technical fields such as electronics and engineering. Now look at the following example from a biology textbook.

A Properly Controlled Experiment to Test the Efficacy of an Aquarium Drug.

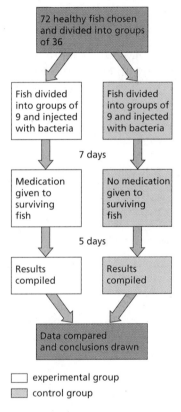

From Joseph S. Levine and Kenneth R. Miller, *Biology.* Lexington, MA: D.C. Heath, 1991, p. 14.

The title tells you that the chart illustrates an experiment to test an aquarium drug. Reading the chart from the top, you can see that the experiment begins with 72 fish that were divided into two groups: an experimental group and a control group. Following the arrows, you can see what happens to the fish. Both groups were injected with bacteria. After seven days, the experimental group was given medication, but the control group got none. After five days on medication, the results of both groups were compared. How many fish from each group lived, and was the medication successful? To find the answers to these questions, you would have to read the explanation in the textbook from which this chart is taken.

Memory Cue

Pie charts show part-to-whole relationships. Organizational charts list information according to its rank or level. Flow charts illustrate processes and show the direction of steps from first to last, from beginning to end.

Exercise 9.1   The following chart is from a business textbook. Use PRT to read the chart and the text that goes with it. The questions will take you through the steps of the strategy.

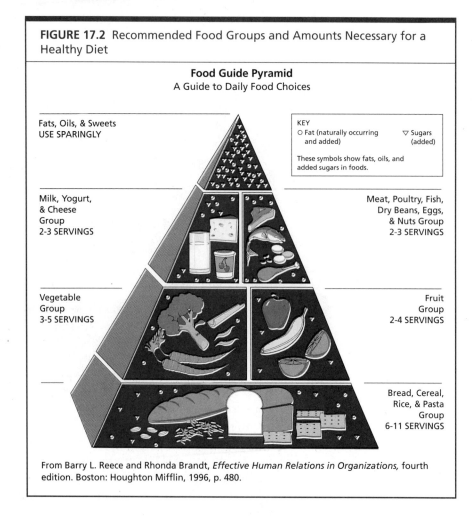

FIGURE 17.2 Recommended Food Groups and Amounts Necessary for a Healthy Diet

Food Guide Pyramid
A Guide to Daily Food Choices

Fats, Oils, & Sweets
USE SPARINGLY

KEY
○ Fat (naturally occurring   ▽ Sugars
   and added)   (added)

These symbols show fats, oils, and added sugars in foods.

Milk, Yogurt,
& Cheese
Group
2-3 SERVINGS

Meat, Poultry, Fish,
Dry Beans, Eggs,
& Nuts Group
2-3 SERVINGS

Vegetable
Group
3-5 SERVINGS

Fruit
Group
2-4 SERVINGS

Bread, Cereal,
Rice, & Pasta
Group
6-11 SERVINGS

From Barry L. Reece and Rhonda Brandt, *Effective Human Relations in Organizations,* fourth edition. Boston: Houghton Mifflin, 1996, p. 480.

Foods high in starch such as breads made with whole grains, dry beans and peas, and potatoes, contain many essential nutrients. Many starches also add dietary fiber to your diet. Some cereals and most fruits and vegetables are good sources of fiber. The National Research Council recommends eating six or more servings of fruits and vegetables as well as six servings of breads or cereals each day to obtain necessary amounts of fiber.

1. What kind of chart is this (pie chart, organizational chart, flow chart)?

   organizational chart

Purpose

2. What is the chart's subject?

   a guide to food choices

3. What is the chart's purpose? (Hint: Read the caption.)

   to illustrate recommended food groups for a healthy diet

Relationship

4. A healthy diet should consist mainly of what food group?

   bread, cereal, rice, and pasta

5. What food group should make up the least amount of a healthy diet?

   fats, oils, and sweets

Text

6. What are three good sources of fiber?

   cereal, fruits, vegetables

Tables

A *table* is a list of facts. Tables often condense a large amount of information into a smaller space. The facts listed in a table may be related in a number of ways. For example, birth control methods could be compared.

Ethnic groups within the United States could be listed according to their population in thousands. Figure 9.1 on page 263 is a table that lists the steps of the graph-reading process: PRT.

A table may have one or more columns of facts. Often the columns are labeled, telling you what kind of information is listed. For example, in Figure 9.1 the first column lists steps, the second column lists how to do the steps, and the third column lists questions to ask.

Tables are widely used, and you will probably find them in all of your textbooks. Now look at the following two examples.

Example 1:
Average annual starting salaries for teachers, 1994–95

Degree in education	Average	Rural	Urban	Suburban
Bachelor's	$22,700	21,400	25,600	25,400
Master's	25,200	23,900	27,500	27,900

Source: Recruiting Trends Survey, 1995–96.

Example 2:
Development of Infant Emotions

Approximate Age (in months)	Emotion
0–1	Social smile
3	Pleasure smile
3–4	Wariness
4–7	Joy, anger
4	Surprise
5–9	Fear
18	Shame

Sources: Izard (1982); Sroufe (1979).

From U.S. Department of Labor, Bureau of Labor Statistics, *Occupational Outlook Quarterly,* Spring 1997, p. 29; from Kelvin L. Seifert and Robert J. Hoffnung, *Childhood and Adolescent Development,* fourth edition. Boston: Houghton Mifflin, 1997, p. 201.

Example 1 from the *Occupational Outlook Quarterly* shows starting salaries for teachers between 1994 and 1995. This table is divided into five columns. The first column lists educational degrees. The second column lists the average salary for all teachers earning a bachelor's or master's degree. The next three columns list teachers' salaries according to whether they work in rural, urban, or suburban areas. As you can see, teachers in rural areas are the lowest paid.

Example 2 from a child development textbook shows the approximate age at which emotions develop in infants. For example, infants begin to smile with pleasure at about 3 months. Fear develops between 5 and 9 months, approximately. To learn more about the significance of the information presented in these tables, you would have to read the explanations in the sources from which they are taken.

Memory Cue

Tables list facts in columns. A table may compare facts or list steps in a process.

Exercise 9.2   The following table is from a finance textbook. Use PRT to read the table and the text that goes with it. The questions will take you through the steps of the strategy.

TABLE 2.1 Careers and Income for Careers That Require a Minimum of a Bachelor's Degree

Occupation	Average Starting Salary	Average Salary of Experienced Individuals
Accountant and auditor	$28,000	$ 58,000
Actuary	32,000	60,000
Airline pilot	40,000	86,000
Architect	28,000	38,000
Chemical engineer	40,000	57,000
Chiropractor	30,000	76,000
Economist	27,000	70,000
Geologist	28,000	54,000
Librarian	28,000	34,000
Metallurgical engineer	38,000	55,000
Physician	85,000	150,000
Professor	37,000	53,000
Public relations	23,000	36,000
Securities sales	30,000	47,000
Social worker	24,000	34,000
Teacher, secondary school	26,000	38,000
Underwriter	27,000	40,000
Veterinarian	30,000	70,000

Source: U.S. Department of Labor, Bureau of Labor Statistics, *Occupational Outlook Handbook* (Washington, DC, various editions); authors' extrapolations to January 1997.
From E. Thomas Garman and Raymond E. Forgue, *Personal Finance,* fifth edition. Boston: Houghton Mifflin, 1997, p. 34.

Table 2.1 gives both the starting salary and the salary for experienced individuals for various careers requiring an educational minimum of a bachelor's degree. In some fields, the starting salary closely matches the salary for more experienced workers, as in the case of librarians and social workers. In other careers, such as those of airline pilots or securities salespeople, experienced workers receive much higher salaries.

Purpose

1. What is the table's subject?

   careers and income for careers requiring at least a Bachelor's Degree

2. What is the table's purpose?

   to compare income for various careers

Relationship

3. What information is provided in the first column?

   occupations

4. What facts in the first and second columns are compared?

   starting salaries and salaries for experienced individuals

5. Which occupations make a starting salary of $28,000?

   accountant and auditor, architect, geologist, librarian

Text

6. In which fields do the starting salaries and the salaries for experienced workers more closely match?

   librarian and social worker

7. In which fields do experienced workers receive much higher salaries?

   airline pilot, chiropractor, economist, veterinarian, securities salesperson

Graphs

A *graph* is a figure that compares quantities or amounts. On a *bar graph,* the amounts or quantities appear as bars running horizontally or verti- cally. On a *line graph,* lines represent the quantities or amounts. If the line runs downward, the amount shows decreases. If the line runs up- ward, the amount shows increases.

The key to reading a graph is to understand all of its parts. The base of the graph is called the *horizontal axis.* The side of the graph is called the *vertical axis.* Different points on each axis represent different quan- tities or amounts. Where a bar or line stops is the point where the ver- tical and horizontal axes intersect.

For an example, look back at the bar graph at the end of the read- ing selection on page 259. The title tells you that the topic is umbilical- cord blood. The numbers on the horizontal axis (bottom) are dates. The numbers on the vertical axis (side) represent the number of cord- blood transplants. The blue bars represent sibling donors of cord- blood. The black bars represent unrelated donors of cord-blood. The caption at the bottom tells you the source of the figures.

If you compare the black bars with the blue bars, you can see that the number of transplants involving unrelated donors has increased since 1992 while the number of transplants involving sibling donors in- creased between 1992 and 1994, stayed the same in 1995, then de- creased in 1996. Also, by 1995, the number of transplants involving un- related donors had outpaced those involving sibling donors. As you can see, one little graph contains a lot of information.

For another example, look at the following line graph.

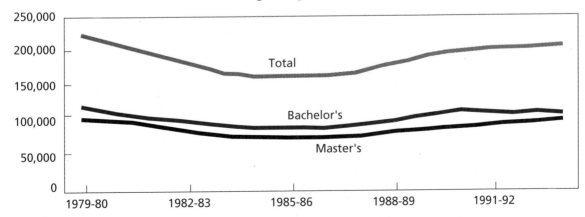

Education degrees granted, 1979-80 to 1991-92

From U.S. Department of Labor, Bureau of Labor Statistics, *Occupational Outlook Quarterly,* Spring 1997, p. 25.

The subject of the graph is educational degrees granted, 1979–80 to 1992–93. The horizontal axis shows dates when degrees were granted. The vertical axis shows the number of degrees granted in thousands. The lines indicate Master's, Bachelor's, and total degrees granted (Master's plus Bachelor's degrees).

If you want to know how many degrees were granted in 1979–80, first look along the horizontal axis to the 1979–80 column. Then, reading up the vertical axis, you can see that 100,000 Master's degrees were awarded, about 125,000 Bachelor's degrees were awarded, and about 225,000 total degrees were awarded. (If a line falls somewhere between two numbers, you have to estimate the number.)

For a more detailed explanation, you would have to read the section of the *Occupational Outlook Quarterly* from which this graph is taken.

Memory Cue

Two types of graphs are bar graphs and line graphs. They both show quantities and amounts, which are listed on the horizontal axis (base) and the vertical axis (side).

Exercise 9.3

The bar graph below is from a history textbook. Use PRT to read the graph and the text that goes with it. The questions will take you through the steps of the strategy.

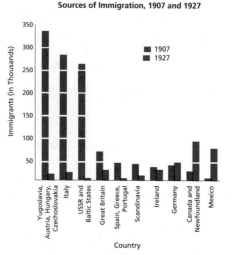

Sources of Immigration, 1907 and 1927

Sources of Immigration, 1907 and 1927 Immigration peaked in the years 1907–1908, when newcomers from southern and eastern Europe poured into the United States. Then, after the immigration restriction laws were passed in the 1920s, the greatest number of immigrants came from the western hemisphere (Canada and Mexico) which was exempted from the quotas, while the number coming from eastern and southern Europe shrank.

From Norton, Katzman, Escott, Chudacoff, Paterson, and Tuttle, *A People and a Nation,* fourth edition. Boston: Houghton Mifflin, 1994, p. 739.

Purpose

1. What is the subject of the graph?

    sources of immigration, 1907 and 1927

2. What is the graph's purpose?

    to show differences in the sources of immigration in 1907 and 1927

Relationship

3. What does the horizontal axis show?

    countries that were the sources of immigrants

4. What does the vertical axis show?

    immigrants (in thousands) from those countries

5. What do the black bars represent?

    people who immigrated in 1907

6. What do the blue bars represent?

    people who immigrated in 1927

7. In which year was immigration the highest?

    _1907_

8. About how many immigrants came from Great Britain in 1907?

    about 75,000

Text

9. What happened during the 1920s that affected the number of immigrants coming into the United States?

    the immigration restriction laws were passed

Diagrams

A *diagram* is a drawing that either illustrates parts and functions or steps in a process. For example, in a biology textbook you might see a drawing of an eye with the parts of the eye labeled. In the same textbook you might see a diagram showing the process by which cells divide. In either case, the diagram helps you form a visual memory of the parts or steps illustrated.

You will find diagrams in most of your textbooks, especially in the sciences. When you read diagrams, be sure you understand the parts and functions or processes they illustrate. Be sure to look at the diagram as you read the text that explains it. The text fills in any information that the diagram leaves out. Now look at the following examples.

Example 1

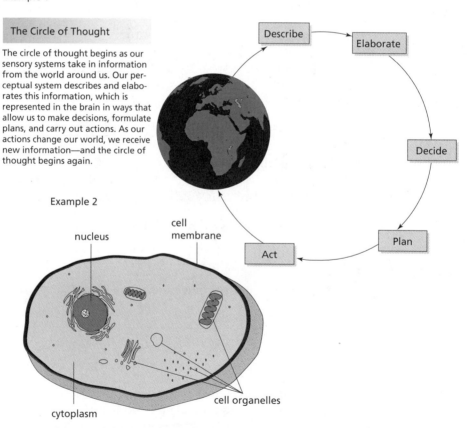

The Circle of Thought

The circle of thought begins as our sensory systems take in information from the world around us. Our perceptual system describes and elaborates this information, which is represented in the brain in ways that allow us to make decisions, formulate plans, and carry out actions. As our actions change our world, we receive new information—and the circle of thought begins again.

Example 2

nucleus

cell membrane

cell organelles

cytoplasm

The "typical" animal cell exhibits familiar structures common to most multicellular animals.

From Bernstein, et al., *Psychology,* fourth edition. Boston: Houghton Mifflin, 1997, p. 265; from Levine and Miller, *Biology.* Lexington, MA: D.C. Heath, 1991, p. 5.

The Circle of Thought is from a psychology textbook. This diagram shows how we process information. The steps of the process are printed in boxes connected by arrows. The arrows show the direction of the process that begins with the first step *describe* and ends with the last step *act*. As you can see from the text beside the diagram, we take in information from the world around us and use it to make decisions and carry out actions.

The second diagram is from a biology textbook. This diagram shows the parts of a typical animal cell. Parts such as the *nucleus* and *cell membrane* are labeled. To learn how these parts function and why they are important, you would have to read the section of the biology textbook from which these diagrams are taken.

Memory Cue

Some diagrams illustrate parts and functions like the parts of a cell. Some diagrams show the steps of a process such as how cells reproduce.

Exercise 9.4   The diagram below is from a biology textbook. Use PRT to read the diagram and the text that goes with it. The questions will take you through the steps of the strategy.

Life Cycle of a Frog

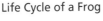

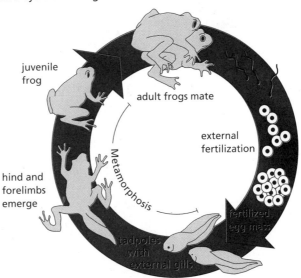

Life cycle: The typical cycle includes a fully aquatic larval stage, or *tadpole.* Frog and toad tadpoles are herbivorous filter feeders whose internal anatomy changes as profoundly as their external anatomy as they metamorphose into carnivorous adults.

From Levine and Miller, *Biology.* Lexington, MA: D.C. Heath, 1991, p. 332.

Purpose

1. What is the subject of the diagram?

    life cycle of a frog

2. What is the diagram's purpose?

    to illustrate the process by which frogs develop

Relationship

3. How many stages are involved in the process?

    six stages

4. What is the first stage?

    Adult frogs mate.

5. What is the next thing that happens after a fertilized egg mass is formed?

    Tadpoles with external gills develop.

6. What stages make up the part of the process called *metamorphosis?*

    tadpoles, hind and forelimbs develop, juvenile frog

Text

7. What do the terms *herbivorous* and *carnivorous* mean?

    Herbivorous means plant eating; carnivorous means flesh eating.

8. At which stage are frogs and toads herbivorous feeders?

    tadpoles

9. When do frogs and toads become carnivorous feeders?

    when they metamorphose into adults

MAKE YOUR OWN GRAPHICS

Graphics enable an author to present the same information in a variety of formats to appeal to readers' different ways of learning. For example, some readers are able to visualize the steps of a process on their own based on what they have read. Others may need a diagram to help them visualize the process.

You too may need to make your own graphics as aids to learning and remembering. As explained in Chapter 8, mapping is a strategy many students use to condense information into a form that has meaning to them. A *map* is a kind of chart such as the ones in Figure 8.4, page 247 and Exercise 8.10, page 248. You could also make tables such as those in Figure 8.1, page 230 and Figure 8.3, page 241. Suppose you wanted to set up a monthly budget as a project for a personal finance class. You could make a table like the one in Figure 9.2 below.

In this figure, the first column lists the student's expenses for one month. The student's *fixed expenses* include things such as rent and car payments that usually do not vary from month to month. The student's *flexible expenses* include things such as the amount spent on entertainment that may vary as the need arises. A good budget will have some money set aside for unexpected expenses such as a visit to the doctor or car repair. This amount is listed on the chart as *other expenses,* and it is

---

FIGURE 9.2 Jane's Monthly Budget

Fixed Expenses	
Rent	$400
Utilities	60
Car	120
Food	200
Flexible Expenses	
Savings	70
Entertainment	30
Other expenses	120
Total Expenses	$1000

also one of the student's flexible expenses. One way to plan a budget is to add up your fixed expenses first. Subtract those from the total amount you have to spend. Whatever is left over can be divided among your flexible expenses.

Whether you make a chart, table, or diagram depends on the kind of information you need to illustrate. For example, if you need to learn the bones of the human skeleton, make a diagram. If you need to remember types of birth control and their rates of effectiveness, make a table. What matters most is that you make the type of graphic that works best for you.

Exercise 9.5   Working with a partner, examine whatever textbooks you have with you for the types of graphics explained in this chapter: charts, tables, bar graph, line graph, and diagrams. Try to find at least one example of each. Share your results with the rest of the class. *(Students' examples will vary.)*

REAL-WORLD CONNECTIONS

As explained in this chapter, graphics aid understanding and memory. Paying attention to graphics as you read will improve your comprehension. Making your own graphics will result in study guides that make learning easier.

Graphics also play a role in everyday life. Diagrams can be used for everything from planning a garden to rearranging the furniture in a room. You can chart your assignments for a week by ranking them in order of most important (what is due first) to least important (what can wait). If you are watching your diet, you can plan your meals on a chart, showing what you will eat for breakfast, lunch, dinner, and snacks. Big families can divide household chores by making a table that lists each person's name and responsibilities. Now apply what you have learned about graphics from this chapter by completing the following activity:

Illustrate your own monthly expenses on a table like the one in Figure 9.2. One way to plan a budget is to add up your fixed expenses first. Subtract those from the total amount you have to spend. Whatever is left over can be divided among your flexible expenses. To make your table, follow these four steps: *(Students' tables will vary but should resemble Figure 9.2.)*

1. In the first column, list your fixed and flexible expenses.

2. In the second column, list the amount spent on each.

3. Try to set aside some money for savings and for emergencies.

4. When you finish, compare your table with a classmate's. Discuss the similarities and differences between your expenditures.

HOW WELL DO YOU REMEMBER?

To review the chapter, read the following summary and fill in the blanks. If you need help with an answer, look back through the chapter to refresh your memory.

Graphics are _____*visual*_____ aids, meaning that they appeal to your sense of sight. PRT, a strategy for reading graphics, stands for _____*purpose*_____, _____*relationship*_____, and _____*text*_____. To determine the subject of a graphic, read the _____*title*_____. In some graphics, a _____*caption*_____ provides a brief explanation. _____*Pie*_____ charts illustrate part-to-whole relationships. _____*Organization*_____ charts show rankings and levels. _____*Flow*_____ charts show steps in a process. A _____*table*_____ lists facts to show their relationship. A _____*bar*_____ or _____*line*_____ graph shows quantities and amounts and how they increase or decrease. A _____*diagram*_____ is a picture or series of pictures that illustrates parts and functions or a process. Always take time to read graphics because they are essential to your understanding of the ideas they illustrate.

WHAT DO YOU THINK?

How has the information presented in this chapter affected the way you will read graphics from now on? Which type of graphic is easiest for you to understand? Which type needs more explanation?

Reflections will vary.

_____

_____

_____

CHAPTER QUIZ 1

Part 1 Terms and Definitions

Match this chapter's special terms in Column A with their definitions in Column B. Use each definition once.

Column A

_c_ 1. graphic

_d_ 2. table

_e_ 3. caption

_a_ 4. map

_b_ 5. diagram

Column B

a. a type of chart or study guide

b. a drawing that shows parts and functions or processes

c. a visual aid

d. list of facts and how they are related

e. brief explanation of a graphic

Part 2 Chapter Review

Read and answer each question below. Write your answer in complete sentences, and use extra paper if needed. *(Answers will vary but should be similar to these.)*

1. Why is it important to read and understand textbook graphics?

   Graphics are important because they illustrate and often simplify

   difficult ideas.

2. What are the steps and purpose of the PRT strategy?

   Determine the graphic's purpose, discover the relationship among ideas,

   and read the text before and after the graphic. This strategy helps you read

   graphics with understanding.

3. How can you use graphics as memory aids?

_____Make your own graphics to use as study guides. Also, study textbook_____

_____graphics and try to visualize them to aid recall on tests._____

Part 3 Using Your Skills

Demonstrate what you have learned about graphics by reading the following examples and answering the questions.

Example 1:

TABLE 2.3 Basic SI (Metric) Units

QUANTITY	UNIT	SYMBOL
Length	meter	m
Mass	kilogram	kg
Time	second	s
Electric current	ampere	A
Temperature	kelvin	K
Light intensity	candela	cd
Amount of substance	mole	mol

From Sherman, Sherman, and Russikoff, _Basic Concepts of Chemistry,_ sixth edition. Boston: Houghton Mifflin, 1996.

a. What is the purpose of the table?

_____to list metric units and the quantities they measure_____

b. What is the unit for measuring _light intensity_ called?

_____candela_____

c. What quantity does _kelvin_ measure?

_____temperature_____

d. What unit of measurement does the symbol _A_ represent?

_____ampere, electric current_____

Example 2:

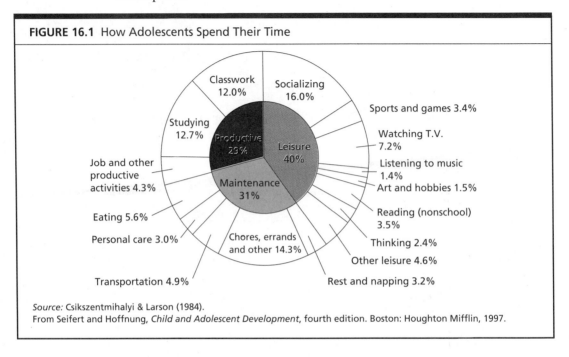

FIGURE 16.1 How Adolescents Spend Their Time

Source: Csikszentmihalyi & Larson (1984).
From Seifert and Hoffnung, *Child and Adolescent Development*, fourth edition. Boston: Houghton Mifflin, 1997.

a. What type of graphic is this?

pie chart

b. What is the graphic's purpose?

to show how adolescents spend their time

c. Adolescents' time is divided into what three *major* divisions?

productive, maintenance, and leisure

d. What percentage of their *productive* time do adolescents spend on studying?

12.7%

e. How much time do adolescents spend on nonschool reading?

3.5%

Score: 100 − 7 for each one missed = _____ %

CHAPTER QUIZ 2

Part 1 Terms and Definitions

Match this chapter's special terms in Column A with their definitions in Column B.

Column A	Column B
_e_ 1. pie chart	a. illustrates a process
_d_ 2. line or bar graph	b. a line reading up and down a graph
_a_ 3. flow chart	c. shows ranks or levels
_b_ 4. vertical axis	d. compares quantities or amounts
_f_ 5. horizontal axis	e. illustrates part-to-whole relationship
_c_ 6. organizational chart	f. a line reading across a graph

Part 2 Chapter Review

Read and answer each question below. Write your answer in complete sentences, and use extra paper if needed. *(Answers will vary but should be similar to these.)*

1. How can you determine the purpose of a chart or table?

   Read the title. Determine the subject of the chart or table and why it is

   important.

2. What is the difference between a bar graph and a line graph?

   Bar and line graphs both compare quantities and amounts. The difference

   is in how they are represented: as bars or lines.

3. What role do graphics play in everyday life?

   You can use charts and diagrams for many types of planning and study

   activities. (Answers may vary.)

Part 3 Using Your Skills

Demonstrate what you have learned about graphics by reading the following examples and answering the questions.

Example 1:

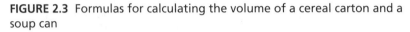

FIGURE 2.3 Formulas for calculating the volume of a cereal carton and a soup can

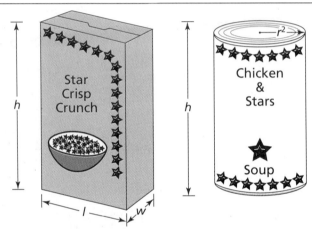

Volume = length × width × height   Volume = π × (radius)² × height

$V = l \times w \times h$ $V = \pi \times r^2 \times h$

$\pi = 3.14$

From Sherman, Sherman, and Russikoff, *Basic Concepts of Chemistry*, sixth edition. Boston: Houghton Mifflin, 1996.

a. What kind of graphic is this?

diagram

b. What is the graphic's purpose?

to illustrate the formula for calculating volume

c. What do *l*, *w*, and *h* stand for?

l = length, w = width, h = height

d. Using the information given in the figure, what is the volume (cubic inches) of a box having the following dimensions: $l = 4$ inches, $w = 2$ inches, and $h = 6$ inches?

_V = 4" × 2" × 6", V = 48 cu. in._

Example 2:

FIGURE 3.3 Federal Grants and State and Local Spending

The dependence of state and local governments on federal grants has shifted significantly over the past several decades.

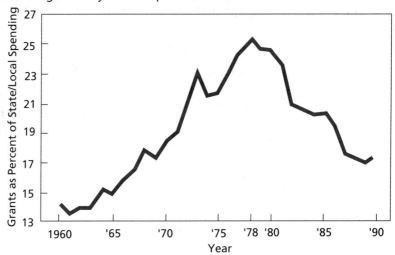

Source: Advisory Commission on Intergovernmental Relations, _Significant Features of Fiscal Federalism, 1991: Volume 2: Revenues and Expenditures_ (Washington, DC: October 1991). From Gitelson, Dudley, and Dubnick, _American Government,_ fourth edition. Boston: Houghton Mifflin, 1996.

a. What kind of graphic is this?

line graph

b. What is the graphic's purpose?

to show how state and local spending on federal grants has changed

over time

c. What does the vertical axis show?

grants as percent of state/local spending

d.   What does the horizontal axis show?

_____*year*_____

e.   When was spending on federal grants the highest?

_____*1978*_____

f.   Approximately what percent was spent on grants in 1965?

_____*about 15%*_____

Score: 100 − 5 for each one missed = _____%

Vocabulary Quiz

Each sentence below contains a word in bold type from the reading
selection on pages 257–260. Read the sentence and the definitions
that follow it. Then circle the correct one. Turn to the vocabulary
preview on pages 257–258 to check your answers.

1. Because Perry likes animals, he is a regular **donor** to several
   wildlife funds.
   a. collector
   b. officer
   c. opponent
   (d.) contributor

2. Because the college team had a winning season, everyone was
   enthusiastic about their chances in the playoffs.
   (a.) excited
   b. fearful
   c. worried
   d. upset

3. A person should be **leery** about eating food that has been sitting
   out too long.
   a. unconcerned
   b. careful
   (c.) suspicious
   d. eager

4. When Ellie's allergy **relapsed,** she decided to try a new medication.
   a. improved
   b. returned
   c. cleared up
   d. went away

5. A robin flew into a window and was knocked unconscious, but we were able to **revive** it.
   a. bury
   b. feed
   c. bring to life
   d. set free

6. Many patients hope they will not need **chemotherapy** because of its unpleasant side effects.
   a. a cancer treatment
   b. bed rest
   c. counseling
   d. over-the-counter drug

7. University cheerleaders are selected for their skill and **vivacious** personalities.
   a. reserved
   b. attractive
   c. lively
   d. healthy

8. A reduction in **platelets** may be the cause of excessive bleeding.
   a. vitamins, minerals, and supplements
   b. blood disks that promote clotting
   c. diseases of the blood
   d. symptoms of disease

9. Some viruses are not **viable** after they are exposed to air.
   a. contagious
   b. dangerous
   c. prone to disease
   d. able to live

10. Fortunately, the tumor was not **invasive,** and it could easily be removed.
   a. cancerous
   b. spreading
   c. large
   d. healthy

Score: 100 − 10 for each one missed = _____%

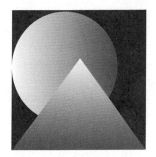

Chapter 10

Developing Your Critical Thinking Skills

*R*eading occurs on two levels: *the literal level* and *the critical level*. To read on the literal level, pay attention to what an author says. Look for a main idea and the details that support it. To read on the critical level, determine what an author means. Make inferences from what the author says.

Critical reading requires critical thinking. When instructors ask your opinion, they expect you to think critically about what you have read or learned. To solve a math problem, you must think critically about what is given, the answer required, and the procedure to use. Suppose you plan to vote in an upcoming election. You must think critically as you read about the candidates' positions on various issues.

In other words, *critical thinking* is logical thinking. It is a natural process you go through to solve problems, make decisions, and make sense of the world. Critical thinking involves many skills, four of which are explained in this chapter. Developing these skills will help you read and think critically not only in college but throughout your life:

- *Determine an author's purpose.*
- *Distinguish facts from opinions.*
- *Make inferences from your reading.*
- *Evaluate what you read.*

WHAT DO YOU ALREADY KNOW?

To prepare yourself for the reading selection that follows, find out what you already know about folk tales. Answer the questions below either on your own or in a group discussion.

1. What is a folk tale?

2. Do you recall reading or hearing a folk tale? What was it about?

3. As far as you know, what is the purpose of folk tales?

4. Read the title, headnote, vocabulary preview, and first two paragraphs of the reading selection. What do you think will follow?

The King of the Frogs

Humphrey Harmon

Humphrey Harmon has spent many years living and teaching in Africa. This folk tale, based on a Nyanza story, is from Harmon's book Tales Told Near a Crocodile.

VOCABULARY PREVIEW

reed	(rēd) a tall stalk of grass
dreadful	(drĕd′fəl) terrible, extremely unpleasant
untidy	(ŭn·tī′dē) not neat, disorderly
commission	(kə·mĭsh′ən) the authority granted to carry out a task
scandalous	(skăn′dl·əs) outrageous, disgraceful
ventured	(vĕn′chərd) took a risk or engaged in dangerous behavior
lithe	(līth) graceful, bends easily
gaped	(gāpt) stared with the mouth open

Pronunciation Key: ă (pat), ā (pay), ĕ (pet), ē (bee), ī (pie), ə (item, about), ŭ (cut), ĭ (pit)

Have you ever been beside a lake in Africa at night and listened to the frogs? You haven't? Then you cannot imagine what the noise is like. And it's not just one kind of noise, it's several. Over there for instance are a thousand creaking doors that have never had their hinges oiled and someone opens and shuts them—and keeps on doing just that. Over *there* are a thousand fat men snoring and one wakes them up. Then there are a thousand carpenters sawing planks and all saws want a touch of grease, and a thousand little bells are being struck and a thousand corks are being pulled out of bottles. 1

Noise! You can hardly hear yourself think. 2

Then you go a little closer until you can just see the edge of the water and perhaps a **reed** or two and there is silence. Just the splash of a frog jumping into the water late because he was asleep and didn't hear you coming. Then nothing, and you can hear the whole world breathe. 3

There's a story about this. 4

Long ago the frogs did as they pleased and the result was **dreadful.** Not one of them would listen to what another said and they all shouted at once. Children wouldn't obey their parents and even wives wouldn't listen to their husbands, which is, indeed, something hardly to be understood. It was all noisy and **untidy** beyond bearing and nothing ever got done. 5

At last a wise, wise old frog called everyone to a meeting and, since he had a very fine voice and went on shouting for long enough, he managed to get them all there at once, for to tell you the truth they were pretty sick of living the way they did. 6

"Frogs!" said the old frog, puffing himself up. "We cannot go on like this. It's no sort of life for anyone and, anyway, when you see how all the other creatures live it makes one ashamed of being a frog. There is only one thing to do. We must get a king. When people have kings there is peace and order and everyone does as he is told." 7

"Agreed!" they all shouted and they stayed long enough to **commission** the old frog to see what he could do about getting them one, before everybody fell to quarreling and pushing and splashing and the meeting broke up in disorder. As usual. 8

Then the wise, wise old frog went to see the Great God Mmumi (you will say the two *m's* correctly if you hum a little before you begin the word). Mmumi happened to be in charge of that part of the world. 9

So the frogs went on as usual, which was badly, until one day Mmumi woke up, remembered his promise, took a great green mossy boulder which had the rough shape of a gigantic frog and threw it into the water. SPLASH! 10

"There you are!" he shouted (it sounded like thunder). "There's your king. His name's Gogo and like me he doesn't want to be disturbed. Respect him and be satisfied." 11

The whole lake was shaken by Gogo's fall. The waves washed through the reeds and tore up the shore, and in the middle of a great cloud of mud Gogo settled on the bottom and the fat green waterweeds curled round and over him. He looked shocking.   12

The frogs were terrified and fled under stones and into dark corners and holes under the bank. Their long white legs streaked behind them as they swam. Parents found their children and husbands their wives and then settled down to explaining what had happened.   13

"This is our king," they said, "and a fine terrible one he seems, and from the splash he made not the sort to fool about with. Now all will be well and this **scandalous** behavior will stop."   14

And so it did, for a while.   15

But although Gogo had made such a wonderful first impression, as time passed they noticed that he never moved. He just sat quietly in the mud and stared in the same direction. Presently they began to get used to him, until finally some young, bold bad, frogs **ventured** to swim close to him and then one of them touched his nose.   16

And still Gogo said and did nothing.   17

"Bah! He's not a king!" they shouted. "He's not even a frog. He's just an old stone and couldn't hurt anyone." And they swam round him until they were dizzy and jumped all over his back and went away and spoke rudely about him to their elders.   18

At first none of the elders believed him. They had told their children Gogo was a king and a king he had to be, but soon it was impossible to deny that the children were right and then . . . Well, the noise began again and things were as they had always been, only worse. Terrible!   19

The wise, wise old frog sighed and set out to see Mmumi again, who was not at all pleased at being woken a second time.   20

"All right!" he shouted in a passion. "*All right!* You aren't satisfied with the king I've given you. Is that the way it is? Very well, you shall have another and I hope you like him."   21

And the very next night he gave them Mamba the Crocodile.   22

Gogo had come to his people with a splash that shook the lake but Mamba slid into the water with only a whisper and left but one small ring spreading gently to show that he had come. Then he swam, silent as a shadow, **lithe** and long and secret, his jaws grinning like a trap. Gogo had never visited the people he had been given to rule but Mamba visited them often and suddenly, and whenever he met a subject the great jaws **gaped** and closed and often it was the last of that frog.   23

The frogs developed the greatest respect for their new king and lived quietly, looking over the backs of their heads as frogs can. Now and again at night they break out but they keep their ears open and if you go near the lake they shut up.   24

They think it's Mamba coming to put a little order into them and they keep quiet.   25

HOW WELL DID YOU COMPREHEND?

Main Idea

1. Which of the following best expresses the main idea of this folk tale?
   a. Even among frogs, someone must be in charge.
   b. Frogs sound differently in Africa than they do in other parts of the world.
   c. There is a reason why frogs sound the way they do at night.
   d. A good king uses fear to rule his people.

2. Which of the following best expresses the main idea of paragraph 1?
   a. Listening to frogs at night is an unusual experience.
   b. You cannot imagine what frogs sound like in Africa.
   c. The sound of frogs is not one sound but many.
   d. Frogs are one of nature's noisiest creatures.

Details

3. The first king of the frogs was a
   a. crocodile.
   b. stone.
   c. snake.
   d. wise old frog.

4. Who is Mmumi?
   a. king of the frogs
   b. one of the elders
   c. a crocodile
   d. a god

Inferences

5. What seems to be the purpose of this folk tale?
   a. to describe the author's experiences while living in Africa.
   b. to explain the different sounds that frogs make.
   c. to contrast the behavior of frogs and crocodiles.
   d. to explain why frogs are sometimes noisy, sometimes quiet at night.

6. Why did the frogs respect their second king?
    a. They were afraid of being eaten.
    b. They thought he was a stone.
    c. Their ancestors taught them respect.
    d. They liked him more than the first king.

Working with Words

Complete the sentences below with these words from the vocabulary preview.

commission	dreadful	scandalous	ventured
gaped	lithe	reed	untidy

1. Flamingoes are known for their bright pink feathers and long _____*lithe*_____ legs.

2. Conditions were _____*dreadful*_____ after the ice storm, which left people without water and electricity.

3. If you look carefully, you may see fish eggs on a _____*reed*_____ down close to the water.

4. A dog that has _____*ventured*_____ too close to the edge of a Florida lake may meet the jaws of an alligator.

5. Because we had left the cover off our boat, we found the inside dirty and _____*untidy*_____.

6. Some elected officials have been accused of _____*scandalous*_____ conduct such as taking bribes or using drugs.

7. The child _____*gaped*_____ and pointed at the water moccasin swimming alongside the boat.

8. Many counties have a game and freshwater fish _____*commission*_____ that is in charge of wildlife management.

Thinking and Writing

Why do you suppose that people in time past used stories like this one to explain natural events?

Answers will vary.

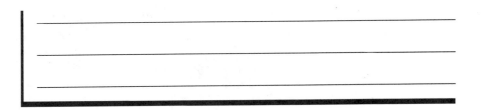

DETERMINE AN AUTHOR'S PURPOSE

Everyone writes for a reason, or *purpose*. An author expects you to respond in certain ways to what you read. Generally speaking, these three purposes motivate most writing:

- To inform
- To persuade
- To entertain

To *inform* means to *teach or explain*. When an author's purpose is to inform, then your response should be to learn the skill or understand the information presented. For example, textbook authors inform students about topics that may be new or unfamiliar. They teach students a skill such as how to do an equation, or they may explain a difficult process such as how an animal becomes infected with disease-causing parasites. Journalists inform the general public about local, national, and international affairs—what is happening at home and abroad. Technical writers provide information on such things as how to build a deck or how to operate a piece of machinery. The next paragraph is an example of writing whose purpose is to *inform*. Read the paragraph and the explanation that follows.

> To balance your checkbook, follow these steps. First, write down the balance shown on your statement. Next, add any deposits you have made that are not listed on your statement. From this amount subtract the sum of all the checks you have written that do not show on your statement. The resulting number should agree with the balance shown in your checkbook.

The author's topic is *balancing a checkbook*. The main idea is stated in the first sentence. The details explain the steps to follow. From the details you can see that the author's purpose is to teach you a process. As a reader, your response should be to learn the steps.

To *persuade* means to *provoke or influence*. When an author's purpose is to persuade, then your response should be to consider the facts, reasons, or opinions that are offered and agree or disagree. For example, authors of political speeches try to influence voters' choices at elections. An author of a newspaper editorial on the suffering of flood victims wants to provoke the public's sympathy—perhaps even move readers to contribute money or time to aid their recovery. Advertisers, of course, want to persuade you to buy their products. The next paragraph is an example of writing whose purpose is to *persuade*. Read the paragraph and the explanation that follows.

> Something should be done to make it safer for people to use automatic teller machines. We have seen too many examples of people who have gotten robbed or assaulted by thugs while making a deposit or withdrawal. Also it is too easy for someone to look over your shoulder and memorize or write down your account number. Later, this scoundrel can come back and wipe out your account.

The author's topic is *automatic teller machines*. The main idea is stated in the first sentence. The author uses emotional language (robbed, assaulted, thugs, scoundrel). The word *should* in the first sentence is also a clue. These details tell you that the author's purpose is to influence the way you think about the safety of using ATMs. As a reader, your response should be to consider the facts or opinions offered and either agree or disagree.

To *entertain* means to *express ideas that arouse or amuse*. When an author's purpose is to entertain, then your response should be to react to the reading in whatever way is appropriate. If a story is funny, you laugh. If it is sad, you cry. If it is thought-provoking, then you try to relate it to what you know or have experienced. The folk tale on pages 292–294 is a good example of writing to entertain. For anyone who has ever listened to frogs at night and wondered why they make so much noise, the story provides a humorous, if not true, explanation. Articles about celebrities entertain readers, sometimes amusing them, sometimes arousing their anger. Novels and other works of fiction are written to entertain readers. The next paragraph is an example of writing whose purpose is to *entertain*. Read the paragraph and the explanation that follows.

> Yesterday, Emily Peterson thought she had won the lottery. When she tried to make a withdrawal from the ATM on her college campus, she got a big surprise. First the machine gave her the $25 she had requested, but then it kept spitting out bills so fast that she could hardly catch them. Something clearly was wrong because she soon had more money than she knew was in her account. The machine thought it was being robbed and sounded an alarm. Emily stood

where she was until security personnel arrived. "This is not my fault," she said, as she handed over all the money. A record of her transaction was still in the machine, and there was no evidence of tampering, so Emily could not be charged with any wrongdoing. Oh yes, she got her $25 back.

The author's topic is *what happened to Emily*. The main idea is stated in the first sentence. The details relate a humorous story about Emily's adventure with the ATM on her campus. Your response should be to feel amused and to put yourself in Emily's place, imagining what you would do.

Finding the purpose may seem difficult at times. An informative article may contain some humor. A persuasive essay may also inform. Some articles written to entertain may also teach you something or even persuade you to change an opinion. When you think you have discovered more than one purpose, ask yourself "What is the *primary*, or most important, purpose?" Finding the main idea will help.

Sometimes an author's purpose is clearly stated near the beginning of an article or a textbook chapter, or in a list of objectives or reading goals. Sometimes you have to figure out the purpose by finding the main idea or looking for clues in the details. If you know the source of the writing then it, too, may serve as a clue to the author's purpose. For example, if the source is a textbook, you can assume that the author's purpose is to inform. If the source is an article or letter on the editorial page of a newspaper, then the purpose may be to persuade. If the source is a novel, the purpose is to entertain. See Figure 10.1 for a summary of the three purposes.

Memory Cue

The three basic purposes are to inform, to persuade, or to entertain. To determine the purpose look near the beginning of the article or chapter. Also consider the main idea, details, and source.

Exercise 10.1   Read and discuss each of the short passages below with a partner. Determine whether the author's purpose is to inform, persuade, or entertain and circle your answer.

1. A mixture and a compound differ in important ways.

   (a.) inform   b. persuade   c. entertain

FIGURE 10.1 The Author's Purpose

Author's Purpose	Types of Details	Your Expected Responses	Common Sources
INFORM (teach or explain)	facts, reasons, examples	to learn, understand, or be able to do something	textbooks, magazines, journals, newspapers, manuals
PERSUADE (provoke or influence)	facts, opinions, strong language, emotional appeals	to consider facts, agree or disagree	editorials, advertisements, political speeches
ENTERTAIN (express ideas)	descriptions, facts that amuse or interest readers	to enjoy the reading, and react appropriately	novels, poems, essays, and articles

2. Teen smoking is a problem we can no longer ignore. We must all work together to help young addicts kick this habit and prevent more teens from taking it up.

   a. inform   b. persuade   c. entertain

3. The U.S. government consists of three branches: the executive, legislative, and judicial. Each branch has separate functions. The three branches act as checks and balances to keep any one branch from gaining too much power.

   a. inform   b. persuade   c. entertain

4. The number of credit card fraud cases has increased dramatically. To avoid being a victim, guard your credit cards carefully. Do not let others use your card. Also, you should keep your carbons and be wary of giving out your credit card numbers over the telephone.

   a. inform   b. persuade   c. entertain

5. The would-be bank robber slipped a note to the teller saying, "Hand over your cash or I'll shoot." He pulled aside his jacket to reveal the butt of his gun. The teller gave him what he asked for, but when he arrived home the police were waiting for him. How did

they know? The note he had given to the teller was written on the back of one of his deposit slips, which listed his name and address.

a. inform   b. persuade   (c.)entertain

6. Frank Sinatra, an entertainer whose popularity spanned several generations, died of a heart attack May 14, 1998, at the age of 82. Although Sinatra made dozens of recordings and starred in many films, he was best known for his unique singing voice.

(a.)inform   b. persuade   c. entertain

7. Employers say that too many graduates lack the basic communication skills required of applicants. We must find ways to include reading and writing activities in all our courses.

a. inform   (b.)persuade   c. entertain

8. To register to win a year's worth of groceries, all you have to do is fill in your name, address, and phone number on one of the blanks available at any of the check-out counters. No purchase is necessary, and you do not have to be present to win.

(a.)inform   b. persuade   c. entertain

9. "Saved by a Dog" read the headline in a Florida newspaper. A child playing too close to shore almost fell into the jaws of a hungry alligator. A neighbor's German shepherd came to the rescue, grabbing the child's diaper in his mouth and pulling him out of danger. In a strange twist of fate, the dog's name is "Gator."

a. inform   b. persuade   (c.)entertain

10. The world's oceans have been overfished to the point that some species are near extinction. Without increased controls on the commercial fishing industry, we may find our choice of seafoods severely limited in the future.

a. inform   (b.)persuade   c. entertain

Exercise 10.2   Read the following passages and determine the author's purpose. Explain how you arrived at your answer. The first one is done as an example.

1. Nick awoke to the sound of bleeping machines and a headache that made him wish that he had not survived. His mouth tasted like it had been filled with hot tar and pigeon droppings. His hands, feet, and nose were as cold as ice. He was conscious of wires leading to his chest and tubes leading in and out of every bodily orifice but one, thank God. . . .

From *Thank You for Smoking,* a novel by Christopher Buckley, New York: Random House, 1994.

a. Author's purpose:

The author's purpose is to entertain.

b. Your explanation:

The source is a novel, and the passage is humorous.

2. Consumers are bombarded with greater and greater volumes of technical information that is difficult to process. Without the advice of experts to guide them, consumers today have difficulty in even understanding which product attributes contribute to quality, durability, safety, and good performance. Thus consumers increasingly rely on the informed judgments of others, particularly product-rating magazines, to help them in decision making. Reliable translators and processors of information include such publications as *Consumer Reports Magazine, Changing Times,* and *Money.*

From *Consumer Economic Issues in America,* E. Thomas Garman, Boston: Houghton Mifflin, 1991.

a. Author's purpose:

The author's purpose is to inform.

b. Your explanation:

The source is a textbook.

3. Their pets may be virtual, but some owners shed real tears when their Tamagotchis die. Like other pets, the handheld electronic hatchlings require plenty of TLC. Neglect kills most, while others die of old age. Comfort and closure can be found in Cornwall, En-

gland, where pet cemetery proprietor Terry Squires has fenced off a special patch just for the digital dearly departed. For less than £4.50, or about $8, each virtual pet will get a 5-by-10-inch wooden coffin, a plot about a foot deep, a headstone and a fistful of flowers. So far 20 graves have been dug. "Kids are very serious about raising them," says Squires. "So we're serious about burying them."

From *Newsweek*, January 12, 1998, "For the Dearly Departed."

a. Author's purpose:

The author's purpose is to entertain.

b. Your explanation:

The source is a magazine that reports newsworthy events, both to inform

and entertain. This one entertains with its humor.

4. Use of the media, particularly television, has almost become a way of life in recent presidential, congressional, and gubernatorial races. A campaign is often organized around media coverage. Candidates make decisions about trips, rallies, and press conferences with an eye to attracting the press and meeting its schedules. Because advertising costs so much, campaign managers work hard to maximize free television-news as well as radio and newspaper coverage to promote their candidates' virtues. Consequently, a candidate's speeches and rallies before large crowds are often scheduled so as to appear on the evening local and network news programs.

From Alan R. Gitelson, Robert L. Dudley, Melvin J. Dubnick, *American Government,* fourth edition. Boston: Houghton Mifflin, 1996.

a. Author's purpose:

The authors' purpose is to inform.

b. Your explanation:

The source is a textbook. In this passage, the authors explain how candidates

use the media.

5. You should share reactions to a work-related problem or issue as soon after the incident as possible. It is often difficult to recapture a feeling once it has passed, and you may distort the incident if you let too much time go by. Your memory is not infallible. The person who caused the hurt feelings is also likely to forget details about the situation.

   If something really bothers you, express your feelings. Clear the air as soon as possible so you can enjoy greater peace of mind. Some people maintain the burden of hurt feelings and resentment for days, weeks, even years. The avoidance of self-disclosure usually has a negative effect on a person's mental and physical health as well as on job performance.

From Barry L. Reece and Rhonda Brandt, *Effective Human Relations in Organizations,* sixth edition. Boston: Houghton Mifflin, 1996.

a. Author's purpose:

  The authors' purpose is to persuade.

b. Your explanation:

  The source is a textbook. The authors want to persuade readers to express

  their feelings about work-related problems. The word "should" is a clue.

DISTINGUISH FACTS FROM OPINIONS

Authors often have strong opinions about topics and issues. To read critically, you must be able to determine whether those opinions are valid. A *valid* opinion is one that can be supported by the details, some of which may be facts and some of which may be other opinions. Therefore, you must be able to distinguish between facts and opinions.

A *fact* is something that can be proven right or wrong. Your birthdate is a fact. Why? Because records are kept of all births, and people have access to the record. Similarly, dates, names of people and places, statistics, and other numerical data are facts as are scientific theories such as gravity and photosynthesis. Such theories have been tested so often that they have gained acceptance by the scientific community and the general public. Matters of law are facts. For example, not everyone believes that all people are equal. However, everyone *is* equal under the law.

An *opinion* is a value, belief, preference, attitude, or feeling. An opinion cannot be proven right or wrong. You may believe that red is a prettier color than blue, but that is a matter of taste. Someone else may like blue better.

But some opinions are so important to us that we think others should share them. People will go to great lengths to persuade others to change their opinions. Consider what happens during presidential elections. Republicans and Democrats alike try to convince the public that their candidate is the best person for the job. However, the "best" candidate is a matter of opinion.

How do you decide whether a statement is a fact or an opinion? Ask yourself, "Where did the author get the information?" Facts can be checked by going to an authoritative source such as an encyclopedia, almanac, the public record, a recognized book or study, or an expert in the field. Opinions are only as good as the facts that back them up.

Now read the following statements and determine which is a fact and which is an opinion.

1. Former President Kennedy said, "Ask not what your country can do for you; ask what you can do for your country."
2. The United States has done so much for us that we should be willing to give back something in return.

The first statement is a fact. The former president did make this statement in one of his speeches. Kennedy's speeches are a matter of public record. A book of quotations such as *Bartlett's* or *Simpson's* is one source you could check. The second statement is an opinion. Although you may agree with the idea that is expressed, you cannot prove it. Words like *should, ought, good, bad, best, preferable,* and others are value words. A statement in which one of these words appears expresses a value or belief and, therefore, an opinion.

Should you dismiss opinions because they are not facts? Not at all. Instead you should question opinions by seeking facts and explanations. Figure 10.2 lists ways to distinguish facts from opinions.

Memory Cue

A fact *is anything that can be proven such as a date, name, or statistic.* Opinions *are value judgments or beliefs, and they cannot be proven.* Value words such as *good,* bad, *or* should *can help you identify opinions.*

FIGURE 10.2 How to Distinguish Facts from Opinions

	Definition	What to Look For	How to Verify
FACT	A fact is anything that can be proven right or wrong.	dates, dollar amounts, names of people and places, statistics and other figures, laws, scientific theories	Check facts by going to an authority: a respected book or periodical, an expert, or the public record.
OPINION	An opinion is a value judgment, belief, or feeling that cannot be proven right or wrong.	value words such as *should, ought, must, good, bad, pretty, ugly,* and so on	Look for the facts, theories, or explanations on which the opinion is based.

Exercise 10.3   Read each statement and circle whether it is a fact or opinion. Then explain your choice. The first one is done as an example.

1. We should not support legislation that would take benefits away from the poor.

   a. fact or (opinion)?

   b. *"Should" is a value word.*

2. I believe that capital punishment is wrong.

   a. fact or (opinion)?

   b. *"Believe" and "wrong" are value words.*

3. In the United States, a person accused of a crime is considered innocent until proven guilty.

   a. (fact) or opinion?

   b. *This statement is common knowledge and is based in the law.*

4. The Fifth Amendment guarantees fair treatment to all under the law.

   a. (fact) or opinion?

   b. *The Fifth Amendment is the source.*

5. If people are going to live and work in the United States, they should be willing to become U.S. citizens.

    a. fact or (opinion)?

    b. *"Should" is a value word.*

6. The fall of the Soviet Union ended the Cold War.

    a. (fact) or opinion?

    b. *This is a fact of history. Textbooks and periodicals are sources.*

7. My company's healthcare plan is a good one that provides the kind of coverage I want.

    a. fact or (opinion)?

    b. *"Good" is a value word.*

8. After hurricane Andrew, Miami received federal aid.

    a. (fact) or opinion?

    b. *This is a fact of history. Periodicals are the sources.*

9. Hurricane Andrew was the worst hurricane anyone has ever seen.

    a. fact or (opinion)?

    b. *"Worst" is a value word.*

10. World War II broke out in August 1914.

    a. (fact) or opinion?

    b. *This is a fact of history. Reference books and others are sources.*

Exercise 10.4 Read each passage below, then answer the questions to identify facts and opinions.

Passage 1

While skeptics still doubt the profitability of e-commerce, Americans are busy shopping. Last year on-line sales topped the $1 billion mark for the first time. Most of that record spending was for books and CDs. But for the adventurous, there's more exciting shopping to be found. For those with a 007 complex, there's Spy Stuff (www.spystuff.com), which sells video cameras disguised as ties. Rather relax than spy? Try CyberBath Catalogue (www.bath.com), which will deliver a sauna to your door. For bargain hunters, the U.S. Treasury Department (www.treas.gov) lists confiscated cars and houses up for auction. If cash isn't an issue, try U.S. Submarines (www.ussubs.com). Personal models sell for $1.2 million to $75 million.

From *Newsweek*, January 12, 1998, "Attention Shoppers."

a. Is the second sentence a fact or an opinion? Why?

Fact. Companies keep records of sales figures.

_____

b. What makes the fourth sentence an opinion?

"Exciting" is a value word.

_____

c. What are three additional facts stated in the passage?

The names, websites, what they provide, and dollar amounts are facts.

(Answers may vary.)

Passage 2

Sometimes when I think back to the Sixties and the heroes I grew up with, it seems that no one is left.   1

President Kennedy is dead. The Beatles can never sing together again. Martin Luther King is dead.   2

But then it occurs to me: one man remains. James Bond is still alive.   3

He is still alive in the person of Sean Connery. Connery no longer portrays Bond in the movies, but to a generation of Americans he was, and is, the only James Bond. His successors were merely imitations . . .   4

From "So . . . We Meet at Last, Mr. Bond," an essay by Bob Greene in *He Was a Midwestern Boy on His Own,* New York: Ballantine, 1991.

a. Is the statement in the first paragraph a fact or opinion? Why?

    Opinion: The author tells you what he thinks.
    _____

b. What facts are stated in paragraph 2? How could you verify them?

    The deaths of Kennedy and King and the breakup of the Beatles can be

    verified by newspapers and reference books.

c. In paragraph 4, the second sentence states both a fact and opinion. What is the fact and what is the opinion?

    That Connery no longer plays Bond is a fact. That his successors were

    imitations is the author's opinion.

Passage 3

When Neil Armstrong stepped onto the moon in 1969, millions of people back on earth heard his radio transmission: "That's one small step for a man, one giant leap for mankind." But if Armstrong had taken off his space helmet and shouted, "Whoo-ee! I can moonwalk!" not even an astronaut three feet away could have heard him. Why? Because he would have been speaking into airless, empty space. **Sound** is a repetitive fluctuation in the pressure of a medium, such as air; in a place like the moon, which has almost no atmospheric medium, sound cannot exist.

From Bernstein, Clarke-Stewart, Roy, and Wickens, *Psychology,* fourth edition. Boston: Houghton Mifflin, 1997.

a. Is it a fact or opinion that millions of people heard Armstrong's radio transmission? Why?

    Fact: Records are available of the transmission and size of audience.
    _____

b. Did Armstrong's quotation express a fact or opinion? Why?

   Opinion: "Small" and "giant" are value words. Armstrong expressed a feeling.

c. Does the last sentence in the passage state a fact or opinion? How do you know?

   Fact: The definition of sound is a scientific fact, as is the conclusion that

   sound cannot exist without an atmospheric medium.

Passage 4

At least four times over the last 3 million years, decreases in world   1
temperatures have triggered ice ages that gripped the entire planet. Vast
ice sheets called glaciers covered much of the northern United States as
recently as 12,000 years ago. . . . At other times—100 million years ago
during the great age of the dinosaurs—for example—the earth became
so warm that even Greenland and Antarctica had tropical climates.

Astronomers, geologists, and climatologists think that two classes of   2
astronomical events—changes in the earth's orbit and encounters with
other heavenly bodies—may be behind some of these phenomena. The
earth's position in orbit around the sun is a critical determinant of the
amount of solar energy the planet receives, so instabilities in the earth's
orbit can cause long-term changes in global temperature. . . .

From Levine and Miller, *Biology.* Lexington, MA: D.C. Heath, 1991.

a. Does the first sentence, paragraph 1, state a fact or opinion? How can you tell?

   Fact: Scientific theories explain the development of ice ages.

b. In paragraph 2, is it a fact or opinion that two classes of astronomical events may be behind the changes in temperature described in paragraph 1? How can you tell?

   Opinion: "May" and "think" suggest that the experts are undecided.

c. Does the last sentence of paragraph 2 state a fact or opinion? Explain your answer.

Fact: The effects stated are scientific facts.

MAKE INFERENCES FROM YOUR READING

An *inference* is an act of reasoning that leads to a conclusion. An inference is an educated guess about something you do not know based on what you do know. Making inferences is what you do when you "read between the lines" to determine an author's meaning.

Some inferences are better than others. A good inference is one that is based on available facts combined with prior knowledge and experience.

Suppose your last test grade was low. You might infer that the instructor does not like you, that the test was too hard, or that you were not well prepared. Which of these inferences is best? It is unlikely that the instructor's grades are based on personal feelings about students. It is also unlikely that the instructor would prepare a test that was too difficult for students who have studied. It is more likely that your lack of preparation led to a poor grade. Perhaps you did not study enough, or perhaps you studied the wrong things. What knowledge and experience would lead to that inference? First of all, you could examine your mistakes. Were they the result of poor studying or a lack of understanding? Second, let your experience guide you. Have you made poor grades in the past? What were the reasons?

The questions instructors ask to test your knowledge are on different levels of difficulty. Some questions ask you to recall stated facts, and they are easy to answer if you have studied the material. Some questions ask you to apply what you have learned to a new situation, and they are more difficult because they force you to make inferences.

Making inferences requires careful reading and critical thinking. To make good inferences, ask yourself three questions:

- What do I already know?
- What experience do I have?
- What new information is given?

In the folk tale on pages 292–294, the author's message is not directly stated. However, you can determine the meaning of the folk tale by making a few inferences. First of all, what do you already know? You may know that some folk tales explain natural events ("How the Camel Got His Hump"), some teach moral lessons ("The Hare and the Tortoise"), and some pass on the traditions of a culture (*Tales from 1001 Arabian Knights*). Also, a folk tale may have more than one message.

What experience do you have? If you have read any folk tales, you can apply what you remember to your reading of "The King of the Frogs." To determine what new information is given, examine the details of the story: What happens? Who is involved? In paragraphs 1–3 the author explains that at night when you hear frogs croaking the sound is interrupted by periods of silence. Why? Paragraph 4 says, "There is a story about this." All the paragraphs following paragraph 4 tell that story. In a nutshell, the frogs quiet down whenever they think "the frog king" (the crocodile) is near because they do not want to be eaten. So this tale's message is to explain a natural event: why the frogs sound the way they do.

Is there another message? Perhaps. Why did the crocodile make a better king than the stone? Your inferences may lead you to discover a moral lesson in "The King of the Frogs."

Why is making inferences an important skill to have? In college, not only do you learn skills and develop knowledge, but you must be able to apply what you have learned to new situations. Throughout your life, you will be faced with having to make decisions and solve problems based on scanty evidence. To make good inferences, you must use what is given, along with your knowledge and experience, to achieve the outcomes you want.

Memory Cue

An inference is an act of reasoning that leads to a conclusion. To make good inferences apply your knowledge and experience to the information that is given.

Exercise 10.5   Read and discuss each passage with a partner. Then using your knowledge, experience, and facts from the passage, circle the best inference. Be prepared to discuss your answers with the rest of the class.

1. After the movie, Dawn watched the people pouring out into the lobby. None of them were smiling. In fact, several people were sniffling and brushing away tears.

a. Some of the people had colds.

(b.) The movie was sad.

c. No one liked the movie.

2. Some mosquitoes transmit diseases such as malaria that are harmful to humans. However, these kinds of mosquitoes are rarely reported in our area.

(a.) We should avoid contact with mosquitoes.

b. We have nothing to fear from mosquitoes.

c. No one in our area has been infected with malaria.

3. When Sarah entered her office, she noticed a sickening odor. The carpet had been pulled up near the corner of the room, and Sarah found some seeds and berries underneath. She also noticed that a mousetrap had been sprung, but it was empty.

a. The plumbing had backed up.

(b.) A mouse may have died somewhere in the building.

c. Sarah's building was old and needed repairs.

4. When asked whether he was in favor of raising taxes to improve education, the candidate said, "We must ensure that our children learn the skills that will enable them to compete in today's marketplace."

a. The candidate is against raising taxes.

b. The candidate has a plan for improving education.

(c.) The candidate does not want to commit himself.

5. The writer of Chris's letter of recommendation stated, "I recommend that you hire the applicant for any position for which he may be qualified."

a. The writer believes that Chris is qualified.

b. The writer believes that Chris is unqualified.

(c.) The writer does not know whether Chris is qualified.

Exercise 10.6 The following passage is from Zora Neale Hurston's autobiography, *Dust Tracks on a Road,* published in 1942. This is the kind of passage you might be required to read in a literature or English composition course. To answer the questions that follow, you must make inferences from the details in the passage. Now read the passage and answer the questions.

I discovered that I was extra strong by playing with other girls near my age. I had no way of judging the force of my playful blows, and so I was always hurting somebody. Then they would say I meant to hurt, and go home and leave me. Everything was all right, however, when I played with boys. It was a shameful thing to admit being hurt among them. Furthermore, they could dish it out themselves, and I was acceptable to them because I was the one girl who could take a good pummeling without running home to tell. The fly in the ointment there, was that in my family it was not ladylike for girls to play with boys. No matter how young you were, no good could come of the thing. I used to wonder what was wrong with playing with boys. Nobody told me. I just mustn't, that was all. What was wrong with my doll-babies? Why couldn't I just sit still and make my dolls some clothes?

1

I never did. Dolls caught the devil around me. They got into fights and leaked sawdust before New Year's. They jumped off the barn and tried to drown themselves in the lake. Perhaps, the dolls bought for me looked too different from the ones I made up myself. The dolls I made up in my mind did everything. Those store-bought things had to be toted and helped around. Without knowing it, I wanted some action. . . .

2

1. What is Hurston's topic?

   Hurston's topic is the way she played as a child.

2. Is her purpose to inform, persuade, or entertain? Explain your reasons.

   Hurston expresses her feelings. Her purpose is to entertain.

   _____

3. How was Hurston different from other girls her age?

   Hurston was extra strong. She preferred to play boys' games. She did not

   want the kind of dolls that other girls played with.

4. Who is asking the questions at the end of paragraph 1, and how can you tell?

    Hurston is asking the questions, but she is repeating the kinds of questions

    the adults asked her.

5. Why do you suppose Hurston's family thought playing with boys was not ladylike?

    When Hurston grew up, little girls and little boys had different roles, games,

    toys, and expected behaviors.

6. What do you think Hurston means by the last line in paragraph 2?

    Hurston wanted to do something with her life. She did not want to do only

    what was expected. (Answers may vary.)

7. How would you compare Hurston as a girl growing up in the early 1900s to girls growing up today? What is different or the same?

    Our ideas about "boys' games" and "girls' games" have changed. Today the

    gender roles are not as distinct in play.

EVALUATE WHAT YOU READ

To *evaluate* what you read means to determine whether the facts are accurate and whether the opinions expressed are valid. Whether you are reading a book, a magazine article, or some information you have accessed through the Internet, you can evaluate it by asking yourself three questions:

- Is it reliable?
- Is it objective?
- Is it useful?

Reliability

A source is *reliable* if it is written by an authority on the subject. A textbook is considered a reliable source. Certain well-respected newspapers and magazines are considered reliable, for example, *The Washington Post, New York Times,* and news magazines such as *Time* and *Newsweek.*

Experts in their fields are reliable sources. For example, when you are sick, you see a doctor; if you think your house may have termite damage, you call an exterminator. Similarly, if you are assigned a research project, you must look for reliable sources of information on your topic. Encyclopedias and other reference tools are reliable. Your instructor or librarian can help you determine which books and articles are the most reliable sources for your topic.

Journals, quarterlies, and magazines devoted to a specific field may also be reliable sources. The *New England Journal of Medicine*, the *Reading Research Quarterly*, and *Science* magazine are a few.

Objectivity

A source is objective if facts and sound reasoning are offered to back up opinions. Objective sources are fair. Their authors acknowledge other viewpoints besides their own. Moreover, objective sources are generally free of bias and slanted language. *Bias* is a strong, usually unreasoned, opinion for or against something. *Slanted language* uses strong words that have an emotional content. For example, the phrase "pro-life" used by those who oppose abortion suggests that their opponents are against life. The phrase "pro-choice" used by those who favor abortion suggests that their opponents wish to deprive others of choices. Use of such language clouds issues, making it difficult for the general public to distinguish facts from opinions on both sides.

Usefulness

A source is *useful* if it improves your understanding of the subject. For example, what have you gained from the reading? Have you learned a skill or gained knowledge that you can use now and in the future? A source is useful if it tells you what you need to know about your topic.

To evaluate your reading, keep these standards in mind: *reliability*, *objectivity*, and *usefulness*. You can also use these same standards to evaluate what you hear in lectures and speeches. As a memory cue, read Figure 10.3, which lists the standards of evaluation and questions to ask that will help you apply them.

Exercise 10.7   Working with a partner, read and discuss each question and possible answers. Then circle your choice. Be prepared to discuss your answers with the rest of the class.

FIGURE 10.3 Use Three Standards to Evaluate What You Read

Standards	Questions to Ask
Reliability	Is the author an expert? What are the author's sources?
Objectivity	Are all sides presented? Are opinions supported with facts? Is the language slanted or biased?
Usefulness	What skill or knowledge have I gained? How can I use the information? Have I learned what I need to know?

---

1. Which of the following would be the most reliable source of a witness's testimony in a controversial trial?
   a. someone who was there
   b. an account of the trial on the evening news
   c. the court record

2. Which of the following would give you the most objective description of the effects of El Niño?
   a. an expert on weather conditions
   b. a spokesperson for the EPA (Environmental Protection Agency)
   c. a politician who supports environmentalism

3. If you wanted to read about a favorite author's life and works, which source would probably be the most useful?
   a. a biographical index
   b. the information printed on the jacket of one of the author's books
   c. a book review printed in a magazine or newspaper

4. To determine whether a candidate for state representative supports an issue that you favor, which would be your most objective source?
   a. the candidate's speech
   b. an interview with the candidate's campaign manager
   c. the candidate's voting record

5. You have an upcoming math test, and you know that you need to review several concepts. Although each of the following sources may be useful, which one is the most reliable?

   a. your notes
   (b.) the textbook
   c. old tests

REAL-WORLD CONNECTIONS

Do you still wonder sometimes "What should I study?" or "How can I tell what is important?" You can use two critical thinking skills to answer these questions.

When you review a chapter, ask yourself, "What is the author's purpose?" If chapter objectives are listed at the beginning, then you know that the author's purpose is for you to learn these objectives. If there are no objectives, look for the author's purpose stated near the introduction to the chapter. For example, suppose you need to study a chapter on the human memory from your psychology text. The introduction tells you that your objective is to learn the functions of memory: how we take in, process, store, and retrieve information for future use. Now you know that you need to study these functions. Later in the chapter, you will probably find a diagram of the functions in addition to a detailed explanation of each. As you can see, the author's purpose is a strong clue to what is important in a chapter.

Making inferences is another skill you can use to determine what to study. Examine old tests. Which questions did you miss? Which ones did you get right? If you are studying for a review test, then you need to review information that you missed on previous tests. If the test covers new information, then you need to look over your notes to determine what your instructor has emphasized. Studying with a partner can help. His or her notes may help you fill any gaps in your memory.

Now try this exercise: Use inferences and the author's purpose to determine what will be covered on an upcoming test in one of your courses. Review your textbook, notes, and old tests. On the following lines, write three questions your instructor is likely to ask. Then answer your questions. Use extra paper as needed. *(Questions and answers will vary.)*

1. Question: _____

   Answer: _____

2. Question: _____

   Answer: _____

3. Question: _____

   Answer: _____

HOW WELL DO YOU REMEMBER?

 To review the chapter, read the following summary and fill in the blanks. If you need help with an answer, look back through the chapter to refresh your memory.

Critical thinking is _____*logical*_____ thinking that involves many skills. Many of your college assignments require critical thinking.

To think critically, you must be able to determine an author's _____*purpose*_____, or reason for writing. For example, if an author expects readers to understand or be able to do something, the purpose is to _____*inform*_____. If an author expects readers to take a stand or change an opinion, the purpose is to _____*persuade*_____. If an author expects readers to enjoy themselves and perhaps learn something in the process, the purpose is to _____*entertain*_____.

To think critically you must be able to distinguish facts from opinions. A _____*fact*_____ is something that can be proven. On the other hand, beliefs, values, and preferences are _____*opinions*_____. A _____*valid*_____ opinion is one that the facts support.

To think critically you must be able to make inferences or read between the lines. An ___*inference*___ is an educated guess about something you do not know based on what you do know.

To think critically, you must evaluate what you read by checking it for ___*objectivity*___ , ___*reliability*___ , and ___*usefulness*___ .

WHAT DO YOU THINK?

Are you a confident reader? Which of the reading strategies covered in this book have been most helpful? Which of your reading skills still need improvement? What will you do to improve these skills and gain even more confidence?

Reflections will vary.

_____

_____

_____

CHAPTER QUIZ 1

Part 1 Terms and Definitions

Match each term in Column A with its definition in Column B.

Column A

___*g*___ 1. literal reading level
___*e*___ 2. critical reading level
___*d*___ 3. critical thinking
___*f*___ 4. purpose
___*b*___ 5. valid
___*a*___ 6. inform
___*h*___ 7. persuade
___*c*___ 8. entertain

Column B

a. to teach or explain
b. can be supported
c. to express ideas
d. logical thinking
e. what an author means
f. a reason for writing
g. what an author says
h. to provoke or influence

Part 2 Chapter Review

Read and answer each question below. Write your answer in complete sentences, and use extra paper if needed. *(Answers will vary but should be similar to these.)*

1. How can you determine an author's purpose? Where do you look for clues?

    Look for clues in the title, details, and opening paragraph. Also, consider

    the source.

2. What is the difference between a fact and an opinion? Give an example of each.

    Facts such as names, dates, and places can be proven. Opinions are values

    and beliefs. They cannot be proven right or wrong.

3. Are some opinions better than others? Why or why not?

    Opinions that are supported with evidence are informed opinions. Such

    opinions are better, or more valid, than uninformed ones.

Part 3 Using Your Skills

1. Identify these statements from the textbook *Childhood and Adolescent Development* as facts or opinions. Write *F* for fact and *O* for opinion.

    __F__ a. "In the United States, some African-Americans use a dialect, or version, of English called *Black English* that differs from the . . . dialect that linguists call *Standard English*." *(A linguist could verify this statement.)*

    __F__ b. "Studies of Black English have found it to be as complex as any other language, including Standard English, and equally capable of expressing the full range of human thought and emotion (Smitherman-Donaldson, 1994)." *(The source of the studies is given.)*

    __O__ c. "Unfortunately, society's attitudes toward it remain rather negative, which has created dilemmas for teachers of students who use Black English." *("Unfortunately" is a value word as is "negative.")*

___F___ d. "Educators typically recommend a compromise: teachers should respect Black English, appreciate its richness, and allow students to use it in class some of the time." *(That educators make this recommendation can be verified.)*

___O___ e. "Teachers should also encourage students to practice Standard English because it probably will help them in situations where they must communicate more formally." *("Should" and "probably" are value words.)*

2. Read each passage and determine whether the author's main purpose is to inform, persuade, or entertain. Write your answer and explanation on the lines provided.

a. For nearly 25 years, the Endangered Species act has held up as the nation's embattled yet enduring shield against wildlife extinction. But today, in an ill-conceived political compromise, Congress is on the verge of diminishing the act's very purpose of protecting animal and plant life from oblivion at the hands of human action.

The shame is that the law could be improved with a different, reasonable, and more widely accepted compromise. . . .

From an article appearing in *National Wildlife*.

Purpose: _Persuade_____

Explanation: _The author's strong language ("ill-conceived," "embattled,"___

*"shame," "oblivion") and the source are clues.*_____

b. For most, afternoon tea in Britain suggests a genteel cup and saucer. But Brooke Bond, the country's largest tea company, now hopes a thirst for convenience will convince Brits to drink their national beverage from a can. The new pop-top restoratives, selling for about 90 cents at corner stores, are kept in heated cabinets at 133 degrees Fahrenheit—the perfect drinking temperature for tea. Purists may not be swayed, but Mav Halai of Cards and Candy, one of

the first shops to stock the tea, says, "Sales have been unbelievable."
What's next: cold beer?

From *Newsweek*

Purpose: *Entertain*

Explanation: *The author writes playfully about canned tea. The question at the end and the lack of seriousness are clues to the purpose.*

c. Both common sense and research suggest that abilities come in many forms. But do these forms add up to one truly general intelligence or to an assortment of "intelligences"? Some theories of intelligence emphasize relatively specific skills; others stress one rather general ability, sometimes called g (Spearman, 1927). In practice most psychologists acknowledge the presence of both general and specific factors, although they differ in emphasis and in the number of specific factors proposed.

From Seifert and Hoffnung, *Childhood and Adolescent Development,* fourth edition. Boston: Houghton Mifflin, 1997.

Purpose: *Inform*

Explanation: *The authors want you to know that there is more than one theory of intelligence.*

d. Most offices today have designated smoking areas, and many prohibit smoking anywhere on the premises. If you smoke, follow the rules strictly. Smoking in public anywhere is increasingly considered bad manners, not to mention a health hazard.

From Ober, *Contemporary Business Communications,* second edition. Boston: Houghton Mifflin, 1995.

Purpose: *persuade*

Explanation: *"Follow the rules" is a clue. The author wants you to avoid the consequences to your health and social acceptance.*

Score: 100 − 5 for each one missed = _____ %

CHAPTER QUIZ 2

Part 1 Terms and Definitions

Match each term in Column A with its definition in Column B.

Column A	Column B
_e_ 1. inference	a. authoritative
_g_ 2. value words	b. strong opinion for or against
_h_ 3. opinion	c. emotionally strong words
_i_ 4. fact	d. revealing all sides
_f_ 5. evaluate	e. an act of reasoning
_c_ 6. slanted language	f. determine accuracy and validity
_a_ 7. reliable	g. "good," "bad," "should," and so on
_d_ 8. objective	h. value judgment or belief
_b_ 9. bias	i. something that can be proven

Part 2 Chapter Review

Read and answer each question below. Write your answer in complete sentences, and use extra paper if needed. *(Answers will vary but should be similar to these.)*

1. To make an inference, what questions should you ask yourself?

   What do I already know? What experience do I have? What new

   information is given?

2. How can you evaluate what you read?

   Evaluate what you read by asking "Is it objective?" "Is it reliable?" "Is it

   useful?"

3. What is slanted language? Give an example.

   Slanted language consists of strong words that have an emotional content.

   (Students' examples will vary.)

Part 3 Using Your Skills

Use your critical thinking skills to read the following passage and answer the questions. Use extra paper as needed.

Giving Gifts

Giving gifts to suppliers, customers, or workers within one's own organization is typical at many firms, especially in December during the holiday period. Although such gifts are often deeply appreciated, you must be sensitive in terms of whom you give a gift to and the type of gift you select. Most people would consider a gift appropriate if it meets these four criteria:

■ It is an impersonal gift. Gifts that can be used in the office or in connection with one's work are always appropriate.

■ It is for past favors. Gifts should be used to thank someone for past favors, business, or performance—*not* to create obligations for the future. A gift to a prospective customer who has never ordered from you before might be interpreted as a bribe.

■ It is given to everyone in similar circumstances. Singling out one person for a gift and ignoring others in similar positions would not only embarrass the one selected but create bad feelings among those who were ignored.

■ It is not extravagant. A very expensive gift might make the recipient uneasy, create a sense of obligation, and call into question the motives of the giver.

Although it is often the custom for a superior to give a subordinate a gift, especially one's secretary, it is less usual for the subordinate to give a personal gift to a superior. More likely, coworkers will contribute to a joint gift for the boss, again selecting one that is neither too expensive nor too personal. As always, follow local customs when giving gifts to international colleagues.

From Ober, *Contemporary Business Communications*, second edition. Boston: Houghton Mifflin, 1995.

1. What is the main idea?

  "Most people would . . ." (first paragraph, third sentence)

2. Is the author's purpose to inform, persuade, or entertain? Explain your answer.

   Inform: The author explains how to choose gifts for people at work.

3. According to the author, under what condition would a gift be considered a bribe?

   A gift to someone who has never ordered from you might be considered a

   bribe.

4. According to the author, under what condition might a gift make someone uneasy or create a sense of obligation?

   Expensive gifts may make someone uneasy or create a sense of obligation.

5. Is the first sentence in the first paragraph a fact or opinion? Why?

   Fact: You can verify it by direct observation.

6. Is the second sentence in the first paragraph a fact or opinion? Why?

   Opinion: "Appreciated" and "sensitive" are value words.

7. What would be an appropriate gift for an international colleague?

   A gift that follows local customs would be appropriate.

8. Would clothing or jewelry be appropriate gifts for a coworker? Why?

   These are personal gifts, so they would not be appropriate.

9. Is the information reliable? Explain your answer.

   The source is a business text by an author who is an expert. (Students should

   consider the source as reliable.)

10. Is the information useful? (How will you use it?)

    Answers will vary.

Score: 100 − 5 for each one missed = _____%

Vocabulary Quiz

Each sentence below contains a word in bold type from the reading selection on pages 292–294. Read the sentence and the definitions that follow it. Then circle the correct one. Turn to the vocabulary preview on page 292 to check your answers.

1. We admired how skilled and **lithe** the ballet dancer's movements were.
   a. clumsy
   b. out of step
   c. graceful
   d. unattractive

2. On his ski vacation, Tim stuck to the beginner's slope and never **ventured** to try the intermediate or advanced ones.
   a. feared
   b. took a risk
   c. avoided
   d. had time

3. The jogger slipped on a rock and took a **dreadful** fall that resulted in a broken nose.
   a. terrible
   b. painless
   c. downhill
   d. wonderful

4. Mosquitoes like to lay their eggs near water, on a **reed** for example.
   a. maple tree
   b. telephone pole
   c. tall stalk of grass
   d. sidewalk

5. All who stopped and **gaped** at the accident scene were told to move along as soon as the police arrived.
   a. passed through
   b. belonged at the scene
   c. responded to calls for help
   d. stared with open mouths

6. The musicians who took off their clothes on stage were arrested for such **scandalous** conduct.
    a. hilarious
    b. artistic
    c. musical
    d. outrageous

7. Mona soon grew tired of cleaning up after the **untidy** tourists who rented her beachfront cottage every summer.
    a. happy
    b. disorderly
    c. loud
    d. playful

8. The organization voted to **commission** the president to hire a speaker for their convention.
    a. stop
    b. prevent
    c. give authority
    d. give praise

Score: 100 − 12 for each one missed = _____ %

Unit

4

Using Your Skills: More Readings

Selection 1

WHAT DO YOU ALREADY KNOW?

To prepare yourself for the reading selection that follows, find out what you already know about making excuses. Answer the questions below either on your own or in a group discussion.

1. In your opinion, do most people seem willing or unwilling to accept blame for their mistakes?

2. When bad things happen to you, are they usually the result of bad luck or bad decisions?

3. When things go wrong, how often do you say, "It's not my fault": most of the time, sometimes, or never?

4. Read the title, headnote, vocabulary preview, and first two paragraphs of the reading selection. What do you think will follow?

It's Not My Fault

Carol Tavris

In this selection, which originally appeared in Vogue *magazine, Carol Tavris suggests that excuse-making has replaced personal responsibility.*

VOCABULARY PREVIEW

perjury   (pûr´jə·rē) false testimony given under oath

obscenity   (ŏb·sĕn´ĭ·tē) something that offends accepted standards of decency or right and wrong

compulsive (kəm·pŭl´sĭv) uncontrollable, acting without restraint

vulnerable (vŭl´nər·ə·bəl) unprotected from harm or personal attack

rationalize (răsh´ə·nə·līz) to give self-satisfying but false reasons for behavior

transgression (trăns·grĕsh´ən) wrongdoing, errors, crimes

attributed (ə·trĭb´yə·tĭd) regarded as the cause

Pronunciation Key: ă (**pat**), ĕ (**pet**), ē (**bee**), ĭ (**pit**), ī (**pie**), ŭ (**cut**), ûr (**urge**), ə(**about, item**), ŏ;(**pot**)

In California, a woman was accused of murdering her infant son. She killed him, the defense claimed, while suffering from postpartum depression. In San Antonio, Texas, a man confessed to raping a woman three times. But the jury agreed that *he* was the victim—of a high testosterone level. Michael Deaver* excused his **perjury** by saying he was "forgetful" due to his drinking problem. We are in the midst of an excuse epidemic in America.   1

William Wilbanks, professor of criminal justice at Florida International University in North Miami, thinks these excuses are all variations on the same theme: "I can't help myself." Wilbanks calls this phrase the "new **obscenity,**" because, he says, "it is offensive to the core concept of humanity": that human beings have free will and are capable of self-discipline and responsibility.   2

Across the country, clinicians are treating the "sexually **compulsive**" man who can't control his sexual desires, the "love-addicted" woman who can't break out of bad relationships, and millions of people addicted to drugs or alcohol—or who are allegedly addicted to those who are.   3

"There is a growing tendency in the scientific community to view human beings as objects who are acted upon by internal and external   4

*Michael Deaver served under President Ronald Reagan.

forces over which they have no control," says Wilbanks. "We mistakenly infer that people *cannot* exercise self-control." We overlook the millions of men with high testosterone levels who do not rape, the depressed women who do not murder their children, and the great majority of addicts who decide to quit and do.

"The new obscenity of 'you can't help yourself' only convinces the person that her problem is hopeless and she might as well give up," says Wilbanks. "It thereby produces the very kind of problem behavior it attempts to explain. The problem with the medical model of misbehavior is that it completely ignores the idea of moral choice and resistance to temptation."

5

At the University of Kansas, C. R. Snyder, Ph.D., and Raymond L. Higgins, Ph.D., are also interested in the growing number of categories the public accepts as legitimate excuses for irresponsible, self-defeating, or criminal behavior. While Wilbanks is concerned about the effect of excuses on the legal system and society at large, Snyder is concerned about the effects of excuses on individual health and well-being.

6

Snyder has been studying the psychology of excuses for years. "Excuses—such as, 'It's not my fault,' 'The dog ate it,' 'I didn't *mean* to break her jaw'—soften the link between you and an unfortunate or negative action," says Snyder. "Of course, without excuses, we would be exposed and **vulnerable.** They protect our self-esteem. But sometimes, people also use excuses to **rationalize** the destructive things they do."

7

Excuses become self-defeating, says Snyder, when their costs outweigh their benefits. "A woman who blames unacceptable behavior on her depression or an 'addiction,'" he says, "finds that her future **transgressions** are automatically **attributed** to her problem— thus, her excuse becomes what's known as a self-handicapping strategy. It excuses her behavior in the short run, but in the long run it undermines her self-esteem and sense of personal control."

8

As a psychotherapist as well as a researcher, Snyder is particularly concerned about people who move from making the excuse to being the excuse. "With some people, the excuse becomes part of their identities," says Snyder. "I couldn't help myself; I *am* an addict/rapist/abuser; I *am* depressed/shy/angry."

9

Snyder observes that it is particularly difficult to treat those with built-in excuses. Once people define themselves as helpless slaves to a problem, they hand over control of the problem to others. Or they find an explanation for the problem that is out of their hands: "I can't help the way I am; my mother made me this way"—an ever-popular choice for blame. (As a client of one of Snyder's colleagues told him: "It's like this: if it's not my fault, it's her fault, and if it's not her fault,

10

it's still not my fault.") For people whose excuses have become a problem, says Snyder, successful therapy depends on breaking down their self-deceptive, self-protective excuses and making them face the link between themselves and their actions.

Both Wilbanks and Snyder recognize that a humane legal system will consider some conditions—such as defending oneself or one's family, or having an organic brain disorder—to be legitimate excuses for a defendant's behavior. But they oppose the growing tendency in psychology and law to excuse behavior we don't like: to confuse moral judgments with scientific ones, and to confuse learned habits with organic deficiencies. 11

Furthermore, Wilbanks believes that for society's sake, as well as for the thousands of people who are being taught to think of themselves as helpless victims of life or biology, it is time to restore confidence in self-control and self-determination. "People can learn to respond to temptations by asking themselves, 'Does this behavior fit my self-image?' " says Wilbanks, "rather than, 'Can I get away with it?' " 12

HOW WELL DID YOU COMPREHEND?

Main Idea

1. Which of the following statements best expresses the central idea of the whole selection?
   a. Making excuses is only one way to handle a difficult situation.
   b. Some scientists believe that we cannot help making mistakes.
   c. Making excuses has become widespread in the United States.
   d. People make many different kinds of excuses.

2. The author's main purpose is to
   a. inform readers about current research in human behavior.
   b. persuade readers that we are becoming a nation of excuse-makers.
   c. entertain readers with stories about people whose excuses have gotten them into trouble.

Details

3. All but one of the following are the author's examples of people who think they have no control. Which one is *not*?
   a. the sexually compulsive man
   b. a love-addicted woman

c. those addicted to alcohol and drugs

(d.) addicts who decide to quit and do

4. According to Snyder, what is the best way to help people whose excuses have become a problem?

   a. Teach them to be more self-protective.

   b. Show them how to rationalize their problems.

   (c.) Make them face the link between themselves and their actions.

   d. Tell them that it is acceptable to blame others for their own mistakes.

5. William Wilbanks calls the excuse "I can't help myself" the "new obscenity" because it offends

   a. standards of right and wrong.

   b. religious beliefs.

   c. our code of justice.

   (d.) the concept of free will.

Inferences

6. What is the author's overall thought pattern?

   a. example

   b. definition

   c. comparison and contrast

   (d.) cause and effect

7. To say that "people have free will and are capable of self-discipline and responsibility" means that

   a. they cannot help making excuses.

   b. they should not blame themselves.

   (c.) they can control their behavior.

   d. they will stop making excuses.

Working with Words

Complete the sentences below with these words from the vocabulary preview:

perjury	compulsive	vulnerable	obscenity
rationalize	transgressions	attributed	

1. The criminal who was convicted of armed robbery in court today was also guilty of many previous _transgressions_ .

2. Lying is wrong, so don't try to _rationalize_ a lie by saying you didn't mean it.

3. People who are ___compulsive___ about getting rid of germs may wash their hands dozens of times each day.

4. A witness who tells one story before a trial and gives a different account in court may be accused of ___perjury___.

5. Many students have ___attributed___ their success in college to effective reading and study habits.

6. A person whose previous relationships have not gone well may feel ___vulnerable___ to being hurt again.

7. "I refuse to have this ___obscenity___ in my house," said the mother who found the pornographic magazine under her child's mattress.

Thinking and Writing

1. According to the author, many people make excuses for bad behavior instead of accepting responsibility for their actions. Do you agree or disagree? Explain your reasons and use extra paper as needed.

   Answers will vary.

   _____

   _____

   _____

2. Both "It's Not My Fault" and "Time Management for College Students" on page 5 are about being responsible. Why is responsible behavior important? What does being responsible have to do with managing time? What other connections do you see between these selections? Use details from the selections to explain your answer, and use extra paper as needed.

   Answers will vary, but here is one example: Responsible behavior is

   important because it puts you in control of your life. By managing your

   time, you are taking control of it. Therefore, you are acting responsibly.

Selection 2

WHAT DO YOU ALREADY KNOW?

To prepare yourself for the reading selection that follows, find out what you already know about children's names. Answer the questions below either on your own or in a group discussion.

1. How do parents choose names for their children?

2. What names are the most popular among your age group?

3. What is an unusual name you have heard recently?

4. Read the title, headnote, vocabulary preview, and first two paragraphs of the reading selection. What do you think will follow?

Parents Creating Unique Names

Cindy Roberts

In recent years, parents, especially African-Americans, have been choosing unusual names for their children, and in some cases creating new names. In this selection by journalist Cindy Roberts, the author explains why.

VOCABULARY PREVIEW

sufficed	(sə·fīst) was enough for
quest	(kwĕst) a search
turbulent	(tûr′byə·lənt) violently disturbed
surname	(sûr′nām) last name
forename	(fôr′nām) first name
appellations	(ăp′ə·lā′shəns) names or titles
unconventional	(ŭn′kən·vĕn′shə·nəl) unusual, out of the ordinary
excluded	(ĭk·sklōōd′ĭd) not included, kept out

Pronunciation Key: ā (**pay**), ă (**pat**), ĕ (**pet**), ē (**bee**), ĭ (**pit**), ī (**pie**), ô (**for**), ōō (**boot**), ŭ (**cut**), ûr (**urge**), ə(**about, item**)

Long before YaMaya Cimone Pugh was born, her mother already had picked her name.   1

"I had known a young lady several years ago named YaMaya, and I always said if I had a daughter I would name her YaMaya. I just named her that because it was different," said LaRhonda Gilstrap, a 22-year-old computer science student.   2

She's not alone. Among those sharing the nursery with YaMaya recently at Crawford Long Hospital: Tria Armania Holloway, Jamecia Thermutus Hawkins and Ja-Min O'Haad Newson.   3

The explosion of originality in naming children has touched nearly every class, race and region, but experts say it is most pronounced among black Americans.   4

"Blacks are refusing to take white people's names," said Leonard Ashley, author of "What's in a Name?" and an English professor at Brooklyn College in New York. "They are saying, 'We are different. We are going to have our own Christmas holiday, we are going to have our own names.' "   5

At the turn of the century, the 10 most popular names in each gender category **sufficed** for half of all boys and girls, Mr. Ashley said.   6

Today, the top 10 account for an estimated 25 percent of all American names, he said. The other 75 percent, he said, are largely names rarely seen in this country until recent years, if at all.   7

The **quest** for originality and individuality began in the politically **turbulent** 1960s and '70s. For black parents, the search has meant going outside the WASP[1] mainstream to invent names or dust off ancestral ones, Mr. Ashley said.   8

"Basically, the majority of African-Americans are now naming outside the tradition," said Jerrilyn McGregory, a professor of African-American studies and English at the University of Georgia.   9

"It's a statement of cultural identity," she said. "Some people predicted it to be a fad, but it seems to be going beyond one generation."   10

No one has had more influence than the late Alex Haley,[2] whose book "Roots" inspired many black Americans to trace their African origins.   11

Kinte, the **surname** of the book's hero Kunta, began popping up across the country, as did Kizzie, the character's daughter, Ms. McGregory said.   12

Nia Damali, owner of Atlanta's Medu Bookstore, was Pat before she changed her name to reflect her African roots in 1986, when she published her book "Golden Names for an African People."   13

Her 6-month-old son, Sekou Ebun Malika, has an African **forename.**   14

"People said, 'Where did you get that name? Is his father African?' I said, 'Well he's African-American,' " said Ms. Damali.   15

Funmilayo Nonye-John, a native of Nigeria who has been a   16
maternity ward nurse at Crawford Long for the past five years, said
black parents frequently ask her to help them choose an African name.

"I try to educate people how to give a name," she said. "People   17
make up names. There's a lot of 'sha' names that are not really
African names."

Some don't care whether a name is African as long as it has a   18
nice ring to it and isn't Anglo-Saxon. The result is a treasure trove of
appellations pieced together from various sources—Swahili, Yoruba,
Spanish, French—and a lot of imagination.[3]

"Blacks are creating names out of bits and pieces of names," Mr.   19
Ashley said. "The main thing they sound is African-American. They're
fake African names, but they are genuine African-American names."

"Da," "La," "Sha" and "Ja" have emerged as among the most   20
popular ingredients. Hence Lavar, LaKeisha, LaTonya, Jabar,
Sheshandra and Daquisha.

For her master's thesis, Ms. McGregory analyzed black birth   21
records from Gary, Ind., from 1945 to 1980. Over the years, there
were more and more **unconventional** names. Of 274 girls born in
1980, 213 had different names. Some names differed only in spelling;
she found 40 versions of Tamika, for example.

The names symbolize the degree to which black Americans have   22
felt **excluded** from American life, she said.

"It's like a gift," Ms. McGregory said. "It's like saying, 'I can't give   23
you much, but I can give you a name no one else will bear.' "

HOW WELL DID YOU COMPREHEND?

Main Idea

1. Which of the following statements best expresses the central
    idea of the whole selection?
    a. Most parents do not want their children to have unusual names.
    b. Originality in names has touched everyone, especially
        African Americans.
    c. Each period of history has its own most popular names for
        boys and girls.
    d. Unique names have many sources, including other languages.

1. Wasp stands for white Anglo-Saxon Protestant.
2. Alex Haley is the author of *Roots*.
3. Swahili and Yoruba are African languages.

2. The author's main purpose is to
   a. inform readers about the trend of choosing original names.
   b. persuade readers that they should give their children unique names.
   c. entertain readers by making fun of unusual names.

Details

3. Today, the top 10 names account for what percent of all American names?
   a. 75 percent
   b. 50 percent
   c. 25 percent
   d. 10 percent

4. When did the quest for original names begin?
   a. before 1900
   b. at the turn of the century
   c. in the 1960s and 1970s
   d. as recently as 1980

5. According to the author, one of the reasons African Americans choose unique names is to
   a. be part of mainstream American life.
   b. reflect their African heritage.
   c. keep up with a trend.
   d. have a name that will be easy to remember.

Inferences

6. What is the author's overall thought pattern?
   a. listing
   b. time order
   c. comparison and contrast
   d. cause and effect

7. As we enter the twenty-first century, the number of people choosing unique names for children probably will
   a. increase.
   b. decrease.
   c. end altogether.
   d. stay the same.

Working with Words

Complete the sentences below with these words from the vocabulary preview:

quest appellations surname sufficed
unconventional forename excluded turbulent

1. Those who had not been asked to join the club felt that they had been unfairly ___*excluded*___ .

2. *Your Highness* and *Your Majesty* are ___*appellations*___ for royalty.

3. The birthday cake ___*sufficed*___ for all the children who were present at the party.

4. *Catherine* is the ___*forename*___ of my mother's sister.

5. The ___*turbulent*___ weather conditions this winter resulted in flooding in many states.

6. Melika's name is both pretty and *unconventional*. In fact, she is the only one I know who has that name.

7. Jeff began his ___*quest*___ for a writing topic by doing research on the Internet.

8. Mr. Willis prefers to be called by his ___*surname*___ than by his first name.

Thinking and Writing

1. Does your name have a story behind it? Were you named for someone in your family? Do you have a unique name like those in Cindy Roberts's article? Write about your name and use extra paper as needed.

___*Answers will vary.*_____

_____

_____

_____

2. In what way are both Selection 2 and "600 New Entries Give Dictionary What Was Missing" on pages 33–34 about adding new words to the English language? What other connections can you make between these selections? Use details from the selections to explain your answer, and use extra paper as needed.

Answers will vary, but here is one example: Both selections are about

words. One is about adding new words to the dictionary. The other is

about adding new names to our language. Both explain cultural and

social changes that give rise to new words or names.

Selection 3

WHAT DO YOU ALREADY KNOW?

To prepare yourself for the reading selection that follows, find out what you already know about the difficulties of being born into one culture and living in another. Answer the questions below either on your own or in a group discussion.

1. What do you think it is like to be born into one culture but to live in another?

2. What are some of the advantages and disadvantages of speaking one language at home and another at school or work?

3. If you were to move to another country, what would you miss the most? What would you want most to learn?

4. Read the title, headnote, vocabulary preview, and first two paragraphs of the reading selection. What do you think will follow?

The Struggle To Be an All-American Girl

Elizabeth Wong

Elizabeth Wong's essays have appeared in magazines and newspapers. In this essay from the Los Angeles Times, *Wong looks back on her childhood, recalling how she was torn between the expectations of Chinese relatives and her desire to be an American.*

VOCABULARY PREVIEW

stoically (stō′ĭ · kəl · ē) without showing emotion, unaffected by pleasure or pain

dissuade (dĭ · swād′) to argue against a desired action or purpose

flanked (flăngkt) placed on one side or beside

kowtow (kou · tou′) to show respect by bowing or kneeling

ideographs (ĭd′ē · ə · grăfs′) written symbols that stand for words or ideas

raunchy (rôn′chē) slang for obscene or vulgar

pedestrian (pə · dĕs′trē · ən) dull, ordinary

chaotic (kā · ŏt′ĭk) disorderly, confused

gibberish (jĭb′ər · ĭsh) nonsense

pidgin (pĭj′ən) speech that mixes two or more languages

Pronunciation Key: ā (**pay**), ă (**pat**), ē (**bee**), ĕ (**pet**), ĭ (**pit**), ō (**toe**), ŏ (**pot**), ô (**for**), ou (**out**), ə (**about, item**)

It's still there, the Chinese school on Yale Street where my brother and I used to go. Despite the new coat of paint and the high wire fence, the school I knew ten years ago remains remarkably, **stoically** the same. 1

Every day at 5 P.M., instead of playing with our fourth- and fifth-grade friends or sneaking out to the empty lot to hunt ghosts and animal bones, my brother and I had to go to Chinese school. No amount of kicking, screaming, or pleading could **dissuade** my mother, who was solidly determined to have us learn the language of our heritage. 2

Forcibly, she walked us the seven long, hilly blocks from our home to school, depositing our defiant tearful faces before the stern principal. My only memory of him is that he swayed on his heels like a palm tree, and he always clasped his impatient twitching hands behind his back. I recognized him as a repressed maniacal child killer, and knew that if we ever saw his hands we'd be in big trouble. 3

We all sat in little chairs in an empty auditorium. The room smelled like Chinese medicine, an imported faraway mustiness. Like ancient mothballs or dirty closets. I hated that smell. I favored crisp new scents. Like the soft French perfume that my American teacher wore in public school. 4

There was a stage far to the right, **flanked** by an American flag   5
and the flag of the Nationalist Republic of China, which was also red,
white, and blue but not as pretty.

Although the emphasis at the school was mainly language—   6
speaking, reading, writing—the lessons always began with an exercise
in politeness. With the entrance of the teacher, the best student
would tap a bell and everyone would get up, **kowtow,** and chant,
"Sing san ho," the phonetic for "How are you, teacher?"

Being ten years old, I had better things to learn than **ideographs**   7
copied painstakingly in lines that ran right to left from the tip of a *moc
but,* a real ink pen that had to be held in an awkward way if blotches
were to be avoided. After all, I could do the multiplication tables, name
the satellites of Mars, and write reports on *Little Women* and *Black
Beauty.* Nancy Drew, my favorite book heroine, never spoke Chinese.

The language was a source of embarrassment. More times than   8
not, I had tried to disassociate myself from the nagging loud voice that
followed me wherever I wandered in the nearby American supermarket
outside Chinatown. The voice belonged to my grandmother, a fragile
woman in her seventies who could outshout the best of the street
vendors. Her humor was **raunchy,** her Chinese rhythmless, patternless.
It was quick, it was loud, it was unbeautiful. It was not like the quiet,
lilting romance of French or the gentle refinement of the American
South. Chinese sounded **pedestrian.** Public.

In Chinatown, the comings and goings of hundreds of Chinese   9
on their daily tasks sounded **chaotic** and frenzied. I did not want to
be thought of as mad, as talking **gibberish.** When I spoke English,
people nodded at me, smiled sweetly, said encouraging words. Even
the people in my culture would cluck and say that I'd do well in life.
"My, doesn't she move her lips fast," they would say, meaning that
I'd be able to keep up with the world outside Chinatown.

My brother was even more fanatical than I about speaking   10
English. He was especially hard on my mother, criticizing her, often
cruelly, for her **pidgin** speech—smatterings of Chinese scattered like
chop suey in her conversation. "It's not 'What it is,' Mom," he'd say in
exasperation. "It's 'What *is* it, what *is* it, what *is* it'!" Sometimes Mom
might leave out an occasional *the* or *a* or perhaps a verb of being. He
would stop her in midsentence: "Say it again, Mom. Say it right."
When he tripped over his own tongue, he'd blame it on her: "See,
Mom, it's all your fault. You set a bad example."

What infuriated my mother most was when my brother cornered   11
her on her consonants, especially *r.* My father had played a cruel joke
on Mom by assigning her an American name that her tongue
wouldn't allow her to say. No matter how hard she tried, "Ruth"
always ended up "Luth" or "Roof."

After two years of writing with a *moc but* and reciting words with multiples of meanings, I finally was granted a cultural divorce. I was permitted to stop Chinese school.   12

I thought of myself as multicultural. I preferred tacos to egg rolls; I enjoyed Cinco de Mayo* more than Chinese New Year.   13

At last, I was one of you; I wasn't one of them.   14

Sadly, I still am.   15

How Well Did You Comprehend?

Main Idea

1. Which of the following statements best expresses the central idea of the whole selection?
   a. The author's mother forced her and her brother to go to Chinese school.
   b. The author was more determined to be an American than to learn the language and culture of China.
   c. As a young girl, the author resented having to go to Chinese school.
   d. In her struggle to be an American girl, the author lost some of her cultural identity.

2. The author's main purpose is to
   a. inform readers about the way Chinese children are educated.
   b. persuade readers of the advantages of learning other languages.
   c. entertain readers by expressing her attitudes about her birth culture.

Details

3. The author says she did not want to learn Chinese for all of the following reasons *except* which one?
   a. She had better things to do.
   b. The language was a source of embarrassment.
   c. She did not want to be thought of as insane.
   d. She liked the way the language sounded.

*On the fifth of May, Cinco deMayo, Mexicans celebrate their independence.

4. The author uses all *except* which one of the following words to describe her grandmother's voice?
   a. quick
   b. quiet
   c. unbeautiful
   d. pedestrian

5. A *moc but* is a(n)
   a. ink pen.
   b. piece of paper.
   c. writing teacher.
   d. blotch or a mistake.

Inferences

6. What is the author's thought pattern in paragraphs 4 and 5?
   a. example
   b. listing
   c. comparison and contrast
   d. cause and effect

7. What inference can you make about the author's meaning in the last two paragraphs of the essay?
   a. She did not want to stop going to Chinese school.
   b. She still struggling to be an all-American girl.
   c. As a girl, she thought of herself as multicultural.
   d. She wishes that she were not Chinese.

Working with Words

Complete the sentences below with these words from the vocabulary preview:

pedestrian   stoically   dissuade   chaotic   kowtow
ideographs   gibberish   raunchy   flanked   pidgin

1. Brenda's uncle tells ____*raunchy*____ stories that some people find embarrassing.

2. The entrance was ____*flanked*____ by two palm trees: one on the left and one on the right.

3. The ____*gibberish*____ of a two-year old is often difficult to understand.

4. When the leaders of two countries meet, they are not expected to _____*kowtow*_____ to one another.

5. I had hoped to read something original, but this story is _____*pedestrian*_____.

6. The accused listened _____*stoically*_____ as the foreman of the jury read the verdict.

7. "I wish I could _____*dissuade*_____ you from wearing that outfit," said my sister, "because it does not look good on you."

8. Brad's room was in a _____*chaotic*_____ mess with old magazines, dirty clothes, and empty food containers spread everywhere.

9. In Chinatown, we had a hard time finding what we wanted because we could not read the _____*ideographs*_____ on the signs outside the stores.

10. Although the two friends' native languages were different, they were able to communicate by using _____*pidgin*_____.

Thinking and Writing

1. Write about one cultural or family tradition, belief, or practice that you learned as a child. Looking back, what was your attitude about the experience? What do you think about it now? Use extra paper as needed.

_____*Answers will vary.*_____

_____

_____

_____

2. The Chinese girl in selection 3 and the Japanese student in "Four Words" on pages 61–62 have problems in school for different reasons. What other differences or similarities do you see between the Chinese girl and the Japanese student? Use details from the selections to explain your answer, and use extra paper as needed.

Answers will vary, but here is one example: The girls' native cultures and

languages are different. One is a Chinese-American; the other is a

Japanese student attending school in the United States. Both are trying

to fit in, to adapt to American ways.

Selection 4

WHAT DO YOU ALREADY KNOW?

To prepare yourself for the reading selection that follows, find out what you already know about spending time alone. Answer the questions below either on your own or in a group discussion.

1. As compared to the amount of time you spend with others, about how much time do you spend alone?

2. Is having time alone very important to you, somewhat important, or not important at all?

3. What kinds of obligations or activities prevent people from spending their time as they would like?

4. Read the title, headnote, vocabulary preview, and first two paragraphs of the reading selection. What do you think will follow?

Solitude Is a Casualty of the War with Time

Cynthia Crossen

In this article from The Wall Street Journal, *Cynthia Crossen explains the need for solitude and why many people have difficulty finding time to be alone.*

VOCABULARY PREVIEW

casualty   (kăzh′ŏŏ·əl·tē) one injured or killed in an accident or military action

solitude   (sŏl′ĭ·tōōd′) being alone

demanding   (dĭ·măn′dĭng) requiring much effort or attention

priority   (prī·ôr′ĭ·tē) order of importance

knack   (năk) a talent for or clever way of doing something

justify   (jŭs′tə·fī′) give reasons, provide evidence

perilously   (pĕr′əl·ŭs·lē) dangerously

restorative   (rĭ·stôr′ə·tĭv) something that restores health or strength

Pronunciation Key: ē (b**ee**), ĕ (p**e**t), ĭ (p**i**t), ī (p**ie**), ŏ (p**o**t), ô (f**or**), ōō (b**oo**t), ŭ (c**u**t), ə (**a**bout, it**e**m), ă (p**a**t)

Americans find time for jobs, friends, family, television, church and school, but they make almost no time for **solitude.**   1

Being alone is an increasingly uncommon state, and many people aren't happy about it. Thirty-one percent of adults polled said they wished they had more time by themselves, and only 6% wanted less. Among people who felt more pressured by time than money, 43% said they wanted more time to be alone. "The only time I get time to myself is if I stay up after midnight, which I do a lot," says Douglas Meeks, a Huntsville, Ala., manager who says he works 50 hours a week.   2

Between **demanding** jobs and demanding children, working parents are especially short on time alone. "There aren't many hours   3

Ideally, would you like to have more time by yourself, less time, or are you satisfied with the amount of time you are by yourself these days?		Thinking about your average seven-day week, how many of your waking hours are you by yourself each week?	
Satisfied with time by yourself	62%	0-10 hours	41%
More time by yourself	31	11-20 hours	20
Less time by yourself	6	More than 30 hours	20
Not sure	1	21-30 hours	12

that I'm here, and no one else is," says Ruth-Ann Wanamaker, a 40-year-old Oaks, Pa., bookkeeper with two children. Now that her children are older, her first **priority** is spending more time reacquainting herself with her husband. "Then I can ask for time off," she says.

Many people have lost the **knack** of being alone, and so are actually uncomfortable when they suddenly have unexpected time. "Busy executives feel guilty if they have unstructured time," says Ruth Klein, a personal time-management trainer in Santa Monica, Calif. "If there's extra time, it's what can I read, maybe I can jump on the Internet, maybe I can make some calls. Very rarely does the thought come into their minds, I'll just take that time for myself."

4

Indeed, experts say time alone is the hardest time to **justify** both to oneself and others. "Being alone comes **perilously** close to looking like you're being selfish," says John White, president of the Rochester, N.Y., office of Priority Management. "But being appropriately selfish is a very healthy thing to do. There's an extremely valuable **restorative** power in being alone."

5

How Well Did You Comprehend?

Main Idea

1. The central idea of the whole selection is stated in the
   a. first paragraph, first sentence.
   b. second paragraph, first sentence.
   c. third paragraph, first sentence.
   d. last paragraph, last sentence.

2. The author's main purpose is to
   a. inform readers by explaining why many Americans have little time for solitude.
   b. persuade readers that everyone needs more solitude.
   c. entertain readers by describing how Americans spend time alone.

Details

3. What percentage of adults polled said they wanted more time alone?
   a. 62 percent
   b. 43 percent
   c. 31 percent
   d. 6 percent

4. Which of the following reasons supports the author's point that people have lost the knack for being alone?
   a. Parents need to make children their first priority.
   b. Some people are not happy spending time alone.
   c. Americans have no time for solitude.
   d. Executives feel guilty about using free time for themselves.

5. According to experts, why is time alone the hardest time to justify?
   a. People do not know what to do with extra time.
   b. Spending time alone may make them seem selfish.
   c. Some selfishness can be healthy.
   d. Time alone has restorative powers.

Inferences

6. What is the author's overall thought pattern?
   a. example
   b. definition
   c. comparison and contrast
   d. cause and effect

7. Based on the article, what do you think the title means?
   a. Employers and employees often seem to be at war with one another.
   b. You cannot spend time alone and still meet your obligations.
   c. In our struggle to find enough time, it is hard to make time for solitude.
   d. Most people have no difficulty making time for themselves.

Working with Words

Complete the sentences below with these words from the vocabulary preview:

| perilously | demanding | solitude | knack |
| restorative | justify | priority | casualty |

1. When asked why he had arrived late to work and had missed two conferences, the employee could not ____justify____ his actions.

2. Because Rachael could not see well in the heavy rain, she came ____perilously____ close to driving off the road.

3. Asked why he did not want to go to the party with his friends, Ramon said, "Tonight I need ____solitude____."

4. Some jobs are so ___demanding___ that they leave little time for family and leisure activities.

5. Have you ever known someone who seemed to have a ____knack____ for saying just the right thing at the right time?

6. Successful college students are willing to make studying their first ____priority____ .

7. Many who suffer from colds believe that a bowl of hot chicken soup acts as a ____restorative____ .

8. The seriously injured child is a ____casualty____ of speed and drunk driving.

Thinking and Writing

1. Examine the two tables that accompany the article. How do your responses to the author's questions compare to the percentages given in the tables? Use extra paper as needed.

   Answers will vary.
   _____
   _____
   _____

2. Both the author of Selection 4 and the author of "Goofing Off Is Fast Becoming a Lost Art" on page 89 discuss the ways Americans use their time. How do these authors' ideas differ? How are they alike? What other connections can you make? Use details from the selections to explain your answer, and use extra paper as needed.

   Answers will vary, but here is one example: Both articles are about

   managing time. "Goofing Off" is about the ways we waste time.

   Selection 4 is about the need for solitude in our busy lives. Both authors

   suggest that we need to set priorities and make better use of our time.

Selection 5

WHAT DO YOU ALREADY KNOW?

To prepare yourself for the reading selection that follows, find out what you already know about the value of public education. Answer the questions below either on your own or in a group discussion.

1. How are you paying for your college education?

2. How many students do you know who must have financial aid in order to go to college?

3. How do free public schools or low-cost community colleges benefit your community?

4. Read the title, headnote, vocabulary preview, and first two paragraphs of the reading selection. What do you think will follow?

The Unwritten American Bargain

General Colin L. Powell

General Colin Powell is the former Chairman of the Joint Chiefs of Staff of the United States and one of this country's foremost leaders. Powell has written numerous articles and an autobiography. In this selection, he explains why he values his education and why we need to make sure that education is always available to future generations.

VOCABULARY PREVIEW

prestigious	(prĕ•stē´jĕs) respected, filled with honor
contemporaries	(kən•tĕm´pə•rĕr´ēs) people of the same age
buoyed	(bōo´ēd) inspired, raised the spirit
implicit	(ĭm plĭs´ĭt) unquestioning, without reservation
abiding	(ə•bī´dĭng) lasting, enduring
disputing	(dĭ•spyōot´ĭng) arguing, questioning, opposing

inclination	(ĭn′klə·nā′shən) a tendency toward
guise	(gīz) outward appearance

Pronunciation Key: ā (**pay**), ĕ (**pet**), ē (**bee**), ĭ (**pit**), ī (**pie**), o͞o (**boot**), ə (**about, item**)

I graduated from Morris High School on Boston Road in the Bronx   1
when I was 16. My parents expected me to go to college—they
expected me to do better than they had done. And I valued my
parents' opinion so highly that there was no question in my mind. I
was going to college. And where to go to college was not an issue
either. I was accepted at New York University and at the City College
of New York. But NYU cost $750 a year, and CCNY cost $10—no
contest for a poor boy from the South Bronx.

I didn't do exceptionally well at CCNY—or at least, I didn't think   2
so at the time. I passed with straight C's and graduated only because
of my superior grades in ROTC, the Reserve Officer Training Corps. It
took me four and one-half years, one summer session and a change
of academic major—plus straight A's in ROTC—but I did graduate.

My CCNY graduating class went off in a thousand and one   3
directions, as do all classes. Many people went the same way I did,
into the Army. The Army was exciting: It promised adventure, it was a
way to serve and most of all it was a job. For me, it turned out to be a
maturing process also.

Between the ages of 16 and 33, something happened to me   4
because later, when I went to George Washington University and got
my Master's degree, I made an A in every course except one, in which
I made a B. I believe the difference was a matter of growing up, the
sense of responsibility the Army had given me, a few years of war and
perhaps a wife and two children.

But I believe it was also the foundation I had gotten at CCNY. In fact,   5
soon after entering the Army, I discovered how important CCNY had
been. I was serving with West Pointers and with other ROTC graduates
who had the benefit of having attended some fairly **prestigious**
universities. But I found out that the education my fellow ROTC cadets
and I had received at CCNY was a great one, notwithstanding my own
failure to drink as deeply from it as I might have. In terms of our ability to
write, to express ourselves, to reflect the skills and mental disciplines of a
liberal arts education, to be knowledgeable of our culture and our values,
to know our history, we were equal to our **contemporaries** from any
school in the nation. And for that I must thank the institution—the

teachers and faculty of the City College. And also the entire public school system of the City of New York—including Public Schools 20 and 39, Junior High School 52, and Morris High School.

My story is not very different from the stories of tens of thousands of other CCNY graduates who received the benefits of a great, free public education. Most of those people fit the same mold I did—kids from working-class immigrant families. Their parents had dreams and ambitions for their children—if not always the means to fulfill those dreams. And we lived in a city that believed in its obligation to educate its youth and to be the dream-maker for those parents.   6

It was sort of an unwritten but intuitively understood three-way bargain: a bargain among parents, kids and schools. The parents were aware of it. The kids weren't so much aware but just sensed it through their parents. The schools strove to hold to it. Entire neighborhoods were **buoyed** by it—how could they not be? Education was the way up.   7

Parents worked long hours, many of them at menial tasks. The kids were often latchkey boys and girls.* There were so many "minorities" that none of us really thought of ourselves as being in a minority. An **implicit** trust in "the bargain" and in one another, person to person and person to institution, was undefined but nonetheless powerful, strong and **abiding.** After all, it was America. And America meant progress. There simply was no **disputing** that—you could get a black eye if you tried.   8

Looking back, I guess if I had to say what was the most important lesson I ever learned—and that's hard because there are several—my first **inclination** would be to say it is the imperative to drink very deeply at the fountain of knowledge wherever, whenever and in whatever **guise** that fountain might appear.   9

But looking more deeply, I believe there's a more vital thing to be learned. It's the obligation we all have to keep the fountain flowing, now and for future generations. The lesson is not simply to get the most we possibly can out of every ounce of education we can get our hands on and never stop learning. That's very important, but there is more. We must ensure there is always a fountain to drink from and no obstacles to drinking.   10

We must ensure there is always some sort of bargain—a mutual promise concerning education—among the parents, schools and children in our cities. This bargain is the single most important building block of our future. It will determine what America will be like in the 21st century. It will shape our future more dramatically than anything else we do.   11

I believe it was Henry Adams who said that the purpose of education is to increase the extent of our ignorance. That sounds a bit crazy until   12

*Children who are left unsupervised while parents are at work.

you give it some long, hard thought. If Adams was right, maybe that's why my teachers at CCNY and elsewhere knew someday I would be sufficiently ignorant to look back and thank them. And sufficiently ignorant to want to protect the imperfect but beautiful process that made me that way.

How Well Did You Comprehend?

Main Idea

1. Which statement best expresses the central idea of this selection?
   a. College provides the foundation all students need to get ahead and achieve their dreams.
   b. Education for all requires a bargain among parents, schools, and children.
   c. Few people in our cities have received the benefits of a liberal arts education.
   d. Because an education must be bargained for, it remains unavailable to some.

2. The author's main purpose is to
   a. inform readers about the benefits of attending public schools and colleges.
   b. persuade readers that providing an education for all is the most important thing we can do.
   c. entertain readers with amusing stories about his years in public school.

Details

3. Which of the following is *not* one of the reasons Powell gives for his improved grades at George Washington University?
   a. the foundation he got at CCNY
   b. the sense of responsibility the Army gave him
   c. his wife and two children
   d. a change in his major

4. Which of the following statements is an opinion?
   a. "I graduated from Morris High School on Boston Road in the Bronx when I was 16."
   b. "I didn't do exceptionally well at CCNY—or at least, I didn't think so at the time."

    c. "I passed with straight C's and graduated only because of my superior grades in ROTC. . . ."

    d. "Many people went the same way I did, into the Army."

5. What does *fountain* refer to in this statement from paragraph 10: "We must ensure there is always a fountain to drink from and no obstacles to drinking"?

    (a.) a source of knowledge

    b. college

    c. liberal arts

    d. public schools

Inferences

6. What is the author's thought pattern in paragraphs 1–5?

    a. example

    (b.) time order

    c. comparison and contrast

    d. cause and effect

7. According to Powell, what was the most important lesson he ever learned?

    a. We must never stop learning.

    b. We must acquire knowledge wherever we can.

    c. We must get the most we can out of our education.

    (d.) We must provide education without obstacles.

Working with Words

Complete the sentences below with these words from the vocabulary preview:

contemporaries	prestigious	implicit	buoyed
inclination	disputing	abiding	guise

1. Some survivors of the airplane crash said that only their _____*abiding*_____ faith in God helped them stay calm.

2. You never agree with me; instead, you are always _____*disputing*_____ what I say.

3. In the fairy tale "Little Red Riding Hood" the wolf appears to the little girl in the _____*guise*_____ of her grandmother.

4. Children have more fun when they are with their _contemporaries_ than when they are with adults.

5. The Oscars that are given for achievements in film are _prestigious_ awards.

6. After so many rainy, gloomy weekends, a sunny Saturday _buoyed_ everyone's spirits.

7. "I have never had any _inclination_ to cheat on an exam," said the student.

8. Many couples' belief in each other's faithfulness is _implicit_, and they do not have to be reassured.

Thinking and Writing

1. Read again paragraphs 1–5 in which the author summarizes his educational history and its importance. Then write a paragraph about your own educational history so far and what it means to you. Use extra paper as needed.

   Answers will vary.

   _____

   _____

   _____

2. In Selection 5, General Colin Powell explains how he felt about his education when he was a student. How does his attitude compare to the attitudes of the students described in "Making the Grade" on pages 118–121? Do the attitudes expressed in either selection reflect your own or those of students you know? What other connections can you make? Use details from the selections to explain your answer, and use extra paper as needed.

   Answers will vary, but here is one example: Powell values his education.

   The students in "Making the Grade" do not. Powell wanted knowledge.

   The students in "Making the Grade" want degrees.

Selection 6

WHAT DO YOU ALREADY KNOW?

To prepare yourself for the reading selection that follows, find out what you already know about Mexican food. Answer the questions below either on your own or in a group discussion.

1. What is a tortilla? How would you describe what it looks or tastes like?

2. Do you like Mexican food? Name some of the dishes you have tried.

3. What foods or dishes are an important part of your culture or background? When are these foods served?

4. Read the title, headnote, vocabulary preview, and first two paragraphs of the reading selection. What do you think will follow?

I Remember Masa

José Antonio Burciaga

José Antonio Burciaga's fiction, poetry, and articles have been published in books and periodicals. In this selection, he looks back on his experiences with a popular Mexican food: tortillas.

VOCABULARY PREVIEW

absconded	(ăb·skônd´ĭd) ran away and hid
mercado	(mər·kä´dō) marketplace
vendors	(věn´dərs) people or companies who offer goods for sale
jalapenos	(hă´lə´păn´yōs) hot peppers used in Mexican cooking
palate	(păl´ĭt) the sense of taste
concocted	(kən·kŏkt´ĭd) prepared by mixing ingredients
Chicano	(chĭ·kä´nō) Mexican or of Mexican descent
whimsical	(hwĭm´zĭ·kəl) playful, odd

distinction   (dĭ·stĭngk′shən) special recognition, honor

Pronunciation Key: ă (**pat**), ä (**father**), ĕ (**pet**), ĭ (**pit**), ŏ (**pot**), ō (**toe**), ô (**for**), ə(**about, item**)

My earliest memory of *tortillas* is my Mama telling me not to play with them. I had bitten eyeholes in one and was wearing it as a mask at the dinner table. 1

As a child, I also used *tortillas* as hand warmers on cold days, and my family claims that I owe my career as an artist to my early experiments with *tortillas*. According to them, my clowning around helped me develop a strong artistic foundation. I'm not so sure though. Sometimes I wore a *tortilla* on my head, like a *yarmulke,** and yet I never had any great urge to convert from Catholicism to Judaism. But who knows? They may be right. 2

For Mexicans over the centuries, the *tortilla* has served as the spoon and the fork, the plate and the napkin. *Tortillas* originated before the Mayan civilizations, perhaps predating Europe's wheat bread. According to Mayan mythology, the great god Quetzalcoatl, realizing that the red ants knew the secret of using maize as food, transformed himself into a black ant, infiltrated the colony of red ants, and **absconded** with a grain of corn. (Is it any wonder that to this day, black ants and red ants do not get along?) Quetzalcoatl then put maize on the lips of the first man and woman, Oxomoco and Cipactonal, so that they would become strong. Maize festivals are still celebrated by many Indian cultures of the Americas. 3

When I was growing up in El Paso, *tortillas* were part of my daily life. I used to visit a *tortilla* factory in an ancient adobe building near the open **mercado** in Ciudad Juarez. As I approached, I could hear the rhythmic slapping of the *masa* as the skilled **vendors** outside the factory formed it into balls and patted them into perfectly round corn cakes between the palms of their hands. The wonderful aroma and the speed with which the women counted so many dozens of *tortillas* out of warm wicker baskets still linger in my mind. Watching them at work convinced me that the most handsome and *deliciosas tortillas* are handmade. Although machines are faster, they can never adequately replace generation-to-generation experience. There's no place in the factory assembly line for the tender slaps that give each *tortilla* character. The best thing that can be said about mass-producing *tortillas* is that it makes it possible for many people to enjoy them. 4

In the *mercado* where my mother shopped, we frequently bought *taquitos de nopalitos,* small tacos filled with diced cactus, onions, 5

---

*A skullcap worn by Jewish men and boys.

tomatoes, and *jalapenos.* Our friend Don Toribio showed us how to make delicious, crunchy *taquitos* with dried, salted pumpkin seeds. When you had no money for the filling, a poor man's *taco* could be made by placing a warm *tortilla* on the left palm, applying a sprinkle of salt, then rolling the *tortilla* up quickly with the fingertips of the right hand. My own kids put peanut butter and jelly on *tortillas,* which I think is truly bicultural. And speaking of fast food for kids, nothing beats a *quesadilla,* a *tortilla* grilled-cheese sandwich.

Depending on what you intend to use them for, *tortillas* may be made in various ways. Even a run-of-the-mill *tortilla* is more than a flat corn cake. A skillfully cooked homemade *tortilla* has a bottom and a top; the top skin forms a pocket in which you put the filling that folds your *tortilla* into a taco. Paper-thin *tortillas* are used specifically for *flautas,* a type of taco that is filled, rolled, and then fried until crisp. The name *flauta* means *flute,* which probably refers to the Mayan bamboo flute; however, the only sound that comes from an edible *flauta* is a delicious crunch that is music to the **palate.** In Mexico *flautas* are sometimes made as long as two feet and then cut into manageable segments. The opposite of *flautas* is *gorditas,* meaning *little fat ones.* These are very thick small tortillas.

The versatility of *tortillas* and corn does not end here. Besides being tasty and nourishing, they have spiritual and artistic qualities as well. The Tarahumara Indians of Chihuahua, for example, **concocted** a corn-based beer called *tesguino,* which their descendants still make today. And everyone has read about the woman in New Mexico who was cooking her husband a *tortilla* one morning when the image of Jesus Christ miraculously appeared on it. Before they knew what was happening, the man's breakfast had become a local shrine.

Then there is *tortilla* art. Various **Chicano** artists throughout the Southwest have, when short of materials or just in a **whimsical** mood, used a dry *tortilla* as a small, round canvas. And a few years back, at the height of the Chicano movement, a priest in Arizona got into trouble with the Church after he was discovered celebrating mass using a *tortilla* as the host. All of which only goes to show that while the *tortilla* may be a lowly corn cake, when the necessity arises, it can reach unexpected **distinction.**

HOW WELL DID YOU COMPREHEND?

Main Idea

1. Which statement best expresses the central idea of this selection?
   a. People in all parts of the world enjoy tortillas.
   b. For Mexicans, tortillas are a part of daily life.

    c. Tortillas are a tasty and nutritional food source.
    d. The tortilla is much more than a flat corn cake.

2. The author's main purpose is to
    a. inform readers about the history of tortillas and other Mexican foods.
    b. persuade readers that everyone should eat foods made with tortillas.
    c. entertain readers by describing both the practical and amusing uses of tortillas.

Details

3. Tortillas originated
    a. before the Mayan civilization.
    b. after European wheat bread.
    c. in Ciudad Juarez
    d. during the twentieth century

4. Tortillas can be made in various ways depending on
    a. their ingredients.
    b. who makes them.
    c. how they will be used.
    d. where they are made.

5. According to the author, tortillas have been used for all of the following *except*
    a. tacos.
    b. flautas.
    c. gorditas.
    d. tesquino.

Inferences

6. What is the author's overall thought pattern?
    a. example
    b. definition
    c. time order
    d. listing

7. Based on the details given in paragraph 4, what is *masa?*
    a. a type of bread
    b. a seasoning
    c. dough for making tortillas
    d. a round, flat table

Working with Words

Complete the sentences below with these words from the vocabulary preview:

distinction   concocted   whimsical   mercado   Chicano
jalapenos   absconded   vendors   palate

1. The burglar ____absconded____ with the cash and the jewels.

2. At the golf tournament, several ____vendors____ provided food, drinks, and souvenirs for the crowds.

3. While on our vacation, we bought tortillas and other foods in the ____mercado____.

4. Only one student can have the ____distinction____ of being first in the class.

5. Please do not season my food with ____jalapenos____ because I think they are too hot.

6. Juan is a ____Chicano____ who lives in my neighborhood.

7. Some citrus fruits are sour to the ____palate____; others are sweet.

8. Linda ____concocted____ a casserole that included potatoes, meat, and several vegetables.

9. The speaker entertained the audience with one ____whimsical____ story after another.

Thinking and Writing

1. The author uses many Spanish words throughout his essay. Which of these words were already familiar to you? Which ones are new? Which ones are defined in context? What reasons can you give for the author's use of these words? Use extra paper as needed?

____*Answers will vary.*____

_____

_____

_____

2. Selection 6 and "What's a Bagel?" on pages 150–153 are each about a different ethnic food. What do the foods described in each selection have in common? Why are these foods important to the authors of these selections? What other connections can you make? Use details from the selections to explain your answer, and use extra paper as needed.

Answers will vary, but here is one example: Both foods are a type of

bread. Both can be used to make various types of dishes. The foods are

important to both authors because they like them and because they

have cultural significance.

Selection 7

WHAT DO YOU ALREADY KNOW?

To prepare yourself for the reading selection that follows, find out what you already know about the ways men and women use language. Answer the questions below either on your own or in a group discussion.

1. What differences, if any, have you noticed in the ways men and women communicate?

2. When a man and a woman are having a conversation, do they communicate differently than when they talk with members of their own sex?

3. What kinds of things do you talk about with friends of your own sex? With members of the opposite sex?

4. Read the title, headnote, vocabulary preview, and first two paragraphs of the reading selection. What do you think will follow?

Can We Talk?

Diane White

In this article, which originally appeared in The Boston Globe, *journalist Diane White reviews a book by Deborah Tannen on the ways men and women communicate.*

VOCABULARY PREVIEW

subordinate (sə·bôr′dn-ĭt) under another's control, of a lower rank or class

intimacy (ĭn′tə·mə·sē) closeness

hierarchical (hi′ə·rär′kə·kəl) arrangement of people or things by ranks or abilities

assert (ə·sûrt′) to put yourself forward boldly and forcefully

persist (pər·sĭst′) continue to exist, keep on

hostilities (hŏ·stĭl′ĭ·tēs) feelings of hatred

systematic (sĭs′tə·ma′tĭk) organized, methodical, interconnected

intently (ĭn·tĕnt′ lē) with concentration, determined

Pronunciation Key: ă (**p**a**t**), ä (**f**a**ther**), ĕ (**p**e**t**), ĭ (**p**i**t**), ŏ (**p**o**t**), ô (**for**), ə (**about, item**), ē (**bee**), û (**urge**)

Recently a friend told me he'd finally discovered the secret of making women happy. "I just shut up and listen," he said.

Imagine, he figured this out all by himself, and he's only 45. But at least he figured it out.

If my friend's discovery strikes me as funny, it's because I used to be a girl, a girl who grew up being told over and over again that if she wanted to be popular with boys she must listen to them, encourage them to talk about themselves, draw them out.

Few boys are given similar instructions about girls. Boys expect girls to listen to them. They don't expect to have to listen to girls. So it isn't surprising that women who want men to listen to them are often disappointed.

In her book "You Just Don't Understand: Women and Men in Conversation," Deborah Tannen writes that many men don't like to listen to anyone, female or male, because they believe that the act of listening is a **subordinate** role. Men never want to be one-down in conversation. It's just the way they are.

Her basic thesis is that men and women use language differently, and that those differences begin when they're children.

Girls play in small groups or pairs, they have best friends and spend a lot of time talking. Girls learn to use language to gain **intimacy,** to make connections. Boys, on the other hand, tend to play competitive games in larger, **hierarchical** groups. Boys grow up

1

2

3

4

5

6

7

learning that other people are going to push them around, and they use language to **assert** themselves.

These separate styles of communicating **persist** into adulthood and, according to Tannen, cause all sorts of confusion and misunderstandings between the sexes. For example, when women marry what they often want and expect in a husband is a new and improved version of a best friend, someone they can tell everything to and who, in turn, will share all his secrets. "This is not what men expect," Tannen said, perhaps unnecessarily.   8

A young man asked [her] why his girlfriend persists in talking about their relationship when he thinks everything is settled. The question, Tannen said, gave her the opportunity to say one of her favorite things about the differences in the way men and women communicate. "Many women feel the relationship is working so long as you keep talking about it," she said. "And many men feel the relationship isn't working if you keep having to work it over."   9

Tannen is not trying to step up **hostilities** in the war between the sexes, on the contrary. One of the points she tries to get across is that many of the misunderstandings in communication between men and women are not the fault of the individual but of cultural conditioning. We must learn to understand our different ways of communicating, she says. "The danger is that if we don't realize that these are **systematic** differences in conversational style we make interpretations that aren't valid."   10

Consider the listening problem. "Sometimes men give [women] the impression they're not listening because they're not looking at them," Tannen said. This, too, is part of the different ways men and women communicate. In videotapes of research she's conducted on the body language of children talking to a friend of the same sex, at every age, from 5 to 15, the girls sit face to face, and look at each other. And at every age the boys sit side by side, talking **intently,** listening, and looking everywhere but at one another. So that man who appears to be ignoring you may in fact be hanging onto your every word. But don't count on it.   11

HOW WELL DID YOU COMPREHEND?

Main Idea

1. Which statement best expresses the author's central idea?
   a. The secret of making women happy is to shut up and listen.
   b. Men and women will probably never be able to understand each other.

    c. Boys are encouraged to talk, but girls are encouraged to listen.

    (d.) From childhood on, men and women use language differently.

2. The author's main purpose is to

    (a.) inform readers of Deborah Tannen's ideas about the ways men and women communicate.

    b. persuade readers that they should change the way they communicate.

    c. entertain readers with bits of men's and women's conversation that she has overheard.

Details

3. Girls use language to

    (a.) gain intimacy.

    b. play competitive games.

    c. assert themselves.

    d. impress their friends.

4. Tannen says that men

    a. prefer to listen to men.

    b. like to listen to themselves.

    (c.) do not like to listen to anyone.

    d. like to listen to both men and women.

5. One of Tannen's points is that misunderstandings in communication between men and women are the fault of

    a. the individual.

    (b.) cultural conditioning.

    c. genetic differences.

    d. psychological factors.

Inferences

6. What is the author's overall thought pattern?

    a. example

    b. definition

    c. cause and effect

    (d.) comparison and contrast

7. Diane White and Deborah Tannen would probably agree that both men and women

    a. seek an equal partnership in marriage.

    b. want someone to share their secrets.

(c.) expect different things from a relationship.

d. expect to talk about their relationship.

Working with Words

Complete the sentences below with these words from the vocabulary preview:

hierarchical	subordinate	intently	persist
hostilities	systematic	intimacy	assert

1. The movie audience watched ____*intently*____ as the Titanic began to sink and everyone rushed toward the lifeboats.

2. I enjoy watching my azaleas bloom, but I wish the flowers would ____*persist*____ a little longer.

3. While visiting popular attractions, rude tourists will often try to ____*assert*____ themselves at the head of a line.

4. She is my supervisor and I am her __*subordinate*__.

5. A best friend is someone with whom you have ____*intimacy*____.

6. A __*hierarchical*__ group is one that has a leader and followers of different ranks.

7. Because of their ____*hostilities*____, the children's games often ended in an argument.

8. Jerome usually does well in his classes because he has a ____*systematic*____ way of studying.

Thinking and Writing

1. Deborah Tannen says that women want a husband who is a best friend, someone to talk to and share secrets with. She also says that men do not expect these qualities in a wife. Do you agree or disagree, and why? Use extra paper as needed.

   ____*Answers will vary.*_____

   _____

_____

_____

_____

2. Selection 7 is about the different ways men and women use language. "How Gender May Bend Your Thinking" on pages 189–191 is about the different ways men and women think. Could it be that the ways men and women think influence how they talk to each other or to members of the same sex? What other connections can you make between these authors' ideas? Use details from the selections to explain your answer, and use extra paper as needed.

Answers will vary, but here is one example: If Gorman is right that brain

differences affect the ways men and women think, then brain differences

probably also affect language use. Tannen seems to emphasize cultural

conditioning more than Gorman does.

_____

_____

Selection 8

WHAT DO YOU ALREADY KNOW?

To prepare yourself for the reading selection that follows, find out what you already know about lotteries and gambling. Answer the questions below either on your own or in a group discussion.

1. What state do you live in, and does it operate a lottery?

2. In your opinion, is gambling right or wrong?

3. Does advertising for lotteries encourage gambling? Why or why not?

4. Read the title, headnote, vocabulary preview, and first two paragraphs of the reading selection. What do you think will follow?

Lotteries: Is It Right to Encourage Gambling?

W. M. Pride and O. C. Ferrell

In this passage from Marketing, *a business textbook, the authors question whether states should encourage gambling by promoting lotteries through advertising.*

VOCABULARY PREVIEW

phenomenon	(fĭ·nŏm´ə·nŏn´) an unusual fact or occurrence
ban	(băn) forbid, prohibit or exclude by law
private sector	(prī´vĭt · sĕk´tər) nongovernment employers and businesses
generate	(jĕn´ə·rāt´) make, produce, bring about
revenues	(rĕv´ə·nōōs) income, monies collected
proclaiming	(prō·klām´ĭng) announcing, declaring
contend	(kən·tĕnd´) to maintain, insist, assert
adversely	(ăd·vûrs´lē) harmfully, unfavorably, negatively
fundamental	(fŭn´də·mĕn´tĭl) basic, most important

Pronunciation Key: ă (**pat**), ā (**pay**), ə(**pet**), ē (**bee**), ĭ (**pit**), ī (**pie**), ŏ (**pot**), ō (**toe**), ōō (**boot**), ŭ (**cut**), ûr (**urge**), ə (**about, item**)

Lotteries are not a recent **phenomenon** in the United States. Holding a lottery financed the settlement of Jamestown, Virginia, in 1612. By the mid-1800s, however, they fell out of favor. In 1894, the last lottery shut down, and lotteries remained illegal until 1964. As states began exploring ways of raising money without raising taxes, lotteries recaptured their appeal and their legal status. Experts predict that by the turn of the century every state but Utah and Nevada will have one.

The odds of being struck by lightning, 1 in 1.9 million, are small, but the odds of winning the top prize in a state lottery, 1 in 12 million, are even smaller. Why then do millions of people line up to spend a hard-earned $22 billion a year on lottery tickets? They take a

1

2

chance because the fantasy of getting rich quick is so appealing. To make that fantasy seem like reality, state governments spend almost $300 million a year on entertaining and imaginative lottery advertising. Outspending Colgate-Palmolive, Nike, Nissan, and American Express, lotteries rank among the top fifty advertisers in the United States. As lottery advertising becomes big business, however, efforts are mounting to limit or **ban** it altogether.

3   Critics complain that most lottery advertising fails to meet the same accuracy and fairness standards required of **private sector** advertising. They believe it is wrong for states to encourage gambling, not only because it advances a something-for-nothing mentality, but because it is addictive. Although supporters maintain that lottery participation is voluntary, experts insist lotteries are the most habit-forming type of gambling. Pointing to statistics that low-income families spend a larger proportion of their income on tickets than other groups, opponents assert that lotteries burden the poor rather than **generate revenues** to help them. With billboards such as those in depressed Chicago neighborhoods **proclaiming** lotteries as "Your Way Out," it is not surprising that many inner-city residents sell their food stamps to buy lottery tickets.

4   The Kansas lottery's slogan is, "Somebody's always winning," and New Yorkers are told, "All you need is a dollar and a dream." These kinds of promises, **contend** those against lottery advertising, mislead consumers about their chances of winning. Duke University economists determined that only 12 percent of TV and radio spots for state lotteries accurately report the odds. Finally, ad opponents believe that it is wrong to encourage gambling as a real alternative to saving, education, and hard work. For example, they point to a New York ad in which a mother tells her daughter that she no longer needs to study to get a college scholarship because they are playing the lottery.

5   At one time, cigarette and alcohol advertisers faced the question, Should advertisers protect people from themselves? Courts eventually answered yes by placing restrictions on advertising of those products. Lottery advertisers now face similar questions. Should governments promote a game in which the vast majority of players lose? Should states sponsor activities that **adversely** affect lower income people? Some see the Supreme Court's recent ruling preventing a radio station in North Carolina, which has no lottery, from broadcasting ads for the Virginia lottery as a forecast of similar restrictions on lottery advertising. For now, marketers continue to insist that they advertise a legal product in a truthful way and continue to bank on advertising as the **fundamental** ingredient in lottery promotion.

HOW WELL DID YOU COMPREHEND?

Main Idea

1. Which statement best expresses the authors' central idea of the whole selection?
   a. Lotteries are not a recent phenomenon in the United States.
   b. Efforts are mounting to limit or ban advertising for lotteries.
   c. We must ask whether governments should promote a game in which most players lose.
   d. Advertising is the fundamental ingredient in lottery promotion.

2. The authors' main purpose is to
   a. inform readers of different tactics states use to promote lotteries.
   b. persuade readers that governments should not promote lotteries.
   c. entertain readers by describing various advertising slogans and campaigns.

Details

3. According to the authors, millions of people buy lottery tickets because
   a. the odds of winning are 1 in 12 million.
   b. playing the lottery is not habit forming.
   c. the get-rich-quick fantasy is appealing.
   d. state governments spend millions on advertising.

4. What do supporters say in favor of lotteries?
   a. Gambling is addictive.
   b. Participation in lotteries is voluntary.
   c. Lotteries burden the poor.
   d. Lotteries advance a something-for-nothing mentality.

5. Which example supports the idea that gambling is an alternative to saving, education, and hard work?
   a. the Kansas lottery's slogan "Somebody's always winning"
   b. the New York lottery's slogan "All you need is a dollar and a dream"
   c. lottery advertising on billboards in depressed Chicago neighborhoods
   d. a daughter who is told she does not need to study for a scholarship because she is playing the lottery

Inferences

6. What is the authors' thought pattern in paragraph 1?
    a. time order
    b. definition
    c. listing
    d. example

7. What do you think is the authors' answer to the question asked in the title?
    a. yes
    b. no
    c. in some neighborhoods
    d. with some restrictions

Working with Words

Complete the sentences below with these words from the vocabulary preview:

private sector	phenomenon	generate	adversely	ban
fundamental	proclaiming	revenues	contend	

1. *Star Wars* is a ___phenomenon___ in the film industry because it has earned more money than any other movie so far.

2. Because of recent tobacco legislation, we no longer see billboards ___proclaiming___ Joe Camel as "Joe Cool."

3. Those who do not want children exposed to ideas with which they disagree may try to ___ban___ books containing those ideas.

4. Tax collectors get more ___revenues___ from lakefront properties than from pasture lands.

5. Brainstorming is a technique many people use to ___generate___ ideas for projects, papers, and speeches.

6. No one has proven conclusively that watching violent movies and T.V. programs ___adversely___ affects audiences.

7. It makes no sense for you to ___contend___ that you are not to blame when I know that you are.

8. Free speech is a ___fundamental___ right guaranteed by the United States Constitution.

9. Some college instructors also work at jobs in the ___private sector___ to enhance their income.

Thinking and Writing

1. Do you believe that it is a good idea for states to operate lotteries? Explain your reasons, and use extra paper as needed.

   Answers will vary.

   _____

   _____

   _____

   _____

2. The authors of Selection 8 and the author of "Biases in Judgment" on pages 224–227 each explain why people play the lottery. What is each author's explanation? How are the explanations similar or different? What other connections can you make between these authors' ideas? Use details from the selections to explain your answer, and use extra paper as needed.

   Answers will vary, but here is an example: The author of "Biases" says

   that people play the lottery because they are overly influenced by T.V.

   ads (availability heuristic). The authors of Selection 8 say people play

   because of the "get-rich-quick fantasy" promoted by advertising. The

   authors of both selections believe that advertising plays a major role in

   people's decision to play the lottery.

   _____

Selection 9

WHAT DO YOU ALREADY KNOW?

To prepare yourself for the reading selection that follows, find out what you already know about the regrowth of animal body parts. Answer the questions below either on your own or in a group discussion.

1. What animals do you know of that can regrow a body part they have lost?

2. What parts of the human body can regenerate, or regrow?

3. Suppose scientists could grow human body parts or organs in laboratories. What would be the benefits of this development?

4. Read the title, headnote, vocabulary preview, and first two paragraphs of the reading selection. What do you think will follow?

Replacement Organs Have Been Grown from Animal Tissue, Say Researchers

Ron Winslow

In this article, Ron Winslow reports on scientists' growth of replacement body parts for animals, a development that may lead to improved organ transplants and treatment of birth defects in humans. Winslow is a staff reporter of The Wall Street Journal *from which the article is taken.*

VOCABULARY PREVIEW

harvest	(här′vĭst) to gather in
culture	(kŭl′chər) *Biol.* the growing of an organism in a specially prepared substance
congenital	(kən·jĕn′ĭ·tl) existing at or before birth
refashion	(rĭ·făsh′ən) remake, adapt to a purpose
induce	(ĭn·do͞os′) influence, persuade, bring about
devised	(dĭ·vīzd′) planned, invented

foster   (fŏ´stər) to promote, encourage

regenerate   (rĭ·jĕn′ə·rāt) regrow, form again, give new life to

Pronunciation Key: ă (**pat**), ā (**pay**), ä (**father**), ĕ (**pet**), ĭ (**pit**), ī (**pie**), ŏ (**pot**), oo (b**oo**t), ŭ (**cut**), ə (**about**, **item**)

Harvard University researchers say they have successfully grown replacement skin, bladders and other body parts for animals using the animals' own tissue in a technique that could open new doors to transplant surgery and treatment of birth defects in humans.   1

The scientists say they have developed a way to **harvest** cells from specific parts of an animal's body, grow the cells in **culture,** mold the resulting tissue into the desired shape, and implant the new part into the animal.   2

Dario Fauza, a fellow at Harvard Medical School's Center for Minimally Invasive Surgery, will be describing some of the research, accomplished with fetal tissue, today at a meeting of the British Association of Pediatric Surgeons in Istanbul, Turkey. But Anthony Atala, a pediatric surgeon at Harvard and at Children's Hospital in Boston says the research team has already constructed such body parts as bladders, windpipes, bone and cartilage in both newborn and older animals.   3

While the technique is obviously experimental, it has been under development for seven years, Dr. Atala says. It may be tried on humans within just a few months.   4

"As a surgeon, my dream is to have body pieces and organs available off the shelf," Dr. Atala says. "With the large organ-donor shortage today, that is something that we would really like to have in order to make our patients better."   5

As pediatric surgeons in particular, the researchers are looking for new ways to correct **congenital** birth defects and related problems in newborns and children. One example is a condition in which a baby is born with a bladder outside the body. Current repair techniques might use a piece of intestine to **refashion** a bladder and require multiple surgeries. Even then, "the child can have a lifetime of problems," Dr. Atala says. "With this technique you could reconstruct the bladder within 48 hours of birth and be done with it."   6

By using cells taken from the same body part that needs repair or replacement, the theory goes, surgeons could "do away with problems of having mismatched tissue or rejection," Dr. Atala says.   7

In the paper being presented in Istanbul, Dr. Fauza describes how researchers performed fetal surgery to **induce** the bladder defect in 10 fetal lambs. They obtained bladder tissue from half of the fetuses and grew it for up to 60 days in the laboratory, and then implanted a   8 re-engineered bladder into those lambs shortly after birth. In the other animals the bladder problems were corrected surgically. After two months, the implanted bladders functioned better, they said.

Use of fetal tissue offers an advantage because of its capacity for growth, Dr. Atala says, but the researchers have used the technique on older animals with success as well.   9

Dr. Atala says that the key to the advance is a way the scientists have **devised** to **foster** the growth of cells outside the body into large pieces of tissue. He said such body parts as skin, bone, kidneys, cartilage and windpipes might be good candidates for replacement with the new technique. So far, he added, researchers haven't succeeded in getting tissue from such critical organs as the liver and pancreas to **regenerate** in the laboratory.   10

HOW WELL DID YOU COMPREHEND?

Main Idea

1. The author's central idea is stated in the
    a. first paragraph.
    b. second paragraph.
    c. third paragraph.
    d. sixth paragraph.

2. The author's main purpose is to
    a. inform readers about a new research development and its possible effects.
    b. persuade readers that they should support research in the growth of human organs.
    c. entertain readers by reporting on the mistakes animal researchers have made.

Details

3. Researchers have been able to construct all of the following body parts from animal tissue *except*
    a. bladders.
    b. livers.
    c. windpipes.
    d. bone and cartilage.

4. According to the author, Harvard researchers have successfully grown replacement body parts from

a. human tissue.
b. animal tissue.
c. artificial tissue.
d. inorganic matter.

5. According to the author, harvested cells are grown in
a. laboratory culture.
b. the animal's own body.
c. the body of another animal.
d. a human body.

Inferences

6. What is the author's overall thought pattern?
a. example
b. time order
c. cause and effect
d. comparison and contrast

7. The best inference you can make from the last sentence in paragraph 10 is that the researchers will
a. eventually succeed.
b. never succeed.
c. keep trying.
d. give up.

Working with Words

Complete the sentences below with these words from the vocabulary preview:

congenital	refashion	harvest	foster
regenerate	devised	culture	induce

1. The generals have ____*devised*____ a plan for achieving peace without war.

2. When Steve restored his antique motorcycle, he had to ____*refashion*____ some of the parts because they were no longer available.

3. Rita signed an agreement that would allow a physician to ____*harvest*____ her organs after her death.

4. Some people believe that allowing prayer in schools will ____*foster*____ moral development; others do not.

5. A doctor may need to grow a ____*culture*____ from diseased tissue to determine what is causing an illness.

6. Diseases that are ____*congenital*____ in nature have been present since birth.

7. "Nothing you say will ____*induce*____ me to cheat on a test," the student declared.

8. If a lizard's tail gets bitten off in a fight, his body will ____*regenerate*____ a new one.

Thinking and Writing

1. Suppose the researchers are successful, and we are able to grow human replacement organs in the future. What do you think would be the possible advantages and disadvantages? Use extra paper as needed.

   Answers will vary.

   _____

   _____

   _____

   _____

2. Both Selection 9 and "Seizing Nature's Lifeline" on pages 257–260 are about new developments in the field of medical research. Which of these developments do you think is of greater importance? Which will benefit the most people? Do you think both developments are worth continued research? Use details from the selections to explain your answer, and use extra paper as needed.

   Answers will vary, but here is an example: Being able to grow replacement

   body parts is probably a more important development because it would

   help more people. However, both developments are worth more

   research since they would both benefit humankind.

Selection 10

WHAT DO YOU ALREADY KNOW?

To prepare yourself for the reading selection that follows, find out what you already know about folk tales and legends. Answer the questions below either on your own or in a group discussion.

1. Do you remember "The King of the Frogs" on pages 292–294 of Chapter 10? Briefly summarize this tale.

2. What other folk tales or stories do you recall that explain animal behavior?

3. What childhood story of any kind do you remember, and what was its moral, message, or lesson for the reader?

4. Read the title, headnote, vocabulary preview, and first two paragraphs of the reading selection. What do you think will follow?

How the Camel Got His Hump
Rudyard Kipling

British author Rudyard Kipling (1865–1936) won the Nobel prize for literature in 1907. The following tale is from Just So Stories, *which he wrote for his daughter. Like many folk tales, this whimsical story has a moral, or message, for the reader.*

VOCABULARY PREVIEW

tamarisks	(tăm´ə·rĭsks´) small tree or bush with white, pink, or red flowers
prickles	(prĭk´əls) small sharp thorns
excruciating	(ĭk·skrōō´shē·ā´tĭng) extremely painful or distressing
idle	(īd´l) lazy, avoiding work
yoke	(yōk) a crossbar with two U-shaped pieces that go around the neck of animals used for pulling a plow or heavy load

> **palaver**   (pə • lăv′ər) idle chatter or talk
>
> **pow-wow**   (pou′-wou) a gathering, or meeting, especially among Native Americans
>
> **Djinn**   (jĭn) in Muslim legend a spirit having magical powers, also *jinn* or *genie*
>
> **lolloping**   (lŏl′əp • ĭng) bobbing up and down
>
> Pronunciation Key: ă (**pat**), ā (**pay**), ē (**bee**), ĭ (**pit**), ī (**pie**), ŏ (**pot**), ō (**toe**), o͞o (**boot**), ou (**out**), ə (**about, item**)

In the beginning of years, when the world was so new and all, and the Animals were just beginning to work for Man, there was a Camel, and he lived in the middle of a Howling Desert because he did not want to work; and besides, he was a Howler himself. So he ate sticks and thorns and **tamarisks** and milkweed and **prickles,** most **'scruciating**[1] **idle;** and when anybody spoke to him he said "Humph!" Just "Humph!" and no more.   1

Presently the Horse came to him on Monday morning, with a saddle on his back and a bit in his mouth, and said, "Camel, O Camel, come out and trot like the rest of us."   2

"Humph!"said the Camel and the Horse went away and told the Man.   3

Presently the Dog came to him, with a stick in his mouth, and said, "Camel, O Camel, come and fetch and carry like the rest of us."   4

"Humph!" said the Camel; and the Dog went away and told the Man.   5

Presently the Ox came to him, with the **yoke** on his neck and said, "Camel, O Camel, come and plow like the rest of us."   6

"Humph!" said the Camel; and the Ox went away and told the Man.   7

At the end of the day the Man called the Horse and the Dog and the Ox together, and said, "Three, O Three, I'm very sorry for you (with the world so new-and-all); but that Humph-thing in the Desert can't work, or he would have been here by now, so I am going to leave him alone, and you must work double time to make up for it."   8

That made the Three very angry (with the world so new-and-all), and they held a **palaver,** and an *indaba,*[2] and a *punchayet,*[3] and a **pow-wow** on the edge of the Desert; and the Camel came chewing milkweed *most* 'scruciating idle, and laughed at them. Then he said "Humph!" and went away again.   9

[1] The first letter of *excruciating* is left off, and the *x* is changed to *s*.
[2] *indaba:* an African word meaning *conference*
[3] *punchayet:* a village council meeting in India

Presently there came along the **Djinn** in charge of All Deserts, rolling in a cloud of dust (Djinns always travel that way because it is Magic), and he stopped to palaver and pow-wow with the Three. 10

"Djinn of All Deserts," said the Horse, "*is* it right for anyone to be idle, with the world so new-and-all?" 11

"Certainly not," said the Djinn. 12

"Well,"said the Horse, "there's a thing in the middle of your Howling Desert (and he's a Howler himself) with a long neck and long legs, and he hasn't done a stroke of work since Monday morning. He won't trot." 13

"Whew!"said the Djinn, whistling. "That's my Camel, for all the gold in Arabia! What does he say about it?" 14

"He says 'Humph!' " said the Dog. "And he won't fetch and carry." 15

"Does he say anything else?" 16

"Only 'Humph!' and he won't plow," said the Ox. 17

"Very good," said the Djinn. "I'll humph him if you will kindly wait a minute." 18

The Djinn rolled himself up in his dustcloak, and took a bearing across the desert, and found the Camel most 'scruciatingly idle, looking at his own reflection in a pool of water. 19

"My long and bubbling friend," said the Djinn, "what's this I hear of your doing no work, with the world so new-and-all?" 20

"Humph!"said the Camel. 21

The Djinn sat down, with his chin in his hand, and began to think a Great Magic, while the Camel looked at his own reflection in the pool of water. 22

"You've given the Three extra work ever since Monday morning, all on account of your 'scruciating idleness," said the Djinn; and he went on thinking Magics, with his chin in his hand. 23

"Humph!"said the Camel. 24

"I shouldn't say that again if I were you," said the Djinn; "you might say it once too often. Bubbles, I want you to work." 25

And the Camel said "Humph!" again; but no sooner had he said it than he saw his back, that he was so proud of, puffing up and puffing up into a great big **lolloping** humph. 26

"Do you see that?" said the Djinn. "That's your very own humph that you've brought upon your very own self by not working. Today is Thursday, and you've done no work since Monday, when the work began. Now you are going to work." 27

"How can I," said the Camel, "with this humph on my back?" 28

"That's made a-purpose," said the Djinn, "all because you missed those three days. You will be able to work now for three days without eating, because you can live on your humph; and don't you ever say I 29 never did anything for you. Come out of the Desert and go to the Three, and behave. Humph yourself!"

And the Camel humphed himself, humph and all, and went away 30 to join the Three. And from that day to this the Camel always wears a humph (we call it "hump" now, not to hurt his feelings); but he has never yet caught up with the three days that he missed at the beginning of the world, and he has never yet learned how to behave.

HOW WELL DID YOU COMPREHEND?

Main Idea

1. Which statement best expresses the central idea of the tale?
   a. What caused the camel's hump is an interesting story.
   b. The camel's hump enables him to go a long time without eating or drinking.
   c. People who live in the desert are very superstitious.
   d. The story of the camel's hump is only one of many legends about this animal.

2. The author's main purpose is to
   a. inform readers of the biological reasons for the camel's hump.
   b. persuade readers that camels are dangerous and unpredictable.
   c. entertain readers with a whimsical story about how the camel got his hump

Details

3. Which of the following is *not* one of "the Three" called by Man?
   a. ox
   b. camel
   c. dog
   d. horse

4. According to the folk tale, the camel got his hump for all of the following reasons *except* which one?
   a. He would not work with the others.
   b. He said "Humph" once too often.
   c. The Djinn worked magic on him.
   d. Camels have always had humps.

5. The phrase "'scrutiating idle" means that the camel is
    a. not talkative.
    b. suffering from pain.
    c. distressingly lazy.
    d. ill-behaved.

Inferences

6. What is the author's overall thought pattern?
    a. example
    b. time order
    c. cause and effect
    d. comparison and contrast

7. The moral of this tale seems to be,
    a. Your reputation follows you.
    b. Be content with who you are.
    c. Never take friends for granted.
    d. Those who are idle get behind.

Working with Words

Complete the sentences below with these words from the vocabulary preview:

excruciating	lolloping	palaver	idle	Djinn
tamarisks	prickles	pow-wow	yoke	

1. When a ____*yoke*____ is fastened around its neck, an animal is not able to turn his head from side to side.

2. On our trip to India, we saw ____*tamarisks*____ blooming beside the road.

3. My sister is so ____*idle*____ that she will not even pick up her clothes from the floor.

4. We watched a small boat ____*lolloping*____ in the water far off shore.

5. If you do not first check for ____*prickles*____ before picking roses, you may get hurt.

6. We need to have a ____*pow-wow*____ with everyone involved in this project to discuss our next step.

7. To the chattering children in the back of the classroom the teacher said "Stop your ____*palaver*____ now."

8. To many people, a burn is the most ____*excruciating*____ of all wounds.

9. Sometimes I wish the ____*Djinn*____ would appear and grant me three wishes.

Thinking and Writing

1. In a way, this tale is about the value of work. In past times, most Americans believed that anything was possible through hard work and individual effort. Do most people still believe this? Do you? Explain your answer and use extra paper as needed.

    Answers will vary.

    _____

    _____

    _____

2. Both Selection 10 and "The King of the Frogs" on pages 292–294 are folk tales about animals. How are the tales different? How are they alike? What is each tale's moral, or message, to readers? Which tale do you think is more entertaining and why? Use details from the selections to explain your answer, and use extra paper as needed.

    Answers will vary, but here is one example: Both tales explain natural

    events: why frogs croak at night and why the camel has a hump. The

    moral of the frog tale is everyone needs leaders. The moral of the camel

    story is that idleness has bad consequences.

Appendix A

Developing Your Library Skills

Whether you need to do some research for an assignment, or whether you simply want to browse for a book or magazine, your college library is the place to go. The library is a storehouse of information and resources. To use them effectively, you must have good library skills. In other words, you must know what kind of information you are looking for and how to find it.

Do your library skills need improving? To find out, read each statement below and check the ones that apply to you. After you finish, read the explanation that follows.

_____ 1. When I go to the library, I usually know exactly what I am looking for.

_____ 2. The library is a confusing place, and I often have difficulty finding what I need.

_____ 3. When I have research to do, I make a plan and follow it.

_____ 4. I do not plan my research. I just go to the shelves and check out the first book I see that covers my topic.

_____ 5. I usually know which sources of information are likely to cover my topic.

_____ 6. I never know whether a source contains what I need until I start reading.

_____ 7. I am familiar with most of my college library's resources.

_____ 8. I am not as familiar with my library's resources as I need to be.

_____   9.   I can evaluate a book or magazine article for its reliability and usefulness.

_____   10.   I do not know which books or articles are more reliable or useful than others.

If you checked mostly odd-numbered statements, you may already have good library skills. If you checked mostly even-numbered statements, you need to develop your skills. Three strategies will help you take advantage of all your library has to offer.

- Seek help from library personnel.
- Learn how to use information retrieval systems.
- Know what resources are available and how to use them.

LIBRARY PERSONNEL

Librarians and their assistants can help you find what you need. An important part of their job is to explain how to use the library's resources. Most librarians are happy to give you a general orientation to the library if it is your first time there. Some libraries provide guided tours, video-cassette recordings, a printed guide, diagram, or handbook that explains what resources are available and where to find them.

If you have a research assignment and do not know where to begin, ask a librarian for help. Be sure to give the librarian any handouts or other information you have about the assignment that will enable him or her to help you.

Although it takes time to find information in a library, you can make that time productive and rewarding. The first step is to ask for help.

INFORMATION RETRIEVAL SYSTEMS

Most libraries today use a *computerized card catalog*. Books and audiovisual materials are classified in the catalog by subject, author, and title and are usually organized according to the Library of Congress system of numbering. Furthermore, your library's catalog may be networked with other libraries' holdings, which greatly increase the number of resources you have available.

To access a listing for a book or videocassette recording from a computerized card catalog, type your responses on a keyboard as you answer questions that come up on the computer screen. First decide which file you want: subject, title, or author. Once you are in a file, use key words to find the information you need. For example, if you type in your topic, a list of your library's holdings on that topic will appear on the screen. If you see a title of a book that interests you, print out the listing. Using the book's call number, which is listed on the printout, go to the stacks and look for the book.

Your library may also have other computerized information retrieval systems. For example, most libraries have *computerized indexes* to newspapers, magazines, journals, and other resources. These too may be networked with other listings, and each may require a different set of commands to access them.

Because systems vary, your best bet is to first find out what systems your library has and what kind of information they contain. Then ask a librarian to demonstrate each system's use. Computerized systems are quick and easy to use, but they are just one of your library's many resources.

YOUR LIBRARY'S RESOURCES

In addition to books, your library also contains *reference works* and *periodicals* (magazines, newspapers, journals). Some of these resources are on shelves; others are collected on microfilm and microfiche. Reference works consist of encyclopedias, dictionaries, almanacs, atlases, books of quotations, government documents, and indexes to periodicals. Using these resources, you can find many types of information as illustrated in Figure A-1 below.

FIGURE A-1 Some Common Resources and What They Contain	
ATLAS	a collection of maps
ALMANAC	statistics on many subjects such as sports, commerce, politics, climate, population, and so on (updated yearly)
GAZETTEER	geographical locations of rivers, volcanoes, mountain ranges, seas, forests, and so on
BOOK OF QUOTATIONS	well-known sayings by noteworthy people (*Bartlett's Familiar Quotations* is one of several such books.)
READER'S GUIDE TO PERIODICAL LITERATURE	magazine, newspaper, and journal articles are listed by subject and by year
GOVERNMENT DOCUMENTS	information on a variety of topics such as AIDS, birth control, education, and statistics on crime, motor vehicle accidents, population, death, and so on
VERTICAL FILE	newspaper clippings, pictures, pamphlets, and other bits of information organized into separate files by subject

The resources listed in Figure A-1 are only a few your library may contain. Many newspapers and magazines have their own indexes. For example, suppose you are looking for an article that you know appeared in the *New York Times* sometime within the last year. To find it, you would look in the index for the *New York Times* under the subject, author, or title of the article. A *biographical index* lists famous people and their accomplishments. *Contemporary Authors* is another index that lists authors, their works, and biographical data. The *Education Index, Humanities Index,* and *Psychological Abstracts* are good places to look for articles in any of these fields. These indexes and many other reference works may be among your library's holdings. Again, it is up to you to find out what resources are available.

HOW TO USE YOUR LIBRARY'S RESOURCES

Because assignments vary and because so many resources are available, it would be impossible to explain how to use them all. Instead, here are a few guidelines to follow if you need to find information on a topic for a report or paper:

1. Begin by looking up your topic in a general reference work such as an encyclopedia. For example, if your topic is "The Civil Rights Movement," an encyclopedia may provide a summary of the major events and figures in the movement.
2. Next, look up your topic in the *Reader's Guide.* For example, if your topic is "Teens Who Kill," you could look for articles under the general topics of "teenagers," "murder," or "crime."
3. Then look up your topic in a specialized periodical index. For example, if your topic is "Bilingual Education," look in the *Education Index* for journal articles on this topic.
4. Finally, you should turn to books for a more in-depth discussion. For example, if your topic is a historical one such as "Watergate" or the conflict between Iraq and the United States known as "Desert Storm," you could read one or more of the many books written on these topics.

Before deciding which of your resources to use, you should evaluate them for objectivity, reliability, and usefulness as explained on pages 315–318. Generally speaking, your librarian or instructor can tell you which resources are likely to meet these standards. In addition, the following questions may be helpful.

- **Is the author an authority?**   Check the author's background for degrees held, colleges attended, major field of expertise, books or articles published, and other relevant accomplishments. *Who's Who* and the *Dictionary of American Biography* are two places to start.
- **Is the author a "name" in the field?**   An author who is a recognized expert will be mentioned in textbooks, reference works, bibliographies, and journal articles and will be well-known among other experts in the field.
- **Is the source current?**   Because information changes so rapidly, especially in scientific and technological fields, recent information may be more reliable.
- **Is the source free of bias?**   Read carefully to determine whether the author's ideas are supported with hard evidence and logical reasoning. Unsupported opinions and emotional language are not characteristic of authoritative research.

Appendix B

Preparing for Tests

*A*sk students what they do not like about college, and most will say, "Tests." Their reasons may vary. Some students have test anxiety, so the very thought of taking a test makes them nervous. Some believe they are not good test takers. Others blame instructors for making tests too difficult. But these reasons ignore the real issues: *attitude* and *preparation*.

To improve your attitude about tests, think of them as opportunities to learn. A test helps you identify your strengths and weaknesses in a subject. To improve the way you prepare for tests, follow these three steps:

- Know what to study.
- Know when to study.
- Know how to study.

WHAT TO STUDY

Instructors will often tell you what chapters a test covers and may even provide time for class review. Review your lecture notes, your underlining and marking of chapters, any study guides you have made, instructor's handouts, and old tests. Especially review items you missed on previous tests.

WHEN TO STUDY

Experts agree that regular study is better than cramming the night before a test. Review your notes immediately after class. At the end of each week, review what you have learned in each course. When you have an upcoming test, begin reviewing a few days before. Organize your materials and go over them several times. Schedule your study time. Set aside a certain time each day to review your notes and other study materials.

HOW TO STUDY

Develop a study system such as SQ3R as explained in Chapter 8. Make study guides and use textbook marking systems. Study with a partner. Choose someone who is serious about learning. If possible, form a study group. Discussing course material with people whose viewpoints and mastery of the information may differ is a good way to broaden your understanding.

These three steps—*know what to study, know when to study,* and *know how to study*—will help you prepare for most of the tests that you encounter in college. However, you may also have to take standardized reading tests. Although you cannot "study" for a standardized test, you can prepare to do your best by using the *SCORE* system.

THE *SCORE* SYSTEM FOR STANDARDIZED TESTS

Standardized reading tests usually consist of several reading selections on different topics followed by multiple-choice questions. The selections may vary in length and difficulty. Some tests contain a separate vocabulary section; others may contain questions throughout that ask you to determine the meaning of a word in context. Two examples of standardized tests are the Scholastic Aptitude Test (SAT) and the Graduate Record Exam (GRE). Standardized tests may have been part of your college entrance requirement, and you may have to take more of these tests, both in college and after, to qualify for certification in certain fields such as nursing or law.

Of course you cannot know in advance the topics covered in the reading selections on a standardized test. However, you can prepare yourself to do your best reading and thinking. The five steps of *SCORE* illustrated in Figure B-1 may help.

Stay focused.   Enter the test with a positive attitude. Focus on the test, not your feelings, not other students. To avoid distractions, keep your eyes on the test. If you start feeling tense, relax. Close your eyes and repeat: "I am calm, I will concentrate, I will do my best." When you are relaxed, return to the test.

FIGURE B-1 The SCORE System

S	Stay focused
C	Come prepared
O	Organize test-taking time
R	Read instructions
E	Eliminate distractors

Come prepared.   Get a good night's sleep, eat a nutritious breakfast, and wear comfortable clothes. Arrive on time so that you get a good seat and have a few minutes to get focused. Do not arrive too early. You do not want other students' negative talk or anxious behavior to rub off on you. In addition, try to find out what type of questions will be on the test. Your college bookstore or library may have a prep manual with sample questions and answers or other practice materials.

Organize test-taking time.   Standardized tests are usually timed. Determine how many sections are on the test and how much time you have for each. Plan to answer questions quickly, skipping difficult ones. If you have time left over, you may be able to return to the questions you skipped. Find out if there is a penalty for guessing. If not, then answer every question, even if you have to guess—you may pick up a few points. Watch your time, and save a few minutes to proofread your answers and erase any stray marks.

Read instructions.   The test monitor may read instructions to you. If not, then read them before you begin. Also, if the test contains several parts, read the instructions before beginning each part. This advice may seem obvious, but many students skip instructions, thinking they will save time. Unfortunately, they usually find out too late that they have not done what the test requires. To be on the safe side, read instructions.

Eliminate distractors.   Multiple-choice questions have two parts: the stem and the options. The *stem* is the part that asks the question. The *options* are the answer choices. One of the options is the correct answer. The incorrect options are called *distractors* because they distract your attention from the right answer. To answer a multiple-choice question correctly, know what the question asks and eliminate distractors.

FIGURE B-2 The Parts of a Multiple-Choice Item

| stem | A balanced diet should include which choice from below? |

o
p
t
i
o
n
s

(distractor)	a. milk, cheese, fruit
(distractor)	b. bread, cereal, whole grains, fruit
(answer)	c. milk, fruit, vegetables, meat, whole grains
(distractor)	d. vegetables, fruit, meat

First, read the stem to determine what the question asks. Are you supposed to find a main idea, a detail, a word meaning, the author's purpose? Look for clues in the stem. Next, try to answer the question without looking at the options. If your answer is correct, one of the options should match it. If not, start eliminating distractors. Read each option and determine whether it answers the question. The more distractors you can rule out, the better chance you have of getting the correct answer. If you cannot determine the answer, leave the question and come back to it later. As a last resort, guess, but only if there is no penalty. Figure B-2 illustrates the parts of a multiple-choice item.

Of the four options in Figure B-2, only *c* is correct. Options *a, b,* and *d* are the distractors because they are only partially correct. Although each distractor lists some foods that are part of a balanced diet, none includes a complete list. Option *c* is correct because it is a more complete answer.

The next time you have to take a standardized test, use the *SCORE* system. The next time you take any multiple-choice test, remember two things:

1. Know what the question asks.
2. Eliminate the distractors.

PARTIAL ANSWER KEY

CHAPTER 1   READING ACTIVELY

How Well Did You Comprehend?

Main Idea: 1. c; 2. b. *Details:* 3. a; 4. d. *Inferences:* 5. b; 6. d. *Working with Words:* 1. incentives; 2. structure; 3. conducive; 4. gorge; 5. retention; 6. eliminate. *Exercise 1.4:* 1. I; 2. E; 3. E; 4. I; 5. E; 6. E; 7. E; 8. I.

Exercise 1.5

1. How to use your dictionary is the topic.
2. You are expected to learn three strategies for using your dictionary effectively.
3. Use your dictionary's guide words.
   Use the parts of a dictionary entry.
   Make note cards for words and terms.
4. etymology, schwa (You may list any of the chapter's special terms.)

CHAPTER 2   USING YOUR DICTIONARY

How Well Did You Comprehend?

Main Idea: 1. d; 2. b. *Details:* 3. a; 4. c. *Inferences:* 5. b; 6. d. *Working with Words:* 1. abundance; 2. strenuous; 3. rife; 4. exploit; 5. innumerable; 6. channeled; 7. etiquette;   8. exasperation; 9. apathetic. *Exercise 2.1:* 1. along; 2. biscuit; 3. churn; 4. fleet; 5. gape; 6. hammer; 7. joiner; 8. perceptive; 9. succotash; 10. york. *Exercise 2.3:* 1. pay; 2. boot; 3. pit; 4. cut; 5. bee. *Exercise 2.5:* 1. ĭk•sĕl´; 2. rĭ•fôrm´ər; 3. kŏn´sĭ•kwĕns; 4. rĭ•mĕm´ bər; 5. fä•tôg´rə fər; 6. rā•dē•ol´ə•jē. *Exercise 2.7:* 1. adj. 12; 2. intr. v. 2; 3. adv. 6; 4. adv. 5; 5. adj. 6b; 6. adv. 1.

CHAPTER 3   USING CONTEXT CLUES

How Well Did You Comprehend?

Main Idea: 1. d. *Details:* 2. c; 3. a; 4. d; 5. b. *Inferences:* 6. c. *Working with Words* 1. humiliated; 2. coed; 3. lousy; 4. naive; 5. perceived; 6. gymnasium;

7. undoubtedly; 8. assured. *Exercise 3.1:* 1. worsen; 2. walked at a leisurely pace; 3. glowing; 4. varied; 5. decrease in value. *Exercise 3.3:* 1. a; 2. c; 3. d; 4. a; 5. c. *Exercise 3.5:* 1. hidden; 2. takeoff; 3. agree; 4. fake; 5. unchanging. *Exercise 3.7:* 1. surprise; 2. arrange or put together; 3. good, helpful; 4. over a period of time; 5. lively.

CHAPTER 4   UNDERSTANDING SENTENCES AND TRANSITIONS

How Well Did You Comprehend?

Main Idea: 1. b. *Details:* 2. d; 3. b; 4. c; 5. d; 6. a. *Inferences:* 7. c. *Working with Words:* 1. mundane; 2. dwarfs; 3. petty; 4. chides; 5. fritter; 6. drudgery; 7. vices; 8. multitasking; 9. cited. *Exercise 4.1:* 1. Nicholas; 2. mother and father; 3. they; 4. Nicholas's sisters; 5. taking care of the dog; 6. Nicholas, his sisters, and his parents; 7. feeding, walking, and brushing; 8. sisters; 9. everyone; 10. caring for a pet; *Exercise 4.2:* 1. could not decide; 2. wanted; 3. talked, took; 4. showed; 5. had earned; 6. require; 7. are; 8. decided; 9. might become; 10. would have. *Exercise 4.5:* 1. also; 2. another; 3. in addition; 4. second; 5. besides; 6. furthermore. *Exercise 4.7:* 1. example; 2. such as; 3. once; 4. for instance; 5. including;   6. to illustrate.

CHAPTER 5   FINDING THE MAIN IDEA

How Well Did You Comprehend?

Main Idea: 1. d. *Details:* 2. a; 3. c. *Inferences:* 4. b; 5. a. *Working with Words:* 1. wheedling; 2. expertise; 3. tentative; 4. eccentric; 5. overwrought; 6. cynicism; 7. superficial; 8. blatant; 9. intrinsically; 10. disgruntled. *Exercise 5.1:* 1. sports; 2. periodical; 3. gemstone; 4. dog; 5. dessert; 6. fruit; 7. flower; 8. music; 9. furniture; 10. tree. *Exercise 5.3:* 1. Mt. Dora Craft Festival; 2. choosing a major; 3. the newest shopping malls. *Exercise 5.5:* 1. Anyone who has ever stood. . . . (first sentence); 2. Miniseries proved able to. . . . (last sentence); 3. Those who view diversity. . . . (first sentence); 4. What is important to realize. . . . (fourth sentence).

Exercise 5.7:

1a. The author's topic is "my job."
 b. The author likes the job.
 c. The details explain the author's reasons.
 d. I like my job for several reasons.

2a. The author's topic is "David Walker."
  b. The author seems to think Walker has led an interesting life.
  c. The details tell you what Walker has done as a pilot and astronaut.
  d. David Walker has had an interesting career.

CHAPTER 6   IDENTIFYING SUPPORTING DETAILS

How Well Did You Comprehend?

Main Idea: 1. c; 2. b. *Details:* 3. a; 4. d; 5. b. *Inferences:* 6. c; 7. a. *Working with Words:* 1. hearth; 2. aficionados; 3. automated; 4. quirky; 5. croissant; 6. spirited; 7. phenomenon; 8. lox; 9. baffling; 10. delicacy; 11. tutus; 12. Yiddish.

Exercise 6.1:

1. Gina knows exactly what she wants in a new apartment.
    a. She wants about 750 square feet of living space.
    b. She wants a bedroom at least 12 feet by 12 feet.
    c. She needs an apartment that is available on December 1.
2. The Bahama Islands enjoy a warm subtropical climate.
    a. Rainfall averages about 30-60 inches a year.
    b. Hurricanes blow from June to November.
    c. Temperatures rarely drop below 70 degrees.
3. Volcanic eruptions occur quite regularly.
    a. Mt. St. Helens erupted in 1991.
    b. During the 1970s and 1980s, 33 eruptions were recorded.
    c. Between 1990 and 1996, eruptions occurred in 12 countries.
    d. Of the world's 42 major volcanoes, only 3 are extinct.

Exercise 6.4:

1. Taking vitamins may be beneficial. . . . (first sentence)
    a. Vitamins provide essential nutrients.
    b. Some vitamins may reduce risk of cancer and other diseases.
    c. Vitamins increase energy and improve well-being.
2. These reasons suggest. . . . (last sentence)
    a. Bookstore chains are opening in major towns and cities.
    b. Best-selling novels sell millions of copies.
    c. People turn out to meet famous authors.
3. But a math course could be. . . . (second sentence)
    a. Math requires logical, critical thinking.
    b. Math teaches you problem-solving skills.

c. A knowledge of math is essential to many careers.

d. Math teaches you discipline and patience.

Exercise 6.7:

1. Rolanda's is a bakery in our neighborhood. . . . (first sentence)
   a. Kids love Rolanda's sugar cookies.
   b. Chocolate chip cookies and macaroons are for chocolate lovers.
   c. Oatmeal raisin are for those who like cookies not too sweet.
2. They wanted something. . . . (second sentence)
   a. They planted pink and white azaleas.
   b. They put in two dogwood trees.
   c. They planted pansies in assorted colors.
3. Our new home. . . . (last sentence)
   a. School is within walking distance.
   b. A mall, restaurants, and theaters are close.
   c. Children have lots of neighborhood kids to play with.
   d. Our street is quiet and shady.

Exercise 6.11:

I. My uncle's restaurant is unusual for two reasons.
   a. First of all, he offers take-out only from a drive-up window.
      1. He saves money by not providing a place for people to sit.
      2. He does not have to clean up after customers.
   b. The second reason is that the menu is different.
      1. Chicken sandwiches are not available.
      2. You will not find chicken parts such as breasts, thighs, wings, and drumsticks.
      3. You can order chicken necks, livers, and gizzards.
      4. Chitlins' are also available.

CHAPTER 7   RECOGNIZING AND FOLLOWING THOUGHT PATTERNS

How Well Did You Comprehend?

Main Idea: 1. b; 2. d. *Details:* 3. a; 4. c. *Inferences:* 5. d. *Working with Words:* 1. tantalizing; 2. uncanny; 3. cerebral; 4. chauvinist; 5. delving; 6. crucial; 7. versatile; 8. predispose; 9. orienting; 10. innately.

Exercise 7.1:

(I.)
1. Many developments. . . . (first sentence)
2a. television
   b. computers
   c. videorecorders
   d. videocameras
   e. CD players
3. One example, another example, three more examples
(II.)
1. Because of advancements in medicine. . . . (second sentence)
2a. Polio is now quite rare.
   b. Yellow fever and scarlet fever have become rare.
   c. Chicken pox occurs less frequently.
3. for instance, two more examples

Exercise 7.3:

(I.)
1. Jim offers these tips. . . . (third sentence)
2a. Decide what to study.
   b. Organize notes and other materials.
   c. Make study guides.
   d. Review notes and study guides.
3. the first step, next, third, the final step
(II.)
1. Diana, the late princess. . . . (first sentence)
2a. She was born in 1961
   b. She married in 1981.
   c. She gave birth in 1982 and 1983.
   d. She was divorced by 1996.
   e. She died on August 29, 1997.
3. 1961, 1981, 1982, 1983, 1996, 1997

Exercise 7.5:

(I.)
1. I used to love. . . . (first sentence)
2a. rent increase
   b. noise
   c. road under construction
   d. utilities no longer included
3. major cause, another cause, because final cause

(II.)
1. Their services not only benefit. . . . (second sentence)
2a. Reading leads to an appreciation of literature.
 b. Sports programs build skills and team spirit.
 c. Volunteers relieve the nursing staff.
 d. They also comfort and cheer patients.
3. effect, leads to, effects

CHAPTER 8   USING TEXTBOOK READING STRATEGIES

How Well Did You Comprehend?

Main Idea: 1. c; 2. a. *Details:* 3. b; 4. a; 5. d. *Inferences:* 6. c. *Working with Words:* 1. random; 2. intuitive; 3. probability; 4. graphic; 5. consequence; 6. symptomatic; 7. bias; 8. relevant; 9. heuristic. *Exercise 8.4:* 1. b; 2. e; 3. g; 4. f; 5. c; 6. d; 7. a.

Exercise 8.6:

1. The preface may explain the author's topic, purpose, organization, and learning aids.
2. The glossary contains terms and definitions.
3. Typographical aids include type size, color, and so on.
4. They provide skill practice and review.
5. They illustrate and condense essential information.
6. The summary reviews the author's most important ideas.
7. Topics are listed in the index.
8. SQ3R is a system for reading textbooks actively.
9. Survey a chapter before you read it or as part of a review.
10. Read title, introduction, objectives, headings and subheadings, and summary.

Exercise 8.7:

1. skim; 2. scan; 3. skim; 4. scan; 5. skim; 6. scan; 7. scan.

CHAPTER 9   READING GRAPHICS WITH UNDERSTANDING

How Well Did You Comprehend?

Main Idea: 1. c; 2. d. *Details:* 3. b; 4. a. *Inferences:* 5. c; 6. b. *Working with Words:* 1. leery; 2. vivacious; 3. enthusiastic; 4. donor; 5. revive; 6. chemotherapy; 7. relapsed; 8. invasive; 9. platelets; 10. viable.

Exercise 9.1:

1. organizational chart
2. a guide to food choices
3. to illustrate recommended food groups for a healthy diet.
4. bread, cereal, rice, and pasta
5. fats, oils, and sweets
6. cereals, fruits, and vegetables

Exercise 9.3:

1. sources of immigration, 1907 and 1927
2. to show differences in the sources of immigration in 1907 and 1927
3. countries that were the sources of immigrants
4. immigrants (in thousands) from those countries
5. people who immigrated in 1907
6. people who immigrated in 1927
7. 1907
8. about 75,000
9. The immigration restriction laws were passed.

CHAPTER 10 DEVELOPING YOUR CRITICAL THINKING SKILLS

How Well Did You Comprehend?

Main Idea: 1. c; 2. c. *Details:* 3. b; 4. d. *Inferences:* 5. d; 6. a. *Working with Words:* 1. lithe; 2. dreadful; 3. reed; 4. ventured; 5. untidy; 6. scandalous; 7. gaped; 8. commission.

Exercise 10.1:

1. a; 2. b; 3. a; 4. b; 5. c; 6. a; 7. b; 8. a; 9. c; 10. b.

Exercise 10.3

1a. opinion
  b. "Should" is a value word.
2a. opinion
  b. "Believe" and "wrong" are value words.
3a. fact
  b. This statement is common knowledge and is based in law.
4a. fact
  b. The Fifth Amendment is the source.

5a. opinion
  b. "Should" is a value word.
6a. fact
  b. This is a fact of history. Textbooks and periodicals are sources.
7a. opinion
  b. "Good" is a value word.
8a. fact
  b. This is a fact of history. Periodicals are sources.
9a. opinion
  b. "Worst" is a value word.
10a. fact
  b. This is a fact of history. Reference books and others are sources.

Exercise 10.5:

1. b; 2. a; 3. b; 4. c; 5. c.

Exercise 10.7:

1. c; 2. a; 3. a; 4. c; 5. b.

ACKNOWLEDGEMENTS

Permission to reprint the following material is gratefully acknowledged:

Page 4: Reprinted with the permission of Macmillan General Reference USA, a division of Ahsuog, Inc., from *College Survival Guide: A Crash Course for Students by Students* by Greg Gottesman. Copyright © 1992 by Greg Gottesman. Page 32: © 1997. Reprinted by permission of the Associated Press. pages 37, 43, 46, 56: Copyright © 1997 by Houghton Mifflin Company. Reproduced by permission from *The American Heritage Dictionary of the English Language, Third Edition*. Page 40: Copyright © 1996 by Houghton Mifflin Company. Reproduced by permission from *The American Heritage Dictionary of the English Language, Third Edition*. Page 44: Copyright © 1997 by Houghton Mifflin Company. Reproduced by permission from *The American Heritage Dictionary of the English Language, Third Edition*. Page 60: Reprinted with the permission of Scribner, a Division of Simon & Schuster Inc., from He Was A Midwestern Boy on His Own by Bob Greene. Copyright © 1991 John Deadline Enterprises, Inc. Page 88: Ellen Graham, "Goofing Off is Fast Becoming a Lost Art," *The Wall Street Journal,* March 8, 1996. Republished by permission of Dow Jones, Inc., via Copyright Clearance Center, Inc. © 1996 Dow Jones and Company, Inc. All Rights Reserved Worldwide. Page 118: Kurt Wiesenfeld, "My Turn: Making the Grade" from *Newsweek,* June 17, 1996. © 1996. All rights reserved. Reprinted by permission. Page 150: Jack Denton Scott, "What's a Bagel?" is reprinted with permission from the June 1988 Reader's Digest. Copyright © 1988 by The Reader's Digest Assn., Inc. Page 181: Reprinted with permission of Simon & Schuster, Inc., from *The Practical Etomologist* by Rick Imes. Copyright © 1992 by Quarto Publishing Plc. Page 189: Christine Gorman, "How Gender May Bend Your Thinking," Time, July 17, 1995. © 1995 *Time,* Inc. Reprinted by permission. Page 224: Kassin, Saul, *Psychology,* First Edition. Copyright © 1995 by Houghton Mifflin Company. Used with permission. Page 257: Claudia Kalb and Melinda Beck, "Seizing Nature's Lifeline" from *Newsweek,* April 29, 1996. © 1996. All rights reserved. Reprinted by permission. Page 259: Claudia Kalb and Melinda Beck, "Seizing Nature's Lifeline" from Newsweek, April 29, 1996. © 1996. All rights reserved. Reprinted by permission. Page 292: Humphrey Harmon, "The King of Frogs," from *Tales Told Near a Crocodile* by Humphrey Harmon. Copyright © 1967 by Humphrey Harmon. Reprinted by permission of Curtis Brown, Ltd. Page 331: *It's Not My Fault,* Copyright © 1989 by Carol Tavris. Originally appeared in *Vogue.* His usage is granted by permission. Page 337: Reprinted by permission of the Associated Press. Page 342: Elizabeth Wong, "The Struggle to Be an All-American Girl," is reprinted by permission of the author. Originally appeared in *The Los Angeles Times,* September, 7, 1980.

Page 348: Cynthia Crossen, "Solitude Is a Casualty of the War with Time" *The Wall Street Journal*, March 8, 1996. Republished by permission of Dow Jones, Inc. via Copyright Clearance Center, Inc. © 1996 Dow Jones and Company, Inc. All Rights Reserved Worldwide. Page 359: Jose Antonio Burciaga, "I Remember Masa." Reprinted by permission of Cecilia Burciaga. Page 364: "Can We Talk?," by Diane White, *The Boston Globe*, March 3, 1992. © 1992. Reprinted Courtesy of *The Boston Globe*. Page 375: Ron Winslow, "Replacement Organs Have Been Grown From Animal Tissue, Say Researchers," *The Wall Street Journal*, July 23 ,1997. Republished by permission of Dow Jones, Inc. via Copyright Clearance Center, Inc. © 1997 Dow Jones and Company, Inc. All Rights Reserved Worldwide. Page 380: "How the Camel Got His Hump" by Rudyard Kipling, excerpted from Bennett's *The Book of Virtues*.

Grateful acknowledgment is also made to the following sources:

Bernstein, Srull, Wickens and Roy, *Psychology*, 4/e, © 1997 Houghton Mifflin Company. Ferrell and Fraedrich, *Business Ethics*, 2/e, © 1994 Houghton Mifflin Company. Garman, *Consumer Economic Issues in America*, 1/e, © 1991 Houghton Mifflin Company. Garman, and Forgue, *Personal Finance*, 5/e, © 1997 Houghton Mifflin Company. Gitelson, Dudley, and Dubnick, *American Government*, 4/e, © 1996 Houghton Mifflin Company. Kanar, *The Confident Student*, 3/e, © 1998 Houghton Mifflin Company. Kassin, *Social Psychology*, 2/e, © 1993 Houghton Mifflin Company. Levine and Miller, *Biology*, 2/e, © 1994 D.C. Heath and Company. Norton, Katzman, Escott, Chudacoff, Paterson, and Tuttle, *A People and a Nation*, 4/e, © 1994 Houghton Mifflin Company. Ober, *Contemporary Business Communications*, 2/e, © 1995 Houghton Mifflin Company. Osborn and Osborn, *Public Speaking*, 4/e, © 1997 Houghton Mifflin Company. Pride and Ferrell, *Marketing*, 9/e, © 1995 Houghton Mifflin Company. Reece and Brandt, *Effective Human Relations in Organizations*, 4/e, © 1990 Houghton Mifflin Company. Seifert and Hoffnung, *Child Adolescent and Development*, 4/e, © 1997 Houghton Mifflin and Company. Sherman, Sherman, and Russikoff, *Basic Concepts of Chemistry*, 6/e, © 1996 Houghton Mifflin and Company.

INDEX

Abbreviations, in dictionary, 44

Accent marks, in dictionary, 41–42, 47

Active reading, 3–30
  controlling concentration for, 14–15
  making time for reading for, 9–14
  positive attitude for, 7–9
  see also Reading strategies/systems

Addition transitions, 98–99, 105

Adjective, in dictionary, 42

Adverb, in dictionary, 42

Almanacs, in libraries, 389

American Heritage College Dictionary, 31, 36, 37, 40, 43, 44, 47

Analyzing sentences, 106–108

Antonyms, as contrast clue, 70, 72

Assignment, time needed for, 9–10

Atlases, in libraries, 389

Attitude, see Positive attitude

Author's opinion
  basis for, see Details
  central idea located with, 131
  implied main idea located with, 133, 134
  topic sentence located with, 127, 128, 129, 133

Author's purpose, 210
  critical thinking determining, 297–304
  studying guided by, 318
  in textbook, 229, 230, 234

Author's topic
  central idea located with, 131
  implied main idea located with, 133, 134
  in longer passage, 132
  main idea located with, 125–126
  in textbook, 229, 230, 234
  topic sentence located with, 127, 128, 129, 133

Background building, as reading strategy, 16, 17–19, 21

Bar graph, 273, 274. See also Graphics

Beck, Melinda, 257–260

Bias, objective sources free of, 316

"Biases in Judgment" (Kassin), 224–227

Biographical indexes, in libraries, 390

Bold type, in textbook, 233

Boredom, ignoring, 14

Brainstorming, building background with, 18

Breaks, concentration enhanced with, 14, 15

Bullets, in textbook, 233

Burciaga, José Antonio, 359–361

"Can We Talk?" (White), 364–366

Caption, with graphics, 263, 264

Card catalog, computerized, 388–389

Cause and effect
  as thought pattern, 188, 194, 195, 203–204
  transitions signaling, 104–105, 195, 203–204

Central idea
  comparison and contrast supporting, 201
  implied, 135
  of longer passage, 131–132, 133, 174

Chapters, see Textbook chapters

Charts, 264–269
  in everyday life, 280
  flow, 265, 267, 268
  organizational, 265, 266, 268
  pie, 264–265, 268
  see also Graphics

Chronological order, see Time order

Communication skills, 59. See also Vocabulary

Comparison and contrast
  as thought pattern, 188, 193, 194, 195, 201–203

transitions signaling, 102–104, 195, 201

Computerized card catalog, in libraries, 388–389

Computerized indexes, in libraries, 389

Concentration
  controlling for active reading, 14–15
  guide questions for, 19

Contemporary Authors, 390

Context, 65–66

Context clues, 59–83
  contrast clue, 70–72
  definition clue, 65, 66–67
  definition of, 65
  example clue, 67–70
  inference clue, 72–74
  for unfamiliar words, 74–75

Contrast clue, as context clue, 70–72

Contrast relationship, 102, 103. See also Comparison and contrast

Critical reading, 291. See also Critical thinking

Critical thinking, 291–328
  author's purpose determined with, 297–304
  facts distinguished from opinions with, 304–311
  inferences made with, 311–315
  reading evaluated with, 315–318
  studying guided with, 318–319

Crossen, Cynthia, 348–350

Definition
  context for, 65–66, see also Context clues
  in dictionary, 42–46, 47
  in glossary, 230, 236, 237
  graphics with, 206
  as thought pattern, 188, 194, 195, 205–208
  transitions signaling, 195, 205

Definition clue, as context clue, 65, 66–67

Details
  author's purpose determined
    with, 299
  central idea located with, 131
  as examples, 156, 164–168, 176
  as facts, 156–160, 168, 176
  implied main idea located with,
    133, 134
  levels of in longer passages,
    173–175
  levels of in paragraphs, 169–172
  listing identifying, 197
  major, 169, 174, 175, 176, 178
  marking, 245
  minor, 169, 175
  note-taking skills and, 177–178
  as reasons, 156, 160–164, 168,
    176
  in sentences, 87, 95–97, 106
  with topic sentence as first
    sentence of paragraph, 128
  with topic sentence as last
    sentence of paragraph, 129
  with topic sentence between first
    and last sentences of
    paragraph, 129
  transitions signaling, 175–177
  types of, 155–168
Development, levels of
  in longer passages, 173–175
  in paragraphs, 169–172
Diagrams, 276–278
  in everyday life, 280
  making own, 280
  note taking and, 178
  see also Graphics
Dictionary, 31–58, 74
  abbreviations in, 44
  accent marks in, 41–42, 47
  definitions and special meanings
    in, 44–46, 47
  entry in, 38–47
  glossary as, 230, 236, 237
  guide words in, 36–38
  parts of speech in, 42–43, 47
  plurals in, 42
  pronunciation in, 39–42, 47
  special meanings in, 44–45
  syllables in, 38–39, 47
  synonyms in, 44
  for unfamiliar words, 74
  word origins in, 46–47
Dictionary entry, 38–47
Disciplines, vocabulary of, 47–49

Distractions, 14
  external, 14, 15
  internal, 14, 15
Distractors, in multiple-choice
    questions, 394–395

Education Index, 390
Effect, *see* Cause and effect
End matter, of textbook chapter, 16
Entertaining, as author's purpose,
    298–299, 300
Etymology, dictionary and, 46–47
Evaluation
  of library resources, 390–391
  of reading, 315–318
Example
  as thought pattern, 188, 194–196
  transitions signaling, 101–102, 195
  as type of detail, 156, 164–168, 176
Example clue, as context clue,
    67–70
Exercises, in textbook, 230,
    235–236, 238, 245
External distractions, 14, 15

Facts
  critical thinking distinguishing
    opinions from, 304–311
  as type of detail, 156–160, 168,
    176
Ferrell, O. C., 370–371
Figures, *see* Graphics
Fixed time, in schedule, 11–13, 14
Flexible time, in schedule, 11–12
Flow chart, 265, 267, 268. *See also*
    Graphics
Focusing, *see* Concentration
"Four Words" (Greene), 60–62

Gazetteers, in libraries, 389
General ideas, specific ideas
    distinguished from, 123–125.
    See also Main idea
Glossary, in textbook, 230, 236,
    237, 238
Goals, staying focused with, 14, 15
"Goofing Off Is Fast Becoming a
    Lost Art" (Graham), 88–89
Gorman, Christine, 189–191, 201
Gottesman, Greg, 4–5, 197
Government documents, in
    libraries, 389
Graduate Record Exam (GRE), 393
Graham, Ellen, 88–89

Graphics, 16, 236–237, 238,
    256–290
  with definitions, 206
  in everyday life, 280–281
  making your own, 279–280
  maps, 279
  marking, 245
  as memory aids, 256, 280
  PRT for reading, 262–264
  purpose of, 262, 263
  relationships illustrated by,
    263–264
  text/caption with, 263, 264
  title of, 262
  see also Charts; Diagrams; Graphs;
    Tables
Graphs, 273–275
  bar, 273, 274
  horizontal axis of, 273, 274
  line, 273, 274
  vertical axis of, 273, 274
  see also Graphics
Greene, Bob, 60–62
Guide questions, as reading
    strategy, 16, 19–20, 21
Guide words, in dictionary, 36–38

Harmon, Humphrey, 292–297
Headings, 16, 230, 231–232, 233,
    234, 238, 239, 240
  central idea located with, 132
  levels of development identified
    with, 173, 174
  marking, 245
  previewing, 232
Highlighting, as marking strategy,
    244
Horizontal axis, of graph, 273, 274
"How Gender May Bend Your
    Thinking" (Gorman),
    189–191, 201
"How the Camel Got His Hump"
    (Kipling), 380–383
Humanities Index, 390
Hunger, elimination of, 14

"I Remember Masa" (Burciaga),
    359–361
Ideas, *see* Central idea; General
    ideas; Main idea; Specific ideas
Implied central idea, 135
Implied main idea, 117, 126
  locating, 133–134
Index(es)

in libraries, 389, 390
in textbook, 230
Index, in textbook, 238
Inference clue, as context clue, 72–74
Inferences, 72–74
critical thinking for, 311–315
studying guided by, 318
informal, dictionary indicating, 44
Information retrieval systems, in libraries, 388–389
Informing, as author's purpose, 297, 299, 300
Interjection, in dictionary, 42
Internal distractions, 14, 15
Introduction, of textbook chapter, 16, 238, 240
Italic type, in textbook, 233
"It's Not My Fault" (Tavris), 331–336

Kalb, Claudia, 257–260
Kassin, Saul, 224–227
Key idea, in sentence, 85, 95–97, 106
Key words
as contrast clue, 70, 72
as definition clue, 66–67
as example clue, 68, 70
"King of the Frogs, The" (Harmon), 292–297
Kipling, Rudyard, 380–383

Language, slanted, 316. *See also* Unfamiliar words; Vocabulary
Learning aids, in textbook, 229, 230, 234
Learning goals/objectives, in textbook chapter, 238, 239, 240
Letters, in textbook, 233
Library, 387–391
computerized card catalog in, 388–389
evaluation of resources in, 390–391
finding information for report in, 390–391
indexes in, 389, 390
information retrieval systems in, 388–389
periodicals in, 389
personnel in, 388
reference works in, 389–390
resources in, 389–391
skill checklist and, 387–388

Line graph, 273, 274. *See also* Graphics
Listing
as thought pattern, 188, 194, 195, 197–199
transitions signaling, 195, 197
Literal level of reading, 291
Longer passages
central idea in, 131–132, 133
definition in, 206
implied central idea in, 135
levels of development in, 173–175
see also Textbook chapters
"Lotteries: Is It Right to Encourage Gambling?" (Pride and Ferrell), 370–371

Magazine articles, *see* Longer passages
Main idea, 117–148, 176
author's purpose determined with, 299
author's topic finding, 125–126
basis for, *see* Details
cause and effect supporting, 203–204
central idea supported by, 131
comparison and contrast supporting, 201
definitions supporting, 205–206
distinguishing between general and specific ideas for, 123–125
examples supporting, 156, 164–168, 176, 194–195
facts supporting, 156–160, 168, 176
as first level of development in paragraph, 169, 175
as implied, 117, 126, 133–134
listing supporting, 197
marking, 245
note taking and, 178
overall, *see* Central idea
reasons supporting, 156, 160–164, 168, 176
table of contents and, 174, 175
time order supporting, 199
see also Topic sentence
Major details, 176
note taking and, 178
in paragraph, 169, 175
table of contents as list of, 174, 175
see also Details
"Making the Grade" (Wiesenfeld), 118–121, 125, 135

Mapping, as reading strategy, 241, 246–249
Maps, 279. *See also* Graphics
Margin notes, as marking strategy, 244
Marking
as reading strategy, 241, 244–246
as studying strategy, 393
Memory aids, graphics as, 256, 280
Minor details, in paragraph, 169, 175. *See also* Details
Multiple-choice test, method for taking, 394–395

Newspaper articles, *see* Longer passages
nonstandard, dictionary indicating, 45
Note cards, for unfamiliar words, 47–49
Note taking, guidelines for, 177–178
Noun, in dictionary, 42
Numbers, in textbook, 233

Objectivity of sources, 316, 317
in library, 390
Opinions, critical thinking distinguishing facts from, 304–311. *See also* Author's opinion
Options, in multiple-choice questions, 394–395
Organization, *see* Thought patterns
Organizational chart, 265, 266, 268. *See also* Graphics
Outline
as reading strategy, 241, 246–247
of report, 249
table of contents as, 231

Paragraphs, 87
levels of development in, 169–172
see also Details; Main idea; Topic sentence
"Parents Creating Unique Names" (Roberts), 337–339
Parts of speech, in dictionary, 42–43, 47
Patterns, *see* Thought patterns
Periodicals
indexes to, 389, 390
in library, 389
Persuading, as author's purpose, 297–298, 299, 300

Phonetic spelling, in dictionary, 39–40

Pictures, *see* Graphics

Pie chart, 264–265, 268. *See also* Graphics

Planning, for reading time, 9–14

Plurals, in dictionary, 42

Positive attitude
  for active reading, 7–9
  for concentration, 14

Powell, Colin, General, 353–356

Preface, in textbook, 229–231, 234

Prereading strategy, *see* Previewing

Previewing, 16–17
  for asking guide questions, 19
  for identifying levels of development, 173–174
  reading summaries for, 21
  for textbook chapters, 16, 18, 232

Pride, W. M., 370–371

Primary accent mark, 41–42

Prior knowledge, building background with, 18

Problems in textbook, *see* Exercises

Pronoun, in dictionary, 42

Pronunciation, in dictionary, 39–42, 47

Pronunciation symbol, in dictionary, 40, 47

PRT, for reading graphics, 262–264

Psychological Abstracts, 390

Punctuation marks, as definition clue, 66–67

Purpose, *see* Author's purpose

Questions
  asking as reading strategy, 19–20, 21
  guide, 16, 19–20, 21
  multiple-choice, 394–395
  in SQ3R, 241, 242
  in textbook, *see* Exercises

Quotations, books of in libraries, 389

Random House Webster's College Dictionary, 31, 32–34

Reader's Guide to Periodical Literature, 389, 390

Reading, in SQ3R, 241–242

Reading enjoyment, finding main ideas and, 137

Reading strategies/systems, 16–22, 240–249
  asking guide questions, 16, 19–20, 21

building background, 16, 17–19, 21

mapping, 241, 246–249

marking, 241, 244–246

outlining, 241, 246–247

reflecting, 16, 21

reviewing, 16, 20–21

scanning, 241, 243–244

skimming, 241, 243–244

SQ3R, 241–243

see also Previewing

Reading tests, *see* Standardized reading tests

Reasons, as type of detail, 156, 160–164, 168, 176

Reciting, in SQ3R, 242

Reference works, in library, 389–390

Reflecting, as reading strategy, 16, 21

Reliability of sources, 315–316, 317
  in library, 390

"Replacement Organs Have Been Grown from Animal Tissue, Say Researchers" (Winslow), 375–377

Report, information in library on, 390–391

Reviewing
  as reading strategy, 16, 20–21
  in SQ3R, 242

Rewards, for completing tasks, 14, 15

Roberts, Cindy, 337–339

Scanning, as reading strategy, 241, 243–244

Schedules, for study time, 9–14

Scholastic Aptitude Test (SAT), 393

Schwa (ə), 40

SCORE system, preparing for standardized reading tests with, 393–395

Scott, Jack Denton, 150–153, 175–176, 206

Secondary accent mark, 41–42

"Seizing Nature's Lifeline" (Kalb and Beck), 257–260

Sentences, 87–116
  analyzing difficult, 106–108
  details in, 87, 95–97, 106
  key ideas in, 87, 95–97, 106
  parts of, 87, 92–95
  subject in, 87, 92–93
  thought standing alone in, 94

verb in, 87, 93–94

writing, 108–109

see also Topic sentence; Transitions

"600 New Entries Give Dictionary What Was Missing," 32–34

Skimming, as reading strategy, 241, 243–244

slang, dictionary indicating, 44, 45

Slanted language, objective sources free of, 316

"Solitude Is a Casualty of the War with Time" (Crossen), 348–350

Specific ideas, general ideas distinguished from, 123–125. *See also* Details

Spelling
  dictionary guide words and, 36, 38
  phonetic, 39–40

SQ3R
  as reading strategy, 241–243
  as study system, 393

Standardized reading tests, *SCORE* system preparing for, 393–395

Stem, in multiple-choice questions, 394–395

Strategy, 16. *See also* Reading strategies/systems

"Struggle To Be an All-American Girl, The" (Wong), 342–345

Study group, 393

Study guides, 393

Studying
  critical thinking for, 318–319
  how to study, 393
  scheduling time for, 9–14
  what to study, 392
  when to study, 392–393
  see also Tests

Subheadings, 230, 231–232, 233, 234, 238, 239, 240
  levels of development identified with, 173, 174
  previewing, 232

Subject, of sentence, 87, 92–93

Summary, in textbook chapter, 16, 21, 239

Supporting details, *see* Details

Surveying, in SQ3R, 241, 242

Syllables, in dictionary, 38–39, 47

Synonyms, 65
  as definition clue, 66–67
  in dictionary, 44

Table of contents, in textbook, 230, 231–232, 234
  levels of development identified with, 173, 174, 175
Tables, 269–272
  in everyday life, 280–281
  making own, 279–280
  see also Graphics
Tavris, Carol, 331–336
Tests, preparation for
  see also Studying
Tests, preparation for, 392–395. *See also* Studying
Textbook, 223–255
  author's purpose in, 229, 230, 234
  author's topics in, 229, 230, 234
  exercises in, 230, 235–236, 238, 245
  glossary in, 230, 236, 237, 238
  index in, 230, 237
  learning aids in, 229, 230, 234
  organization of, 229, 230, 231, 238–239
  preface in, 229–231, 234
  as reliable source, 315
  table of contents in, 173, 174, 175, 230, 231–232, 234
  typographical aids in, 230, 233–235, *see also* Headings; Subheadings
  see also Graphics; Reading strategies/systems; Textbook chapters
Textbook chapters
  calculating time needed to read, 9–10
  endmatter of, 16
  introduction of, 16, 238, 240
  learning goals/objectives in, 238, 239, 240
  organization of, 238–240
  previewing, 16, 18, 232
  summary of, 16, 21, 239
  title of, 16, 238, 240
  see also Central idea; Headings; Longer passages; Subheadings; Textbook
Thought patterns, 188–219
  cause and effect, 188, 194, 195, 203–204
  comparison and contrast, 188, 193, 194, 195, 201–203
  definition, 188, 194, 195, 205–208
  example, 188, 194–196

listing, 188, 194, 195, 197–199
  time order, 188, 193, 195, 199–201
  transitions signaling, 194, 195, 197, 199, 201, 203–204, 205
  for writing, 210–211
"Time Management for College Students" (Gottesman), 4–5, 197
Time order
  as thought pattern, 188, 193, 195, 199–201
  transitions signaling, 99–101, 195, 199
Tiredness, elimination of, 14
Title
  central idea located with, 132, 133
  of graphics, 262
  levels of development identified with, 173, 174
  of textbook chapter, 16, 238, 240
Topic
  information on in library, 390–391
  note taking and, 178
  for writing, 210
  see also Author's topic
Topic sentence, 117, 126–131, 133
  author's opinion located for, 127, 128, 129, 133
  author's topic located for, 127, 128, 129, 133
  between first and last sentences, 129
  as first sentence, 128
  as last sentence, 128–129
  main idea as, 117, 126–131
Transitions, 87, 97–106
  addition, 98–99, 105
  analyzing sentences with, 106
  cause and effect, 104–105, 195, 203–204
  comparison and contrast, 102–104
  definition signaled by, 195, 205
  details signaled by, 175–177
  example, 101–102, 195
  listing signaled by, 195, 197
  marking, 245
  note taking and, 178
  thought patterns signaled by, 194, 195, 197, 199, 201, 203–204, 205

time, 99–101, 195, 199
  writing, 108–109
Typographical aids, in textbook, 16, 233–235
  marking, 245
  see also Headings; Subheadings

Underlining, as marking strategy, 244
Unfamiliar words
  context clues for, 74–75
  defining for analyzing difficult sentences, 106
  dictionary for, 74
  in longer passages, 174
  note cards for, 47–49
  see also Context clues; Dictionary
Unstated main idea, *see* Implied main idea
"Unwritten American Bargain, The" (Powell), 353–356
Usefulness of sources, 316–317
  in library, 390

Verb
  in dictionary, 42
  in sentence, 87, 93–94
Vertical axis, of graph, 273, 274
Vertical file, in libraries, 389
Visual aids, *see* Graphics
Vocabulary, 31
  impressions based on, 49, 59
  see also Dictionary; Unfamiliar words

Weekly schedules, study time in, 9–14
"What's a Bagel?" (Scott), 150–153, 175–176, 206
White, Diane, 364–366
Wiesenfeld, Kurt, 118–121, 125, 135
Winslow, Ron, 375–377
Wong, Elizabeth, 342–345
Word meanings, *see* Context clues; Dictionary; Glossary; Unfamiliar words; Vocabulary
Word origins, in dictionary, 46–47
Writing
  sentences and, 108–109
  thought patterns for, 210–211
  transitions and, 108–109